LOOKING AHEAD

The Vision of Science Fiction

Edited by Dick Allen
University of Bridgeport

Lori Allen

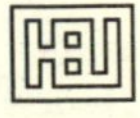

Harcourt Brace Jovanovich, Inc.
New York Chicago San Francisco Atlanta

ISBN: 0-15-551184-X

Library of Congress Catalog Card Number: 74-22511

Printed in the United States of America

Copyrights and Acknowledgments

COVER PHOTO: Alex Harsley

ACE BOOKS for "Utopia" from *Science Fiction: What It's All About* by Sam Lundwall. Copyright © 1971 by Ace Books. Reprinted by permission of the publisher.

THE DIAL PRESS for *The Fall of Japan*. Excerpted from *The Fall of Japan* by William Craig. Copyright © 1967 by William Craig. Used with permission of The Dial Press. For "Tomorrow and Tomorrow and Tomorrow," copyright 1954 by Kurt Vonnegut, Jr. Originally published in *Galaxy* as "The Big Trip Up Yonder." Reprinted from the book, *Welcome to the Monkey House* by Kurt Vonnegut, Jr. with permission of Delacorte Press/Seymour Lawrence.

EDGE PRESS for "A New Age" by Dick Allen from *Edge*. First appeared in *SF Directions*, The Edge Press, 1972. Reprinted by permission of the publisher.

LESLIE FIEDLER for "Cross the Border, Close the Gap" by Leslie Fiedler. Reprinted by permission of the author.

GALAXY PUBLISHING CO. for "The Year of the Jackpot" by Robert A. Heinlein. Copyright © 1952, Galaxy Publishing Co. Reprinted by permission of Lurton Blassingame, the author's agent.

HARPER'S MAGAZINE for "Survival U.: Prospectus for a Really Relevant University" by John Fischer. Copyright 1969 by Harper's Magazine. Reprinted from the September 1969 issue by special permission.

HARPER & ROW for "The Obsolescence of Man" from *Profiles of the Future*, Revised Edition, by Arthur C. Clarke. Copyright © 1961 by H.M.H. Publishing Co. By permission of Harper & Row Publishers, Inc.

HOLT, RINEHART AND WINSTON, INC. for "The Star-Splitter" from *The Poetry of Robert Frost*, edited by Edward Connery Lathem. Copyright 1923, © 1969 by Holt, Rinehart and Winston, Inc. Copyright 1951 by Robert Frost. Reprinted by permission of Holt, Rinehart and Winston, Inc.

VIRGINIA KIDD for "Interurban Queen" by R. A. Lafferty. Copyright © 1970 by Damon Knight; originally appeared in *Orbit 8*, edited by Damon Knight. For "The

To
Richard Negridge Allen

Preface

Looking Ahead: The Vision of Science Fiction is a multipurpose sourcebook/anthology designed for use in college Freshman English courses, Science Fiction courses, and courses in Studies of the Future. Its selections provide basic, or "core," readings for these offerings. Although *Looking Ahead* is meant to be supplemented by science fiction novels, other anthologies, films, and works on the future—and strongly encourages the assigning of such additional works—we have planned it to be also "self-teaching," a basic introduction to the genre.

The selections introduce most of the main themes of science fiction, including ones that lead into questions of ecology, time travel, responsibility of the scientist, overpopulation, space travel, mythology, future shock, man-machine relationships, the alien encounter. All selections were chosen for their literary merit as well as for their interest as outstanding SF or SF-related commentary. The focus in the fiction is on science rather than on fantasy, since we are convinced that one of the primary strengths of this genre is its ability to make realistic and useful extrapolations from basic technology-caused changes in society.

The book contains extensive apparatus, from Introduction through section introductions and headnotes, to questions for discussion, topics for writing papers, bibliography, and an SF and Future Shock Chronology. The apparatus was carefully planned to raise issues essential to contemporary awareness. Instructors and students should find the book "open-ended," designed to motivate explorations, not narrowly direct them. If *Looking Ahead* is used primarily for research and critical papers, instructors and students should find that the basic material they require is covered.

We are convinced that SF is, in itself, a respectable and important genre of literature, which has finally won its right to be taught alongside such other standard genre courses as Tragedy and Satire. Although rooted in "popular" literature, it has come of age and taken on increasing sophistication of style and literary complexity. But it is its usefulness as a "mind-expanding" form of literature, a literature that increases the readers' world- and- time perspective, that has impelled us to construct this book.

Additionally, we would be remiss if we did not warn readers that, like Anne and Paul Erlich, Robert L. Heilbroner, and William Irwin Thompson, we are personally convinced that vast and tragic changes lie shortly ahead, for humankind and particularly for Western civilization. Pessimistic, we envision continuing energy crises, a wildly fluctuating economy, minor and major wars, mass starvation, finally a near-complete societal breakdown within the lifetimes of most readers of this book. Regrettably, it is no longer very controversial to express this conviction —a conviction many SF writers have held for years.

We are not without hope; we feel much can be done to reduce the impact of an inevitable end-of-the-century crisis. Yet we also think that it is best to be forewarned and prepared, as a nation as well as individuals. Nonfiction studies of the future, of "how to be a survivor," abound. But it is *fiction* that can best make us *feel* a sense of what may be ahead, convince us emotionally when our minds refuse to confront the dimensions of Future Shock, expand our consciousness sufficiently so we can imagine and perhaps act on hard and nontraditional solutions that will be necessary. Thus, in effect, *Looking Ahead* is our contribution to the growing literature of preparation.

Since the text refers frequently to Hugo and Nebula awards, a short explanation seems necessary. The Hugo Awards were instituted in 1955 by readers of the genre who attend the World Science Fiction Conventions. Awards are given annually to the best novel, novelette, and short story of the year, among other categories. The Nebula Awards are voted on by the members of the Science Fiction Writers of America. First given in 1965, they generally cover best novel, novelette, novella, and short story.

We would like to offer our thanks to William A. Pullin, Vice President of Harcourt Brace Jovanovich, for encouraging us to prepare this volume and for giving us a free hand in choosing its selections and emphasis; to Paula Lewis, also of Harcourt Brace Jovanovich, whose conscientious and perceptive copyediting contributed much to the book; to the staff of the Fairfield Woods library—one of the country's finest community libraries—for their help in locating selections as well as their acquisition of many books that have shaped our understandings of both SF and the future; to the students in "English 250: Science Fiction" at the University of Bridgeport, who helped us learn what really "taught" and what did not, and whose deep questioning expanded ours; and especially to the man who worked tirelessly on this sourcebook, Sidney Zimmerman of Harcourt Brace Jovanovich, a painstaking and dedicated editor who helped us through our time of personal crisis during the work's preparation and whose own understanding contribution to *Looking Ahead* is deeply felt.

Dick Allen
Lori Allen

Contents

III. Breaking Outward

IV. Aftermath

V. Theories

Introduction

Allen Ginsberg's statement that "we're all in science fiction now" has been vindicated by current history.

- A successful space program resulted in an end to manned flights.
- A rumor—invented as a gag by a television star—resulted in a nationwide shortage of toilet paper.
- The feasibility of cloning, a process by which it may be possible to create complete individuals from a single cell, has been successfully proven in a laboratory.
- Enraged bulls became tame after electrodes were implanted in their brains, thus enabling researchers to influence their behavior by remote control.
- Two American girls were sterilized because a welfare agency decided they were not intelligent enough to pass on their genes.
- With the aid of a telephone and a small briefcase it became possible to hook into the major computers of the country.
- Men waving red flags on superhighways proved, only after close inspection, to be robots.

Want to know what will happen next? There is one promising way to find out—read science fiction. The reader, however, should be prepared to think critically, for science fiction's major purpose is not to predict but to entertain analytically. It offers apparently logical answers to many planetary problems, but the answers are often conflicting and sometimes bizarre. One story may "solve" overpopulation by showing a world where murder is legalized, while another story makes gigantic high-rise buildings, covering almost all the planet's land surface, seem practical. Solar power "solves" the energy crisis in one story; in another, giant windmills provide sufficient energy for world industry.

Thus, readers should be warned not to accept the basic tenets of every story they read, but they should also know that they can learn the various possibilities inherent in the current developments in science, economics, technology, politics, and social organization. At its best, science fiction can teach us to think algebraically in terms of multiple unknowns and multiple solutions. It trains the thinking mind to extrapolate and to judge the extrapolations of others. It is the analytical process rather than the creative imagination that turns the science fiction writer into a prognosticator.

Still, many of the events on our list drawn from the early 1970s were anticipated by science fiction writers. Harry Harrison, in *Make Room Make Room*, published in 1966, foresaw diseases caused by protein deficiency, resulting in part from the use of ersatz food. And indeed today our muffins have artificial blueberries and our children's breakfast cereals are prepared in laboratories rather than kitchens. Food experts, testifying before congressional committees, claim that children fed only popular, brand-name foods may be inadequately nourished.

The science fiction writers of the 1940s did not waste their energies dwelling on such inevitable future occurrences as an energy crisis in the early 1970s, but they did allude to the problem. In "The Roads Must Roll," published in 1940, Robert A. Heinlein predicted vast shortages of oil in the second half of the twentieth century ("petroleum to be an essential and limited material of war"). He described one way to circumvent the effect of the shortages (the civilian population riding on giant conveyor belts), then built his story around what could go wrong with his solution.

It is fairly obvious by now that we need this kind of analytic ability in Washington. But few elected officials would admit they read science fiction, much less write it. Politicians are supposed to be practical, realistic, and levelheaded; science fiction is supposed to be merely escape literature. Escape literature is most commonly looked on as a legal and cheap substitute for liquor and drugs, with no connection to the real world and its problems. However, one can argue that escape is more easily achieved in mainstream literature (what SF fans call everything that isn't SF) than in science fiction.

We now come to a problem of terms. There are many adequate definitions of science fiction; none are completely satisfactory. "Mainstream" literature is even more elusive. We do not wish to add to the list of definitions; a standard dictionary will clear up any confusion for the time being sufficient to our purpose. We are concerned here only with the simplest examples of the broadest of categories. Moreover, we are being antediluvian. Science fiction began changing in the 1960s; that which was once true for most stories is now true for only a small proportion, a phenomenon that will be discussed later in this introduction. The business at hand is to purge, at least partially, the term "escape" literature from science fiction.

The first problem is the reader's identification with the hero or heroine. The classic mainstream character is generally a "rounded" figure, that is, a man or a woman who possesses a complex set of physical and psychological features that gives the reader the illusion of "reality." When the character is successfully drawn, the reader says to himself or herself, "I know someone like that," or "I've felt like that myself," or ultimately, "how true to life that is." For the space of the story, the reader's reality is a fiction created by the author. It matters little how distant the story may be from the reader's actual life experiences; he or she will usually share the author's vision and the main character's problems. Few of us are princes of Denmark, and perhaps even fewer have had our uncles kill our fathers and marry our mothers, but most of us can share with Hamlet his anguish at discovering the truth of his father's death. For several hours we have "escaped" into Hamlet's mind and Shakespeare's world.

In contrast, science fiction characters are simply conceived. Often, they are described in terms of a single physical feature and a character trait. Whether it be because of oversized ears, a limp, excessive greed, self-sacrificing devotion, height or shortness, obesity or leanness, gentle stupidity or cruel intelligence, they are set apart from ordinary humans. And when the classic science fiction hero appears, he is handsome, strong, honest, blue eyed, square jawed, with one or two interesting but not disfiguring scars artistically placed. He is a fitting companion for the classic science fiction woman, who measures 48-12-34 inches of poreless complexion, peerless compassion, and recurring virginity. To *truly* identify with such images takes a prodigious strength of imagination or an extraordinary amount of wish fulfillment. We're not likely to ever be that astronaut or that spacewoman or even that monster. And our telepathy isn't too good either. Objectivity—that is, psychological distance from the story and its characters—is not likely to be totally lost. There is no full "escape" into the Other.

Second, to "escape" we must be convinced, at least for the time being, that we are not where we are but are instead in another place—in effect, we have been "transported." The setting in mainstream literature is always somewhere believable and on this world. A few choice words by the author and we can close our eyes and be wherever the story dictates. If we've never been there, we've probably seen someplace like it on television or in pictures. Everything is at least slightly familiar and completely believable. Very easy to escape to.

In contrast, the settings of science fiction are its least believable aspects. Worlds change with every story. We are never at home in any of them; they are far too alien, even when the depicted world is the Earth. The chairs have no legs and the tables are retractable, keeping us on our toes literally and figuratively. The differences between the worlds of science fiction and our own are continually stressed. We are constantly reminded of our present environment and the ways in which it conflicts with the setting of the SF story.

Third, plot in much mainstream literature, especially in contemporary works, is often fragmented: the "normal," chronological, order of events is rearranged, interrupted by flashbacks, even, in "plotless" stories, ignored. The author's focus is on such things as tone, free association, and imagery. Plot, or lack of it, can become symbolic—its use or "misuse" reflecting the author's conception of a nonlinear universe. At its extreme, a plotless work can show the author's despair with logic and reason; these "tools" are then seen as no longer useful in handling contemporary human experience.

In contrast, classic science fiction is a literature of calculated adventure. Its plots can usually be diagrammed as neatly as a sentence from a 1930s grammar. There is the beginning exposition, in which the situation and characters are introduced; the middle section, or complication, where the main character goes through the ups and downs of suspense; the climax, the point of highest tension as the situation is resolved; and the denouement—a few sentences or paragraphs in which we are gentled out of the story, left-over elements are wrapped up, and we get some indications of what might happen to the characters after the time of the particular story. Straight-line plotting is characteristic of "pop" literature. The traditional plot outline in science fiction is similar to that used in the detective story. For instance, much of Isaac Asimov's early writing consists of the introduction of the basic premise (commission of the crime), the problematic effects or side effects of the premise (the search for clues), and the eventual solution of the predicament (apprehension of the criminal).

The clarity and simplicity of the plot force SF readers to extrapolate, to take the story's ideas one step further. Readers are not puzzled by plot devices; things happen in the traditional order of "popular" fiction, and they can let their attention go to other matters. Similarly, the classic SF writer—not very concerned with unique plotting devices—works on the *science* of science fiction, on the ideas stemming from the science, rather than on carefully worked out plot effects. He or she brings up questions and once we start asking questions, we're not running away, we're meeting our problems head on. We have come to realize that the problems dramatized in science fiction are critical and can no longer be evaded; if they can be solved, we will be that much closer to utopia, and if they can't, we will go down with the spaceship. If reading science fiction starts our minds going, we have done more than not escape, we have eliminated escape as a desirable goal.

Finally we come to the question of personal involvement and reader criticism. The majority of mainstream readers, excluding educators, exceptional students, and those whose lives revolve around literature, are usually rather a passive lot. When asked an opinion of a story they have casually read, they will answer "good," "bad," or "mediocre," unless pressed for details. They have experienced the story as a whole and with little question.

True science fiction fans, however, not only question, they argue. Ask them what they think of a story and they will not only discuss what is possible, improbable, and impossible, but they will also discriminate between an original idea and an imitative one. And they might even trace the imitation to the original that was written twenty years before.

Thousands subscribe to or originate fan magazines ("fanzines")—a phenomenon perhaps unique to science fiction, in which readers address themselves to Isaac Asimov, Robert Heinlein, or andrew j. offutt, criticizing their stories, pointing out the weak and strong points, disagreeing even with themselves. But these readers are alert and thinking and very much alive in their unlimited little worlds.

Mainstream stories, at least considered from this admittedly generalized and risky perspective, can be thought of as escape literature. They drown us. We react to the best stories emotionally, we lose ourselves in them. They leave us with an explanation of something we almost thought of, with the memory of a feeling, with a realization. But with a new *thought?* Hardly. Mainstream literature feigns reality so well that its readers totally believe; imitates its readers' experiences so closely that they forget the need for objectivity. A mainstream story is complete and finished and a good experience to have, but it is seldom even potentially world-shaking.

We have been writing, throughout this introduction, about "classic" or "traditional" science fiction—the type from which the fiction selections in *Looking Ahead* are mainly drawn. These are the kind of stories in which the science is "hard," that is, plays a major role in the story, is discussed in such a way that it appears accurate in light of current scientific knowledge and extrapolation. It is this type that has generally been most successful in exploring the large problems we face now, in the present and are anticipating in the near and far future.

Paradoxically, however, a major reason for the increasing acceptance of science fiction as literature suitable for serious classroom study is the movement toward the mainstream by numerous SF writers. The term "science fiction" has been shortened to "SF" or expanded to "speculative fiction." The characteristics of mainstream literature mentioned earlier, as well as other "mainstream" characteristics, are found in a significant number of recently published SF novels and short stories. Thus we have fragmented plot in the fiction of Barry Malzberg and Kurt Vonnegut, Jr.; intricate characterization in Samuel R. Delany, Kit Reed, and Judith Merril; surrealistic satire in Ron Goulart; heavy symbolism in Arthur C. Clarke; explicit sexuality in Harlan Ellison's *Dangerous Visions* anthologies; stream-of-consciousness writing in J. G. Ballard; meticulously described settings in Ursula LeGuin's works; concentration on "emotion" rather than "thought" in fiction by Thomas M. Disch and James Sallis; the present world seen as SF in Donald Barthleme's allegories. Fantasy, which we'll define as the "literature of the impossible," in contrast to the "possible" elements of classic science fiction, is widely popular. And many mainstream writers, such as Doris Lessing, John Hersey, and Wright Morris, use SF elements in their work, finding them necessary since "we're all in science fiction now."

It is difficult to forecast the result of the increasing assimilation of contemporary science fiction to mainstream literature. Most likely, "classic" science fiction will always be written. It will exist side by side with "speculative fiction"—much as the classic detective novel exists comfortably alongside the work of John Le Carré. Perhaps speculative fiction will be completely absorbed by the mainstream. This could leave science fiction better characterized, more intricate, containing a more sophisticated style, yet continuing to deal primarily with mass sociological and psychological problems, just as it has so successfully dealt with early problems of physical, biological, and technical science.

With the advent of the new style SF writer, the gains for literature per se are obvious. The danger is that SF writers—who have taught us so much because of their concern for large effects, for societies, for the planet, and for the future as a whole—may come to substitute the multinuance concern with the individual for the mighty concern with the destinies, massive difficulties, and potential accomplishments of the entire human (and hopefully universal) family.

Kurt Vonnegut, Jr.'s Eliot Rosewater, in *God Bless You, Mr. Rosewater,* said it best. As he addresses a group of SF writers in Milford, Pennsylvania, he says, "You're the only ones who'll talk about the *really* terrific changes going on, the only ones crazy enough to know that life is a space voyage, and not a short one, either, but one that'll last for billions of years. You're the only ones with guts enough to *really* care about the future, who *really* notice what machines do to us, what wars do to us, what cities do to us, what big, simple ideas do to us, what tremendous misunderstandings, mistakes, accidents and catastrophies do to us. You're the only ones zany enough to agonize over time and distances without limit, over mysteries that will never die, over the fact that we are right now determining whether the space voyage for the next billion years or so is going to be Heaven or Hell."

part 1

About Now

It is increasingly apparent that there has been an enormous change in human consciousness since the Second World War—a change exhilarating for some but terrifying for most. Certainly it was felt earlier in the century by poets like T. S. Eliot and Robinson Jeffers, and was expressed in works ranging from Joseph Wood Krutch's collection of essays *The Modern Temper* and Aldous Huxley's novel *Brave New World* to Oswald Spengler's and Arnold Toynbee's massive studies of human history. But since the Second World War this new awareness "gathers soundlessly, like evidence"—to borrow the poet W. D. Snodgrass's phrase—and enters the daily thoughts and conversations of millions of people.

Put simply, the future has fallen on us all and left us with no escape. Critics who disagree with present doomsday prophecies have said that our situation is not new, that civilizations have tottered on the edge of destruction before and either survived or been replaced by other societies that were ultimately better. Yet it is difficult for others not to feel that this time it is different—that Yeats's rough beast is slouching toward us at last.

The human race has already undergone such horror, developed such a capacity for self-destruction and evil that, having gone to extremes of behavior, we now provide ourselves with apocalyptic metaphors warning us of the brink to which we have already ventured. Such, certainly, is suggested by the passage from *The Fall of Japan* and by the account of a concentration camp in this section.

Closer to the immediate present is the great period of outer space exploration that started with Sputnik in 1957 and culminated in our arrival on the moon. The selections from Norman Mailer's epic work about the first moon landing in 1969 explore the meanings that adventure had and continues to have. We have made "the giant leap forward." The event seems to grow more and more awesome as we fade back from its point in chronological time. Yet what meaning does this event hold for us? Will it help the human race somehow survive its present crisis?

If the situation illustrated so graphically in *The Limits to Growth* is even approximately accurate, it seems clear that we *must* undertake drastic global changes affecting the entire human race. Otherwise, there will be nothing much at all after—at the latest—the year 2100. Numerous doomsayers are already forecasting a return to ages darker than the Dark Ones—assuming, that is, the air of the planet is still breathable and the land still able to yield crops.

Science fiction provides us with our current images of the predicament described in *The Limits to Growth.* In the movie *Marooned,* a spaceship circles the Earth with its astronauts trapped in orbit and running out of oxygen. A rescue mission is planned—vehicles are made ready. But a hurricane is moving toward Cape Kennedy. Despair—until a bright scientist remembers the eye of the hurricane, that brief period of calm at the center. The rescue mission must be launched through the eye, before the forces of nature unleash a greater fury. We are in the eye of a hurricane now. According to such groups as the Club of Rome (authors of *The Limits to Growth*), we have only a few years in which to launch the rescue of ourselves.

Hope might be placed in the young. This optimistic view emerged from the Earth Days of the late 1960s, when numerous youth groups began pressing for pollution controls and saner ways of living in harmony with the Earth. "Ecology" became a byword. Still, mass attention turned to other matters in the early 1970s. In America, the end of the Vietnam War, the Watergate scandal, and economic problems took precedence.

However, the ecological problems—though for a brief time ignored—return, somewhat changed, somewhat enlarged, somewhat more exacerbated than before. This section of *Looking Ahead* presents some of the events and problems that have contributed to the present consciousness of human capabilities and ecological dangers. The cumulative consciousness reflected in these selections serves as a prelude to the later sections devoted to "science fiction." The SF writers have faced, rather than ignored, the changes brought about by past decades. Their stories and the implications of these stories grow from their apprehension and wonder at the possibilities that lie before Earth people in the *far* future if we can somehow survive the near one.

The Listeners

Walter de la Mare

Walter de la Mare's poem expresses forcefully the questioning, troubled quality of the twentieth century. Although the poem can be interpreted in many ways, for our purposes it might best be used to pose the problem of human loneliness. "The Listeners" can make us realize vividly the strangeness of a universe in which we exist with almost painful fragility.

Walter de la Mare was the author of many poems blending reality and fantasy. The critic F. R. Leavis calls him "the belated last poet of the Romantic tradition," and J. B. Priestley has said that de la Mare has " 'kept innocency,' though his spirit should walk the awful borderlands and proclaim its despair."

Is there anybody there?" said the Traveller,
  Knocking on the moonlit door;
And his horse in the silence champed the grasses
  Of the forest's ferny floor:
And a bird flew up out of the turret,
  Above the Traveller's head:
And he smote upon the door again a second time;
  "Is there anybody there?" he said.
But no one descended to the Traveller;
  No head from the leaf-fringed sill 10
Leaned over and looked into his grey eyes,
  Where he stood perplexed and still.
But only a host of phantom listeners
  That dwelt in the lone house then
Stood listening in the quiet of the moonlight
  To that voice from the world of men:
Stood thronging the faint moonbeams on the dark stair
  That goes down to the empty hall,
Hearkening in an air stirred and shaken
  By the lonely Traveller's call. 20
And he felt in his heart their strangeness,
  Their stillness answering his cry,

While his horse moved, cropping the dark turf,
'Neath the starred and leafy sky;
For he suddenly smote on the door, even
Louder, and lifted his head:—
"Tell them I came, and no one answered,
That I kept my word," he said.
Never the least stir made the listeners,
Though every word he spake 30
Fell echoing through the shadowiness of the still house
From the one man left awake:
Ay, they heard his foot upon the stirrup,
And the sound of iron on stone,
And how the silence surged softly backward,
When the plunging hoofs were gone.

QUESTIONS

1. Who or what are the listeners?

2. What does the house represent?

3. What is the traveler a metaphor of? What is he seeking at the house?

4. How does point of view work in this poem? Who is the speaker? Could the entire poem have been spoken by one of the "phantom listeners"? Explain your answer.

5. What words and images evoke a sense of mystery and possible dread?

6. How is the horse used to balance the poem's quality of unreality? What contributes to this unreality?

7. Discuss the sound effects of the poem, especially those in the last four lines.

8. How would you interpret the meaning of " 'Tell them I came, and no one answer'd,/ That I kept my word,' he said."?

from The Fall of Japan

William Craig

It is still almost impossible to realize the full horror of atomic warfare. Our minds boggle at the prospect. Yet the following report is fact, not fiction. Technology has gone out of control. A weapon has been invented that—generations after it has been used—continues to kill and maim. Our concepts of "reality" have undergone a radical change directly because we have experienced such gigantic destruction. Those born after the A bomb have never known a time when the sword of Damocles did not hang over them. Is it any wonder that the doomsday vision of science fiction now seems to us all too "realistic"?

This selection comes from William Craig's documentary account of the last few weeks of the Second World War in the Pacific. Craig has also published an espionage novel, The Tashkent Crisis, *and another documentary work,* Enemy at the Gates: The Battle for Stalingrad.

When the atomic bomb left the B-29, arming wires were extracted, enabling the weapon to run on its own internal power. Safe-separation timing clocks held switches open so that the bomb could not detonate near the aircraft. As it fell farther toward earth, additional switches were closed by barometric pressure. Then radar fuses were actuated to sense the exact height above ground. As the shiny black weapon neared an altitude of 1,540 feet, arming and firing switches closed, and the high voltages already built up in massive condensers were released to a series of detonators attached to a layer of high explosive. The detonators triggered an implosion, a bursting inward. The resultant shock wave quickly pressed the separate sections of plutonium together. In turn, the now dense plutonium sphere compressed a tiny "initiator," composed of particles of beryllium and polonium. Alpha rays emitted by the polonium acted on the beryllium, which sent a shower of neutrons out into the surrounding dark gray metal. In a millisecond, Nagasaki became a graveyard.

The Fat Man was detonated over the northwest leg of the X, just northeast of the stadium in the Urakami Valley. At the moment of ignition, there was an intense bluish-white flash as though a large amount of magnesium had exploded. The entire area grew hazy with smoke. Simultaneously there was a tremendous roar, a crushing blast wave and searing heat.

Twenty-four hundred feet to the northeast, the roof and masonry of the Catholic cathedral fell on the kneeling worshipers. All of them died.

At the Nagasaki Branch Prison, just north of the explosion, 118 guards and convicts saw the brilliant light but nothing more. There were no survivors.

The baggage master at the railroad station never rose to meet the incoming train. The roof of the building dropped onto his head. His assistant, torn by flying glass, ran into the street where people were beginning to jump headlong into the river to find relief from burns.

The approaching train had stopped for a moment to discharge passengers near the entrance to the Urakami Valley. Most of the people never left their seats as the white light flooded over them. The windows blew in and ripped flesh into flayed meat. Severed heads rolled down the aisles as uninjured Japanese stumbled over the dead and ran from the train, too stunned to offer any help to others.

Out in the harbor, two and a half miles from the center of the blast, a seaman watched the explosion from his boat. As he stood transfixed, a small craft near him burst into flames and burned to the waterline. Beside him on his own deck, crew members screamed from burns on exposed portions of flesh.

Four and a half miles to the south of the blast, a wooden barracks at Kamigo simply fell down.

When the bomb exploded, Fusa Kawauchi was working inside a cave pumping out water. She did not see the intense flash but heard a noise like the sound of machinery running. She looked at a girl across from her and noticed that her face was streaked with dirt and soot. The two girls got up and went to the mouth of the cave. What they saw was unbelievable.

The fireball of the bomb had broadened in seconds to fill the valley. It lapped at the ridges on either side. The blast wave leaped the crests and raced through the seaport. People by the hundreds lay on the streets, in the fields, in wreckage, and screamed for water. Creatures that barely resembled human beings walked dazedly, skin hanging down in huge flaps, torsos blackened.

A mile and a half north of the center of the fireball, Ensign Jolly of the Netherlands Navy lay under a table in a prisoner-of-war camp. He had seen the parachutes drop, and he had seen the flash. Instinctively he plunged under the furniture as the building crashed around him. He lived, but several of his fellow prisoners died in the first seconds.

Another prisoner of war was an American, Motorman's Machinist Mate Second-class Jack Madison, captured three years before at Corregidor. He was standing before a coal-washing pit nearly two miles away. Guarding him and six other prisoners was a solitary Japanese policeman, who glanced idly into the sky as *Bock's Car* passed by. None of the captives paid much attention to that one plane as it headed over the Urakami Valley. Madison continued working and neither felt the blast nor saw the light as Fat Man burst below the layer of clouds. He was thrown to the bottom of the pit, unconscious.

At the Nagasaki Medical College, southeast of the epicenter, Dr. Shirabe heard the plane and started for the door of his offices. The room collapsed behind him and left him in total darkness. When the light returned, Shirabe stumbled to the corridor and walked outside to join survivors struggling to reach the high ground behind the building. At their backs were the terror-filled cries of patients trapped in their beds by crackling fire.

Over the wreckage of the Urakami Valley towered a monstrous expanding pillar of smoke shooting upward from the middle of the explosion at incredible speed. Like a genie released after countless ages of captivity, the column writhed and twisted toward the stratosphere. At its feet lay incredible devastation, as though the living thing had wreaked a special vengeance on its jailers. The deadly apparition seethed up toward the circling planes. It changed faces, it changed colors from purple to salmon to gold to soft white. It escaped into the boundless sky where it sprouted a new head and hovered menacingly over the dying valley.

QUESTIONS

1. Discuss why the editors have included this and the following selection.

2. Compare the opening description of the bomb's mechanism and the following description of the havoc it caused.

   a. What are the differences in tone between the two descriptions?

   b. What moral judgment can you infer from the difference in tone?

   c. How did the people react to the bomb? Did anyone try to help anyone else?

3. The final paragraph of the selection is a description of the famous A-bomb cloud. Here the author has shifted from a straightforward prose narrative to the use of a poetic device, personification. What is the effect of this device?

4. The author is very careful to indicate spatial relationships throughout the description. Why did he do this?

5. What has the atom bomb come to symbolize? in terms of modern ethical values? in terms of modern technology?

The Ultimate Horror

R. W. Thompson

The atomic bomb was not the only instrument to change human consciousness after the Second World War. The Nazi concentration camps did the same. Humanity had to come to terms with the slaughter of millions of innocent people by one insane government. We could no longer think of the goodness of the human race in any simplified fashion. The benign advances of scientific progress were turned inside out and made to seem like the horrors of the Gothic tale: mad scientists experimented on living beings, humans were forced to act like animals. Since this did actually happen, was not all else possible? We are just now beginning to realize the implications the Second World War had for the present and future time of man.

This report, by the London Sunday Times *war correspondent, describes Bergen-Belsen.*

The blue smoke of many fires hangs thickly in the pine woods along the road from Winsen to Belsen. In the clearings the young corn is green and all the loveliness of spring, of budding life, is in the air, and the smouldering grasses of the pine woods bring a wonderful tang to the nostrils so that you expand your chest and feel your youth still in you, and are glad to be alive. Then suddenly a new tang creeps into the odours of burning. It is the stench of death. It is the stench from the great charnel-house our armies have overrun so that all mankind shall know—and this time neither to balk nor forget—the appalling crime Hitler and the Nazis have done against humanity, against the very basis of life and faith itself. . . .

I began the unforgettable walk that you must read about. At first it was little worse than a kind of enormous hutted camp with here and there the wooden towers where the guards had watched. The whole enormous area hidden in lovely pine woods divided into barbed-wire enclosures each containing about thirty long huts to house, on military standards, less than 50 men. Here the inmates, men, women and children, were new, but recently brought in. For the first time for days there was water, and for the first time for weeks these people were washing themselves and their clothes. The only odd thing was that here and there men and women were excreting—just casually anywhere. There is no sanitation in this hell in the woods.

And now before my eyes was the slow destruction of human beings, stripped of all human dignity, forced down to the level of the beasts, and so to die in utter ruin. This thing, this hell far beyond the wild dreams of Dante, holds some 60,000 souls—souls! These are not souls, these tragic travesties of humanity that sit and rot in their own excrement, these things that were human once, reduced now to skeleton death by slow deliberate starvation, but first stripped of all remnants of human dignity so that in truth they are dead before they die. By the barbed wire lie the dead, some bits of clothing, others naked, men, women and children, almost unrecognisable as the remains of human kind though they died but an hour since. . . .

They lie down and they die. Now deep into the camp the dead lie in bundles, neat bundles, grotesque limbs in terrible positions. Here is a small cart loaded with a dozen corpses of men, women and children, the faces like parchment tight against the skulls. They are only just dead. A brown stocking is limply around a leg that a small black garter less than 4 inches diameter cannot clasp. A shock of auburn hair crowns the dead face of this woman that stares sightless to the blue sky. The normal world of life is receding. Horror is not yet too deep for an individual to mean something. This woman had a life, a purpose, was beloved of someone. But now the dead are in hundreds, the dead, the living and the near-living. The dead in small bundles of threes or fours under the shadow of the pines, the dying in attitudes of sleep by the roadside, some dying peacefully, some suddenly sitting up chattering. Here a woman sits with eyes round in deep sockets, and a younger woman tries to quiet her babbling. She is babbling like a grotesque travesty of a child. If you did not know, she might be asking for a toy to play with, but she is asking for death. . . .

And so slowly the Chaplain takes me to the great burial ground where our soldiers are scooping pits with bulldozers to accommodate all this dead and putrefying human wreckage, deliberately, slowly, brought to this pass by Adolf Hitler and the German race. Morning and night the heavy truck with its trailers brings its cargoes of bodies to the great pits. Stand with me at the brink of this death pit. It is my job, your job, and the world's job. It is about 30 feet deep, but you cannot see how deep because it is nearly filled now with human bodies, littered together in the embrace of death. Here are girls, boys, men, women, naked, half-naked, upside down, sideways, all ways, some staring up to the sky, others with their heads buried in human remains. So stare in silence and let this crime beyond expression sink in. Across the sandy clearing is the incinerator, but it ran out of petrol. A rough record by the chief burner of bodies records seventeen thousand burned last month. They say each body was roughly clubbed as it went in, for there is so little difference between the dead and the near-dead. There is no difference in the faces even. . . .

Germany was deadly for me. I loathed it. It clamped down upon my spirit. . . . I found it difficult to speak to Germans at all. I used to walk through crowds of them—civilians or prisoners—as though they weren't there, yet feeling a kind of flaming wall around me. . . . The monstrous thing changed me. My outlook on life has changed—or developed—so that all my thoughts on social, political, and economic affairs have crystallised. I am now a complete idealist. I have given up all the "isms." I believe in the human spirit above all things, and that only by a change of heart can civilization be saved.

For although it is the Germans who have done this thing, it is not only the Germans who can do it. Prisoners of Germans did it to other prisoners. Mankind can do this thing to mankind.

QUESTIONS

1. As in the preceding selection there are marked differences between the opening description and the rest of the essay. What are these differences? What effect do they have?

2. Why does the author say of the former inmates of Bergen-Belsen that "they are dead before they die"? What does this imply about both the prisoners and those who imprisoned them?

3. The author says that the horrors of the concentration camp changed his entire view of life and that he is now an idealist. What does he mean by this and the statement that "only by a change of heart can civilization be saved"? What is actually involved in "a change of heart"? Relate this desired change to ethical and material values, to social, political, and economic organization, to belief systems such as religion, science, or the "isms" mentioned by the author.

4. Much of the horror in the concentration camps was perpetrated in the name of science. What does this imply about the scientific attitude?

5. Are the questions about this selection and the preceding one secondary to the larger questions of "Why?" and "How could humankind do this?" Explain your answer.

from The Limits to Growth

Donella H. Meadows, Dennis L. Meadows,
Jørgen Randers, William W. Behrens III

Humans have created weapons capable of wiping out most of the earth's population; we have exhibited a massive potential—individually and nationally—for depravity; we have broken away from the planet's soil. And now, in addition, we must face the prospect of our own planet soon becoming uninhabitable; our current civilization catapulting toward collapse. Few works have so convincingly shown the relentless thrust toward self-destruction as does the pioneer study, The Limits to Growth. *Arguments rage over the pessimistic picture drawn here, but most commentators agree that we are now in the midst of a planetary crisis. Every problem, it seems, has to be solved at once—overpopulation, pollution, depletion of natural resources, inflation—or there is little hope for the future of an operational world.*

Although the history of human effort contains numerous incidents of mankind's failure to live within physical limits, it is success in overcoming limits that forms the cultural tradition of many dominant people in today's world. Over the past three hundred years, mankind has compiled an impressive record of pushing back the apparent limits to population and economic growth by a series of spectacular technological advances. Since the recent history of a large part of human society has been so continuously successful, it is quite natural that many people expect technological breakthroughs to go on raising physical ceilings indefinitely. These people speak about the future with resounding technological optimism.

> There are no substantial limits in sight either in raw materials or in energy that alterations in the price structure, product substitution, anticipated gains in technology and pollution control cannot be expected to solve.[35]

> Given the present capacity of the earth for food production, and the potential for additional food production if modern technology were

[35] Frank W. Notestein, "Zero Population Growth: What Is It?" *Family Planning Perspectives* 2 (June 1970): 20.

> more fully employed, the human race clearly has within its grasp the capacity to chase hunger from the earth—within a matter of a decade or two.[36]

> Humanity's mastery of vast, inanimate, inexhaustible energy sources and the accelerated doing more with less of sea, air, and space technology has proven Malthus to be wrong. Comprehensive physical and economic success for humanity may now be accomplished in one-fourth of a century.[37]

. . . Will new technologies alter the tendency of the world system to grow and collapse? Before accepting or rejecting these optimistic views of a future based on technological solutions to mankind's problems, one would like to know more about the global impact of new technologies, in the short term and the long term, and in all five interlocking sectors of the population-capital system.

TECHNOLOGY IN THE WORLD MODEL

There is no single variable called "technology" in the world model. We have not found it possible to aggregate and generalize the dynamic implications of technological development because different technologies arise from and influence quite different sectors of the model. Birth control pills, high-yield grains, television, and off-shore oil-drilling rigs can all be considered technological developments, but each plays a distinct role in altering the behavior of the world system. Therefore we must represent each proposed technology separately in the model, considering carefully how it might affect each of the assumptions we have made about the model elements. In this section we shall present some examples of this approach to global, long-term "technology assessment."

Energy and Resources

The technology of controlled nuclear fission has already lifted the impending limit of fossil fuel resources. It is also possible that the advent of fast breeder reactors and perhaps even fusion nuclear reactors will considerably extend the lifetime of fissionable fuels, such as uranium.

---

[36] Donald J. Bogue, *Principles of Demography* (New York: John Wiley and Sons, 1969), p. 828.

[37] R. Buckminster Fuller, *Comprehensive Design Strategy*, World Resources Inventory, Phase II (Carbondale, Ill.: University of Illinois, 1967), p. 48.

Does this mean that man has mastered "vast, inanimate, inexhaustible energy sources" that will release unlimited raw materials for his industrial plants? What will be the effect of increasing use of nuclear power on resource availability in the world system?

Some experts believe that abundant energy resources will enable mankind to discover and utilize otherwise inaccessible materials (in the sea bed, for example); to process poorer ores, even down to common rock; and to recycle solid waste and reclaim the metals it contains. Although this is a common belief, it is by no means a universal one, as the following quotation by geologist Thomas Lovering indicates.

> Cheaper energy, in fact, would little reduce the total costs (chiefly capital and labor) required for mining and processing rock. The enormous quantities of unusable waste produced for each unit of metal in ordinary granite (in a ratio of at least 2,000 to 1) are more easily disposed of on a blueprint than in the field. . . . To recover minerals sought, the rock must be shattered by explosives, drilled for input and recovery wells, and flooded with solutions containing special extractive chemicals. Provision must then be made to avoid the loss of solutions and the consequent contamination of groundwater and surface water. These operations will not be obviated by nuclear power.[38]

Let us assume, however, that the technological optimists are correct and that nuclear energy will solve the resource problems of the world. The result of including that assumption in the world model is shown in figure 37. To express the possibility of utilizing lower grade ore or mining the seabed, we have doubled the total amount of resources available, as in figure 36. We have also assumed that, starting in 1975, programs of reclamation and recycling will reduce the input of virgin resources needed per unit of industrial output to only one-fourth of the amount used today. Both of these assumptions are, admittedly, more optimistic than realistic.

In figure 37 resource shortages indeed do not occur. Growth is stopped by rising pollution, as it was in figure 36. The absence of any constraint from resources allows industrial output, food, and services to rise slightly higher than in figure 36 before they fall. Population reaches about the same peak level as it did in figure 36, but it falls more suddenly and to a lower final value.

"Unlimited" resources thus do not appear to be the key to sustaining growth in the world system. Apparently the economic impetus such resource availability provides must be accompanied by curbs on pollution if a collapse of the world system is to be avoided.

---

[38] Thomas S. Lovering, "Mineral Resources from the Land," in *Committee on Resources and Man* (San Francisco, Calif.: W. H. Freeman and Co., 1969), pp. 122–23.

Figure 36
WORLD MODEL WITH NATURAL RESOURCE RESERVES DOUBLED

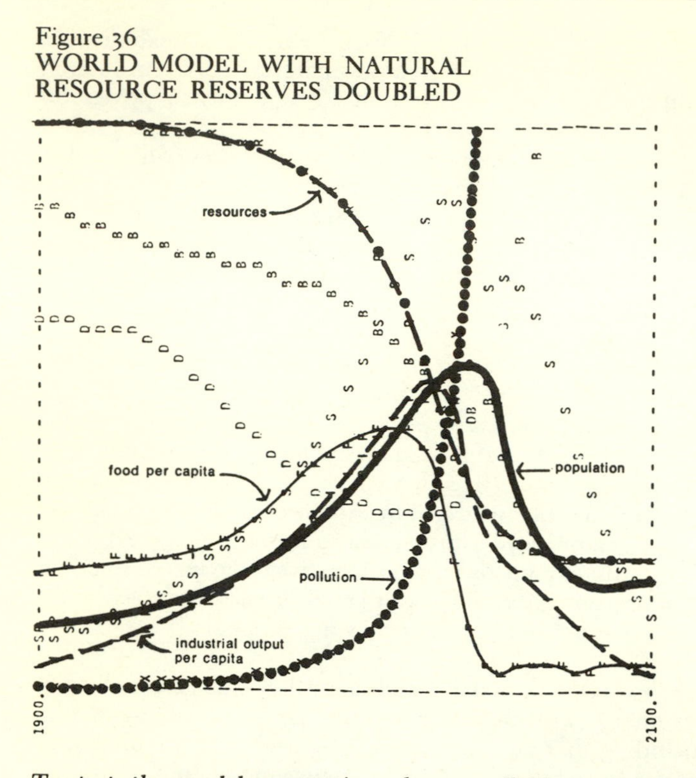

To test the model assumption about available resources, we doubled the resource reserves in 1900, keeping all other assumptions identical to those in the standard run. Now industrialization can reach a higher level since resources are not so quickly depleted. The larger industrial plant releases pollution at such a rate, however, that the environmental pollution absorption mechanisms become saturated. Pollution rises very rapidly, causing an immediate increase in the death rate and a decline in food production. At the end of the run resources are severely depleted in spite of the doubled amount initially available.

Pollution Control

We assumed in figure 37 that the advent of nuclear power neither increased nor decreased the average amount of pollution generated per unit of industrial output. The ecological impact of nuclear power is not yet clear. While some by-products of fossil fuel consumption, such as CO_2 and sulfur dioxide, will be decreased, radioactive by-products will be increased. Resource recycling will certainly decrease pollution from solid waste and from some toxic metals. However, a changeover to nuclear power will probably have little effect on most other kinds of pollution,

Figure 37
WORLD MODEL WITH "UNLIMITED" RESOURCES

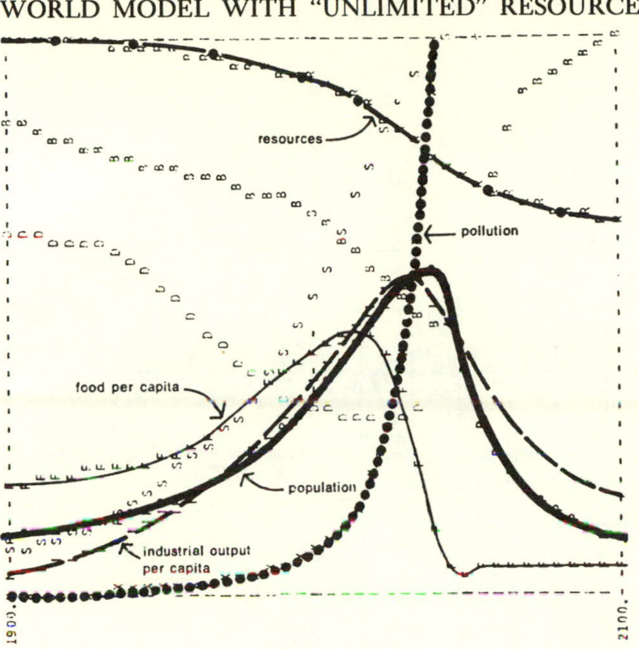

The problem of resource depletion in the world model system is eliminated by two assumptions: first, that "unlimited" nuclear power will double the resource reserves that can be exploited and, second, that nuclear energy will make extensive programs of recycling and substitution possible. If these changes are the only ones introduced in the system, growth is stopped by rising pollution, as it was in figure 36.

including by-products of most manufacturing processes, thermal pollution, and pollution arising from agricultural practices.

It is likely, however, that a world society with readily available nuclear power would be able to control industrial pollution generation by technological means. Pollution control devices are already being developed and installed on a large scale in industrialized areas. How would the model behavior be changed if a policy of strict pollution control were instituted in, say, 1975?

Strict pollution control does not necessarily mean *total* pollution control. It is impossible to eliminate all pollution because of both technological and economic constraints. Economically, the cost of pollution control soars as emission standards become more severe. Figure 38 shows the cost of reducing water pollution from a sugar-processing

Figure 38
COST OF POLLUTION REDUCTION

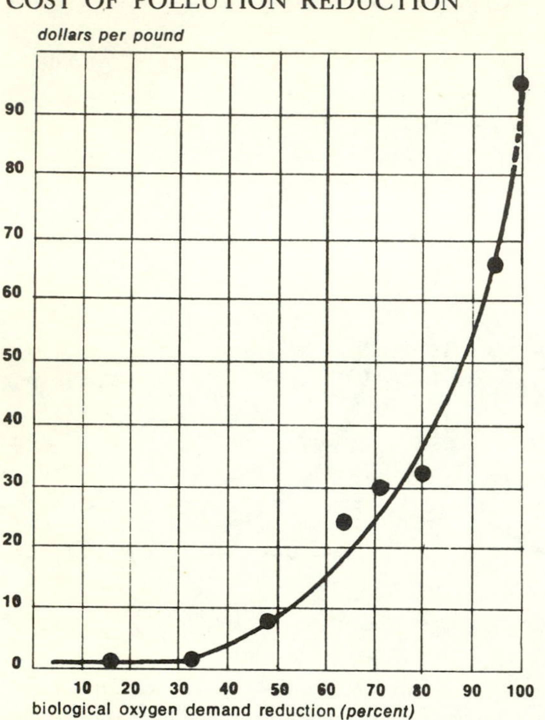

Incremental cost of reducing organic wastes from a 2,700-ton-per-day beet sugar plant rises steeply as emission standards approach complete purity. Reduction of biological oxygen demand (a measure of the oxygen required to decompose wastes) costs less than $1 a pound up to 30 percent reduction. Reduction beyond 65 percent requires more than $20 for each additional pound removed, and at 95 percent reduction, each pound removed costs $60.

SOURCE: *Second Annual Report of the Council on Environmental Quality* (Washington, DC: Government Printing Office, 1971).

plant as a function of organic wastes removed. If *no* organic wastes were allowed to leave the plant, the cost would be 100 times greater than if only 30 percent of the wastes were removed from the effluent. Table 6 on page 23 shows a similar trend in the projected costs of reducing air pollution in a US city.[39]

[39] *Second Annual Report of the Council on Environmental Quality*, p. 118.

In figure 39 the world model output is plotted assuming *both* the reduction in resource depletion of figure 37 *and* a reduction in pollution generation from all sources by a factor of four, starting in 1975. Reduction to less than one-fourth of the present rate of pollution generation is probably unrealistic because of cost, and because of the difficulty of eliminating some kinds of pollution, such as thermal pollution and radioisotopes from nuclear power generation, fertilizer runoff, and asbestos particles from brake linings. We assume that such a sharp reduction in pollution generation could occur globally and quickly for purposes of experimentation with the model, not because we believe it is politically feasible, given our present institutions.

Table 6
COST OF REDUCING
AIR POLLUTION IN A US CITY

Percent reduction in SO_2	*Percent reduction in particulates*	*Projected cost*
5	22	$ 50,000
42	66	7,500,000
48	69	26,000,000

As figure 39 shows, the pollution control policy is indeed successful in averting the pollution crisis of the previous run. Both population and industrial output per person rise well beyond their peak values in figure 37, and yet resource depletion and pollution never become problems. The overshoot mode is still operative, however, and the collapse comes about this time from food shortage.

As long as industrial output is rising in figure 39, the yield from each hectare of land continues to rise (up to a maximum of seven times the average yield in 1900) and new land is developed. At the same time, however, some arable land is taken for urban-industrial use, and some land is eroded, especially by highly capitalized agricultural practices. Eventually the limit of arable land is reached. After that point, as population continues to rise, food per capita decreases. As the food shortage becomes apparent, industrial output is diverted into agricultural capital to increase land yields. Less capital is available for investment, and finally the industrial output per capita begins to fall. When food per capita sinks to the subsistence level, the death rate begins to increase, bringing an end to population growth.

Figure 39
WORLD MODEL WITH "UNLIMITED"
RESOURCES AND POLLUTION CONTROLS

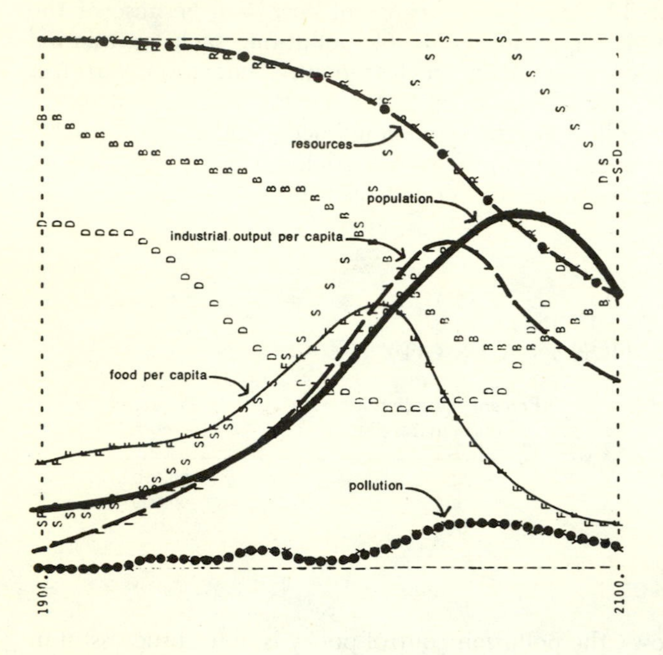

A further technological improvement is added to the world model in 1975 to avoid the resource depletion and pollution problems of previous model runs. Here we assume that pollution generation per unit of industrial and agricultural output can be reduced to one-fourth of its 1970 value. Resource policies are the same as those in figure 37. These changes allow population and industry to grow until the limit of arable land is reached. Food per capita declines, and industrial growth is also slowed as capital is diverted to food production.

Increased Food Yield and Birth Control

The problem in figure 39 could be viewed either as too little food or as too many people. The technological response to the first situation would be to produce more food, perhaps by some further extension of the principles of the Green Revolution. (The development of the new, high-yield grain varieties which constitutes the Green Revolution has

Figure 40
WORLD MODEL WITH "UNLIMITED" RESOURCES, POLLUTION CONTROLS, AND INCREASED AGRICULTURAL PRODUCTIVITY

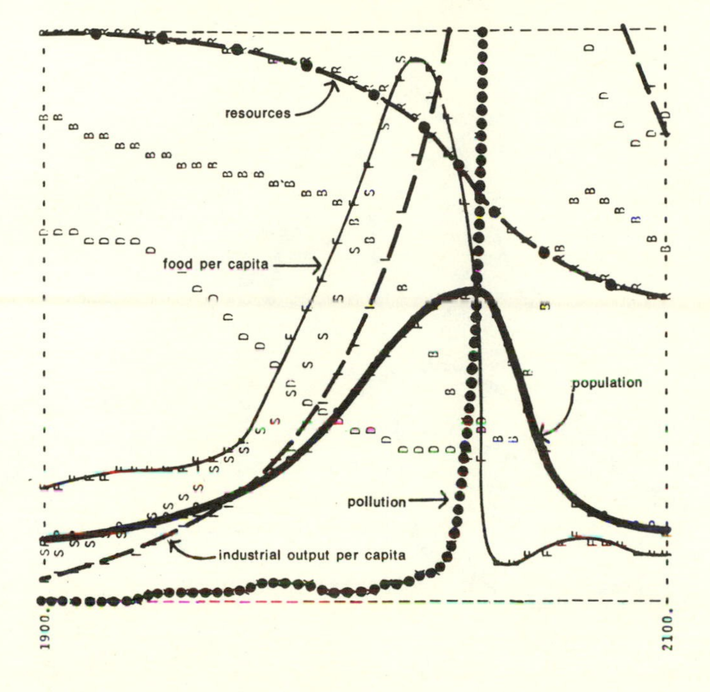

To avoid the food crisis of the previous model run, average land yield is doubled in 1975 in addition to the pollution and resource policies of previous figures. The combination of these three policies removes so many constraints to growth that population and industry reach very high levels. Although each unit of industrial production generates much less pollution, total production rises enough to create a pollution crisis that brings an end to growth.

been included in the original model equations.) The technological solution to the second problem would be to provide better methods of birth control. The results of these two changes, instituted in 1975 along with the changes in resource use and pollution generation we have already discussed, are shown both separately and simultaneously in figures 40, 41, and 42.

Figure 41
WORLD MODEL WITH "UNLIMITED" RESOURCES, POLLUTION CONTROLS, AND "PERFECT" BIRTH CONTROL

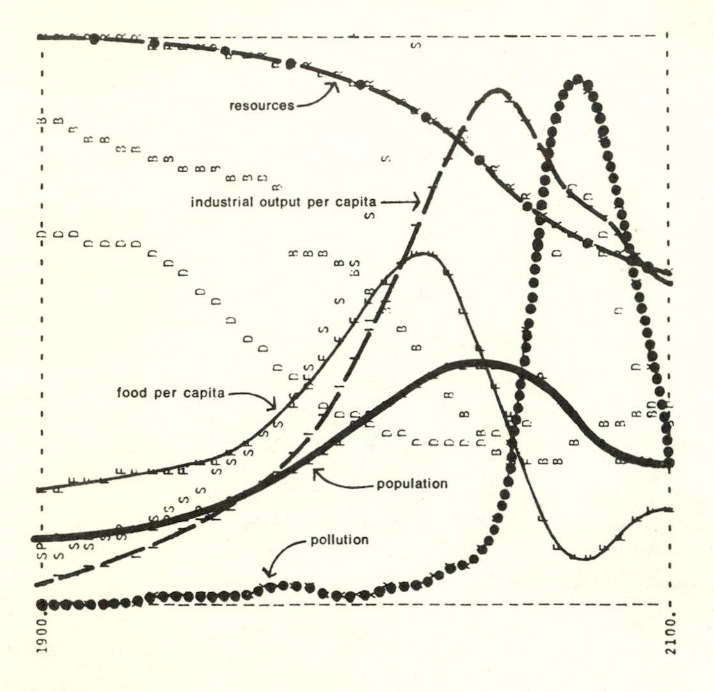

Instead of an increase in food production, an increase in birth control effectiveness is tested as a policy to avert the food problem. Since the birth control is voluntary and does not involve any value changes, population continues to grow, but more slowly than it did in figure 39. Nevertheless, the food crisis is postponed for only a decade or two.

In figure 40 we assume that the normal yield per hectare of all the world's land can be further increased by a factor of two. The result is an enormous increase in food, industrial output, and services per capita. Average industrial output per person for all the world's people becomes nearly equal to the 1970 US level, but only briefly. Although a strict pollution control policy is still in effect, so that pollution per unit of output is reduced by a factor of four, industry grows so quickly that soon it is producing four times as much output. Thus the level of pollution rises in spite of the pollution control policy, and a pollution crisis stops further growth, as it did in figure 37.

Figure 42
WORLD MODEL WITH "UNLIMITED" RESOURCES, POLLUTION CONTROLS, INCREASED AGRICULTURAL PRODUCTIVITY, AND "PERFECT" BIRTH CONTROL

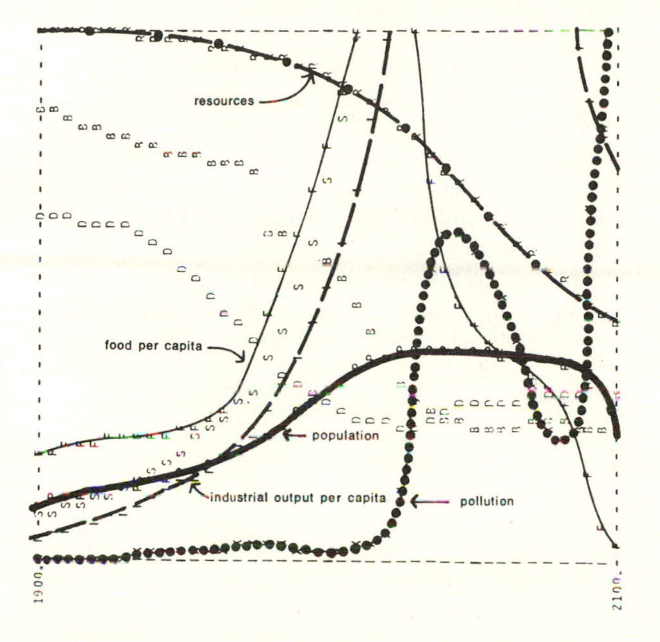

Four simultaneous technological policies are introduced in the world model in an attempt to avoid the growth-and-collapse behavior of previous runs. Resources are fully exploited, and 75 percent of those used are recycled. Pollution generation is reduced to one-fourth of its 1970 value. Land yields are doubled, and effective methods of birth control are made available to the world population. The result is a temporary achievement of a constant population with a world average income per capita that reaches nearly the present US level. Finally, though, industrial growth is halted, and the death rate rises as resources are depleted, pollution accumulates, and food production declines.

Figure 41 shows the alternate technological policy—perfect birth control, practiced voluntarily, starting in 1975. The result is not to stop population growth entirely because such a policy prevents only the births of *unwanted* children. The birth rate does decrease markedly, however, and the population grows more slowly than it did in figures 39 and 40. In this run growth is stopped by a food crisis occurring about 20 years later than in figure 39.

In figure 42 we apply increased land yield and perfect birth control simultaneously. Here we are utilizing a technological policy in every sector of the world model to circumvent in some way the various limits to growth. The model system is producing nuclear power, recycling resources, and mining the most remote reserves; withholding as many pollutants as possible; pushing yields from the land to undreamed-of heights; and producing only children who are actively wanted by their parents. The result is still an end to growth before the year 2100. In this case growth is stopped by three simultaneous crises. Overuse of land leads to erosion, and food production drops. Resources are severely depleted by a prosperous world population (but not as prosperous as the present US population). Pollution rises, drops, and then rises again dramatically, causing a further decrease in food production and a sudden rise in the death rate. The application of technological solutions alone has prolonged the period of population and industrial growth, but it has not removed the ultimate limits to that growth.

The Overshoot Mode

Given the many approximations and limitations of the world model, there is no point in dwelling glumly on the series of catastrophes it tends to generate. We shall emphasize just one more time that none of these computer outputs is a prediction. We would not expect the real world to behave like the world model in any of the graphs we have shown, especially in the collapse modes. The model contains dynamic statements about only the physical aspects of man's activities. It assumes that social variables—income distribution, attitudes about family size, choices among goods, services, and food—will continue to follow the same patterns they have followed throughout the world in recent history. These patterns, and the human values they represent, were all established in the growth phase of our civilization. They would certainly be greatly revised as population and income began to decrease. Since we find it difficult to imagine what new forms of human societal behavior might emerge and how quickly they would emerge under collapse conditions, we have not attempted to model such social changes. What validity our model has holds up only to the point in each output graph at which growth comes to an end and collapse begins.

Although we have many reservations about the approximations and simplifications in the present world model, it has led us to one conclusion that appears to be justified under all the assumptions we have tested so far. *The basic behavior mode of the world system is exponential growth of population and capital, followed by collapse.* As we have shown in the model runs presented here, this behavior mode occurs if we assume no change in the present system or if we assume any number of technological changes in the system.

The unspoken assumption behind all of the model runs we have presented in this chapter is that population and capital growth should be allowed to continue until they reach some "natural" limit. This assumption also appears to be a basic part of the human value system currently operational in the real world. Whenever we incorporate this value into the model, the result is that the growing system rises above its ultimate limit and then collapses. When we introduce technological developments that successfully lift some restraint to growth or avoid some collapse, the system simply grows to another limit, temporarily surpasses it, and falls back. Given that first as assumption, that population and capital growth should not be deliberately limited but should be left to "seek their own levels," we have not been able to find a set of policies that avoids the collapse mode of behavior.

It is not really difficult to understand how the collapse mode comes about. Everywhere in the web of interlocking feedback loops that constitutes the world system we have found it necessary to represent the real-world situation by introducing time delays between causes and their ultimate effects. These are natural delays that cannot be controlled by technological means. They include, for example, the delay of about fifteen years between the birth of a baby and the time that baby can first reproduce itself. The time delay inherent in the aging of a population introduces a certain unavoidable lag in the ability of the population to respond through the birth rate to changing conditions. Another delay occurs between the time a pollutant is released into the environment and the time it has a measurable influence on human health. This delay includes the passage of the pollutant through air or rivers or soil and into the food chain, and also the time from human ingestion or absorption of the pollutant until clinical symptoms appear. This second delay may be as long as 20 years in the case of some carcinogens. Other delays occur because capital cannot be transferred instantly from one sector to another to meet changing demands, because new capital and land can only be produced or developed gradually, and because pollution can only slowly be dispersed or metabolized into harmless forms.

Delays in a dynamic system have serious effects only if the system itself is undergoing rapid changes. Perhaps a simple example will clarify that statement. When you drive a car there is a very short, unavoidable delay between your perception of the road in front of you and your reaction to it. There is a longer delay between your action on the accelerator or brakes and the car's response to that action. You have learned to deal with those delays. You know that, because of the delays, it is unsafe to drive too fast. If you do, you will certainly experience the overshoot and collapse mode, sooner or later. If you were blindfolded and had to drive on the instructions of a front-seat passenger, the delay between perception and action would be considerably lengthened. The only safe way to handle the extended delay would be to slow down. If you tried to drive your normal speed, or if you tried to accelerate continuously (as in exponential growth), the result would be disastrous.

In exactly the same way, the delays in the feedback loops of the world system would be no problem if the system were growing very slowly or not at all. Under those conditions any new action or policy could be instituted gradually, and the changes could work their way through the delays to feed back on every part of the system before some other action or policy would have to be introduced. Under conditions of rapid growth, however, the system is forced into new policies and actions long before the results of old policies and actions can be properly assessed. The situation is even worse when the growth is exponential and the system is changing ever more rapidly.

Thus population and capital, driven by exponential growth, not only reach their limits, but temporarily shoot beyond them before the rest of the system, with its inherent delays, reacts to stop growth. Pollution generated in exponentially increasing amounts can rise past the danger point, because the danger point is first perceived years after the offending pollution was released. A rapidly growing industrial system can build up a capital base dependent on a given resource and then discover that the exponentially shrinking resource reserves cannot support it. Because of delays in the age structure, a population will continue to grow for as long as 70 years, even after average fertility has dropped below the replacement level (an average of two children for each married couple).

TECHNOLOGY IN THE REAL WORLD

The hopes of the technological optimists center on the ability of technology to remove or extend the limits to growth of population and capital. We have shown that in the world model the application of technology to apparent problems of resource depletion or pollution or food shortage has no impact on the *essential* problem, which is exponential growth in a finite and complex system. Our attempts to use even the most optimistic estimates of the benefits of technology in the model did not prevent the ultimate decline of population and industry, and in fact did not in any case postpone the collapse beyond the year 2100. Before we go on in the next chapter to test other policies, which are not technological, let us extend our discussion of technological solutions to some aspects of technology that could not be included in the world model.

Technological Side-Effects

Dr. Garrett Hardin has defined side-effects as "effects which I hadn't foreseen or don't want to think about."[40] He has suggested that, since such effects are actually inseparable from the principal effect, they should not be labeled *side*-effects at all. Every new technology has side-effects, of course, and one of the main purposes of model-building is to anticipate those effects. The model runs in this chapter have shown some of the side-effects of various technologies on the world's physical and economic systems. Unfortunately the model does not indicate, at this stage, the *social* side-effects of new technologies. These effects are often the most important in terms of the influence of a technology on people's lives.

A recent example of social side-effects from a successful new technology appeared as the Green Revolution was introduced to the agrarian societies of the world. The Green Revolution—the utilization of new seed varieties, combined with fertilizers and pesticides—was designed to be a technological solution to the world's food problems. The planners of this new agricultural technology foresaw some of the social problems it might raise in traditional cultures. The Green Revolution was intended not only to produce more food but to be labor-intensive—to provide jobs and not to require large amounts of capital. In some areas of the world, such as the Indian Punjab, the Green Revolution has indeed increased the number of agricultural jobs faster than the rate of growth of the total population. In the East Punjab there was a real wage increase of 16 percent from 1963 to 1968.[41]

The principal, or intended, effect of the Green Revolution—increased food production—seems to have been achieved. Unfortunately the social side-effects have not been entirely beneficial in most regions where the new seed varieties have been introduced. The Indian Punjab had, before the Green Revolution, a remarkably equitable system of land distribution. The more common pattern in the nonindustrialized world is a wide range in land ownership, with most people working very small farms and a few people in possession of the vast majority of the land.

Where these conditions of economic inequality already exist, the

[40] Garrett Hardin, "The Cybernetics of Competition: A Biologist's View of Society," *Perspectives in Biology and Medicine* 7 (Autumn 1963): 58. Reprinted in Paul Shepard and Daniel McKinley, eds., *The Subversive* Science (Boston: Houghton Mifflin, 1969), p. 275.

[41] S. R. Sen, *Modernizing Indian Agriculture*, Vol. 1, Expert Committee on Assessment and Evaluation (New Delhi: Ministry of Food, Agriculture, Community Development, and Cooperatives, 1969).

Green Revolution tends to cause widening inequality. Large farmers generally adopt the new methods first. They have the capital to do so and can afford to take the risk. Although the new seed varieties do not require tractor mechanization, they provide much economic incentive for mechanization, especially where multiple cropping requires a quick harvest and replanting. On large farms, simple economic considerations lead almost inevitably to the use of labor-displacing machinery and to the purchase of still more land.[42] The ultimate effects of this socio-economic positive feedback loop are agricultural unemployment, increased migration to the city, and perhaps even increased malnutrition, since the poor and unemployed do not have the means to buy the newly produced food.

A specific example of the social side-effects of the Green Revolution in an area where land is unequally distributed is described below.

> A landless laborer's income in West Pakistan today is still just about what it was five years ago, less than $100 a year. In contrast, one landlord with a 1,500-acre wheat farm told me when I was in Pakistan this winter that he had cleared a net profit of more than $100,000 on his last harvest.[43]

Statistics from Mexico, where the Green Revolution began in the 1940's, provide another example. From 1940 to 1960 the average growth rate of agricultural production in Mexico was 5 percent per year. From 1950 to 1960, however, the average number of days worked by a landless laborer fell from 194 to 100, and his real income decreased from $68 to $56. Eighty percent of the increased agricultural production came from only 3 percent of the farms.[44]

These unexpected social side-effects do not imply that the technology of the Green Revolution was unsuccessful. They do imply that social side-effects must be anticipated and forestalled *before* the large-scale introduction of a new technology.

> As agriculture emerges from its traditional subsistence state to modern commercial farming . . . it becomes progressively more important to ensure that adequate rewards accrue directly to the man who tills the soil. Indeed, it is hard to see how there can be any meaningful modernization of food production in Latin America and Africa south

---

[42] For an excellent summation of this problem see Robert D'A. Shaw, *Jobs and Agricultural Development* (Washington, D.C.: Overseas Development Council, 1970).

[43] Richard Critchfield, "It's a Revolution All Right," Alicia Paterson Fund Paper (New York: Alicia Paterson Fund, 1971).

[44] Robert D'A. Shaw, *Jobs and Agricultural Development*, p. 440.

of the Sahara unless land is registered, deeded, and distributed more equitably.[45]

Such preparation for technological change requires, at the very least, a great deal of time. Every change in the normal way of doing things requires an adjustment time, while the population, consciously or unconsciously, restructures its social system to accommodate the change. While technology can change rapidly, political and social institutions generally change very slowly. Furthermore, they almost never change *in anticipation* of a social need, but only in response to one.

We have already mentioned the dynamic effect of physical delays in the world model. We must also keep in mind the presence of social delays—the delays necessary to allow society to absorb or to prepare for a change. Most delays, physical or social, reduce the stability of the world system and increase the likelihood of the overshoot mode. The social delays, like the physical ones, are becoming increasingly more critical because the processes of exponential growth are creating additional pressures at a faster and faster rate. The world population grew from 1 billion to 2 billion over a period of more than one hundred years. The third billion was added in 30 years and the world's population has had less than 20 years to prepare for its fourth billion. The fifth, sixth, and perhaps even seventh billions may arrive before the year 2000, less than 30 years from now. Although the rate of technological change has so far managed to keep up with this accelerated pace, mankind has made virtually no new discoveries to increase the rate of social (political, ethical, and cultural) change.

Problems with No Technical Solutions

When the cities of America were new, they grew rapidly. Land was abundant and cheap, new buildings rose continuously, and the population and economic output of urban regions increased. Eventually, however, all the land in the city center was filled. A physical limit had been reached, threatening to stop population and economic growth in that section of the city. The technological answer was the development of skyscrapers and elevators, which essentially removed the constraint of land area as a factor in suppressing growth. The central city added more people and more businesses. Then a new constraint appeared. Goods and workers could not move in and out of the dense center city quickly enough. Again the solution was technological. A network of expressways,

[45] Lester R. Brown, *Seeds of Change: The Green Revolution and Development in the 1970's* (New York: Praeger, 1970), p. 112.

mass transit systems, and helicopter ports on the tops of the tallest buildings was constructed. The transportation limit was overcome, the buildings grew taller, the population increased.

Now most of the larger US cities have stopped growing. (Of the ten largest, five—New York, Chicago, Philadelphia, Detroit, and Baltimore—decreased in population from 1960 to 1970. Washington, DC, showed no change. Los Angeles, Houston, Dallas, and Indianapolis continued to grow, at least in part by annexing additional land.)[46] The wealthier people, who have an economic choice, are moving to the ever-expanding ring of suburbs around the cities. The central areas are characterized by noise, pollution, crime, drug addiction, poverty, labor strikes, and breakdown of social services. The quality of life in the city core has declined. Growth has been stopped in part by problems with no technical solutions.

A technical solution may be defined as "one that requires a change only in the techniques of the natural sciences, demanding little or nothing in the way of change in human values or ideas of morality."[47] Numerous problems today have no technical solutions. Examples are the nuclear arms race, racial tensions, and unemployment. Even if society's technological progress fulfills all expectations, it may very well be a problem with no technical solution, or the interaction of several such problems, that finally brings an end to population and capital growth.

A Choice of Limits

Applying technology to the natural pressures that the environment exerts against any growth process has been so successful in the past that a whole culture has evolved around the principle of fighting against limits rather than learning to live with them. This culture has been reinforced by the apparent immensity of the earth and its resources and by the relative smallness of man and his activities.

But the relationship between the earth's limits and man's activities is changing. The exponential growth curves are adding millions of people and billions of tons of pollutants to the ecosystem each year. Even the ocean, which once appeared virtually inexhaustible, is losing species after species of its commercially useful animals. Recent FAO statistics indicate that the total catch of the world's fisheries decreased in 1969 for the first time since 1950, in spite of more mechanized and intensive

[46] U.S. Bureau of the Census 1970, *Census of Population and Housing, General Demographic Trends of Metropolitan Areas, 1960–70* (Washington, D.C.: Government Printing Office, 1971).

[47] Garrett Hardin, "The Tragedy of the Commons," *Science* 162 (1968): 1243.

fishing practices. (Among commercial species becoming increasingly scarce are Scandinavian herring, menhaden, and Atlantic cod.)[48]

Yet man does not seem to learn by running into the earth's obvious limits. The story of the whaling industry (shown in figure 43) demonstrates, for one small system, the ultimate result of the attempt to grow forever in a limited environment. Whalers have systematically reached one limit after another and have attempted to overcome each one by increases in power and technology. As a result, they have wiped out one species after another. The outcome of this particular grow-forever policy can only be the final extinction of both whales and whalers. The alternative policy is the imposition of a *man-determined limit* on the number of whales taken each year, set so that the whale population is maintained at a steady-state level. The self-imposed limit on whaling would be an unpleasant pressure that would prevent the growth of the industry. But perhaps it would be preferable to the gradual disappearance of both whales and whaling industry.

The basic choice that faces the whaling industry is the same one that faces any society trying to overcome a natural limit with a new technology. *Is it better to try to live within that limit by accepting a self-imposed restriction on growth? Or is it preferable to go on growing until some other natural limit arises, in the hope that at that time another technological leap will allow growth to continue still longer?* For the last several hundred years human society has followed the second course so consistently and successfully that the first choice has been all but forgotten.

There may be much disagreement with the statement that population and capital growth must stop *soon*. But virtually no one will argue that material growth on this planet can go on forever. At this point in man's history, the choice posed above is still available in almost every sphere of human activity. Man can still choose his limits and stop when he pleases by weakening some of the strong pressures that cause capital and population growth, or by instituting counterpressures, or both. Such counterpressures will probably not be entirely pleasant. They will certainly involve profound changes in the social and economic structures that have been deeply impressed into human culture by centuries of growth. The alternative is to wait until the price of technology becomes more than society can pay, or until the side-effects of technology suppress growth themselves, or until problems arise that have no technical solutions. At any of those points the choice of limits will be gone. Growth will be stopped by pressures that are not of human choosing, and that, as the world model suggests, may be very much worse than those which society might choose for itself.

[48] UN Food and Agriculture Organization, *The State of Food and Agriculture* (Rome: UN Food and Agriculture Organization, 1970), p. 6.

Figure 43
MODERN WHALING

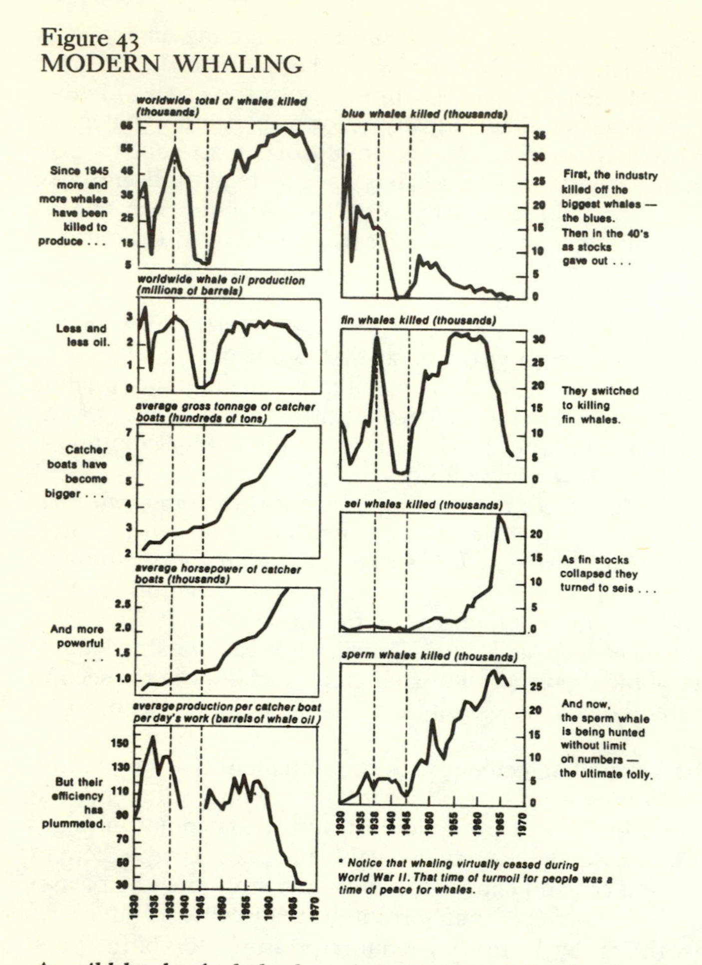

As wild herds of whales have been destroyed, finding the survivors has become more difficult and has required more effort. As larger whales are killed off, smaller species are exploited to keep the industry alive. Since there have never been species limits, however, large whales are always taken wherever and whenever encountered. Thus small whales are used to subsidize the extermination of large ones.

SOURCE: Roger Payne, "Among Wild Whales," in *The New York Zoological Society Newsletter*, November 1968.

We have felt it necessary to dwell so long on an analysis of technology here because we have found that technological optimism is the most common and the most dangerous reaction to our findings from the world model. Technology can relieve the symptoms of a problem without affecting the underlying causes. Faith in technology as the ultimate solution to all problems can thus divert our attention from the most fundamental problem—the problem of growth in a finite system—and prevent us from taking effective action to solve it.

On the other hand, our intent is certainly not to brand technology as evil or futile or unnecessary. We are technologists ourselves, working in a technological institution. We strongly believe, as we shall point out in the following chapter, that many of the technological developments mentioned here—recycling, pollution control devices, contraceptives—will be absolutely vital to the future of human society *if they are combined with deliberate checks on growth.* We would deplore an unreasoned rejection of the benefits of technology as strongly as we argue here against an unreasoned acceptance of them. Perhaps the best summary of our position is the motto of the Sierra Club: "Not blind opposition to progress, but opposition to blind progress."

We would hope that society will receive each new technological advance by establishing the answers to three questions *before* the technology is widely adopted. The questions are:

1. What will be the side-effects, both physical and social, if this development is introduced on a large scale?

2. What social changes will be necessary before this development can be implemented properly, and how long will it take to achieve them?

3. If the development is fully successful and removes some natural limit to growth, what limit will the growing system meet next? Will society prefer its pressures to the ones this development is designed to remove?

Let us go on now to investigate nontechnical approaches for dealing with growth in a finite world.

QUESTIONS

1. What is the "collapse mode of behavior"?
2. Why do most people feel that an end to growth is a prelude to the end of the world? In your view, what are the psychological overtones of the word "growth"?
3. Is it possible to predict *ultimate* effects and side effects? What might interfere?
4. *The Limits to Growth* is presented as a highly rational and factual article. Is the relatively dispassionate prose more persuasive than a more heated

rhetoric would be? What of the charts? Do they lend greater credibility to the prose than it might otherwise have? If so, why?

5. Can you think of psychological factors that might have been overlooked in this study? Parallel these to the discussion of social side effects.

6. According to the authors, it all comes down to the multiple problem of overpopulation and unlimited capital growth. Do you think it possible for the nations and peoples of the world to solve this dual problem, short of imposing worldwide dictatorship?

7. The authors of this essay are well grounded in the techniques and concepts of science, perhaps one of the largest "growth industries" of the twentieth century. Is it not ironic that perhaps the most severe criticism of "technological optimism"—the result of the growth of science—should come from within the community of scientists? What does this imply about the rest of the intellectual community, such as philosophers, poets, religious theorists, and the like? What does it imply about the organization of knowledge?

from Of a Fire on the Moon

Norman Mailer

In this section from Of a Fire on the Moon, *Mailer provides an epic dimension to still another event that has brought us into "future shock." We have literally taken the first steps outward, we have voyaged from this planet and walked on another pebble of the universe. The very event, the consciousness of our achievement, must inevitably change forever our view of Earth.*

There is a strong likelihood that Norman Mailer's Of a Fire on the Moon, *with its strong parallels to Herman Melville's* Moby Dick, *will eventually be recognized as one of the greatest literary works of the century.*

Orbits are not difficult to comprehend. It is gravity which stirs the depths of insomnia. We can remind ourselves that the idea that what goes up must come down is still a momentous discovery to an infant (who finds every balloon a magical beast). An adult on the contrary builds the bedrock of his common sense on the certain fall of an unsupported object. What goes up *must* come down. Of course the Lem in Apollo 10 would never come down again—it was off in orbit around the sun, and Mariner would not be back again, nor Ranger, nor Lunar Orbiter. And Surveyor I had landed on the moon and there it had stayed. So the moon apparently had its own kind of gravity, as did Mars, and Venus, and the planets and the sun. Every heavenly body had its domain of gravity, its field of attractive influence. Indeed every physical body did. There was a force which drew bodies together, and physics had calculated it neatly as in reverse proportion to the distance between, which was another way of saying that attraction accelerated as bodies drew nearer, it increased as the inverse function of the square of the distance. Two feet apart, bodies were only attracted to one another with one quarter of the power the same bodies would feel at one foot apart. At three feet, it was one-ninth the power, at five feet one-twenty-fifth. Of course if the bodies were only six inches apart, the force of attraction was four times as great as at one foot. That was the first part of an extraordinary relation. The second was that no matter how attracted, whether by much or little, they were attracted in inverse relation to their mass, which crudely is to say in opposite proportion to their weight. Heavy bodies would attract light bodies toward them faster than light bodies would induce movement in heavy bodies. Very heavy bodies would hardly move at all as light bodies accelerated toward them. It was more than theory: the laws of gravity were the soundest laws of behavior in the kingdom of physics—it required only that one not personify the bodies, not give them private will or curiosity or whim, no independent desire or independent resistance. Obviously, a theory of sexual mechanics could never be based on gravity. Still, gravity was a damnable mystery—why did inanimate or dead objects attract each other? And why did animate objects like human beings act like inanimate objects under certain conditions, such as jumping off a high building? Then the human body entered the laws of physics at a weight of two hundred pounds. Since the earth had a literal weight of six billion trillion tons, there was no visible reciprocity. Dispensing with all sizable calculations of air resistance, the body fell at an increasing rate of thirty-two feet per second every second, which was the accleration gravity gave to falling objects. From a fall of a hundred feet the two-hundred pound man would be moving about sixty-five feet a second when he hit the ground—the earth, with all of its six billion trillion tons, would not be quivering at any perceptible rate of acceleration up toward the body. Still by the width of a hair taken from an electron it had been moving toward the body which approached. Because we cannot see the movement, we tend to think it does not exist, that bodies merely fall, but in fact the reason a two-hundred pound man exhibits much the same behavior as any inanimate object in a ten-story fall is that the power with which the earth pulls on him is enormous, and the muscles which express his will are not equipped to be effective in air. So it is not so much that he falls as that he is *drawn* by an intense and accelerating introduction to the earth. And indeed anyone who has ever had a high fall has felt such a fierce force pulling on him. "The earth came up and socked me," is the good tough statement a child gives to witnesses. What a ringing in the ear, what a memory of the lightning bolt!

Metaphors then arise of a charged and libidinous universe with heavenly bodies which attract each other across the silences of space. If they do not all gather together in assembly at a point, it is because they do not act simply upon each other, but are each in relation with many bodies in many directions, and all are moving as well. If they are moving fast enough and with enough force, they can resist powers of attraction calling to them from vastly larger bodies. An airplane need not descend so long as it has fuel to give its motor strength.

We are preparing, however, to brood upon the astronauts in orbit, and that is another case. They are now not flying with engines, they are coasting with motors off. They are a hundred miles up in the air, and their motors are off, and yet they do not fall. They merely continue to circle the earth once every hour and twenty-eight minutes.

Of course they are traveling fast, at eighteen thousand miles an hour we can remember, and while that is nowhere near the speed of light, 186,000 miles a second (a speed which is probably the walls of the vessel which contains the time of our universe), it is still interesting to note that eighteen thousand miles an hour is as many times greater than the rate at which a baby crawls (or Apollo-Saturn began its trip from the VAB to the pad) as the speed of light is greater than the present velocity of the spacecraft. If men could move out of infancy at half a mile an hour and get up to eighteen thousand miles an hour in one lifetime, well, who was to assume that the walls of the universe were safe from future men?

At any rate, the spacecraft was traveling at eighteen thousand miles an hour, and that speed was just great enough to keep it in orbit a hundred miles above the earth. It was of course falling, it was in fact in free fall and in a virtual vacuum (for the presence of air at one hundred miles of altitude is next to nonexistent) but it was also traveling so fast in a forward direction that it fell forward like a ball thrown into an endless chasm, and as it fell forward it fell around the curve of the earth. The earth pulled on it of course, it pulled on the spaceship with all the force of its gravity, but only succeeded in bending its path around the circumference of the earth.

It is easier if we conceive of gravity as a general condition of which magnetism is a special case. Magnetism only works a force of attraction on iron objects, whereas gravity works on all objects. Think of a cylindrical ring highly magnetized, and a steel bullet fired from a revolver which passes the ring in just such a way that the intense force of the magnetism bends the path of the bullet around the cylinder. The bullet would whip around until air resistance had slowed its speed to the point where it would circle in and touch the ring. Orbit was comparable. Even better, at one hundred miles up, air resistance was next to nonexistent, so the spaceship could stay in orbit for a long time. What peace and communality to drift over the earth from such a height, to see nations appear below on the extended field of a continent, nations no larger to the eye from a hundred miles up than the spread of a city from a passenger plane, and oceans the size of a cove. Clouds covered the earth like the wet white feathers of a bird just born, clouds with lines of logic and reentrant curves of thought, clouds gathered in nodes of spiral to signify a shift of atmospheric being—a storm was blowing across a thousand miles of sea. A planet manifest beneath, filling the window out which the astronauts would look, a planet blue and brown with white trailings of celestial ripple and wake, hints of green and dark gray and silver in the curvings and stuffings and pumpings of thousand-mile odysseys of cloud, caravans of weather, pulsations of weather. What a peace, what a calm, what a silence!

Not a chance! The sound of static filled the module, the crackling of questions and answers from earth to spacecraft, from air to ground. Into the ear of each astronaut came burning searching spitting sounds, the unclassifiable sounds of static, so much like the rush of crackling air, the consumption of something vital in space. If smell, Aquarius long had thought, was related to time, then sound was some current in space. But what was static, what special case of space? Static was a form of speech man did not comprehend. Like the dialogue of the dolphin, the communication was faster than the ear. But what fury of irritabilities was loose in the ether at this harshness perpetrated upon it!

Below the astronauts was the earth. Above them, behind them, around them, was a sky no longer blue but dark, dark as the endless night of space. They would not always see that black sky. Sometimes the shine from the earth, the moon, or the light of the sun would reflect from their module, and the sky—almost impossible to see stars in such curious reflected light—would seem a dark rose, a hellish color with glare and plays of transparency and curtains of dark. They were weightless. As their ship fell in its ever continuing circle about the earth, so they fell too. If not strapped down, or with hands on a grip, or with Velcro-soled shoes hooked to a Velcro mat, they floated through the fall of free fall as a man will fall and turn in the air before he opens his parachute. They could do small dives inside the locked spaces of the module, twists and tucks and ever revolving turns, disport like seals and monkeys and otters. That very weightlessness, that absence of gravity which space doctors worried might produce profound deteriorations of the organs and the flesh in a trip of some months' duration was for now a delight, a languor. Think of reaching to dispose of a full can of beer. To one's surprise it is empty. How languorous is the arm as it comes up. John Glenn experiencing weightlessness in his first orbit had said, "Contrary to this being a problem, I think I have finally found the element in which I belong." Of course, years later, Glenn had slipped in a tub and almost been killed. Who knew what price was in the pounds lost to weightlessness—for in every intoxication was some kind of price. Otherwise, nothing divine to economy.

Now, however, they did not have time to play. There was static in their ear, and systems and subsystems to monitor, align, check out, adjust, a Puritan ethic in the whisper of the empty spaces—keep busy in the empyrean was the whisper of those empty spaces. So they kept busy for those two and a half hours before they took off for the moon. Names and duties came their way. Alignments, static, stations.

Ground stations ready to receive their communications and relay them to Houston came into range as they moved around the earth, acquired signal, then lost signal when they moved further on. The tracking ship *Vanguard* in the Caribbean lost contact, the Canary Island Station acquired it, Tananarive in the Indian Ocean was next, then Carnarvon in Australia, Honeysuckle in Australia, Goldstone in California. Somewhat later, starting from an altitude of ten thousand miles, on all the way to the moon, there would be but three stations for radio communication, each one hundred and twenty degrees apart on the circumference of the earth, stations with enormous eighty-five foot dish-shaped antennae located in Madrid; in Goldstone; and Canberra, Australia; but for now the stations were more modest, the antennae were no larger than thirty feet, the communication was close, and the data received was fed by relay into computers at Mission Control at Houston, there to go up on the wall to show in display the position of the ship.

They passed the other tracking stations in their orbit, passed them at Hawaii, at Guaymas in Mexico, Corpus Christi, in the Bermudas, the Bahamas, the tracking ship *Redstone,* in all there were seventeen ground stations, plus six units from ARIA (Apollo Range Instrumented Aircraft, what an acronym was ARIA!), six jets which could be used for voice relay in emergency or on unusual azimuths if Apollo passed over in unconventional orbit. But nothing was out of the ordinary today. The orbit and a half before Trans-Lunar Injection was a time of testing out communications and making their checks. The rocket thrusters which would give their spaceship its attitude, put its nose up or down, left or right, or leave it to roll, were fired in brief maneuvers, and studied by instruments in Mission Control in Houston to pass on the results. The temperature of one rocket thruster was soon discovered to be lower than the others. Queries came up from the ground.

> CAPCOM: *Would you confirm that your RCS heater switch for quad BRAVO is in primary? Over.*
>
> ALDRIN: *You're correct. It was not in primary. It was off. It's on now. Thank you.*
>
> CAPCOM: *Roger. Thank you.*

The time-line lengthened. They were in second orbit. At a point somewhere near the Gilbert Islands, about halfway between Australia and Hawaii, they would ignite the engine on the third and remaining stage of the launch vehicle, and proceed into Trans-Lunar Injection, which is to say they would quit their earth orbit and fire up to the moon.

This is the transcript on that mighty event:

> CAPCOM: *Apollo 11, this is Houston. We are slightly less than one minute to ignition and everything is GO.*
>
> COLLINS: *Roger.*
>
> ARMSTRONG: *Ignition. (The sound of rocket motors are faintly heard.)*
>
> CAPCOM: *We confirm ignition and the thrust is Go.*
>
> CAPCOM: *Apollo 11, this is Houston at 1 minute. Trajectory and guidance look good and the stage is good. Over.*
>
> COLLINS: *Apollo 11. Roger.*
>
> CAPCOM: *Apollo 11, this is Houston. Thrust is good. Everything is still looking good. . . .*

COLLINS: Roger.

CAPCOM: *Apollo 11, this is Houston. Around three and a half minutes. You're still looking good. Your predicted cutoff is right on the nominal.*

ARMSTRONG: *Roger. Apollo 11's GO.*

CAPCOM: *Apollo 11, this is Houston. You are GO at five minutes.*

ARMSTRONG: *Roger, We're GO.*

CAPCOM: *Apollo 11, this is Houston. We show cutoff and we copy the numbers in Noun 62 . . .*

COLLINS: *Roger, Houston, Apollo 11. We're reading the VI 35579 and the EMS was plus 3.3. Over.*

CAPCOM: *Roger. Plus 3.3. on the EMS. And we copy the VI.*

ARMSTRONG: *Hey Houston. Apollo 11. This Saturn gave us a magnificent ride.*

CAPCOM: *Roger, 11, we'll pass that on, and it looks like you are well on your way now.*

. . .

. . . Four minutes after ignition . . . the Lem turned over on its back and the astronauts approaching the moon looked across a quarter of a million miles to earth. The comments are laconic, the difficulties are doubtless still ahead, but the radio is giving trouble again. They have passed through a minute where their remarks are garbled.

CAPCOM: *Eagle, Houston. You are GO. Take it all at four minutes. Roger, you are GO—you are GO to continue power descent.*

ALDRIN: *Roger.*

PAO: *Altitude 40,000.*

CAPCOM: *And Eagle, Houston. We've got data dropout. You're still looking good.*

ALDRIN: *PGNCS. We got good lock on. Altitude light is out. Delta H is minus 2900.*

CAPCOM: *Roger, we copy.*

ALDRIN: *Got the earth right out our front window.*

How powerful must have been such a sight to draw comment when the radio is working poorly, and a garbled remark can throw confusion back and forth. Perhaps it suggests some hint of happiness that they are finally at the beginning of the entrance to the last tunnel.

In the next moment Aldrin's voice speaks. "Houston, you're looking at our Delta H program alarm?"

"That's affirmative," replies the Capcom. "It's looking good to us. Over."

Aldrin's voice calls out, "1202, 1202." It was an alarm from the computer—"Executive Overflow" was its title. What a name! One thinks of seepage on the corporation president's bathroom floor. In fact it meant the computer was overloaded, and so unable to perform all its functions. In such a case the computer stops, then starts over again. It has recalculated its resources. Now it will take on only the most important functions, drop off the others. But what a moment at Mission Control! They have worked on this alarm in the day Kranz devoted to emergency situations. They know that if 1202 keeps blinking, the activities of the computer will soon deteriorate. The automatic pilot will first be lost, then control over the thrust of the engine, then Navigation and Guidance—the pilots will have to abort. In fifteen seconds it can all happen.

Picture Aldrin on his back looking up at the DSKY. "Give us the reading on the 1202 program alarm." It is his way of saying, "Is it serious?"

Thirty seconds go by. Duke speaks up the quarter of a million miles. "Roger, we got . . ." Pause. "We're GO on that alarm."

Kranz has been quizzing his Guidance officers and his Flight Dynamics officers. It is a ten-second roll call, and each one he queries says GO. The words come in, "GO. GO. GO. GO." The key word is from Guidance Officer Stephen G. Bales. It is on his console that the 1202 is also blinking. But they have been over the permissible rate of alarm on which they can continue to fly a mission, and the 1202 is coming in not that fast—the Executive Overflow is not constant. So Bales' voice rings out GO. Listening to it on a tape recorder later, there is something like fear in the voice, it is high-pitched, but it rings out. In the thirty seconds between Aldrin's request for a reading and the reply that they were GO, the decision has been taken.

Capcom: "Eagle, Houston. We'll monitor your Delta H." Mission Control would take over part of Pings. Data from the landing radar would no longer be fed to the computer on the Eagle, it would be sent uniquely to the ground. Eagle would be able to continue with the computer eased of some of its burden. But if telemetry failed again, and Pings could not reassume the burden, they would still have to turn back.

So they were obliged to proceed through the long braking burn with their minds on thoughts of Abort all the way, their eyes on the instrument panel, Armstrong's eyes as much as Aldrin's, searching for a clue to what had caused the overload, six hundred dials and switches to consider and eliminate in blocks and banks—a hopeless activity: the cause of the malfunction might reveal itself on no dial, and in fact could derive from the load of the rendezvous radar in addition to the landing radar, and that introduced still another fear, for the rendezvous radar would have even more work on the trip up from the moon. As Duke said: "Here we are with a computer that seems to be saturated during descent and my gosh, we might be asking it to perform a more complicated task during ascent." And periodically Kranz queried his FIDO, his GUIDO, his TelCom and his EECOM, and the voices came back, "GO, GO, GO,

GO," and Eagle descended, now at twenty-one thousand feet, now at sixteen thousand, thirteen thousand five hundred. "Stand by," said the Capcom. "You're looking great at eight minutes." Altitude ninety-two hundred feet.

In another twelve seconds they were at high gate. Now their horizontal speed was very low, their thrust was reduced, and they began to sit up from their near horizontal position. Slowly the astronauts' legs inclined with the legs of the Lem toward the ground, slowly their heads came up. And as they did, so returned a view of the moon through the bottom of the window now that the Lem inclined back toward the vertical. There were markings on their windows, horizontal lines to line up against the horizon of the moon and so serve to pinpoint the area where they would land, but as the ground of the Sea of Tranquility came into sight from four thousand feet, from three thousand feet, as their angle shifted and more and more of the moon was visible through that slanted window, so to their distress was the terrain unrecognizable. Quick glimpses showed no landmarks, no particular craters on the flat desert of Tranquility which might bear familiar relation to the photographs and charts Apollo 10 had prepared for them, and Armstrong memorized, no, now they were in another place, whether four miles or fourteen away from the selected landing site was impossible to tell. And at that instant a new alarm blinks on the computer. "Twelve alarm," says Aldrin, "1201." The Capcom answers, "Roger. 1201 alarm."

When nothing further is said, Aldrin's voice comes in again. "We're GO. Hang tight. We're GO. Two thousand feet . . ."

Capcom: "Roger."

Eagle: "Forty-seven degrees."

Capcom: "Eagle looking great. You're GO."

And the flight controllers at Mission Control are screwed to the parameters of the consoles, the roll calls come in for GO. There is always attention to Bales' answer to Kranz's query. "GO," Bales' voice will pipe out against the alarms.

Kranz is a leader. He is a man who gives others the feeling that they are about to go through the door together into the stadium where they are each going to play the best game of their life. Kranz, like Slayton, has the look of a man who had lived for years in space, and Bales is a young engineer with a large round face and large horn-rimmed glasses, destiny sits on him with a moist touch, but the limits of decision had been clarified that June morning a month ago and Bales had done the work to separate a total crisis from a partial crisis on 1202 and 1201, and now, distinguishing the differences—no time to ask for confirmation—calls GO. The mission continues.

But the astronauts continue without the division of labor Aldrin has specified as tidy. They come down toward the gray wife of the earth's ages with their eyes riveted to the instruments. There are no more than peeps and glimpses of the oncoming ground. At two thousand feet, Armstrong finally leaves the dials, studies the view from the window. He can land by hand if necessary now.

But he cannot locate himself. No landmarks are familiar. From one thousand feet up it is apparent that Eagle is headed for a wretched crater with a boulder field of rocks and "the rocks seemed to be coming up at us awfully fast." Fast and mean are those rocks accelerating to the eye like the zoom of a camera down to the ground. "The clock runs about triple speed in a situation like that." And now Aldrin is calling out relevant computer and instrument readings. Here they come at Armstrong! "750, coming down at 23." That was altitude seven hundred and fifty feet, rate of descent twenty-three feet per second. "700 feet, 21 down. 600 feet, down at 19. 540 feet down at 30—down at 15." In the tension Aldrin has miscalled a number for an instant. "400 feet, down at 9." Something is now garbled. Then the voice again. It is quiet, it is almost sad. "350, down at 4. 330 feet, 3½ down. We're pegged on horizontal velocity."

They are drifting horizontally over the boulder fields, skittering like a water bug debating which pad it will light on. Armstrong has taken over all of attitude control and part of throttle control—his commands are now inserted in with computer commands. The descent rate has reduced from ten feet a second to three feet, then only a foot a second. They hover, Armstrong searching for a spot in the boulder field, "because I'm sure some of the ejecta coming out of such a large crater would have been lunar bedrock, and as such, fascinating to the scientists. I was tempted, but my better judgment took over . . ." No, he is not rushing in. He has gone through the computer alerts, the loss of all landmarks, has descended into that narrow field of vision where the horizon of the moon is always near, now drops down toward those boulders, hovers and skims, he has not had his recurring dreams as a boy night after night without tutoring the synapses of his growth into a thousand simulations of deliberate entrance into a dark space.

At last there is a place, "the size of a big house lot" between craters and a boulder field, and drifting almost done, they see the shadow of their Lem slanting across the moon ground like a giant prehistoric bird of destiny and "200 feet," says Aldrin, "4½ down, 5½ down. 160, 6½ down, 5½ down, 9 forward. 5 percent. Quantity light. 73 feet. Things looking good. Down a half. 6 forward."

"Sixty seconds," says the Capcom. That is the limit of their fuel.

"Lights on," returns Eagle. Now their landing lights burn down on the sunlit moon ground to beam through the dust, and now comes the dust. At thirty feet above the ground, a great amount blows out in all directions like an underwater flower of the sea and the ground is partially visible beneath as if "landing in a very fast-moving ground fog," and the fuel gauges almost empty, and still he drifts forward. "Thirty seconds," calls out the Capcom for warning. And in a murk of dust and sunlight and landing lights, the Eagle settles in. Contact lights light up on the board to register the touch of the probes below her legs. Aldrin's voice speaks softly, "Okay, engine stop. ACA out of detente. Modes control both auto. Descent engine command override off. Engine arm off. 413 is in."

Capcom: "We copy you down, Eagle."

Armstrong: "Houston, Tranquility Base here. The Eagle has landed."

Then was it that the tension broke for fifty million people or was it five hundred million, or some sum of billions of eyes and ears around a world which had just come into contact with another world for what future glory, disaster, blessing or curse nobody living could know. And Armstrong and Aldrin, never demonstrative, shook hands or clapped each other on the back—they did not later remember—and back at Mission Control, Charley Duke said, "Roger, Tranquility, we copy you on the ground. You've got a bunch of guys about to turn blue. We're breathing again. Thanks a lot."

And Kranz, who had issued every order to Duke, and queried his controllers in a voice of absolute calm for the entire trip down, now tried to speak and could not. And tried to speak, and again could not, and finally could unlock his lungs only by smashing his hand on a console so hard his bones were bruised for days. But then if his throat had constricted and his lungs locked, his heart stopped, he would have been a man who died at the maximum of his moments on earth and what a spring might then have delivered him to the first explorers of the moon. Perhaps it is the function of the dream to teach us those moments when we are GO or NO GO for the maximum thrust into death. They were down, they were on the moon ground, and who could speak?

"All right," said Kranz. "Everybody settle down, and let's get ready for a T-1 Stay–No Stay."

. . .

It was almost three-thirty in the morning when the astronauts finally prepared for sleep. They pulled down the shades and Aldrin stretched out on the floor, his nose near the moon dust. Armstrong sat on the cover of the ascent engine, his back leaning against one of the walls, his legs supported in a strap he had tied around a vertical bar. In front of his face was the eyepiece of the telescope. The earth was in its field of view, and the earth "like a big blue eyeball" stared back at him. They could not sleep. Like the eye of a victim just murdered, the earth stared back at him.

. . .

It used to be said that men in the hour of their triumph knew the sleep of the just, but a modern view might argue that men sleep in order to dream, sleep in order to invoke that mysterious theater where regions of the unconscious reach into communication with one another, and charts and portraits of the soul and the world outside are subtly retouched from the experience of the day. If this is so, what a gargantuan job of ingestion had fallen upon the unconscious mind of the two astronauts, for the experience of their world would not include the moon. Deep in a state of exaltation and exhaustion, tonight—it is now four in the morning—was hardly the time to embark upon the huge work of a dream which could begin to feed into the wisdom of the unconscious those huge productions of the day behind. If their senses had been witness to sights and sensations never experienced before, their egos were also in total perturbation, for on the previous day their names had been transported to the eternal moonlight of the ego—they were now immortal. It is not so easy for men to sleep on such a night, for they know their lives have been altered forever—what a dislocation of the character's firm sense of itself; in fact it is precisely in the character of strong egos that they are firmly rooted. Now, they are uprooted and in a state of glory. What confusion! A disorientation of the senses and coronation of the ego are the problems to be approached this night by the dream, and that while lying in the most uncomfortable positions possible in the foreign skin of a pressure garment while the temperature grew chilly inside that stiff sack, for even with water circulation down to a minimum, the suits insisted on cooling their tired heat-depleted bodies. How indeed to go past the threshold and enter the great chamber where the kingdoms of sleep will greet them with a revel equal to the hour, no, no man in a state of exhaustion would dare to chance the rigors of a powerful night of dreams, for important decisions which may shape the future can be decided on bad nights by the poor artwork of dreams not sufficiently energetic or well enough conceived to offer the unconscious a real depth of answer—which is why perhaps insomnia is self-cycling, for, too tired or fearful to engage in serious dreams one night, we are even more exhausted for the next, and do not dare to sleep. Who will be the first to swear that deep contracts of the soul are never sworn to in the darkest exchanges of slumber, or failure too quickly accepted in the once ambitious hearts of exhausted men? No, the astronauts were in no shape to sleep. Just so quickly ask a computer to work when its power supply is erratic, its mechanical parts need oiling, and it has just been instructed to compute all further trajectories as if earth gravity did not exist and the moon were motionless before the sun!

Yet, all of this—this kaleidoscope of impressions, this happiness of the heart, sore and tender and merry in the very pumping of its walls, these thrifty ducts of aviator's love for family, children and mate open now if ever open, the patriotic incandescence of a dialogue with the President, the delivery of a job promised to the team—these tributaries of happiness carrying the uprooted tree of the ego and the mysterious house of the moon downstream in full flood are still only half of their inability to sleep. Few men could sleep with such happiness flowing unaccustomed in them, but now add a fear which has been kept in the vaults, a firm well-regulated natural concern of the executive mind, yet a fear not even primitive, but primeval in its uncharted depths: are they going to be able to ascend from the moon? It is one thing to shatter a taboo, it is another to escape the retribution which follows the sacrilege—where is the savage society whose folklore is not crowded with tales of the subtlety of every outraged curse? It is a fear which still lives in many an athlete and celebrity, in many an excessive modesty in any poor man who has found at last some luck, it is in the groveling of a dog at what comes next after he has won a fierce fight. The danger is always greatest just beyond victory—in some men that is a deeper belief than any other, for not yet at climax they can see themselves as deserving; once triumphant their balance has shifted, they know guilt, they are now not deserving. Well, whether the astronauts were deeply superstitious in this fashion or barely superstitious at all, we can be certain that any residual of this prime and hallowed fear would be awake in them tonight, for they were not by any measure yet free of the moon. In the morning, after all preparations were taken, a moment would still come when they would have to fire up their engines and lift off in the upper half of the Lem from the descent stage left behind. The ascent stage would rise if the ascent motor functioned—they were doomed if it did not, for all the redundancies of the equipment passed here through the bottleneck of one and only one piece of mechanism. There was no substitute for the ascent engine. Double tanks of fuel, and double tanks of oxidizer; double containers of helium to put pressure on fuel and oxygen; valves and cutoff valves in a plenitude of substitutions and alternate paths; but, finally, there was only one motor with only one throat and one bell, and that motor would have to flame up to 90 percent of its full thrust in the first three-tenths of a second after it ignited so that the ascent stage would lift and not settle back—no refinements to blast-off here!

There had been tests beyond measure on that motor, tests in vacuums and tests in fast-descending elevators to simulate lunar gravity; there had been refinements inserted within refinements to make certain that when a fuel spray of hydrazine and unsymmetrical dimethylhydrazine came through the injectors to meet a spray of nitrogen tetroxide the combustion would take place.

Since it had been designed for ignition in a lunar vacuum, so there was no air to feed the fires of the fuel. The equivalent of air was supplied by the nitrogen tetroxide, whose oxygen would sustain the burning hydrogen, whose oxygen would indeed ignite the hydrogen by merely meeting it. The very elements of water were here the elements of a fire so contagious it needed no match, merely the mating of the gases, a fire so explosive that a motor with a nozzle only two and a half feet across could lift the ascent stage and the men inside, lift them and fling them into orbit, all ten thousand pounds and more.

Still, this motor had never been fired before on the moon. It had been fired in vacuums, yes, but they were artificial vacuums on earth and not the pure vacuum of the moon where who knew what subtleties atomic particles, subparticles, and cosmic rays could present upon ignition? Nothing in any theory or working hypothesis of physics even began to suggest there was any reason why a moon vacuum should not prove the practical equal of an earth vacuum, but nobody could be certain, nobody could swear there were not unforeseen conditions which could inhibit the flame or cause it to flame out. Who knew the dispositions of fire on the moon when the air we breathed was also the stuff of fire, and hydrogen and oxygen could make water or electricity or fire? Yes, the real explanation of the flames remain as much a mystery as man's first hour in a forest after lightning struck a tree.

Primeval fears inspire primeval thoughts. There in the Lem, one body on a floor, the other with his heroic posterior carefully spotted on the very cover of that ascent engine which would lift them off in the morning, how they must have drifted on runs of happiness and rills of deep-veined fear. How easily they must have passed into large sleep-deprived inchoate thoughts of a world of men and women back on earth secretly wishing them well or ill, intervening in the long connected night of the world's sleep with whatever gods' or powers were sitting upon the ignition of the engine in the morning. So scourged and exalted, hovering on that ultimate edge of moral balance where one wonders if the sum of one's life has been for good or ill and if the morning will return a fair and just verdict, fingers crossed, ready fair enough to laugh or cry, dopey, exhausted, chilled, feverish no doubt with desire for morning to come, alert, high on the empty holes of the numbers they would punch into the computer in the morning, ears alert to the quiet pumps of the nocturnal Lem whose skin was baking in the moon morning heat, there in a cave of chilly isolation, happy, numb, and full of a fear of dreams, not knowing if their glory was to be doubled by the next night or if they would be at one among the martyred dead yes, how were they to sleep and dare to dream when the future must look either to a transformation of the psyche, or a trip down the underground river of them all? Yet, if they were to die on the moon—was there an underground river there? or would they be forced, full strangers, to wander together, a queer last place for the mortal bones. Who, indeed, could sleep?

. . .

It is almost sixty hours before reentry for the astronauts, and their return will be without events of the largest scope. Collins will grow a mustache, and Mission Control will report that the crime rate in Italy was at a low for the year on the night they walked the moon. A girl will be born in Memphis who is christened Module McGhee, and a boy named Greg Force will fix a bearing on the huge antenna in Guam because he is the only one whose arm is small enough to reach into the hole. The Capcom on duty the following night will mistake the moon for the earth on a murky television screen and the astronauts will have the experience of seeing the earth and moon looking equal in size out opposite windows. Slowly the earth will grow in the window. Blue she will gleam and brown and gray and silver and rose and red. Her clouds will cover her like curls of white hair, her clouds will turn dark as smoky pearls and the lavender of orchid, her clouds will be brown and green like marsh grass wet by the sea, and the sea will appear beneath like pools of water in the marsh grass. The earth will look like a precious stone, blue as sapphire, blue as a diamond, the earth will be an eye to look at them in curious welcome as they return. They have been as far as Achilles and Odysseus, as far as Jason who sailed to meet the argonauts, far as Magellan and Columbus, they have been far. And their fingertips are smooth from plastic, their lungs are leather from days of bottled gas. What does an astronaut give up of the ultimate tastes to travel so far? We are back to Aquarius moldering on flatlands not far from the sea.

QUESTIONS

1. How does Mailer utilize imagery and rhythm to make you feel the difference between gravity and free fall?

2. Are the astronauts ready for the experience of traveling to the moon, or has technology gone so fast that humanity's comprehension cannot keep pace? If and when we have manned flights to other planets, in what ways might we expect our astronauts to be more sophisticated? Are they likely to also be more poetic in their appreciation? Is this a contradiction of terms? What reactions do you think will remain the same?

3. Is Mailer's description of the landing exciting? Why or why not?

4. If this selection was fiction, would it be believable? Has Mailer succeeded in making the "unbelievable" believable? How?

5. Should we have gone to the moon, or should we have spent the money making the earth a better place to live?

6. Discuss point of view in this selection, especially the reasons Mailer shifted from the first person to the third person point of view.

7. Do you think that the very act of walking on the moon has altered human consciousness, much in the same way consciousness was altered by the microscope, the telescope, the voyages of Columbus and Magellan? Explain.

8. What different devices does Mailer use to dramatize the Trans-Lunar Injection and the section on sleep?

9. Discuss the ways in which "space consciousness"—the ability to see the earth as a giant blue marble, floating alone in the darkness—may help humanity to collectively face its most urgent planetary problems. In what way is this kind of awareness "ecological"?

10. How would you describe Mailer's style? What characteristics make it epic?

Survival U: Prospectus for a Really Relevant University

John Fischer

Near the conclusion of William Faulkner's speech on his acceptance of the Nobel Prize for Literature, he proclaimed his belief that man "will not merely endure: he will prevail." Many people, however, have asked if our desire to prevail is not itself the problem, saying we must rather attain a state of harmony with the planet's resources and size limitations if we are to even "merely endure." The problem is huge: how do we feed, clothe, and shelter humanity and at the same time keep the world fit for decent human habitation? Most other long-range difficulties fade before this problem.

"Survival U.," by a contributing editor of Harper's *magazine, is one of many proposals urging us to rethink, reevaluate our priorities, to look ahead in order to salvage the near and far future.*

> It gets pretty depressing to watch what is going on in the world and realize that your education is not equipping you to do anything about it.
>
> —*From* a letter by a University of California senior

She is not a radical, and has never taken part in any demonstration. She will graduate with honors, and profound disillusionment. From listening to her—and a good many like-minded students at California and East Coast campuses—I think I am beginning to understand what they mean when they say that a liberal-arts education isn't relevant.

They mean it is incoherent. It doesn't cohere. It consists of bits and pieces which don't stick together, and have no common purpose. One of our leading Negro educators, Arthur Lewis of Princeton, recently summed it up better than I can. America is the only country, he said, where youngsters are required "to fritter away their precious years in meaningless peregrination from subject to subject . . . spending twelve weeks getting some tidbits of religion, twelve weeks learning French, twelve weeks seeing whether the history professor is stimulating, twelve weeks seeking entertainment from the economics professor, twelve weeks confirming that one is not going to be able to master calculus."

These fragments are meaningless because they are not organized around any central purpose, or vision of the world. The typical liberal-arts college has no clearly defined goals. It merely offers a smorgasbord of courses, in hopes that if a student nibbles at a few dishes from the humanities table, plus a snack of science, and a garnish of art or anthropology, he may emerge as "a cultivated man"—whatever that means. Except for a few surviving church schools, no university even pretends to have a unifying philosophy. Individual teachers may have personal ideologies—but since they are likely to range, on any given campus, from Marxism to worship of the scientific method to exaltation of the irrational (*à la* Norman O. Brown), they don't cohere either. They often leave a student convinced at the end of four years that any given idea is probably about as valid as any other—and that none of them has much relationship to the others, or to the decisions he is going to have to make the day after graduation.

Education was not always like that. The earliest European universities had a precise purpose: to train an elite for the service of the Church. Everything they taught was focused to that end. Thomas Aquinas had spelled it all out: what subjects had to be mastered, how each connected with every other, and what meaning they had for man and God.

Later, for a span of several centuries, Oxford and Cambridge had an equally clear function: to train administrators to run an empire. So too did Harvard and Yale at the time they were founded; their job was to produce the clergymen, lawyers, and doctors that a new country needed. In each case, the curriculum was rigidly prescribed. A student learned what he needed, to prepare himself to be a competent priest, district officer, or surgeon. He had no doubts about the relevance of his courses—and no time to fret about expanding his consciousness or currying his sensual awareness.

This is still true of our professional schools. I have yet to hear an engineering or medical student complain that his education is meaningless. Only in the liberal-arts colleges—which boast that "we are not trade schools"—do the youngsters get that feeling that they are drowning in a cloud of feathers.

For a long while some of our less complacent academics have been trying to restore coherence to American education. When Robert Hutchins was at Chicago, he tried to use the Great Books to build a comprehensible framework for the main ideas of civilized man. His experiment is still being carried on, with some modifications, at St. John's—but it has not proved irresistibly contagious. Sure, the thoughts of Plato and Machiavelli are still pertinent, so far as they go—but somehow they don't seem quite enough armor for a world beset with splitting atoms, urban guerrillas, nineteen varieties of psychotherapists, amplified guitars, napalm, computers, astronauts, and an atmosphere polluted simultaneously with auto exhaust and TV commercials.

Another strategy for linking together the bits-and-pieces has been attempted at Harvard and at a number of other universities. They require their students to take at least two years of survey courses, known variously as core studies, general education, or world civilization. These too have been something less than triumphantly successful. Most faculty members don't like to teach them, regarding them as superficial and synthetic. (And right they are, since no survey course that I know of has a strong unifying concept to give it focus.) Moreover, the senior professors shun such courses in favor of their own narrow specialties. Consequently, the core studies which are meant to place all human experience—well, at least the brightest nuggets—into One Big Picture usually end up in the perfunctory hands of resentful junior teachers. Naturally the undergraduates don't take them seriously either.

Any successful reform of American education, I am now convinced, will have to be far more revolutionary than anything yet attempted. At a minimum, it should be:

1. Founded on a single guiding concept—an idea capable of knotting together all strands of study, thus giving them both coherence and visible purpose.

2. Capable of equipping young people to do something about "what is going on in the world"—notably the things which bother them most, including war, injustice, racial conflict, and the quality of life.

Maybe it isn't possible. Perhaps knowledge is proliferating so fast, and in so many directions, that it can never again be ordered into a coherent whole, so that molecular biology, Robert Lowell's poetry, and highway engineering will seem relevant to each other and to the lives of ordinary people. Quite possibly the knowledge explosion, as Peter F. Drucker has called it, dooms us to scholarship which grows steadily more specialized, fragmented, and incomprehensible.

The Soviet experience is hardly encouraging. Russian education is built on what is meant to be a unifying ideology: Marxism-Leninism. In theory, it provides an organizing principle for all scholarly activity—whether history, literature, genetics, or military science. Its purpose is explicit: to train a Communist elite for the greater power and glory of the Soviet state, just as the medieval universities trained a priesthood to serve the Church.

Yet according to all accounts that I have seen, it doesn't work very well. Soviet intellectuals apparently are almost as restless and unhappy as our own. Increasing numbers of them are finding Marxism-Leninism too simplistic, too narrowly doctrinaire, too oppressive; the bravest are risking prison in order to pursue their own heretical visions of reality.

Is it conceivable, then, that we might hit upon another idea which could serve as the organizing principle for many fields of scholarly inquiry; which is relevant to the urgent needs of our time; and which would not, on the other hand, impose an ideological strait jacket, as both ecclesiastical and Marxist education attempted to do?

Just possibly it could be done. For the last two or three years I have been probing around among professors, college administrators, and students—and so far I have come up with only one idea which might fit the specifications. It is simply the idea of survival.

For the first time in history, the future of the human race is now in serious question. This fact is hard to believe, or even think about—yet it is the message which a growing number of scientists are trying, almost frantically, to get across to us. Listen, for example, to Professor Richard A. Falk of Princeton and of the Center for Advanced Study in the Behavioral Sciences:

> The planet and mankind are in grave danger of irreversible catastrophe. . . . Man may be skeptical about following the flight of the dodo into extinction, but the evidence points increasingly to just such a pursuit. . . . There are four interconnected threats to the planet—wars of mass destruction, overpopulation, pollution, and the depletion of resources. They have a cumulative effect. A problem in one area renders it more difficult to solve the problems in any other area. . . . The basis of all four problems is the inadequacy of the sovereign states to manage the affairs of mankind in the twentieth century.

Similar warnings could be quoted from a long list of other social scientists, biologists, and physicists, among them such distinguished thinkers as Rene Dubos, Buckminster Fuller, Loren Eiseley, George Wald, and Barry Commoner. They are not hopeless. Most of them believe that we still have a chance to bring our weapons, our population growth, and the destruction of our environment under control before it is too late. But the time is short, and so far there is no evidence that enough people are taking them seriously.

That would be the prime aim of the experimental university I'm suggesting here: to look seriously at the interlinking threats to human existence, and to learn what we can do to fight them off.

Let's call it Survival U. It will not be a multiversity, offering courses in every conceivable field. Its motto—emblazoned on a life jacket rampant—will be: "What must we do to be saved?" If a course does not help to answer that question, it will not be taught here. Students interested in musicology, junk sculpture, the Theater of the Absurd, and the literary *dicta* of Leslie Fiedler can go somewhere else.

Neither will our professors be detached, dispassionate scholars. To get hired, each will have to demonstrate an emotional commitment to our cause. Moreover, he will be expected to be a moralist; for this generation of students, like no other in my lifetime, is hungering and thirsting after righteousness. What it wants is a moral system it can believe in—and that is what our university will try to provide. In every class it will preach the primordial ethic of survival.

The biology department, for example, will point out that it is sinful for anybody to have more than two children. It has long since become glaringly evident that unless the earth's cancerous growth of population can be halted, all other problems—poverty, war, racial strife, uninhabitable cities, and the rest—are beyond solution. So the department naturally will teach all known methods of birth control, and much of its research will be aimed at perfecting cheaper and better ones.

Its second lesson in biological morality will be: "Nobody has a right to poison the environment we live in." This maxim will be illustrated by a list of public enemies. At the top will stand the politicians, scientists, and military men—of whatever country—who make and deploy atomic weapons; for if these are ever used, even in so-called defensive systems like the ABM, the atmosphere will be so contaminated with strontium 90 and other radioactive isotopes that human survival seems most unlikely. Also on the list will be anybody who makes or tests chemical and biological weapons—or who even attempts to get rid of obsolete nerve gas, as our Army recently proposed, by dumping the stuff in the sea.

Only slightly less wicked, our biology profs will indicate, is the farmer who drenches his land with DDT. Such insecticides remain virulent indefinitely, and as they wash into the streams and oceans they poison fish, water fowl, and eventually the people who eat them. Worse yet—as John Hay noted in his recently published *In Defense of Nature*—"The original small, diluted concentrations of these chemicals tend to build up in a food chain so as to end in a concentration that may be thousands of times as strong." It is rapidly spreading throughout the globe. DDT already has been found in the tissues of Eskimos and of Antarctic penguins, so it seems probable that similar deposits are gradually building up in your body and mine. The minimum fatal dosage is still unknown.

Before he finishes this course, a student may begin to feel twinges of conscience himself. Is his motorcycle exhaust adding carbon monoxide to the smog we breathe? Is his sewage polluting the nearest river? If so, he will be reminded of two proverbs. From Jesus: "Let him who is without sin among you cast the first stone." From Pogo: "We have met the enemy and he is us."

In like fashion, our engineering students will learn not only how to build dams and highways, but where *not* to build them. Unless they understand that it is immoral to flood the Grand Canyon or destroy the Everglades with a jetport, they will never pass the final exam. Indeed, our engineering graduates will be trained to ask a key question about every contract offered them: "What will be its effect on human life?" That obviously will lead to other questions which every engineer ought to comprehend as thoroughly as his slide rule. Is this new highway really necessary? Would it be wiser to use the money for mass transit—or to decongest traffic by building a new city somewhere else? Is an offshore oil well really a good idea, in view of what happened to Santa Barbara?

Our engineering faculty also will specialize in training men for a new growth industry: garbage disposal. Americans already are spending $4.5 billion a year to collect and get rid of the garbage which we produce more profusely than any other people (more than five pounds a day for each of us). But unless we are resigned to stifling in our own trash, we are going to have to come up with at least an additional $835 million a year.* Any industry with a growth rate of 18 percent offers obvious attractions to a bright young man—and if he can figure out a new way to get rid of our offal, his fortune will be unlimited.

Because the old ways no longer work. Every big city in the United States is running out of dumping grounds. Burning won't do either, since the air is dangerously polluted already—and in any case, 75 percent of the incinerators in use are inadequate. For some 150 years Californians happily piled their garbage into San Francisco Bay, but they can't much longer. Dump-and-fill operations already have reduced it to half its original size, and in a few more decades it would be possible to walk dry-shod from Oakland to the Embarcadero. Consequently San Francisco is now planning to ship garbage 375 miles to the yet-uncluttered deserts of Lassen County by special train—known locally as "The Twentieth Stenchery Limited" and "The Excess Express." The city may actually get away with this scheme, since hardly anybody lives in Lassen County except Indians, and who cares about them? But what is the answer for the metropolis that doesn't have an unspoiled desert handy?

A few ingenious notions are cropping up here and there. The Japanese are experimenting with a machine which compacts garbage, under great heat and pressure, into building blocks. A New York businessman is thinking of building a garbage mountain somewhere upstate, and equipping it with ski runs to amortize the cost. An aluminum company plans to collect and reprocess used aluminum cans—which, unlike the old-fashioned tin can, will not rust away. Our engineering department will try to Think Big along these lines. That way lies not only new careers, but salvation.

---

* According to Richard D. Vaughn, chief of the Solid Wastes Program of HEW, in his recent horror story entitled "1968 Survey of Community Solid Waste Practices."

Survival U's Department of Earth Sciences will be headed—if we are lucky—by Dr. Charles F. Park, Jr., now professor of geology and mineral engineering at Stanford. He knows as well as anybody how fast mankind is using up the world's supply of raw materials. In a paper written for the American Geographical Society he punctured one of America's most engaging (and pernicious) myths: our belief that an ever-expanding economy can keep living standards rising indefinitely.

It won't happen; because, as Dr. Park demonstrates, the tonnage of metal in the earth's crust won't last indefinitely. Already we are running short of silver, mercury, tin, and cobalt—all in growing demand by the high-technology industries. Even the commoner metals may soon be in short supply. The United States alone is consuming one ton of iron and eighteen pounds of copper every year, for each of its inhabitants. Poorer countries, struggling to industrialize, hope to raise their consumption of these two key materials to something like that level. If they should succeed—and if the globe's population doubles in the next forty years, as it will at present growth rates—then the world will have to produce, somehow, *twelve times* as much iron and copper every year as it does now. Dr. Park sees little hope that such production levels can even be reached, much less sustained indefinitely. The same thing, of course—doubled in spades—goes for other raw materials: timber, oil, natural gas, and water, to note only a few.

Survival U, therefore, will prepare its students to consume less. This does not necessarily mean an immediate drop in living standards—perhaps only a change in the yardstick by which we measure them. Conceivably Americans might be happier with fewer automobiles, neon signs, beer cans, supersonic jets, barbecue grills, and similar metallic fluff. But happy or not, our students had better learn how to live The Simpler Life, because that is what most of them are likely to have before they reach middle age.

To help them understand how very precious resources really are, our mathematics department will teach a new kind of bookkeeping: social accounting. It will train people to analyze budgets—both government and corporate—with an eye not merely to immediate dollar costs, but to the long-range costs to society.

By conventional bookkeeping methods, for example, the coal companies strip-mining away the hillsides of Kentucky and West Virginia show a handsome profit. Their ledgers, however, show only a fraction of the true cost of their operations. They take no account of destroyed land which can never bear another crop; of rivers poisoned by mud and seeping acid from the spoil banks; of floods which sweep over farms and towns downstream, because the ravaged slopes can no longer hold the rainfall. Although these costs are not borne by the mining firms, they are nevertheless real. They fall mostly on the taxpayers, who have to pay for disaster relief, flood-control levees, and the resettlement of Appalachian farm families forced off the land. As soon as our students (the taxpayers of tomorrow) learn to read a social balance sheet, they obviously will throw the strip miners into bankruptcy.

Another case study will analyze the proposal of the Inhuman Real Estate Corporation to build a fifty-story skyscraper in the most congested area of midtown Manhattan. If 90 percent of the office space can be rented at $12 per square foot, it looks like a sound investment, according to antique accounting methods. To uncover the true facts, however, our students will investigate the cost of moving 12,000 additional workers in and out of midtown during rush hours. The first (and least) item is $8 million worth of new city buses. When they are crammed into the already clogged avenues, the daily loss of man-hours in traffic jams may run to a couple of million more. The fumes from their diesel engines will cause an estimated 9 percent increase in New York's incidence of emphysema and lung cancer: this requires the construction of three new hospitals. To supply them, plus the new building, with water—already perilously short in the city—a new reservoir has to be built on the headwaters of the Delaware River, 140 miles away. Some of the dairy farmers pushed out of the drowned valley will move promptly into the Bronx and go on relief. The subtraction of their milk output from the city's supply leads to a price increase of two cents a quart. For a Harlem mother with seven hungry children, that is the last straw. She summons her neighbors to join her in riot, seven blocks go up in flames, and the Mayor demands higher taxes to hire more police. . . .

Instead of a sound investment, Inhuman Towers now looks like criminal folly, which would be forbidden by any sensible government. Our students will keep that in mind when they walk across campus to their government class.

Its main goal will be to discover why our institutions have done so badly in their efforts (as Dr. Falk put it) "to manage the affairs of mankind in the twentieth century." This will be a compulsory course for all freshmen, taught by professors who are capable of looking critically at every political artifact, from the Constitution to the local county council. They will start by pointing out that we are living in a state of near-anarchy because we have no government capable of dealing effectively with public problems.

Instead we have a hodgepodge of 80,000 local governments—villages, townships, counties, cities, port authorities, sewer districts, and special purpose agencies. Their authority is so limited, and their jurisdictions so confused and overlapping, that most of them are virtually impotent. The states, which in theory could put this mess into some sort of order, usually have shown little interest and less competence. When Washington is called to help out—as it increasingly has been for the last thirty-five years—it often has proved ham-handed and entangled in its own archaic bureaucracy. The end result is that nobody in authority has been able to take care of the country's mounting needs. Our welfare rolls keep growing, our air and water get dirtier, housing gets scarcer, airports jam up, road traffic clots, railways fall apart, prices rise, ghettos burn, schools turn out more illiterates every year, and a war nobody wants drags on and on. Small wonder that so many young people are losing confidence in American institutions. In their present state, they don't deserve much confidence.

The advanced students of government at Survival U will try to find out whether these institutions can be renewed and rebuilt. They will take a hard look at the few places—Jacksonville, Minnesota, Nashville, Appalachia—which are creating new forms of government. Will these work any better, and if so, how can they be duplicated elsewhere? Can the states be brought to life, or should we start thinking about an entirely different kind of arrangement? Ten regional prefectures, perhaps, to replace the fifty states? Or should we take seriously Norman Mailer's suggestion for a new kind of city-state to govern our great metropolises? (He merely called for New York City to secede from its state; but that isn't radical enough. To be truly governable, the new Republic of New York City ought to include chunks of New Jersey and Connecticut as well.) Alternatively, can we find some way to break up Megalopolis, and spread our population into smaller and more livable communities throughout the continent? Why should we keep 70 percent of our people crowded into less than 2 percent of our land area, anyway?

Looking beyond our borders, our students will be encouraged to ask even harder questions. Are nation-states actually feasible, now that they have power to destroy each other in a single afternoon? Can we agree on something else to take their place, before the balance of terror becomes unstable? What price would most people be willing to pay for a more durable kind of human organization—more taxes, giving up national flags, perhaps the sacrifice of some of our hard-won liberties?

All these courses (and everything else taught at Survival U) are really branches of a single science. Human ecology is one of the youngest disciplines, and probably the most important. It is the study of the relationship between man and his environment, both natural and technological. It teaches us to understand the consequences of our actions—how sulfur-laden fuel oil burned in England produces an acid rain that damages the forests of Scandinavia, why a well-meant farm subsidy can force millions of Negro tenants off the land and lead to Watts and Hough. A graduate who comprehends ecology will know how to look at "what is going on in the world," and he will be equipped to do something about it. Whether he ends up as a city planner, a politician, an enlightened engineer, a teacher, or a reporter, he will have had a relevant education. All of its parts will hang together in a coherent whole.

And if we can get enough such graduates, man and his environment may survive a while longer, against all the odds.

QUESTIONS

1. Defend the concept of a liberal arts college. Include a definition of a "cultivated" man. What, from your point of view, is the purpose of "education"?

2. What place has the lone individual in Survival U? Should the arts be incorporated into Fischer's concept of university education? If yes, why? If no, why not?

3. In your opinion, would the moral education described by Fischer enable the graduates of Survival U. to help save the world, or would profit motives and outside pressures cause them to make the same old mistakes? Explain your answer.

4. Survival U. teaches its students to ask questions, to consider all possible results and side effects before taking any actions. Could this approach be self-defeating and paralyzing? Why?

5. Could the results of building a fifty-story skyscraper described by Fischer truly be anticipated? Is this exaggeration for dramatic effect, or is Fischer serious?

6. Can education be relevant in a constantly changing world? If Fischer's basic ideas are not followed, what then?

7. What would be the effect of having a "unifying" concept in a university? Can you reasonably have a unifying concept in a school without also having it in the broader society the school serves?

part 2

Earthbound

Science fiction is often mistakenly thought of as "space fiction," those unfamiliar with the genre believing that most of its tales take place on other planets and in other galaxies. However, a respectable number of SF stories are "Earthbound." They take place on Earth past, present, and future. They examine what has happened to the human race, what might have happened, what may yet happen. By taking the science fiction perspective, the reader may come to perceive the planet as a place of magic, wonder, infinite possibility, and change. Science fiction—to borrow Robert Frost's words—allows us "to get away from Earth awhile/And then come back to it and begin over." We gain a broad view as we examine large events or life-changing inventions.

Dick Allen's poem "A New Age" begins the section by envisioning two people who are slightly conscious that a phase of human history is over and another beginning. The implication is that change, at the exact time it occurs, is not, as a rule, radical in its effect on personal lives. The two characters express some uneasiness, a brief awareness that a turning point may have been reached—perhaps as a result of those events dealt with in the preceding section of this book.

"The Artist of the Beautiful" moves us backward in time. Here is a familiar setting with recognizable characters. And yet, something miraculous is happening: an exceptional craftsman, a watchmaker, creates a living soul in a tiny piece of machinery. Another way of examining the past and present of human life is the "alternate path" story, a common science fiction device. Humans have always dreamed of making this Earth into a utopia. In R. A. Lafferty's "Interurban Queen" they seem to have succeeded. Yet, Lafferty expresses a characteristically modern skepticism about our yearning for heaven on Earth. In his lovely land of trolley cars everything seems *too* regulated, controlled, and contrived.

Lee, in Samuel R. Delaney's "Corona," is also tightly regulated, but in a future time on Earth. She is literally locked into a hospital and kept from killing herself. In this story, her ESP indicates a broadened human potential that carries with it many problems. A marvelous and unusual ability gives its possessor terrible suffering that can be relieved only by a kind of love. C. M. Kornbluth's "The Marching Morons" presents another possible future on Earth. Here the dire warnings about overpopulation have proven accurate, and something drastic must be done. The story is a bitter, unpleasant warning of the straits the human race may be in; one wonders if the solution is any better than the problem.

Earth is also in trouble when "The Forever People" arrive from Supertown. The comic book—long a staple of the SF genre—is often the place where our changing consciousness becomes most apparent. In current comic books, the human dimension, the sense of the individual, is finally recognized. Even Superman is lonely and isolated. What does it indicate about the modern age when even our pop and superheroes are characterized as disillusioned and doubting?

Finally, we are reminded by Robert Frost's "The Star-Splitter" of how enormously isolated the Earth itself seems. This poem suggests that the individual, perhaps earthbound now, is driven to peer outward toward the stars, which seem to contain mysteries within mysteries.

A New Age

Dick Allen

If one looks back into history, one can sense the exact time when certain "ages," time frames for ways of behavior and belief, changed. It may even seem that most of the people living during these ages were aware of what was happening around them and saw the changes as violent and disturbing. The following poem, however, proposes another view; perhaps the transition between different ways of life, between "ages," is much more gentle than we realize. The poet, one of the editors of this book, has won numerous national awards for his "SF-oriented" poetry, many collected in Regions with No Proper Names.

We walk into a new age
carrying knapsacks, twin sleeping bags.

The colours of the trees slightly turn.
We have stepped from one photograph
into a print almost but not quite perfect.

Your voice has a small new tone
to it; I feel
a slight new texture when I touch your hand.

I am not sure if this age
is darker or lighter. 10
The sun appears smaller,
shadows in the pines seem looser.

We do nothing to adjust. We walk a mile
and the difference goes forever.

I was thinking of having married another woman.
You were thinking of having married another man.

We lie down in the shade
of an oak with faded initials carved

ten feet up its trunk. Nothing, you say,
is wrong. It is just a new age. 20

QUESTIONS

1. What is the tone of the poem? Why does the poet use so many qualifying words?

2. Do you feel that the imagery of a backpacking trip is appropriate to a poem about entering a new age? Why?

3. What does the poet mean when he says "the difference goes forever"?

4. Throughout the poem there are images that evoke the past through indirection. What are they? What view of the past do they imply?

5. Do the poem's final lines reflect a happy or sad acceptance of the "new age"? How does the woman interpret the man's state of mind?

The Artist of the Beautiful

Nathaniel Hawthorne

The term "science fiction" did not exist when Nathaniel Hawthorne was writing. Yet Hawthorne was one of the first American writers to concern himself deeply with the vision, the perceptions peculiar to science fiction. Many of his stories deal with hostile attitudes toward the independent thinker or the unconventional visionary, as well as with the complex areas of good and evil, beauty, truth, or falsehood that lie just beyond normal human comprehension. The following short story is one of Hawthorne's recognized masterpieces—a story about time, about nourishing unique ideas, about spiritual values that can be imparted to technology.

An elderly man, with his pretty daughter on his arm, was passing along the street, and emerged from the gloom of the cloudy evening into the light that fell across the pavement from the window of a small shop. It was a projecting window; and on the inside were suspended a variety of watches, pinchbeck, silver, and one or two of gold, all with their faces turned from the streets, as if churlishly disinclined to inform the wayfarers what o'clock it was. Seated within the shop, sidelong to the window, with his pale face bent earnestly over some delicate piece of mechanism on which was thrown the concentrated lustre of a shade lamp, appeared a young man.

"What can Owen Warland be about?" muttered old Peter Hovenden, himself a retired watchmaker, and the former master of this same young man whose occupation he was now wondering at. "What can the fellow be about? These six months past I have never come by his shop without seeing him just as steadily at work as now. It would be a flight beyond his usual foolery to seek for the perpetual motion; and yet I know enough of my old business to be certain that what he is now so busy with is no part of the machinery of a watch."

"Perhaps, father," said Annie, without showing much interest in the question, "Owen is inventing a new kind of timekeeper. I am sure he has ingenuity enough."

"Poh, child! He has not the sort of ingenuity to invent anything better than a Dutch toy," answered her father, who had formerly been put to much vexation by Owen Warland's irregular genius. "A plague on such ingenuity! All the effect that ever I knew of it was to spoil the accuracy of some of the best watches in my shop. He would turn the sun out of its orbit and derange the whole course of time, if, as I said before, his ingenuity could grasp anything bigger than a child's toy!"

"Hush, father! He hears you!" whispered Annie, pressing the old man's arm. "His ears are as delicate as his feelings; and you know how easily disturbed they are. Do let us move on."

So Peter Hovenden and his daughter Annie plodded on without further conversation, until in a by-street of the town they found themselves passing the open door of a blacksmith's shop. Within was seen the forge, now blazing up and illuminating the high and dusky roof, and now confining its lustre to a narrow precinct of the coal-strewn floor, according as the breath of the bellows was puffed forth or again inhaled into its vast leathern lungs. In the intervals of brightness it was easy to distinguish objects in remote corners of the shop and the horseshoes that hung upon the wall; in the momentary gloom the fire seemed to be glimmering amidst the vagueness of unenclosed space. Moving about in this red glare and alternate dusk was the figure of the blacksmith, well worthy to be viewed in so picturesque an aspect of light and shade, where the bright blaze struggled with the black night, as if each would have snatched his comely strength from the other. Anon he drew a white-hot bar of iron from the coals, laid it on the anvil, uplifted his arm of might, and was soon enveloped in the myriads of sparks which the strokes of his hammer scattered into the surrounding gloom.

"Now, that is a pleasant sight," said the old watchmaker. "I know what it is to work in gold; but give me the worker in iron after all is said and done. He spends his labor upon a reality. What say you, daughter Annie?"

"Pray don't speak so loud, father," whispered Annie, "Robert Danforth will hear you."

"And what if he should hear me?" said Peter Hovenden. "I say again, it is a good and a wholesome thing to depend upon main strength and reality, and to earn one's bread with the bare and brawny arm of a blacksmith. A watchmaker gets his brain puzzled by his wheels within a wheel, or loses his health or the nicety of his eyesight, as was my case, and finds himself at middle age, or a little after, past labor at his own trade and fit for nothing else, yet too poor to live at his ease. So I say once again, give me main strength for my money. And then, how it takes the nonsense out of a man! Did you ever hear of a blacksmith being such a fool as Owen Warland yonder?"

"Well said, uncle Hovenden!" shouted Robert Danforth from the forge, in a full, deep, merry voice, that made the roof reëcho. "And what says Miss Annie to that doctrine? She, I suppose, will think it a genteeler business to tinker up a lady's watch than to forge a horseshoe or make a gridiron."

Annie drew her father onward without giving him time for reply.

But we must return to Owen Warland's shop, and spend more meditation upon his history and character than either Peter Hovenden, or probably his daughter Annie, or Owen's old school-fellow, Robert Danforth, would have thought due to so slight a subject. From the time that his little fingers could grasp a penknife, Owen had been remarkable for a delicate ingenuity, which sometimes produced pretty shapes in wood, principally figures of flowers and birds, and sometimes seemed to aim at the hidden mysteries of mechanism. But it was always for purposes of grace, and never with any mockery of the useful. He did not, like the crowd of school-boy artisans, construct little windmills on the angle of a barn or watermills across the neighboring brook. Those who discovered such peculiarity in the boy as to think it worth their while to observe him closely, sometimes saw reason to suppose that he was attempting to imitate the beautiful movements of Nature as exemplified in the flight of birds or the activity of little animals. It seemed, in fact, a new development of the love of the beautiful, such as might have made him a poet, a painter, or a sculptor, and which was as completely refined from all utilitarian coarseness as it could have been in either of the fine arts. He looked with singular distaste at the stiff and regular processes of ordinary machinery. Being once carried to see a steam-engine, in the expectation that his intuitive comprehension of mechanical principles would be gratified, he turned pale and grew sick, as if something monstrous and unnatural had been presented to him. This horror was partly owing to the size and terrible energy of the iron laborer; for the character of Owen's mind was microscopic, and tended naturally to the minute, in accordance with his diminutive frame and the marvellous smallness and delicate power of his fingers. Not that his sense of beauty was thereby diminished into a sense of prettiness. The beautiful idea has no relation to size, and may be as perfectly developed in a space too minute for any but microscopic investigation as within the ample verge that is measured by the arc of the rainbow. But, at all events, this characteristic minuteness in his objects and accomplishments made the world even more incapable than it might otherwise have been of appreciating Owen Warland's genius. The boy's relatives saw nothing better to be done—as perhaps there was not—than to bind him apprentice to a watchmaker, hoping that his strange ingenuity might thus be regulated and put to utilitarian purposes.

Peter Hovenden's opinion of his apprentice has already been expressed. He could make nothing of the lad. Owen's apprehension of the professional mysteries, it is true, was inconceivably quick; but he altogether forgot or despised the grand object of a watchmaker's business, and cared no more for the measurement of time than if it had been merged into eternity. So long, however, as he remained under his old master's care, Owen's lack of sturdiness made it possible, by strict injunctions and sharp oversight, to restrain his creative eccentricity within bounds; but when his apprenticeship was served out, and he had taken the little shop which Peter Hovenden's failing eyesight compelled him to relinquish, then did people recognize how unfit a person was Owen Warland to lead old blind Father Time along his daily course. One of his most rational projects was to connect a musical operation with the machinery of his watches, so that all the harsh dissonances of life might be rendered tuneful, and each flitting moment fall into the abyss of the past in golden drops of harmony. If a family clock was intrusted to him for repair,—one of those tall, ancient clocks that have grown nearly allied to human nature by measuring out the lifetime of many generations,—he would take upon himself to arrange a dance or funeral procession of figures across its venerable face, representing twelve mirthful or melancholy hours. Several freaks of this kind quite destroyed the young watchmaker's credit with that steady and matter-of-fact class of people who hold the opinion that time is not to be trifled with, whether considered as the medium of advancement and prosperity in this world or preparation for the next. His custom rapidly diminished—a misfortune, however, that was probably reckoned among his better accidents by Owen Warland, who was becoming more and more absorbed in a secret occupation which drew all his science and manual dexterity into itself, and likewise gave full employment to the characteristic tendencies of his genius. This pursuit had already consumed many months.

After the old watchmaker and his pretty daughter had gazed at him out of the obscurity of the street, Owen Warland was seized with a fluttering of the nerves, which made his hand tremble too violently to proceed with such delicate labor as he was now engaged upon.

"It was Annie herself!" murmured he. "I should have known it, by this throbbing of my heart, before I heard her father's voice. Ah, how it throbs! I shall scarcely be able to work again on this exquisite mechanism to-night! Annie! dearest Annie! thou shouldst give firmness to my heart and hand, and not shake them thus; for if I strive to put the very spirit of beauty into form and give it motion, it is for thy sake alone. O throbbing heart, be quiet! If my labor be thus thwarted, there will come vague and unsatisfied dreams which will leave me spiritless to-morrow."

As he was endeavoring to settle himself again to his task, the shop door opened and gave admittance to no other than the stalwart figure which Peter Hovenden had paused to admire, as seen amid the light and shadow of the blacksmith's shop. Robert Danforth had brought a little anvil of his own manufacture, and peculiarly constructed, which the young artist had recently bespoken. Owen examined the article and pronounced it fashioned according to his wish.

"Why, yes," said Robert Danforth, his strong voice filling the shop as with the sound of a bass viol, "I consider myself equal to anything in the way of my own trade; though I should have made but a poor figure at yours with such a fist as this," added he, laughing, as he laid his vast hand beside the delicate one of Owen. "But what then? I put more main strength into one blow of my sledge hammer than all that you have expended since you were a 'prentice. Is not that the truth?"

"Very probably," answered the low and slender voice of Owen. "Strength is an earthly monster. I make no pretensions to it. My force, whatever there may be of it, is altogether spiritual."

"Well, but, Owen, what are you about?" asked his old school-fellow, still in such a hearty volume of tone that it made the artist shrink, especially as the question related to a subject so sacred as the absorbing dream of his imagination. "Folks do say that you are trying to discover the perpetual motion."

"The perpetual motion? Nonsense!" replied Owen Warland, with a movement of disgust; for he was full of little petulances. "It can never be discovered. It is a dream that may delude men whose brains are mystified with matter, but not me. Besides, if such a discovery were possible, it would not be worth my while to make it only to have the secret turned to such purposes as are now effected by steam and water power. I am not ambitious to be honored with the paternity of a new kind of cotton machine."

"That would be droll enough!" cried the blacksmith, breaking out into such an uproar of laughter that Owen himself and the bell glasses on his workboard quivered in unison. "No, no, Owen! No child of yours will have iron joints and sinews. Well, I won't hinder you any more. Good night, Owen, and success, and if you need any assistance, so far as a downright blow of hammer upon anvil will answer the purpose, I'm your man."

And with another laugh the man of main strength left the shop.

"How strange it is," whispered Owen Warland to himself, leaning his head upon his hand, "that all my musings, my purposes, my passion for the beautiful, my consciousness of power to create it,—a finer, more ethereal power, of which this earthly giant can have no conception,—all, all, look so vain and idle whenever my path is crossed by Robert Danforth! He would drive me mad were I to meet him often. His hard, brute force darkens and confuses the spiritual element within me; but I, too, will be strong in my own way. I will not yield to him."

He took from beneath a glass a piece of minute machinery, which he set in the condensed light of his lamp, and, looking intently at it through a magnifying glass, proceeded to operate with a delicate instrument of steel. In an instant, however, he fell back in his chair and clasped his hands, with a look of horror on his face that made its small features as impressive as those of a giant would have been.

"Heaven! What have I done?" exclaimed he. "The vapor, the influence of that brute force,—it has bewildered me and obscured my perception. I have made the very stroke—the fatal stroke—that I have dreaded from the first. It is all over—the toil of months, the object of my life. I am ruined!"

And there he sat, in strange despair, until his lamp flickered in the socket and left the Artist of the Beautiful in darkness.

Thus it is that ideas, which grow up within the imagination and appear so lovely to it and of a value beyond whatever men call valuable, are exposed to be shattered and annihilated by contact with the practical. It is requisite for the ideal artist to possess a force of character that seems hardly compatible with its delicacy; he must keep his faith in himself while the incredulous world assails him with its utter disbelief; he must stand up against mankind and be his own sole disciple, both as respects his genius and the objects to which it is directed.

For a time Owen Warland succumbed to this severe but inevitable test. He spent a few sluggish weeks with his head so continually resting in his hands that the towns-people had scarcely an opportunity to see his countenance. When at last it was again uplifted to the light of day, a cold, dull, nameless change was perceptible upon it. In the opinion of Peter Hovenden, however, and that order of sagacious understandings who think that life should be regulated, like clockwork, with leaden weights, the alteration was entirely for the better. Owen now, indeed, applied himself to business with dogged industry. It was marvellous to witness the obtuse gravity with which he would inspect the wheels of a great old silver watch; thereby delighting the owner, in whose fob it had been worn till he deemed it a portion of his own life, and was accordingly jealous of its treatment. In consequence of the good report thus acquired, Owen Warland was invited by the proper authorities to regulate the clock in the church steeple. He succeeded so admirably in this matter of public interest that the merchants gruffly acknowledged his merits on 'Change; the nurse whispered his praises as she gave the potion in the sick-chamber; the lover blessed him at the hour of appointed interview; and the town in general thanked Owen for the punctuality of dinner time. In a word, the heavy weight upon his spirits kept everything in order, not merely within his own system, but wheresoever the iron accents of the church clock were audible. It was a circumstance, though minute, yet characteristic of his present state, that, when employed to engrave names or initials on silver spoons, he now wrote the requisite letters in the plainest possible style, omitting a variety of fanciful flourishes that had heretofore distinguished his work in this kind.

One day, during the era of this happy transformation, old Peter Hovenden came to visit his former apprentice.

"Well, Owen," said he, "I am glad to hear such good accounts of you from all quarters, and especially from the town clock yonder, which speaks in your commendation every hour of the twenty-four. Only get rid altogether of your nonsensical trash about the beautiful, which I nor nobody else, nor yourself to boot, could ever understand,—only free yourself of that, and your success in life is as sure as daylight. Why, if you go on in this way, I should even venture to let you doctor this precious old watch of mine; though, except my daughter Annie, I have nothing else so valuable in the world."

"I should hardly dare touch it, sir," replied Owen, in a depressed tone; for he was weighed down by his old master's presence.

"In time," said the latter,—"in time, you will be capable of it."

The old watchmaker, with the freedom naturally consequent on his former authority, went on inspecting the work which Owen had in hand at the moment, together with other matters that were in progress. The artist, meanwhile, could scarcely lift his head. There was nothing so antipodal to his nature as this man's cold, unimaginative sagacity, by contact with which everything was converted into a dream except the densest matter of the physical world. Owen groaned in spirit and prayed fervently to be delivered from him.

"But what is this?" cried Peter Hovenden abruptly, taking up a dusty bell glass, beneath which appeared a mechanical something, as delicate and minute as the system of a butterfly's anatomy. "What have we here? Owen! Owen! there is witchcraft in these little chains, and wheels, and paddles. See! with one pinch of my finger and thumb I am going to deliver you from all future peril."

"For Heaven's sake," screamed Owen Warland, springing up with wonderful energy, "as you would not drive me mad, do not touch it! The slightest pressure of your finger would ruin me forever."

"Aha, young man! And is it so?" said the old watchmaker, looking at him with just enough of penetration to torture Owen's soul with the bitterness of worldly criticism. "Well, take your own course; but I warn you again that in this small piece of mechanism lives your evil spirit. Shall I exorcise him?"

"You are my evil spirit," answered Owen, much excited,—"you and the hard, coarse world! The leaden thoughts and the despondency that you fling upon me are my clogs, else I should long ago have achieved the task that I was created for."

Peter Hovenden shook his head, with the mixture of contempt and indignation which mankind, of whom he was partly a representative, deem themselves entitled to feel towards all simpletons who seek other prizes than the dusty one along the highway. He then took his leave, with an uplifted finger and a sneer upon his face that haunted the artist's dreams for many a night afterwards. At the time of his old master's visit, Owen was probably on the point of taking up the relinquished task; but, by this sinister event, he was thrown back into the state whence he had been slowly emerging.

But the innate tendency of his soul had only been accumulating fresh vigor during its apparent sluggishness. As the summer advanced he almost totally relinquished his business, and permitted Father Time, so far as the old gentleman was represented by the clocks and watches under his control, to stray at random through human life, making infinite confusion among the train of bewildered hours. He wasted the sunshine, as people said, in wandering through the woods and fields and along the banks of streams. There, like a child, he found amusement in chasing butterflies or watching the motions of water insects. There was something truly mysterious in the intentness with which he contemplated these living playthings as they sported on the breeze or examined the structure of an imperial insect whom he had imprisoned. The chase of butterflies was an apt emblem of the ideal pursuit in which he had spent so many golden hours; but would the beautiful idea ever be yielded to his hand like the butterfly that symbolized it? Sweet, doubtless, were these days, and congenial to the artist's soul. They were full of bright conceptions, which gleamed through his intellectual world as the butterflies gleamed through the outward atmosphere, and were real to him, for the instant, without the toil, and perplexity, and many disappointments of attempting to make them visible to the sensual eye. Alas that the artist, whether in poetry, or whatever other material, may not content himself with the inward enjoyment of the beautiful, but must chase the flitting mystery beyond the verge of his ethereal domain, and crush its frail being in seizing it with a material grasp. Owen Warland felt the impulse to give external reality to his ideas as irresistibly as any of the poets or painters who have arrayed the world in a dimmer and fainter beauty, imperfectly copied from the richness of their visions.

The night was now his time for the slow progress of re-creating the one idea to which all his intellectual activity referred itself. Always at the approach of dusk he stole into the town, locked himself within his shop, and wrought with patient delicacy of touch for many hours. Sometimes he was startled by the rap of the watchman, who, when all the world should be asleep, had caught the gleam of lamplight through the crevices of Owen Warland's shutters. Daylight, to the morbid sensibility of his mind, seemed to have an intrusiveness that interfered with his pursuits. On cloudy and inclement days, therefore, he sat with his head upon his hands, muffling, as it were, his sensitive brain in a mist of indefinite musings; for it was a relief to escape from the sharp distinctness with which he was compelled to shape out his thoughts during his nightly toil.

From one of these fits of torpor he was aroused by the entrance of Annie Hovenden, who came into the shop with the freedom of a customer, and also with something of the familiarity of a childish friend. She had worn a hole through her silver thimble, and wanted Owen to repair it.

"But I don't know whether you will condescend to such a task," she said, laughing, "now that you are so taken up with the notion of putting spirit into machinery."

"Where did you get that idea, Annie?" said Owen, starting in surprise.

"Oh, out of my own head," answered she, "and from something that I heard you say, long ago, when you were but a boy and I a little child. But come; will you mend this poor thimble of mine?"

"Anything for your sake, Annie," said Owen Warland,—"anything, even were it to work at Robert Danforth's forge."

"And that would be a pretty sight!" retorted Annie, glancing with imperceptible slightness at the artist's small and slender frame. "Well; here is the thimble."

"But that is a strange idea of yours," said Owen, "about the spiritualization of matter."

And then the thought stole into his mind that this young girl possessed the gift to comprehend him better than all the world besides. And what a help and strength would it be to him in his lonely toil if he could gain the sympathy of the only being whom he loved! To persons whose pursuits are insulated from the common business of life—who are either in advance of mankind or apart from it—there often comes a sensation of moral cold that makes the spirit shiver as if it had reached the frozen solitudes around the pole. What the prophet, the poet, the reformer, the criminal, or any other man with human yearnings, but separated from the multitude by a peculiar lot, might feel, poor Owen felt.

"Annie," cried he, growing pale as death at the thought, "how gladly would I tell you the secret of my pursuit! You, methinks, would estimate it rightly. You, I know, would hear it with a reverence that I must not expect from the harsh, material world."

"Would I not? to be sure I would!" replied Annie Hovenden, lightly laughing. "Come; explain to me quickly what is the meaning of this little whirligig, so delicately wrought that it might be a plaything for Queen Mab.[1] See! I will put it in motion."

"Hold!" exclaimed Owen, "hold!"

Annie had but given the slightest possible touch, with the point of a needle, to the same minute portion of complicated machinery which has been more than once mentioned, when the artist seized her by the wrist with a force that made her scream aloud. She was affrighted at the convulsion of intense rage and anguish that writhed across his features. The next instant he let his head sink upon his hands.

"Go, Annie," murmured he; "I have deceived myself, and must suffer for it. I yearned for sympathy, and thought, and fancied, and dreamed that you might give it me; but you lack the talisman, Annie, that should

[1] A fairy queen of English folklore, associated with dreams.

admit you into my secrets. That touch has undone the toil of months and the thought of a lifetime! It was not your fault, Annie; but you have ruined me!"

Poor Owen Warland! He had indeed erred, yet pardonably; for if any human spirit could have sufficiently reverenced the processes so sacred in his eyes, it must have been a woman's. Even Annie Hovenden, possibly, might not have disappointed him had she been enlightened by the deep intelligence of love.

The artist spent the ensuing winter in a way that satisfied any persons who had hitherto retained a hopeful opinion of him that he was, in truth, irrevocably doomed to inutility as regarded the world, and to an evil destiny on his own part. The decease of a relative had put him in possession of a small inheritance. Thus freed from the necessity of toil, and having lost the steadfast influence of a great purpose,—great, at least, to him,—he abandoned himself to habits from which it might have been supposed the mere delicacy of his organization would have availed to secure him. But when the ethereal portion of a man of genius is obscured, the earthly part assumes an influence the more uncontrollable, because the character is now thrown off the balance to which Providence had so nicely adjusted it, and which, in coarser natures, is adjusted by some other method. Owen Warland made proof of whatever show of bliss may be found in riot. He looked at the world through the golden medium of wine, and contemplated the visions that bubble up so gayly around the brim of the glass, and that people the air with shapes of pleasant madness, which so soon grow ghostly and forlorn. Even when this dismal and inevitable change had taken place, the young man might still have continued to quaff the cup of enchantments, though its vapor did but shroud life in gloom and fill the gloom with spectres that mocked at him. There was a certain irksomeness of spirit, which, being real, and the deepest sensation of which the artist was now conscious, was more intolerable than any fantastic miseries and horrors that the abuse of wine could summon up. In the latter case he could remember, even out of the midst of his trouble, that all was but a delusion; in the former, the heavy anguish was his actual life.

From this perilous state he was redeemed by an incident which more than one person witnessed, but of which the shrewdest could not explain or conjecture the operation on Owen Warland's mind. It was very simple. On a warm afternoon of spring, as the artist sat among his riotous companions with a glass of wine before him, a splendid butterfly flew in at the open window and fluttered about his head.

"Ah," exclaimed Owen, who had drank freely, "are you alive again, child of the sun and playmate of the summer breeze, after your dismal winter's nap? Then it is time for me to be at work!"

And, leaving his unemptied glass upon the table, he departed and was never known to sip another drop of wine.

And now, again, he resumed his wanderings in the woods and fields. It might be fancied that the bright butterfly, which had come so spirit-like into the window as Owen sat with the rude revellers, was indeed a spirit commissioned to recall him to the pure, ideal life that had so etherealized him among men. It might be fancied that he went forth to seek this spirit in its sunny haunts; for still, as in the summer time gone by, he was seen to steal gently up wherever a butterfly had alighted, and lose himself in contemplation of it. When it took flight his eyes followed the winged vision, as if its airy track would show the path to heaven. But what could be the purpose of the unseasonable toil, which was again resumed, as the watchman knew by the lines of lamplight through the crevices of Owen Warland's shutters? The towns-people had one comprehensive explanation of all these singularities. Owen Warland had gone mad! How universally efficacious—how satisfactory, too, and soothing to the injured sensibility of narrowness and dulness—is this easy method of accounting for whatever lies beyond the world's most ordinary scope! From St. Paul's days down to our poor little Artist of the Beautiful, the same talisman had been applied to the elucidation of all mysteries in the words or deeds of men who spoke or acted too wisely or too well. In Owen Warland's case the judgment of his towns-people may have been correct. Perhaps he was mad. The lack of sympathy—that contrast between himself and his neighbors which took away the restraint of example—was enough to make him so. Or possibly he had caught just so much of ethereal radiance as served to bewilder him, in an earthly sense, by its intermixture with the common daylight.

One evening, when the artist had returned from a customary ramble and had just thrown the lustre of his lamp on the delicate piece of work so often interrupted, but still taken up again, as if his fate were embodied in its mechanism, he was surprised by the entrance of old Peter Hovenden. Owen never met this man without a shrinking of the heart. Of all the world he was most terrible, by reason of a keen understanding which saw so distinctly what it did see, and disbelieved so uncompromisingly in what it could not see. On this occasion the old watchmaker had merely a gracious word or two to say.

"Owen, my lad," said he, "we must see you at my house to-morrow night."

The artist began to mutter some excuse.

"Oh, but it must be so," quoth Peter Hovenden, "for the sake of the days when you were one of the household. What, my boy! don't you know that my daughter Annie is engaged to Robert Danforth? We are making an entertainment, in our humble way, to celebrate the event."

"Ah!" said Owen.

That little monosyllable was all he uttered; its tone seemed cold and unconcerned to an ear like Peter Hovenden's; and yet there was in it the stifled outcry of the poor artist's heart, which he compressed within him like a man holding down an evil spirit. One slight outbreak, however, imperceptible to the old watchmaker, he allowed himself. Raising the instrument with which he was about to begin his work, he let it fall upon the little system of machinery that had, anew, cost him months of thought and toil. It was shattered by the stroke!

Owen Warland's story would have been no tolerable representation of the troubled life of those who strive to create the beautiful, if, amid all other thwarting influences, love had not interposed to steal the cunning from his hand. Outwardly he had been no ardent or enterprising lover; the career of his passion had confined its tumults and vicissitudes so entirely within the artist's imagination that Annie herself had scarcely more than a woman's intuitive perception of it; but, in Owen's view, it covered the whole field of his life. Forgetful of the time when she had shown herself incapable of any deep response, he had persisted in connecting all his dreams of artistical success with Annie's image; she was the visible shape in which the spiritual power that he worshipped, and on whose altar he hoped to lay a not unworthy offering, was made manifest to him. Of course he had deceived himself; there were no such attributes in Annie Hovenden as his imagination had endowed her with. She, in the aspect which she wore to his inward vision, was as much a creature of his own as the mysterious piece of mechanism would be were it ever realized. Had he become convinced of his mistake through the medium of successful love,—had he won Annie to his bosom, and there beheld her fade from angel into ordinary woman,—the disappointment might have driven him back, with concentrated energy, upon his sole remaining object. On the other hand, had he found Annie what he fancied, his lot would have been so rich in beauty that out of its mere redundancy he might have wrought the beautiful into many a worthier type than he had toiled for; but the guise in which his sorrow came to him, the sense that the angel of his life had been snatched away and given to a rude man of earth and iron, who could neither need nor appreciate her ministrations, —this was the very perversity of fate that makes human existence appear too absurd and contradictory to be the scene of one other hope or one other fear. There was nothing left for Owen Warland but to sit down like a man that had been stunned.

He went through a fit of illness. After his recovery his small and slender frame assumed an obtuser garniture of flesh than it had ever before worn. His thin cheeks became round; his delicate little hand, so spiritually fashioned to achieve fairy task-work, grew plumper than the hand of a thriving infant. His aspect had a childishness such as might have induced a stranger to pat him on the head—pausing, however, in the act, to wonder what manner of child was here. It was as if the spirit had gone out of him, leaving the body to flourish in a sort of vegetable existence. Not that Owen Warland was idiotic. He could talk, and not irrationally. Somewhat of a babbler, indeed, did people begin to think him; for he was apt to discourse at wearisome length of marvels of mechanism that he had read about in books, but which he had learned to consider as absolutely fabulous. Among them he enumerated the Man of Brass, constructed by Albertus Magnus, and the Brazen Head of Friar Bacon; and, coming down to later times, the automata of a little coach and horses, which it was pretended had been manufactured for the Dauphin of France; together with an insect that buzzed about the ear like a living fly, and yet was but a contrivance of minute steel springs. There was a story, too, of a duck that waddled, and quacked, and ate; though, had any honest citizen purchased it for dinner, he would have found himself cheated with the mere mechanical apparition of a duck.

"But all these accounts," said Owen Warland, "I am now satisfied are mere impositions."

Then, in a mysterious way, he would confess that he once thought differently. In his idle and dreamy days he had considered it possible, in a certain sense, to spiritualize machinery, and to combine with the new species of life and motion thus produced a beauty that should attain to the ideal which Nature has proposed to herself in all her creatures, but has never taken pains to realize. He seemed, however, to retain no very distinct perception either of the process of achieving this object or of the design itself.

"I have thrown it all aside now," he would say. "It was a dream such as young men are always mystifying themselves with. Now that I have acquired a little common sense, it makes me laugh to think of it."

Poor, poor and fallen Owen Warland! These were the symptoms that he had ceased to be an inhabitant of the better sphere that lies unseen around us. He had lost his faith in the invisible, and now prided himself, as such unfortunates invariably do, in the wisdom which rejected much that even his eye could see, and trusted confidently in nothing but what his hand could touch. This is the calamity of men whose spiritual part dies out of them and leaves the grosser understanding to assimilate them more and more to the things of which alone it can take cognizance; but in Owen Warland the spirit was not dead nor passed away; it only slept.

How it awoke again is not recorded. Perhaps the torpid slumber was broken by a convulsive pain. Perhaps, as in a former instance, the butterfly came and hovered about his head and reinspired him,—as indeed this creature of the sunshine had always a mysterious mission for the artist,—reinspired him with the former purpose of his life. Whether it were pain or happiness that thrilled through his veins, his first impulse was to thank Heaven for rendering him again the being of thought, imagination, and keenest sensibility that he had long ceased to be.

"Now for my task," said he. "Never did I feel such strength for it as now."

Yet, strong as he felt himself, he was incited to toil the more diligently by an anxiety lest death should surprise him in the midst of his labors.

This anxiety, perhaps, is common to all men who set their hearts upon anything so high, in their own view of it, that life becomes of importance only as conditional to its accomplishment. So long as we love life for itself, we seldom dread the losing it. When we desire life for the attainment of an object, we recognize the frailty of its texture. But, side by side with this sense of insecurity, there is a vital faith in our invulnerability to the shaft of death while engaged in any task that seems assigned by Providence as our proper thing to do, and which the world would have cause to mourn for should we leave it unaccomplished. Can the philosopher, big with the inspiration of an idea that is to reform mankind, believe that he is to be beckoned from this sensible existence at the very instant when he is mustering his breath to speak the word of light? Should he perish so, the weary ages may pass away—the world's, whose life sand may fall, drop by drop—before another intellect is prepared to develop the truth that might have been uttered then. But history affords many an example where the most precious spirit, at any particular epoch manifested in human shape, has gone hence untimely, without space allowed him, so far as mortal judgment could discern, to perform his mission on the earth. The prophet dies, and the man of torpid heart and sluggish brain lives on. The poet leaves his song half sung, or finishes it, beyond the scope of mortal ears, in a celestial choir. The painter—as Allston[2] did—leaves half his conception on the canvas to sadden us with its imperfect beauty, and goes to picture forth the whole, if it be no irreverence to say so, in the hues of heaven. But rather such incomplete designs of this life will be perfected nowhere. This so frequent abortion of man's dearest projects must be taken as a proof that the deeds of earth, however etherealized by piety or genius, are without value, except as exercises and manifestations of the spirit. In heaven, all ordinary thought is higher and more melodious than Milton's song. Then, would he add another verse to any strain that he had left unfinished here?

But to return to Owen Warland. It was his fortune, good or ill, to achieve the purpose of his life. Pass we over a long space of intense thought, yearning effort, minute toil, and wasting anxiety, succeeded by an instant of solitary triumph: let all this be imagined; and then behold the artist, on a winter evening, seeking admittance to Robert Danforth's fireside circle. There he found the man of iron, with his massive substance thoroughly warmed and attempered by domestic influences. And there was Annie, too, now transformed into a matron, with much of her husband's plain and sturdy nature, but imbued, as Owen Warland still believed, with a finer grace, that might enable her to be the interpreter between strength and beauty. It happened, likewise, that old

[2] Washington Allston (1779–1843), American landscape painter.

Peter Hovenden was a guest this evening at his daughter's fireside; and it was his well-remembered expression of keen, cold criticism that first encountered the artist's glance.

"My old friend Owen!" cried Robert Danforth, starting up, and compressing the artist's delicate fingers within a hand that was accustomed to gripe bars of iron. "This is kind and neighborly to come to us at last. I was afraid your perpetual motion had bewitched you out of the remembrance of old times."

"We are glad to see you," said Annie, while a blush reddened her matronly cheek. "It was not like a friend to stay from us so long."

"Well, Owen," inquired the old watchmaker, as his first greeting, "how comes on the beautiful? Have you created it at last?"

The artist did not immediately reply, being startled by the apparition of a young child of strength that was tumbling about on the carpet,—a little personage who had come mysteriously out of the infinite but with something so sturdy and real in his composition that he seemed moulded out of the densest substance which earth could supply. This hopeful infant crawled towards the new-comer, and setting himself on end, as Robert Danforth expressed the posture, stared at Owen with a look of such sagacious observation that the mother could not help exchanging a proud glance with her husband. But the artist was disturbed by the child's look, as imagining a resemblance between it and Peter Hovenden's habitual expression. He could have fancied that the old watchmaker was compressed into this baby shape, and looking out of those baby eyes, and repeating, as he now did, the malicious question:—

"The beautiful, Owen! How comes on the beautiful? Have you succeeded in creating the beautiful?"

"I have succeeded," replied the artist, with a momentary light of triumph in his eyes and a smile of sunshine, yet steeped in such depth of thought that it was almost sadness. "Yes, my friends, it is the truth. I have succeeded."

"Indeed!" cried Annie, a look of maiden mirthfulness peeping out of her face again. "And is it lawful, now, to inquire what the secret is?"

"Surely; it is to disclose it that I have come," answered Owen Warland. "You shall know, and see, and touch, and possess the secret! For, Annie,—if by that name I may still address the friend of my boyish years,—Annie, it is for your bridal gift that I have wrought this spiritualized mechanism, this harmony of motion, this mystery of beauty. It comes late, indeed; but it is as we go onward in life, when objects begin to lose their freshness of hue and our souls their delicacy of perception, that the spirit of beauty is most needed. If,—forgive me, Annie,—if you know how to value this gift, it can never come too late."

He produced, as he spoke, what seemed a jewel box. It was carved richly out of ebony by his own hand, and inlaid with a fanciful tracery of pearl, representing a boy in pursuit of a butterfly, which, elsewhere, had become a winged spirit, and was flying heavenward; while the boy, or youth, had found such efficacy in his strong desire that he ascended from earth to cloud, and from cloud to celestial atmosphere, to win the beautiful. This case of ebony the artist opened, and bade Annie place her finger on its edge. She did so, but almost screamed as a butterfly fluttered forth, and, alighting on her finger's tip, sat waving the ample magnificence of its purple and gold-speckled wings, as if in prelude to a flight. It is impossible to express by words the glory, the splendor, the delicate gorgeousness which were softened into the beauty of this object. Nature's ideal butterfly was here realized in all its perfection; not in the pattern of such faded insects as flit among earthly flowers, but of those which hover across the meads of paradise for child-angels and the spirits of departed infants to disport themselves with. The rich down was visible upon its wings; the lustre of its eyes seemed instinct with spirit. The firelight glimmered around this wonder—the candles gleamed upon it; but it glistened apparently by its own radiance, and illuminated the finger and outstretched hand on which it rested with a white gleam like that of precious stones. In its perfect beauty, the consideration of size was entirely lost. Had its wings overreached the firmament, the mind could not have been more filled or satisfied.

"Beautiful! beautiful!" exclaimed Annie. "Is it alive? Is it alive?"

"Alive? To be sure it is," answered her husband. "Do you suppose any mortal has skill enough to make a butterfly, or would put himself to the trouble of making one, when any child may catch a score of them in a summer's afternoon? Alive? Certainly! But this pretty box is undoubtedly of our friend Owen's manufacture; and really it does him credit."

At this moment the butterfly waved its wings anew, with a motion so absolutely lifelike that Annie was startled, and even awe-stricken; for, in spite of her husband's opinion, she could not satisfy herself whether it was indeed a living creature or a piece of wondrous mechanism.

"Is it alive?" she repeated, more earnestly than before.

"Judge for yourself," said Owen Warland, who stood gazing in her face with fixed attention.

The butterfly now flung itself upon the air, fluttered round Annie's head, and soared into a distant region of the parlor, still making itself perceptible to sight by the starry gleam in which the motion of its wings enveloped it. The infant on the floor followed its course with his sagacious little eyes. After flying about the room, it returned in a spiral curve and settled again on Annie's finger.

"But is it alive?" exclaimed she again; and the finger on which the gorgeous mystery had alighted was so tremulous that the butterfly was forced to balance himself with his wings. "Tell me if it be alive, or whether you created it."

"Wherefore ask who created it, so it be beautiful?" replied Owen Warland. "Alive? Yes, Annie; it may well be said to possess life, for it has absorbed my own being into itself; and in the secret of that butterfly, and in its beauty,—which is not merely outward, but deep as its whole system,—is represented the intellect, the imagination, the sensibility, the soul of an Artist of the Beautiful! Yes; I created it. But"—and here his countenance somewhat changed—"this butterfly is not now to me what it was when I beheld it afar off in the daydreams of my youth."

"Be it what it may, it is a pretty plaything," said the blacksmith, grinning with childlike delight. "I wonder whether it would condescend to alight on such a great clumsy finger as mine? Hold it hither, Annie."

By the artist's direction, Annie touched her finger's tip to that of her husband; and, after a momentary delay, the butterfly fluttered from one to the other. It preluded a second flight by a similar, yet not precisely the same, waving of wings as in the first experiment; then, ascending from the blacksmith's stalwart finger, it rose in a gradually enlarging curve to the ceiling, made one wide sweep around the room, and returned with an undulating movement to the point whence it had started.

"Well, that does beat all nature!" cried Robert Danforth, bestowing the heartiest praise that he could find expression for; and, indeed, had he paused there, a man of finer words and nicer perception could not easily have said more. "That goes beyond me, I confess. But what then? There is more real use in one downright blow of my sledge hammer than in the whole five years' labor that our friend Owen has wasted on this butterfly."

Here the child clapped his hands and made a great babble of indistinct utterance, apparently demanding that the butterfly should be given him for a plaything.

Owen Warland, meanwhile, glanced sidelong at Annie, to discover whether she sympathized in her husband's estimate of the comparative value of the beautiful and the practical. There was, amid all her kindness towards himself, amid all the wonder and admiration with which she contemplated the marvellous work of his hands and incarnation of his idea, a secret scorn—too secret, perhaps, for her own consciousness, and perceptible only to such intuitive discernment as that of the artist. But Owen, in the latter stages of his pursuit, had risen out of the region in which such a discovery might have been torture. He knew that the world, and Annie as the representative of the world, whatever praise might be bestowed, could never say the fitting word nor feel the fitting sentiment which should be the perfect recompense of an artist who, symbolizing a lofty moral by a material trifle,—converting what was earthly to spiritual gold,—had won the beautiful into his handiwork. Not at this latest moment was he to learn that the reward of all high performance must be sought within itself, or sought in vain. There was, however, a view of the matter which Annie and her husband, and even Peter Hovenden, might fully have understood, and which would have satisfied them that the toil of years had here been worthily bestowed. Owen Warland might have told them that this butterfly, this plaything, this bridal gift of a poor watchmaker to a blacksmith's wife, was, in truth, a gem of art that a monarch would have purchased with honors and abundant wealth, and have treasured it among the jewels of his kingdom as the most unique and wondrous of them all. But the artist smiled and kept the secret to himself.

"Father," said Annie, thinking that a word of praise from the old watchmaker might gratify his former apprentice, "do come and admire this pretty butterfly."

"Let us see," said Peter Hovenden, rising from his chair, with a sneer upon his face that always made people doubt, as he himself did, in everything but a material existence. "Here is my finger for it to alight upon. I shall understand it better when once I have touched it."

But, to the increased astonishment of Annie, when the tip of her father's finger was pressed against that of her husband, on which the butterfly still rested, the insect drooped its wings and seemed on the point of falling to the floor. Even the bright spots of gold upon its wings and body, unless her eyes deceived her, grew dim, and the glowing purple took a dusky hue, and the starry lustre that gleamed around the blacksmith's hand became faint and vanished.

"It is dying! it is dying!" cried Annie, in alarm.

"It has been delicately wrought," said the artist, calmly. "As I told you, it has imbibed a spiritual essence—call it magnetism, or what you will. In an atmosphere of doubt and mockery its exquisite susceptibility suffers torture, as does the soul of him who instilled his own life into it. It has already lost its beauty; in a few moments more its mechanism would be irreparably injured."

"Take away your hand, father!" entreated Annie, turning pale. "Here is my child; let it rest on his innocent hand. There, perhaps, its life will revive and its colors grow brighter than ever."

Her father, with an acrid smile, withdrew his finger. The butterfly then appeared to recover the power of voluntary motion, while its hues assumed much of their original lustre, and the gleam of starlight, which was its most ethereal attribute, again formed a halo round about it. At first, when transferred from Robert Danforth's hand to the small finger of the child, this radiance grew so powerful that it positively threw the little fellow's shadow back against the wall. He, meanwhile, extended his plump hand as he had seen his father and mother do, and watched the waving of the insect's wings with infantine delight. Nevertheless, there was a certain odd expression of sagacity that made Owen Warland feel as if here were old Peter Hovenden, partially, and but partially, redeemed from his hard scepticism into childish faith.

"How wise the little monkey looks!" whispered Robert Danforth to his wife.

"I never saw such a look on a child's face," answered Annie, admiring her own infant, and with good reason, far more than the artistic butterfly. "The darling knows more of the mystery than we do."

As if the butterfly, like the artist, were conscious of something not entirely congenial in the child's nature, it alternately sparkled and grew dim. At length it arose from the small hand of the infant with an airy motion that seemed to bear it upward without an effort, as if the ethereal instincts with which its master's spirit had endowed it impelled this fair vision involuntarily to a higher sphere. Had there been no obstruction, it might have soared into the sky and grown immortal. But its lustre gleamed upon the ceiling; the exquisite texture of its wings brushed against that earthly medium; and a sparkle or two, as of stardust, floated downward and lay glimmering on the carpet. Then the butterfly came fluttering down, and, instead of returning to the infant, was apparently attracted towards the artist's hand.

"Not so! not so!" murmured Owen Warland, as if his handiwork could have understood him. "Thou has gone forth out of thy master's heart. There is no return for thee."

With a wavering movement, and emitting a tremulous radiance, the butterfly struggled, as it were, towards the infant, and was about to alight upon his finger; but while it still hovered in the air, the little child of strength, with his grandsire's sharp and shrewd expression in his face, made a snatch at the marvellous insect and compressed it in his hand. Annie screamed. Old Peter Hovenden burst into a cold and scornful laugh. The blacksmith, by main force, unclosed the infant's hand, and found within the palm a small heap of glittering fragments, whence the mystery of beauty had fled forever. And as for Owen Warland, he looked placidly at what seemed the ruin of his life's labor, and which was yet no ruin. He had caught a far other butterfly than this. When the artist rose high enough to achieve the beautiful, the symbol by which he made it perceptible to mortal senses became of little value in his eyes while his spirit possessed itself in the enjoyment of the reality.

QUESTIONS

1. The names of Hawthorne's characters are allusive. Trace their origins and then discuss the story as allegory.
2. Does Owen Warland seem "feminine"? Explain your answer.
3. What advice does Hawthorne give to the "ideal artist"? Aside from Hawthorne's concern, does the artist have a duty to society? If so, what is it? If not, why not?
4. In Hawthorne's view, can a work of art hope to equal the original model? What did Hawthorne consider the "original model" to be?
5. In your opinion, did Owen Warland come close to insanity? Support your opinion from the text.

6. Since, on three separate occasions, Owen considered his work ruined by the gentlest touch, is it possible that he did not want to finish it at those times? Why?

7. Does Hawthorne deal harshly with Peter Hovenden, Robert Danforth, and the child? If yes, in what way is his treatment harsh? If no, how does Hawthorne present these characters?

8. Discuss the meanings of the phrases "the beautiful idea has no relation to size"; "main strength" versus "spiritual strength"; and "that [the artificial butterfly, the work of art] does beat all nature."

9. What is the conception of time in the story?

10. Hawthorne uses the word "reality" in several different contexts within this work. What are the various meanings he gives this word?

Interurban Queen

R. A. Lafferty

This work belongs to the subgenre of science fiction sometimes known as the "alternate path" story. Stories of this sort explore the consequences following on the development of society in a direction other than the one it has actually taken. "Interurban Queen" contains a good deal of nostalgia as well as some pointed observations on the way in which the automobile has affected contempora: y life. It raises the question of "turning back the clock" and pursuing other possibilities. The question is extremely important in approaching a period of scarcity or overdevelopment. But the story might also convince us that whatever way we might have turned there would have been problems. Lafferty's perspective here is an example of what John Fischer has called "ecological humanism," a perspective common to most contemporary SF writers.

Raphael Aloysius Lafferty rode streetcars as a child in Tulsa. He still lives in the same house as he did at that time. Lafferty has published many works in the SF genre and a large number of his short stories are included in "best of the year" anthologies.

"It was the year 1907 when I attained my majority and came into a considerable inheritance," the old man said. "I was a very keen young man, keen enough to know that I didn't know everything. I went to knowledgeable men and asked their advice as to how I might invest this inheritance.

"I talked with bankers and cattlemen and the new oilmen. These were not stodgy men. They had an edge on the future, and they were excited and exciting about the way that money might be made to grow. It was the year of statehood and there was an air of prosperity over the new state. I wished to integrate my patrimony into that new prosperity.

"Finally I narrowed my choice to two investments which then seemed about of equal prospect, though you will now smile to hear them equated. One of them was the stock-selling company of a certain Harvey Goodrich, a rubber company, and with the new automobile coming into wider use, it seemed that rubber might be a thing of the future. The other was a stock-selling transportation company that proposed to run an interurban railway between the small towns of Kiefer and Mounds. It also proposed (at a future time) to run branches to Glenpool, to Bixby, to Kellyville, to Slick, to Bristow, to Beggs, even to Okmulgee and Sapulpa. At that time it also seemed that these little interurban railways might be things of the future. An interurban already ran between Tulsa and Sand Springs, and one was building between Tulsa and Sapulpa. There were more than one thousand of these small trolley railroads operating in the nation, and thoughtful men believed that they would come to form a complete national network, might become the main system of transportation."

But now the old man Charles Archer was still a young man. He was listening to Joe Elias, a banker in a small but growing town.

"It is a riddle you pose me, young man, and you set me thinking," Elias said. "We have dabbled in both, thinking to have an egg under every hen. I begin to believe that we were wrong to do so. These two prospects are types of two futures, and only one of them will obtain. In this state with its new oil discoveries, it might seem that we should be partial to rubber which has a tie-in with the automobile which has a tie-in with petroleum fuel. This need not be. I believe that the main use of oil will be in powering the new factories, and I believe that rubber is already oversold as to industrial application. And yet there *will be* a new transportation. Between the horse and the main-line railways there is a great gap. I firmly believe that the horse will be eliminated as a main form of transportation. We are making no more loans to buggy or buckboard manufacturers nor to harness makers. I have no faith in the automobile. It destroys something in me. It is the interurbans that will go into the smallest localities, and will so cut into the main-line railroads as to leave no more than a half dozen of the long-distance major lines in America. Young man, I would invest in the interurban with complete confidence."

Charles Archer was listening to Carl Bigheart, a cattleman.

"I ask you, boy, how many head of cattle can you put into an automobile? Or even into what they call a lorry or truck? Then I ask you how many you can put into an honest cattle car which can be coupled onto any interurban on a country run? The interurban will be the salvation of us cattlemen. With the fencing regulations we cannot drive cattle even twenty miles to a railroad; but the little interurbans will go into the deep country, running along every second or third section line.

"And I will tell you another thing, boy: there is no future for the automobile. *We cannot let there be!* Consider the man on horseback, and I have been a man on horseback for most of my life. Well, mostly he is a good man, but there is a change in him as soon as he mounts. Every man on horseback is an arrogant man, however gentle he may be on foot. I know this in myself and in others. He was necessary in his own time, and I believe that time is ending. There was always extreme danger from the man on horseback.

"Believe me, young man, the man in the automobile is one thousand times as dangerous. The kindest man in the world assumes an incredible arrogance when he drives an automobile, and this arrogance will increase still further if the machine is allowed to develop greater power and sophistication. I tell you, it will engender absolute selfishness in mankind if the driving of automobiles becomes common. It will breed violence on a scale never seen before. It will mark the end of the family as we know it, the three or four generations living happily in one home. It will destroy the sense of neighborhood and the true sense of nation. It will create giantized cankers of cities, false opulence of suburbs, ruinized countryside, and unhealthy conglomeration of specialized farming and manufacturing. It will breed rootlessness and immorality. It will make every man a tyrant. I believe the private automobile will be suppressed. *It will have to be!* This is a moral problem, and we are a moral nation and world; we will take moral action against it. And without the automobile, rubber has no real future. Opt for the interurban stock, young man."

Young Charles Archer was listening to Nolan Cushman, an oilman. "I will not lie to you, young fellow, I love the automobile, the motorcar. I have three, custom-built. I am an emperor when I drive. Hell, I'm an emperor anyhow! I bought a castle last summer that had housed emperors. I'm having it transported, stone by stone, to my place in the Osage. Now, as to the motorcar, I can see how it should develop. It should develop with the roads, they becoming leveled and metaled or concreted, and the cars lower and lower and faster and faster. We would develop them so, if we were some species other than human. It is the logical development, but I hope it will not come, and it will not. That would be to make it common, and the commonality of men cannot be trusted with this power. Besides, I love a high car, and I do not want there to be very many of them. They should only be allowed to men of extreme wealth and flair. How would it be if the workingmen were ever permitted them? It would be murderous if they should come into the hands of ordinary men. How hellish a world would it be if all men should become as arrogant as myself! No, the automobile will never be anything but a rich man's pride, the rubber will never be anything but a limited adjunct to that special thing. Invest in your interurban. It is the thing of the future, or else I dread that future."

Young Charles Archer knew that this was a crossroads of the world. Whichever turning was taken, it would predicate a certain sort of nation and world and humanity. He thought about it deeply. Then he decided. He went out and invested his entire inheritance in his choice.

"I considered the two investments and I made my choice," said Charles Archer, the old man now in the now present. "I put all I had into it, thirty-five thousand dollars, a considerable sum in those days. You know the results."

"I am one of the results, Great-grandfather," said Angela Archer. "If you had invested differently you would have come to different fortune, you would have married differently, and I would be different or not at all. I like me here and now. I like everything as it is."

Three of them were out riding early one Saturday morning, the old man Charles Archer, his great-granddaughter Angela, and her fiancé Peter Brady. They were riding through the quasiurbia, the rich countryside. It was not a main road, and yet it had a beauty (partly natural and partly contrived) that was as exciting as it was satisfying.

Water always beside the roadway, that was the secret! There were the carp ponds one after another. There were the hatcheries. There were the dancing rocky streams that in a less enlightened age might have been mere gutter runs or roadway runs. There were the small and rapid trout streams, and boys were catching big trout from them.

There were the deep bush-trees there, sumac, witch hazel, sassafras—incense trees they might almost have been. There were the great trees themselves, pecan and hickory and black walnut, standing like high backdrops; and between were the lesser trees, willow, cottonwood, sycamore. Catheads and sedge grass and reeds stood in the water itself, and tall Sudan grass and bluestem on the shores. And always the clovers there, and the smell of wet sweet clover.

"I chose the wrong one," said old Charles Archer as they rode along through the textured country. "One can now see how grotesque was my choice, but I was young. In two years, the stock-selling company in which I had invested was out of business and my loss was total. So early and easy riches were denied me, but I developed an ironic hobby: keeping track of the stock of the enterprise in which I did *not* invest. The stock I could have bought for thirty-five thousand dollars would now make me worth nine million dollars."

"Ugh, don't talk of such a thing on such a beautiful day," Angela objected.

"They heard another of them last night," Peter Brady commented. "They've been hearing this one, off and on, for a week now, and haven't caught him yet."

"I always wish they wouldn't kill them when they catch them," Angela bemoaned. "It doesn't seem quite right to kill them."

A goose-girl was herding her white honking charges as they gobbled weeds out of fields of morning onions. Flowering kale was shining green-purple, and okra plants were standing. Jersey cows grazed along the roadway, and the patterned plastic (almost as patterned as the grasses) filled the roadway itself.

There were clouds like yellow dust in the air. Bees! Stingless bees they were. But dust itself was not. That there never be dust again!

"They will have to find out and kill the sly klunker makers," said old man Charles Archer. "Stop the poison at its source."

"There's too many of them, and too much money in it," said Peter Brady. "Yes, we kill them. One of them was found and killed Thursday, and three nearly finished klunkers were destroyed. But we can't kill them all. They seem to come out of the ground like snakes."

"I wish we didn't have to kill them," Angela said.

There were brightly colored firkins of milk standing on loading stoas, for this was a milk shed. There were chickens squawking in nine-story-high coops as they waited the pickups, but they never had to wait long. Here were a thousand dozen eggs on a refrigeration porch; there a clutch of piglings, or of red steers.

Tomato plants were staked two meters high. Sweet corn stood, not yet come to tassel. They passed cucumber vines and canteloupe vines, and the potato hills rising up blue-green. Ah, there were grapevines in their tight acres, deep alfalfa meadows, living fences of Osage orange and white-thorn. Carrot tops zephyred like green lace. Cattle were grazing fields of red clover and of peanuts—that most magic of all clovers. Men mowed hay.

"I hear him now!" Peter Brady said suddenly.

"You couldn't. Not in the daytime. Don't even think of such a thing," Angela protested.

Farm ducks were grazing with their heads under water in the roadway ponds and farm ponds. Bower oaks grew high in the roadway parks. Sheep fed in hay grazer that was higher than their heads; they were small white islands in it. There was local wine and choc beer and cider for sale at small booths, along with limestone sculpture and painted fruitwood carvings. Kids danced on loading stoas to little post-mounted music canisters, and goats licked slate outcroppings in search of some new mineral.

The Saturday riders passed a roadway restaurant with its tables out under the leaves and under a little rock overhang. A one-meter-high waterfall gushed through the middle of the establishment, and a two-meter-long bridge of set shale stone led to the kitchen. Then they broke onto view after never-tiring view of the rich and varied quasiurbia. The roadway forms, the fringe farms, the berry patches! In their seasons: Juneberries, huckleberries, blueberries, dewberries, elderberries, highbush cranberries, red raspberries, boysenberries, loganberries, nine kinds of blackberries, strawberries, greenberries.

Orchards! Can there ever be enough orchards? Plum, peach, sand plum and chokecherry, black cherry, apple and crab apple, pear, blue-fruited pawpaw, persimmon, crooked quince. Melon patches, congregations of beehives, pickle patches, cheese farms, flax farms, close clustered towns (twenty houses in each, twenty persons in a house, twenty of the little settlements along every mile of roadway, country honkey-tonks, as well as high-dog clubs already open and hopping with action in the early morning; roadway chapels with local statuary and with their rich-box-poor-boxes (one dropped money in the top if one had it and the spirit to give it, one tripped it out the bottom if one needed it), and the little refrigeration niches with bread, cheese, beef rolls, and always the broached cask of country wine: that there be no more hunger on the roadways forever!

"I hear it too!" old Charles Archer cried out suddenly. "High-pitched and off to the left. And there's the smell of monoxide and—gah—rubber. Conductor, conductor!"

The conductor heard it, as did others in the car. The conductor stopped the cars to listen. Then he phoned the report and gave the location as well as he might, consulting with the passengers. There was rough country over to the left, rocks and hills, and someone was driving there in broad daylight.

The conductor broke out rifles from the locker, passing them out to Peter Brady and two other young men in the car, and to three men in each of the other two cars. A competent-seeming man took over the communication, talking to men on a line further to the left, beyond the mad driver, and they had him boxed into a box no more than half a mile square.

"You stay, Angela, and you stay, Grandfather Archer," Peter Brady said. "Here is a little thirty carbine. Use it if he comes in range at all. We hunt him down now." Then Peter Brady followed the conductor and the rifle-bearing men, ten men on a death hunt. And there were now four other groups out on the hunt, converging on their whining, coughing target.

"Why do they have to kill them, Great-grandfather? Why not turn them over to the courts?"

"The courts are too lenient. All they give them is life in prison."

"But surely that should be enough. It will keep them from driving the things, and some of the unfortunate men might even be rehabilitated."

"Angela, they are the greatest prison breakers ever. Only ten days ago, Mad Man Gudge killed three guards, went over the wall at State Prison, evaded all pursuit, robbed the cheesemakers' cooperative of fifteen thousand dollars, got to a sly klunker maker, and was driving one of the things in a wild area within thirty hours of his breakout. It was four days before they found him and killed him. They are insane, Angela, and the mental hospitals are already full of them. Not one of them has ever been rehabilitated."

"Why is it so bad that they should drive? They usually drive only in the very wild places, and for a few hours in the middle of the night."

"Their madness is infectious, Angela. Their arrogance would leave no room for anything else in the world. Our country is now in balance, our communication and travel is minute and near perfect, thanks to the wonderful trolleys and the people of the trolleys. We are all one neighborhood, we are all one family! We live in love and compassion, with few rich and few poor, and arrogance and hatred have all gone out from us. We are the people with roots, and with trolleys. We are one with our earth."

"Would it hurt that the drivers should have their own limited place to do what they wanted, if they did not bother sane people?"

"Would it hurt if disease and madness and evil were given their own limited place? But they will not stay in their place, Angela. There is the diabolical arrogance in them, the rampant individualism, the hatred of order. There can be nothing more dangerous to society than the man in the automobile. Were they allowed to thrive, there would be poverty and want again, Angela, and wealth and accumulation. And cities."

"But cities are the most wonderful things of all! I love to go to them."

"I do not mean the wonderful Excursion Cities, Angela. There would be cities of another and blacker sort. They were almost upon us once when a limitation was set on them. Uniqueness is lost in them; there would be mere accumulation of rootless people, of arrogant people, of duplicated people, of people who have lost their humanity. Let them never rob us of our involuted countryside, or our quasiurbia. We are not perfect; but what we have, we will not give away for the sake of wild men."

"The smell! I cannot stand it!"

"Monoxide. How would you like to be born in the smell of it, to live every moment of your life in the smell of it, to die in the smell of it?"

"No, no, not that."

The rifleshots were scattered but serious. The howling and coughing of the illicit klunker automobile were nearer. Then it was in sight, bouncing and bounding weirdly out of the rough rock area and into the tomato patches straight toward the trolley interurban.

The klunker automobile was on fire, giving off ghastly stench of burning leather and rubber and noxious monoxide and seared human flesh. The man, standing up at the broken wheel, was a madman, howling, out of his head. He was a young man, but sunken-eyed and unshaven, bloodied on the left side of his head and the left side of his breast, foaming with hatred and arrogance.

"Kill me! Kill me!" he croaked like clattering broken thunder. "There will be others! We will not leave off driving so long as there is one desolate place left, so long as there is one sly klunker maker left!"

He went rigid. He quivered. He was shot again. But he would die howling.

"Damn you all to trolley haven! A man in an automobile is worth a thousand men on foot! He is worth a million men in a trolley car! You never felt your black heart rise up in you when you took control of one of the monsters! You never felt the lively hate choke you off in rapture as you sneered down the whole world from your bouncing center of the universe! Damn all decent folks! I'd rather go to hell in an automobile than to heaven in a trolley car!"

A spoked wheel broke, sounding like one of the muted volleys of rifle fire coming from behind him. The klunker automobile pitched onto its nose, upended, turned over, and exploded in blasting flames. And still in the middle of the fire could be seen the two hypnotic eyes with their darker flame, could be heard the demented voice:

"The crankshaft will still be good, the differential will still be good, a sly klunker maker can use part of it, part of it will drive again—*ahhhiiii.*"

Some of them sang as they rode away from the site in the trolley cars, and some of them were silent and thoughtful. It had been an unnerving thing.

"It curdles me to remember that I once put my entire fortune into that future," Great-grandfather Charles Archer moaned. "Well, that is better than to have lived in such a future."

A young couple had happily loaded all their belongings onto a baggage trolley and were moving from one of the Excursion Cities to live with kindred in quasiurbia. The population of that Excursion City (with its wonderful theaters and music halls and distinguished restaurants and literary coffeehouses and alcoholic oases and amusement centers) had now reached seven thousand persons, the legal limit for any city. Oh, there were a thousand Excursion Cities and all of them delightful! But a limit must be kept on size. A limit must be kept on everything.

It was a wonderful Saturday afternoon. Fowlers caught birds with collapsible kite-cornered nets. Kids rode free out to the diamonds to play Trolley League ball. Old gaffers rode out with pigeons in pigeon boxes, to turn them loose and watch them race home. Shore netters took shrimp from the semisaline Little Shrimp Lake. Banjo players serenaded their girls in grassy lanes.

The world was one single bronze gong song with the melodious clang of trolley cars threading the country on their green-iron rails, with the sparky fire following them overhead and their copper gleaming in the sun. By law there must be a trolley line every mile, but they were oftener. By law no one trolley line might run for more than twenty-five miles.

This was to give a sense of locality. But transfers between the lines were worked out perfectly. If one wished to cross the nation, one rode on some one hundred and twenty different lines. There were no more long-distance railroads. They also had had their arrogance, and they also had had to go.

Carp in the ponds, pigs in the clover, a unique barn-factory in every hamlet and every hamlet unique, bees in the air, pepper plants in the lanes, and the whole land as sparky as trolley fire and right as rails.

QUESTIONS

1. Is Lafferty for the klunker or the trolley? Is he completely committed to one position or the other? Describe the positive and negative features of both the klunkers and the trolleys.

2. Discuss the significance of a "lynching party" in a well-regulated society such as Lafferty describes. Is this society "utopian" or "antiutopian"?

3. Consider the klunker as an "instrument of the devil." What "evil" qualities does it possess?

4. Would you say that today's automobile driver is an arrogant person behind the wheel? Is arrogance necessarily "bad"? Justify your answer. In your view, is the society of "Interurban Queen" arrogant? Why?

5. What is the mood and tone of this story? Describe the story's nostalgic and idyllic elements, its use of time, and its development of dramatic interest. How does Lafferty's style contribute to these qualities?

6. Is it correct to blame as many of our modern woes as we do on the automobile? Explain your answer.

7. There is a similarity in theme between Lafferty's story and Hawthorne's. What is it? In what way do the driver of the klunker and the artist of the beautiful resemble one another? In what way is their relationship to the rest of society similar?

Corona

Samuel R. Delany

The golden touch presented certain difficulties, as King Midas discovered. Telepathy is also a mixed blessing. In the following short story, Samuel R. Delany—a leading younger SF author—shows how an individual can be affected both positively and negatively by possession of uncommon powers. Delany's story is notable for its style, its infusion of "youth culture" elements into the narrative fabric. These characteristics are also found in other Delany works, such as his novel The Einstein Intersection *and his award-winning short stories collected in* Driftglass.

Pa ran off to Mars Colony before Buddy was born. Momma drank. At sixteen Buddy used to help out in a copter repair shop outside St. Gable below Baton Rouge. Once he decided it would be fun to take a copter, some bootleg, a girl named Dolores-jo, and sixty-three dollars and eighty-five cents to New Orleans. Nothing taken had ever, by any interpretation, been his. He was caught before they raised from the garage roof. He lied about his age at court to avoid the indignity of reform school. Momma, when they found her, wasn't too sure ("Buddy? Now, let me see, that's Laford. And James Robert Warren—I named him after my third husband who was not living with me at the time—now my little James, he came along in . . . two thousand and thirty-*two*, I do believe. Or thirty-*four*—you sure now, it's Buddy?") when he was born. The constable was inclined to judge him younger than he was, but let him go to grown-up prison anyway. Some terrible things happened there. When Buddy came out three years later he was a gentler person than before; still, when frightened, he became violent. Shortly he knocked up a waitress six years his senior. Chagrined, he applied for emigration to one of Uranus's moons. In twenty years, though, the colonial economy had stabilized. They were a lot more stringent with applicants than in his pa's day: colonies had become almost respectable. They'd started barring people with jail records and things like that. So he went to New York instead and eventually got a job as an assistant servicer at the Kennedy spaceport.

There was a nine-year-old girl in a hospital in New York at that time who could read minds and wanted to die. Her name was Lee.

Also there was a singer named Bryan Faust.

Slow, violent, blond Buddy had been at Kennedy a year when Faust's music came. The songs covered the city, sounded on every radio, filled the title selections on every jukebox and scopitone. They shouted and whispered and growled from the wall speaker in the spacehangar. Buddy ambled over the catwalk while the cross-rhythms, sudden silences, and moments of pure voice were picked up by jangling organ, whining oboe, bass and cymbals. Buddy's thoughts were small and slow. His hands, gloved in canvas, his feet, rubber booted, were big and quick.

Below him the spaceliner filled the hangar like a tuber an eighth of a mile long. The service crew swarmed the floor, moving over the cement like scattered ball bearings. And the music—

"Hey, kid."

Buddy turned.

Bim swaggered toward him, beating his thigh to the rhythms in the falls of sound. "I was just looking for you, kid." Buddy was twenty-four, but people would call him 'kid' after he was thirty. He blinked a lot.

"You want to get over and help them haul down that solvent from upstairs? The damn lift's busted again. I swear, they're going to have a strike if they don't keep the equipment working right. Ain't safe. Say, what did you think of the crowd outside this morning?"

"Crowd?" Buddy's drawl snagged on a slight speech defect. "Yeah, there was a lot of people, huh. I been down in the maintenance shop since six o'clock, so I guess I must've missed most of it. What was they here for?"

Bim got a lot of what-are-you-kidding-me on his face. Then it turned to a tolerant smile. "For Faust." He nodded toward the speaker: the music halted, lurched, then Bryan Faust's voice roared out for love and the violent display that would prove it real. "Faust came in this morning, kid. You didn't know? He's been making it down from moon to moon through the outer planets. I hear he broke 'em up in the asteroids. He's been to Mars, and the last thing I heard, they love him on Luna as much as anywhere else. He arrived on Earth this morning, and he'll be up and down the Americas for twelve days." He thumbed toward the pit and shook his head. "That's his liner." Bim whistled. "And did we have a hell of a time! All them kids, thousands of 'em, I bet. And people old enough to know better, too. You should have seen the police! When we were trying to get the liner in here, a couple of hundred kids got through the police block. They wanted to pull his ship apart and take home the pieces. You like his music?"

Buddy squinted toward the speaker. The sounds jammed into his ears, pried around his mind, loosening things. Most were good things, touched on by a resolved cadence, a syncopation caught up again, feelings sounded on too quickly for him to hold, but good feelings. Still, a few of them . . .

Buddy shrugged, blinked. "I like it." And the beat of his heart, his lungs, and the music coincided. "Yeah. I like that." The music went faster; heart and breathing fell behind; Buddy felt a surge of disorder. "But it's . . . strange." Embarrassed, he smiled over his broken tooth.

"Yeah. I guess a lot of other people think so too. Well, get over with those solvent cans."

"Okay." Buddy turned off toward the spiral staircase. He was on the landing, about to go up, when someone yelled down, "Watch it—!"

A ten gallon drum slammed the walkway five feet from him. He whirled to see as the casing split—

(Faust's sonar drums slammed.)

—and solvent, oxidizing in the air, splattered.

Buddy screamed and clutched his eye. He had been working with the metal rasp that morning, and his gloves were impregnated with steel flakes and oil. He ground his canvas palm against his face.

(Faust's electric bass ground against a suspended dissonance.)

As he staggered down the walk, hot solvent rained on his back. Then something inside went wild and he began to swing his arms.

(The last chorus of the song swung toward the close. And the announcer's voice, not waiting for the end, cut over, "All *right* all you little people *out* there in music land . . .")

"What in the—"

"Jesus, what's wrong with—"

"What happened? I told you the damn lift was broken!"

"Call the infirmary! Quick! Call the—"

Voices came from the level above, the level below. And footsteps. Buddy turned on the ramp and screamed and swung.

"Watch it! What's with that guy—"

"Here, help me hold . . . Owww!—"

"He's gone berserk! Get the doc up from the infirm—"

(". . . *that* was Bryan Faust's mind-*twisting*, brain-*blowing*, brand new release, *Corona!* And you know it will be a *hit!* . . .")

Somebody tried to grab him, and Buddy hit out. Blind, rolling from the hips, he tried to apprehend the agony with flailing hands. And couldn't. A flash bulb had been jammed into his eye socket and detonated. He knocked somebody else against the rail, and staggered, and shrieked.

(". . . And he's come down to Earth at *last*, all you baby-mommas and baby-poppas! The little man from Ganymede who's been putting *the* music of *the* spheres through *so* many changes this past year arrived *in* New York this morning. And all *I* want to say, Bryan . . .")

Rage, pain, and music.

(". . . is, how do you *dig* our Earth!")

Buddy didn't even feel the needle stab his shoulder. He collapsed as the cymbals died.

Lee turned and turned the volume nob till it clicked.

In the trapezoid of sunlight over the desk from the high, small window, open now for August, lay her radio, a piece of graph paper with an incomplete integration for the area within the curve $X^4 + Y^4 = k^4$, and her brown fist. Smiling, she tried to release the tension the music had built.

Her shoulders lowered, her nostrils narrowed, and her fist fell over on its back. Still, her knuckles moved to the remembered rhythm of *Corona.*

The inside of her forearm was webbed with raw pink. There were a few marks on her right arm too. But those were three years old; from when she had been six.

Corona!

She closed her eyes and pictured the rim of the sun. Centered in the flame, with the green eyes of his German father and the high cheekbones of his Arawak mother, was the impudent and insousiant, sensual and curious face of Bryan Faust. The brassy, four-color magazine with its endless hyperbolic prose was open on her bed behind her.

Lee closed her eyes tighter. If she could reach out, and perhaps touch—no, not him; that would be too much—but someone standing, sitting, walking near him, see what seeing him close was like, hear what hearing his voice was like, through air and light: she reached out her mind, reached for the music. And heard—

—your daughter getting along?

They keep telling me better and better every week when I go to visit her. But, oh, I swear, I just don't know. You have no idea how we hated to send her back to that place.

Of course I know! She's your own daughter. And she's such a cute little thing. And so smart. Did they want to run some more tests?

She tried to kill herself. Again.

Oh, *no!*

She's got scars on her wrist halfway to her elbow! What am I doing wrong? The doctors can't tell me. She's not even ten. I can't keep her here with me. Her father's tried; he's about had it with the whole business. I know because of a divorce a child may have emotional problems, but that a little girl, as intelligent as Lee, can be so—confused! She had to go back, I know she had to go back. But what is it I'm doing wrong? I hate myself for it, and sometimes, just because she can't tell me, I hate her—

Lee's eyes opened; she smashed the table with her small, brown fists, tautening the muscles of her face to hold the tears. All musical beauty was gone. She breathed once more. For a while she looked up at the window, its glass door swung wide. The bottom sill was seven feet from the floor.

Then she pressed the button for Dr. Gross, and went to the bookshelf.

She ran her fingers over the spines: *Spinoza, The Bobsy Twins at Spring Lake, The Decline of the West, The Wind in the Wil—*

She turned at the sound of the door unbolting. "You buzzed for me, Lee?"

"It happened. Again. Just about a minute ago."

"I noted the time as you rang."

"Duration, about forty-five seconds. It was my mother, and her friend who lives downstairs. Very ordinary. Nothing worth noting down."

"And how do you feel."

She didn't say anything, but looked at the shelves.

Dr. Gross walked into the room and sat down on her desk. "Would you like to tell me what you were doing just before it happened?"

"Nothing. I'd just finished listening to the new record. On the radio."

"Which record?"

"The new Faust song, *Corona*."

"Haven't heard that one." He glanced down at the graph paper and raised an eyebrow. "This yours, or is it from somebody else?"

"You told me to ring for you every time I . . . got an attack, didn't you?"

"Yes—"

"I'm doing what you want."

"Of course, Lee. I didn't mean to imply you hadn't been keeping your word. Want to tell me something about the record? What did you think of it?"

"The rhythm is very interesting. Five against seven when it's there. But a lot of the beats are left out, so you have to listen hard to get it."

"Was there anything, perhaps in the words, that may have set off the mind reading?"

"His colonial Ganymede accent is so thick that I missed most of the lyrics, even though it's basically English."

Dr. Gross smiled. "I've noticed the colonial expressions are slipping into a lot of young people's speech since Faust has become so popular. You hear them all the time."

"I don't." She glanced up at the doctor quickly, then back to the books.

Dr. Gross coughed; then he said, "Lee, we feel it's best to keep you away from the other children at the hospital. You tune in most frequently on the minds of people you know, or those who've had similar experiences and reactions to yours. All the children in the hospital are emotionally disturbed. If you were to suddenly pick up all their minds at once, you might be seriously hurt."

"I wouldn't!" she whispered.

"You remember you told us about what happened when you were four, in kindergarten, and you tuned into your whole class for six hours? Do you remember how upset you were?"

"I went home and tried to drink the iodine." She flung him a brutal glance. "I remember. But I hear mommy when she's all the way across the city. I hear strangers too, lots of times! I hear Mrs. Lowery, when she's teaching down in the classroom! I hear her! I've heard people on other planets!"

"About the song, Lee—"

"You want to keep me away from the other children because I'm smarter than they are! I know. I've heard you think too—"

"Lee, I want you to tell me more about how you felt about this new song—"

"You think I'll upset them because I'm so smart. You won't let me have any friends!"

"What did you feel about the song, Lee?"

She caught her breath, holding it in, her lids batting, the muscle in the back of her jaw leaping.

"What did you *feel* about the song; did you like it, or did you dislike it?"

She let the air hiss through her lips. "There are three melodic motifs," she began at last. "They appear in descending order of rhythmic intensity. There are more silences in the last melodic line. His music is composed of silence as much as sound."

"Again, what did you feel? I'm trying to get at your emotional reaction, don't you see?"

She looked at the window. She looked at Dr. Gross. Then she turned toward the shelves. "There's a book here, a part in a book, that says it, I guess, better than I can." She began working a volume from the half-shelf of Nietzsche.

"What book?"

"Come here." She began to turn the pages. "I'll show you."

Dr. Gross got up from the desk. She met him beneath the window.

Dr. Gross took it and, frowning, read the title heading: "*The Birth of Tragedy from the Spirit of Music* . . . death lies only in these dissonant tones—"

Lee's head struck the book from his hands. She had leapt on him as though he were a piece of furniture and she a small beast. When her hand was not clutching his belt, shirt front, lapel, shoulder, it was straining upward. He managed to grab her just as she grabbed the window ledge.

Outside was a nine story drop.

He held her by the ankle as she reeled in the sunlit frame. He yanked, and she fell into his arms, shrieking, "Let me die! Oh, please! Let me die!"

They went down on the floor together, he shouting, "No!" and the little girl crying. Dr. Gross stood up, now panting.

She lay on the green vinyl, curling around the sound of her own sobs, pulling her hands over the floor to press her stomach.

"Lee, isn't there *any* way you can understand this? Yes, you've been exposed to more than any nine-year-old's mind should be able to bear. But you've got to come to terms with it, somehow! That isn't the answer, Lee. I wish I could back it up with something. If you let me help, perhaps I can—"

She shouted, with her cheek pressed to the floor, "But you can't help! Your thoughts, they're just as clumsy and imprecise as the others! How can you—*you* help people who're afraid and confused because their own minds have formed the wrong associations! How! I don't want to have to stumble around in all your insecurities and fears as well! I'm not a child! I've lived more years and places than any ten of you! Just go away and let me alone—"

Rage, pain, and music.

"Lee—"

"Go away! Please!"

Dr. Gross, upset, swung the window closed, locked it, left the room, and locked the door.

Rage, pain . . . below the chaos she was conscious of the infectious melody of *Corona.* Somebody—not her—somebody else was being carried into the hospital, drifting in the painful dark, dreaming over the same sounds. Exhausted, still crying, she let it come.

The man's thoughts, she realized through her exhaustion, to escape pain had taken refuge in the harmonies and cadences of *Corona.* She tried to hide her own mind there. And twisted violently away. There was something terrible there. She tried to pull back, but her mind followed the music down.

The terrible thing was that someone had once told him not to put his knee on the floor.

Fighting, she tried to push it aside to see if what was underneath was less terrible. ("Buddy, stop that whining and let your momma alone. I don't feel good. Just get out of here and leave me *alone!*" The bottle shattered on the door jamb by his ear, and he fled. She winced. There couldn't be anything that bad about putting your knee on the floor. And so she gave up and let it swim toward her—

—Suds wound on the dirty water. The water was under his knees. Buddy leaned forward and scrubbed the wire brush across the wet stone. His canvas shoes were already soaked.

"Put your blessed knee on the floor, and I'll get you! Come on, move your . . ." Somebody, not Buddy, got kicked. "And don't let your knee touch that floor! Don't, I say." And got kicked again.

They waddled across the prison lobby, scrubbing. There was a sign over the elevator: Louisiana State Penal Correction Institute, but it was hard to make out because Buddy didn't read very well.

"Keep up with 'em, kid. Don't you let 'em get ahead'n you!" Bigfoot yelled. "Just 'cause you little, don't think you got no special privileges." Bigfoot slopped across the stone.

"When they gonna get an automatic scrubber unit in here?" somebody complained. "They got one in the county jail."

"This Institute"—Bigfoot lumbered up the line—"was built in nineteen hundred and forty-seven! We ain't had no escape in ninety-four years. We run it the same today as when it was builded back in nineteen hundred and *forty*-seven. The first time it don't do its job right of keepin' you all inside—then we'll think about running it different. Get on back to work. *Watch* your knee!"

Buddy's thighs were sore, his insteps cramped. The balls of his feet burned and his pants cuffs were sopping.

Bigfoot had taken off his slippers. As he patrolled the scrubbers, he slapped the soles together, first in front of his belly, then behind his heavy buttocks. *Slap* and *slap*. With each *slap*, one foot hit the soapy stone. "Don't bother looking up at me. You look at them stones! But don't let your knee touch the floor."

Once, in the yard latrine, someone had whispered, "Bigfoot? You watch him, kid! Was a preacher, with a revival meeting back in the swamp. Went down to the Emigration Office in town back when they was taking everyone they could get and demanded they make him Pope or something over the colony on Europa they was just setting up. They laughed him out of the office. Sunday, when everyone came to meeting, they found he'd sneaked into the town, busted the man at the Emigration Office over the head, dragged him out to the swamp, and nailed him up to a cross under the meeting tent. He tried to make everybody pray him down. After they prayed for about an hour, and nothing happened, they brought Bigfoot here. He's a trustee now."

Buddy rubbed harder with his wire brush.

"Let's see you rub a little of the devil out'n them stones. And don't let me see your knee touch the—"

Buddy straightened his shoulders. And slipped.

He went over on his backside, grabbed the pail; water splashed over him, sluiced beneath. Soap stung his eyes. He lay there a moment.

Bare feet slapped toward him. "Come on, kid. Up you go, and back to work."

With eyes tight Buddy pushed himself up.

"You sure are one clums—"

Buddy rolled to his knees.

"I *told* you not to let your knee touch the floor!"

Wet canvas whammed his ear and cheek.

"Didn't I?"

A foot fell in the small of his back and struck him flat. His chin hit the floor and he bit his tongue, hard. Holding him down with his foot,

Bigfoot whopped Buddy's head back and forth, first with one shoe, then the other. Buddy, blinded, mouth filled with blood, swam on the wet stone, tried to duck away.

"Now don't let your knees touch the floor *again.* Come on, back to work, all of you." The feet slapped away.

Against the sting, Buddy opened his eyes. The brush lay just in front of his face. Beyond the bristles he saw a pink heel strike in suds.

His action took a long time to form. *Slap* and *slap.* On the third *slap* he gathered his feet, leapt. He landed on Bigfoot's back, pounding with the brush. He hit three times, then he tried to scrub off the side of Bigfoot's face.

The guards finally pulled him off. They took him into a room where there was an iron bed with no mattress and strapped him, ankles, wrists, neck, and stomach, to the frame. He yelled for them to let him up. They said they couldn't because he was still violent. "How'm I gonna eat!" he demanded. "You gonna let me up to eat?"

"Calm down a little. We'll send someone in to feed you."

A few minutes after the dinner bell rang that evening, Bigfoot looked into the room. Ear, cheek, neck, and left shoulder were bandaged. Blood had seeped through at the tip of his clavicle to the size of a quarter. In one hand Bigfoot held a tin plate of rice and fatback, in the other an iron spoon. He came over, sat on the edge of Buddy's bed, and kicked off one canvas shoe. "They told me I should come in and feed you, kid." He kicked off the other one. "You real hungry?"

When they unstrapped Buddy four days later, he couldn't talk. One tooth was badly broken, several others chipped. The roof of his mouth was raw; the prison doctor had to take five stitches in his tongue.

Lee gagged on the taste of iron.

Somewhere in the hospital, Buddy lay in the dark, terrified, his eyes stinging, his head filled with the beating rhythms of *Corona.*

Her shoulders bunched; she worked her jaw and tongue against the pain that Buddy remembered. She wanted to die.

Stop it! she whispered, and tried to wrench herself from the inarticulate terror which Buddy, cast back by pain and the rhythm of a song to a time when he was only twice her age, remembered. Oh, stop it! But no one could hear her, the way she could hear Buddy, her mother. Mrs. Lowery in the schoolroom.

She had to stop the fear.

Perhaps it was the music. Perhaps it was because she had exhausted every other way. Perhaps it was because the only place left to look for a way out was back inside Buddy's mind—

—When he wanted to sneak out of the cell at night to join a card game down in the digs where they played for cigarettes, he would take a piece of chewing gum and the bottle cap from a *Doctor Pepper* and stick it over the bolt in the top of the door. When they closed the doors after free-time, it still fitted into place, but the bolt couldn't slide in—

Lee looked at the locked door of her room. She could get the chewing gum in the afternoon period when they let her walk around her own floor. But the soft drink machine by the elevator only dispensed in cups. Suddenly she sat up and looked at the bottom of her shoe. On the toe and heel were the metal taps that her mother had made the shoe maker put there so they wouldn't wear so fast. She had to stop the fear. If they wouldn't let her do it by killing herself, she'd do it another way. She went to the cot, and began to work the tap loose on the frame.

Buddy lay on his back, afraid. After they had drugged him, they had brought him into the city. He didn't know where he was. But he couldn't see, and he was afraid.

Something fingered his face. He rocked his head to get away from the spoon—

"Shhhh! It's all right . . ."

Light struck one eye. There was still something wrong with the other. He blinked.

"You're all right," she—it was a *she* voice, though he still couldn't make out a face—told him again. "You're not in jail. You're not in the . . . the joint anymore. You're in New York. In a hospital. Something's happened to your eye. That's all."

"My eye . . . ?"

"Don't be afraid anymore. Please. Because I can't stand it."

It was a kid's voice. He blinked again, reached up to rub his vision clear.

"Watch out," she said. "You'll get—"

His eye itched and he wanted to scratch it. So he shoved at the voice.

"Hey!"

Something stung him and he clutched at his thumb with his other hand.

"I'm sorry," she said. "I didn't mean to bite your finger. But you'll hurt the bandage. I've pulled the one away from your right eye. There's nothing wrong with that. Just a moment." Something cool swabbed his blurred vision.

It came away.

The cutest little colored girl was kneeling on the edge of the bed with a piece of wet cotton in her hand. The light was nowhere near as bright as it had seemed, just a nightlight glowing over the mirror above the basin. "You've got to stop being so frightened," she whispered. "You've *got* to."

Buddy had spent a good deal of his life doing what people told him, when he wasn't doing the opposite on purpose.

The girl sat back on her heels. "That's better."

He pushed himself up in the bed. There were no straps. Sheets hissed over his knees. He looked at his chest. Blue pajamas: the buttons were in the wrong holes by one. He reached down to fix them, and his fingers closed on air.

"You've only got one eye working so there's no parallax for depth perception."

"Huh?" He looked up again.

She wore shorts and a red and white polo shirt.

He frowned, "Who are you?"

"Dianne Lee Morris," she said. "And you're—" Then she frowned too. She scrambled from the bed, took the mirror from over the basin and brought it back to the bed. "Look. Now who are you?"

He reached up to touch with grease crested nails the bandage that sloped over his left eye. Short, yellow hair lapped the gauze. His forefinger went on to the familiar scar through the tow hedge of his right eyebrow.

"Who are you."

"Buddy Magowan."

"Where do you live?"

"St. Gab—" He stopped. "A hun' ni'tee' stree' 'tween Se'on and Thir' A'nue."

"Say it again."

"A hundred an' nineteenth street between Second an' Third Avenue." The consonants his nightschool teacher at P.S. 125 had laboriously inserted into his speech this past year returned.

"Good. And you work?"

"Out at Kennedy. Service assistant."

"And there's nothing to be afraid of."

He shook his head, "Naw," and grinned. His broken tooth reflected in the mirror. "Naw. I was just having a bad . . . dream."

She put the mirror back. As she turned back, suddenly she closed her eyes and sighed.

"What'sa matter?"

She opened them again. "It's stopped. I can't hear inside your head any more. It's been going on all day."

"Huh? What do you mean?"

"Maybe you read about me in the magazine. There was a big article about me in *New Times* a couple of years ago. I'm in the hospital too. Over on the other side, in the psychiatric division. Did you read the article?"

"Didn't do much magazine reading back then. Don't do too much now either. What'd they write about?"

"I can hear and see what other people are thinking. I'm one of the three they're studying. I do it best of all of them. But it only comes in spurts. The other one, Eddy, is an idiot. I met him when we were getting all the tests. He's older than you and even dumber. Then there's Mrs. Lowery. She doesn't hear. She just sees. And sometimes she can make other people hear her. She works in the school here at the hospital. She can come and go as she pleases. But I have to stay locked up."

Buddy squinted. "You can hear what's in my head?"

"Not now. But I could. And it was . . ." Her lip began to quiver; her brown eyes brightened. ". . . I mean when that man tried to . . . with the . . ." And overflowed. She put her fingers on her chin and twisted. ". . . when he . . . cutting in your . . ."

Buddy saw her tears, wondered at them. "Aw, honey—" he said, reached to take her shoulder.

Her face struck his chest and she clutched his pajama jacket. "It hurt so much!"

Her grief at his agony shook her.

"I had to stop you from hurting! Yours was just a dream, so I could sneak out of my room, get down here, and wake you up. But the others, the girl in the fire, or the man in the flooded mine . . . those weren't dreams! I couldn't do anything about them. I couldn't stop the hurting there. I couldn't stop it at all, Buddy. I wanted to. But one was in Australia and the other in Costa Rica!" She sobbed against his chest. "And one was on Mars! And I couldn't get to Mars. I couldn't!"

"It's all right," he whispered, uncomprehending, and rubbed her rough hair. Then, as she shook in his arms, understanding swelled. "You came . . . down here to wake me up?" he asked.

She nodded against his pajama jacket.

"Why?"

She shrugged against his belly. "I . . . I don't . . . maybe the music."

After a moment he asked, "Is this the first time you ever done something about what you heard?"

"It's not the first time I ever tried. But it's the first time it ever . . . worked."

"Then why did you try again?"

"Because . . ." She was stiller now. ". . . I hoped maybe it would hurt less if I could get—through." He felt her jaw moving as she spoke. "It does." Something in her face began to quiver. "It does hurt less." He put his hand on her hand, and she took his thumb.

"You knew I was . . . was awful scared?"

She nodded. "I knew, so I was scared just the same."

Buddy remembered the dream. The back of his neck grew cold, and the flesh under his thighs began to tingle. He remembered the reality behind the dream—and held her more tightly and pressed his cheek to her hair. "Thank you." He couldn't say it any other way, but it didn't seem enough. So he said it again more slowly. "*Thank* you."

A little later she pushed away, and he watched her sniffling face with depthless vision.

"Do you like the song?"

He blinked. And realized the insistent music still worked through his head. "You can—hear what I'm thinking again?"

"No. But you were thinking about it before. I just wanted to find out."

Buddy thought awhile. "Yeah." He cocked his head. "Yeah. I like it a lot. It makes me feel . . . good."

She hesitated, then let out: "Me *too!* I think it's beautiful. I think Faust's music is so," and she whispered the next word as though it might offend, "*alive!* But with life the way it should be. Not without pain, but with pain contained, ordered, given form and meaning, so that it's almost all right again. Don't you feel that way?"

"I . . . don't know. I *like* it . . ."

"I suppose," Lee said a little sadly, "people like things for different reasons."

"You like it a lot." He looked down and tried to understand how she liked it. And failed. Tears had darkened his pajamas. Not wanting her to cry again, he grinned when he looked up. "You know, I almost saw him this morning."

"Faust? You mean you saw Bryan Faust?"

He nodded. "Almost. I'm on the service crew out at Kennedy. We were working on his liner when . . ." He pointed to his eye.

"*His* ship? *You* were?" The wonder in her voice was perfectly childish, and enchanting.

"I'll probably see him when he leaves," Buddy boasted. "I can get in where they won't let anybody else go. Except people who work at the port."

"I'd give—" she remembered to take a breath, "—anything to see him. Just anything in the world!"

"There was a hell of a crowd out there this morning. They almost broke through the police. But I could've just walked up and stood at the bottom of the ramp when he came down. If I'd thought about it."

Her hands made little fists on the edge of the bed as she gazed at him.

"Course I'll probably see him when he goes." This time he found his buttons and began to put them into the proper holes.

"I wish I could see him too!"

"I suppose Bim—he's foreman of the service crew—he'd let us through the gate, if I said you were my sister." He looked back up at her brown face. "Well, my cousin."

"Would you take me? Would you really take me?"

"Sure." Buddy reached out to tweak her nose, missed. "You did something for me. I don't see why not, if they'd let you leave—"

"Mrs. Lowery!" Lee whispered and stepped back from the bed.

"—the hospital. Huh?"

"They know I'm gone! Mrs. Lowery is calling for me. She says she's seen me, and Dr. Gross is on his way. They want to take me back to my room." She ran to the door.

"Lee, there you are! Are you all right?" In the doorway Dr. Gross grabbed her arm as she tried to twist away.

"Lemme *go!*"

"Hey!" bellowed Buddy. "What are you doin' with that little girl!" Suddenly he stood up in the middle of the bed, shedding sheets.

Dr. Gross's eyes widened. "I'm taking her back to her room. She's a patient in the hospital. She should be in another wing."

"She wanna go?" Buddy demanded, swaying over the blankets.

"She's very disturbed," Dr. Gross countered at Buddy, towering on the bed. "We're trying to help her, don't you understand? I don't know who you are, but we're trying to keep her alive. She has to go back!"

Lee shook her head against the doctor's hip. "Oh, Buddy . . ."

He leapt over the foot of the bed, swinging. Or at any rate, he swung once. He missed wildly because of the parallax. Also because he pulled the punch in, half completed, to make it seem a floundering gesture. He was not in the Louisiana State Penal Correction Institute: the realization had come the way one only realizes the tune playing in the back of the mind when it stops. "Wait!" Buddy said.

Outside the door the doctor was saying, "Mrs. Lowery, take Lee back up to her room. The night nurse knows the medication she should have."

"Yes, doctor."

"Wait!" Buddy called. "Please!"

"Excuse me," Dr. Gross said, stepping back through the door. Without Lee. "But we have to get her upstairs and under a sedative, immediately. Believe me, I'm sorry for this inconvenience."

Buddy sat down on the bed and twisted his face. "What's . . . the matter with her?"

Dr. Gross was silent a moment. "I suppose I do have to give you an explanation. That's difficult, because I don't know exactly. Of the three proven telepaths that have been discovered since a concerted effort has been made to study them, Lee is the most powerful. She's a brilliant, incredibly creative child. But her mind has suffered so much trauma—from all the lives telepathy exposes her to—she's become hopelessly suicidal. We're trying to help her. But if she's left alone for any length of time, sometimes weeks, sometimes hours, she'll try to kill herself."

"Then when's she gonna be better?"

Dr. Gross put his hands in his pockets and looked at his sandals. "I'm afraid to cure someone of a mental disturbance, the first thing you have to do is isolate them from the trauma. With Lee that's impossible. We don't even know which part of the brain controls the telepathy, so we couldn't even try lobotomy. We haven't found a drug that affects it yet." He shrugged. "I wish we could help her. But when I'm being objective, I can't see her ever getting better. She'll be like this the rest of her life. The quicker you can forget about her, the less likely you are to hurt her. Goodnight. Again, I'm very sorry this had to happen."

"G'night." Buddy sat in his bed a little while. Finally he turned off the light and lay down. He had to masturbate three times before he finally fell asleep. In the morning, though, he still had not forgotten the dark little girl who had come to him and awakened—so much in him.

The doctors were very upset about the bandage and talked of sympathetic opthalmia. They searched his left cornea for any last bits of metal dust. They kept him in the hospital three more days, adjusting the pressure between his vitreous and aqueous humors to prevent his till now undiscovered tendency toward glaucoma. They told him that the thing that had occasionally blurred the vision in his left eye was a vitreous floater and not to worry about it. Stay home at least two weeks, they said. And wear your eyepatch until two days before you go back to work. They gave him a hassle with his workmen's compensation papers too. But he got it straightened out—he'd filled in a date wrong. He never saw the little girl again.

And the radios and jukeboxes and scopitones in New York and Buenos Aires, Paris and Istanbul, in Melbourne and Bangkok, played the music of Bryan Faust.

The day Faust was supposed to leave Earth for Venus, Buddy went back to the spaceport. It was three days before he was supposed to report to work, and he still wore the flesh colored eyepatch.

"Jesus," he said to Bim as they leaned at the railing of the observation deck on the roof of the hangar, "just look at all them people."

Bim spat down at the hot macadam. The liner stood on the take-off pad under the August sun.

"He's going to sing before he goes," Bim said. "I hope they don't have a riot."

"Sing?"

"See that wooden platform out there and all them loudspeakers? With all those kids, I sure hope they don't have a riot."

"Bim, can I get down onto the field, up near the platform?"

"What for?"

"So I can see him up real close."

"You were the one talking about all the people."

Buddy, holding the rail, worked his thumb on the brass. The muscles in his forearm rolled beneath the tattoo: *To Mars I Would Go for Dolores-jo*, inscribed on Saturn's rings. "But I got to!"

"I don't see why the hell—"

"There's this little nigger girl, Bim—"

"Huh?"

"Bim!"

"Okay. Okay. Get into a coverall and go down with the clocker crew. You'll be right up with the reporters. But don't tell anybody I sent you. You know how many people want to get up there. Why you want to get so close for anyway?"

"For a . . ." He turned in the doorway. "For a friend." He ran down the stairs to the lockers.

Bryan Faust walked across the platform to the microphones. Comets soared over his shoulders and disappeared under his arms. Suns novaed on his chest. Meteors flashed around his elbows. Shirts of polarized cloth with incandescent, shifting designs were now being called *Fausts*. Others flashed in the crowd. He pushed back his hair, grinned, and behind the police-block hundreds of children screamed. He laughed into the microphone; they quieted. Behind him a bank of electronic instruments glittered. The controls were in the many jeweled rings hanging bright and heavy on his fingers. He raised his hands, flicked his thumbs across the gems, and the instruments, programmed to respond, began the cascading introduction to *Corona*. Bryan Faust sang. Across Kennedy, thousands—Buddy among them—heard.

On her cot in the hospital, Lee listened. "Thank you, Buddy," she whispered. "Thank you." And felt a little less like dying.

QUESTIONS

1. The kind of violence in "Corona" was, until very recently, unusual for science fiction. Why might this kind of explicit and socially conscious violence have been generally lacking in SF? Is it justified here?

2. How does style and characterization in this story differ from that of "classic" science fiction? On the basis of your own reading and the description in the Introduction, what are the major stylistic features of traditional science fiction?

3. Buddy is described as blond and violent. Is he actually violent at the time the story takes place?

4. Lee is black. What effect, if any, does the racial contrast between Buddy and Lee have on the story? Are there other contrasts between them? What purpose do the contrasts serve?

5. Lee wants to commit suicide. Is she therefore as violent as Buddy? If they are equally violent, what motivates their violence? Against whom or what is their violence directed?

6. Both Lee and Buddy are victims. What has victimized them? What view of the world is implied in the answer to this question and to the preceding one?

7. "Corona" ends on a hopeful note. What is the nature of this "happy ending" and what does it imply for the real world?

8. Relate this story to "The Listeners," *The Fall of Japan,* and "The Ultimate Horror" in Part I.

The Marching Morons

C. M. Kornbluth

Although "The Marching Morons," unlike "Corona," does not serve as a Christian parable of redemption in modern terms, it too offers a prospect of hope. The hope it offers, however, is grounded in death and deception, reflecting a grim view of our present realities and future possibilities.

Planned parenthood is seen by many people today as the chief solution to overpopulation and the world food crisis.

C. M. Kornbluth takes a skeptic's view in this story of a logical and possible outcome of Zero Population Growth. The Science Fiction Writers of America consider "The Marching Morons" to be one of the finest works in the genre.

Some things had not changed. A potter's wheel was still a potter's wheel and clay was still clay. Efim Hawkins had built his shop near Goose Lake, which had a narrow band of good fat clay and a narrow beach of white sand. He fired three bottle-nosed kilns with willow charcoal from the wood lot. The wood lot was also useful for long walks while the kilns were cooling; if he let himself stay within sight of them, he would open them prematurely, impatient to see how some new shape or glaze had come through the fire, and—*ping!*—the new shape or glaze would be good for nothing but the shard pile back of his slip tanks.

A business conference was in full swing in his shop, a modest cube of brick, tile-roofed, as the Chicago-Los Angeles "rocket" thundered overhead—very noisy, very swept back, very fiery jets, shaped as sleekly swift-looking as an airborne barracuda.

The buyer from Marshall Fields was turning over a black-glazed one-liter carafe, nodding approval with his massive, handsome head. "This is real pretty," he told Hawkins and his own secretary, Gomez-Laplace. "This has got lots of what ya call real est'etic principles. Yeah, it is real pretty."

"How much?" the secretary asked the potter.

"Seven-fifty in dozen lots," said Hawkins. "I ran up fifteen dozen last month."

"They are real est'etic," repeated the buyer from Fields. "I will take them all."

"I don't think we can do that, doctor," said the secretary. "They'd cost us $1,350. That would leave only $532 in our quarter's budget. And we still have to run down to East Liverpool to pick up some cheap dinner sets."

"Dinner sets?" asked the buyer, his big face full of wonder.

"Dinner sets. The department's been out of them for two months now. Mr. Garvy-Seabright got pretty nasty about it yesterday. Remember?"

"Garvy-Seabright, that meat-headed bluenose," the buyer said contemptuously. "He don't know nothin' about est'etics. Why for don't he lemme run my own department?" His eye fell on a stray copy of *Whambozambo Comix* and he sat down with it. An occasional deep chuckle or grunt of surprise escaped him as he turned the pages.

Uninterrupted, the potter and the buyer's secretary quickly closed a deal for two dozen of the liter carafes. "I wish we could take more," said the secretary, "but you heard what I told him. We've had to turn away customers for ordinary dinnerware because he shot the last quarter's budget on some Mexican piggy banks some equally enthusiastic importer stuck him with. The fifth floor is packed solid with them."

"I'll bet they look mighty est'etic."

"They're painted with purple cacti."

The potter shuddered and caressed the glaze of the sample carafe.

The buyer looked up and rumbled, "Ain't you dummies through yakkin' yet? What good's a seckertary for if'n he don't take the burden of *de*-tail off'n my back, harh?"

"We're all through, doctor. Are you ready to go?"

The buyer grunted peevishly, dropped *Whambozambo Comix* on the floor and led the way out of the building and down the log corduroy road to the highway. His car was waiting on the concrete. It was, like all contemporary cars, too low slung to get over the logs. He climbed down into the car and started the motor with a tremendous sparkle and roar.

"Gomez-Laplace," called out the potter under cover of the noise, "did anything come of the radiation program they were working on the last time I was on duty at the Pole?"

"The same old fallacy," said the secretary gloomily. "It stopped us on mutation, it stopped us on culling, it stopped us on segregation, and now it's stopped us on hypnosis."

"Well, I'm scheduled back to the grind in nine days. Time for another firing right now. I've got a new luster to try . . ."

"I'll miss you. I shall be 'vacationing'—running the drafting room of the New Century Engineering Corporation in Denver. They're going to put up a two-hundred-story office building, and naturally somebody's got to be on hand."

"Naturally," said Hawkins with a sour smile.

There was an ear-piercingly sweet blast as the buyer leaned on the horn button. Also, a yard-tall jet of what looked like flame spurted up from the car's radiator cap; the car's power plant was a gas turbine and had no radiator.

"I'm coming, doctor," said the secretary dispiritedly. He climbed down into the car and it whooshed off with much flame and noise.

The potter, depressed, wandered back up the corduroy road and contemplated his cooling kilns. The rustling wind in the boughs was obscuring the creak and mutter of the shrinking refractory brick. Hawkins wondered about the number two kiln—a reduction fire on a load of lusterware mugs. Had the clay chinking excluded the air? Had it been a properly smoky blaze? Would it do any harm if he just took one close—?

Common sense took Hawkins by the scruff of the neck and yanked him over to the tool shed. He got out his pick and resolutely set off on a prospecting jaunt to a hummocky field that might yield some oxides. He was especially low on coppers.

The long walk left him sweating hard, with his lust for a peek into the kiln quiet in his breast. He swung his pick almost at random into one of the hummocks; it clanged on a stone which he excavated. A largely obliterated inscription said:

ERSITY OF CHIC
OGICAL LABO
ELOVED MEMORY OF
KILLED IN ACT

The potter swore mildly. He had hoped the field would turn out to be a cemetery, preferably a once-fashionable cemetery full of once-massive bronze caskets moldered into oxides of tin and copper.

Well, hell, maybe there was some around anyway.

He headed lackadaisically for the second largest hillock and sliced into it with his pick. There was a stone to undercut and topple into a trench, and then the potter was very glad he'd stuck at it. His nostrils were filled with the bitter smell and the dirt was tinged with the exciting blue of copper salts. The pick went *clang!*

Hawkins, puffing, pried up a stainless steel plate that was quite badly stained and was also marked with incised letters. It seemed to have pulled loose from rotting bronze; there were rivets on the back that brought up flakes of green patina. The potter wiped off the surface dirt with his sleeve, turned it to catch the sunlight obliquely and read:

HONEST JOHN BARLOW

Honest John, famed in university annals, represents a challenge which medical science has not yet answered: revival of a human being accidentally thrown into a state of suspended animation.

In 1988 Mr. Barlow, a leading Evanston real estate dealer, visited his dentist for treatment of an impacted wisdom tooth. His dentist requested and received permission to use the experimental anesthetic Cycloparadimethanol-B-7, developed at the University.

After administration of the anesthetic, the dentist resorted to his drill. By freakish mischance, a short circuit in his machine delivered 220 volts of 60-cycle current into the patient. (In a damage suit instituted by Mrs. Barlow against the dentist, the University and the makers of the drill, a jury found for the defendants.) Mr. Barlow never got up from the dentist's chair and was assumed to have died of poisoning, electrocution or both.

Morticians preparing him for embalming discovered, however, that their subject was—though certainly not living—just as certainly not dead. The University was notified and a series of exhaustive tests was begun, including attempts to duplicate the trance state on volunteers. After a bad run of seven cases which ended fatally, the attempts were abandoned.

Honest John was long an exhibit at the University museum and livened many a football game as mascot of the University's Blue Crushers. The bounds of taste were overstepped, however, when a pledge to Sigma Delta Chi was ordered in '03 to "kidnap" Honest John from his loosely guarded glass museum case and introduce him into the Rachel Swanson Memorial Girls' Gymnasium shower room.

On May 22, 2003, the University Board of Regents issued the following order: "By unanimous vote, it is directed that the remains of Honest John Barlow be removed from the University museum and conveyed to the University's Lieutenant James Scott III Memorial Biological Laboratories and there be securely locked in a specially prepared vault. It is further directed that all possible measures for the preservation of these remains be taken by the Laboratory administration and that access to these remains be denied to all persons except qualified scholars authorized in writing by the Board. The Board reluctantly takes this action in view of recent notices and photographs in the nation's press which, to say the least, reflect but small credit upon the University."

It was far from his field, but Hawkins understood what had happened—an early and accidental blundering onto the bare bones of the Levantman shock anesthesia, which had since been replaced by other methods. To bring subjects out of Levantman shock, you let them have a squirt of simple saline in the trigeminal nerve. Interesting. And now about that bronze—

He heaved the pick into the rotting green salts, expecting no resistance, and almost fractured his wrist. *Something* down there was *solid*. He began to flake off the oxides.

A half hour of work brought him down to phosphor bronze, a huge casting of the almost incorruptible metal. It had weakened structurally over the centuries; he could fit the point of his pick under a corroded boss and pry off great creaking and grumbling striae of the stuff.

Hawkins wished he had an archaeologist with him but didn't dream of returning to his shop and calling one to take over the find. He was an all-around man: by choice, and in his free time, an artist in clay and glaze; by necessity, an automotive, electronics and atomic engineer who could also swing a project in traffic control, individual and group psychology, architecture or tool design. He didn't yell for a specialist every time something out of his line came up; there were so few with so much to do . . .

He trenched around his find, discovering that it was a great brick-shaped bronze mass with an excitingly hollow sound. A long strip of moldering metal from one of the long vertical faces pulled away, exposing red rust that went *whoosh* and was sucked into the interior of the mass.

It had been de-aired, thought Hawkins, and there must have been an inner jacket of glass which had crystallized through the centuries and quietly crumbled at the first clang of his pick. He didn't know what a vacuum would do to a subject of Levantman shock, but he had hopes, nor did he quite understand what a real estate dealer was, but it might have something to do with pottery. And *anything* might have a bearing on Topic Number One.

He flung his pick out of the trench, climbed out and set off at a dog-trot for his shop. A little rummaging turned up a hypo and there was a plastic container of salt in the kitchen.

Back at his dig, he chipped for another half hour to expose the juncture of lid and body. The hinges were hopeless; he smashed them off.

Hawkins extended the telescopic handle of the pick for the best leverage, fitted its point into a deep pit, set its built-in fulcrum, and heaved. Five more heaves and he could see, inside the vault, what looked like a dusty marble statue. Ten more and he could see that it was the naked body of Honest John Barlow, Evanston real estate dealer, uncorrupted by time.

The potter found the apex of the trigeminal nerve with his needle's point and gave him 60 cc.

In an hour Barlow's chest began to pump.

In another hour, he rasped, "Did it work?"

"*Did* it!" muttered Hawkins.

Barlow opened his eyes and stirred, looked down, turned his hands before his eyes—

"I'll sue!" he screamed. "My clothes! My fingernails!" A horrid suspicion came over his face and he clapped his hands to his hairless scalp. "My hair!" he wailed. "I'll sue you for every penny you've got!

That release won't mean a damned thing in court—I didn't sign away my hair and clothes and fingernails!"

"They'll grow back," said Hawkins casually. "Also your epidermis. Those parts of you weren't alive, you know, so they weren't preserved like the rest of you. I'm afraid the clothes are gone, though."

"What is this—the University hospital?" demanded Barlow. "I want a phone. No, you phone. Tell my wife I'm all right and tell Sam Immerman—he's my lawyer—to get over here right away. Greenleaf 7-4022. Ow!" He had tried to sit up, and a portion of his pink skin rubbed against the inner surface of the casket, which was powdered by the ancient crystallized glass. "What the hell did you guys do, boil me alive? Oh, you're going to pay for this!"

"You're all right," said Hawkins, wishing now he had a reference book to clear up several obscure terms. "Your epidermis will start growing immediately. You're not in the hospital. Look here."

He handed Barlow the stainless steel plate that had labeled the casket. After a suspicious glance, the man started to read. Finishing, he laid the plate carefully on the edge of the vault and was silent for a spell.

"Poor Verna," he said at last. "It doesn't say whether she was stuck with the court costs. Do you happen to know—"

"No," said the potter. "All I know is what was on the plate, and how to revive you. The dentist accidentally gave you a dose of what we call Levantman shock anesthesia. We haven't used it for centuries; it was powerful, but too dangerous."

"Centuries . . ." brooded the man. "Centuries . . . I'll bet Sam swindled her out of her eyeteeth. Poor Verna. How long ago was it? What year is this?"

Hawkins shrugged. "We call it 7-B-936. That's no help to you. It takes a long time for these metals to oxidize."

"Like that movie," Barlow muttered. "Who would have thought it? Poor Verna!" He blubbered and sniffled, reminding Hawkins powerfully of the fact that he had been found under a flat rock.

Almost angrily, the potter demanded, "How many children did you have?"

"None yet," sniffed Barlow. "My first wife didn't want them. But Verna wants one—wanted one—but we're going to wait until—we *were* going to wait until—"

"Of course," said the potter, feeling a savage desire to tell him off, blast him to hell and gone for his work. But he choked it down. There was The Problem to think of; there was always The Problem to think of, and this poor blubberer might unexpectedly supply a clue. Hawkins would have to pass him on.

"Come along," Hawkins said. "My time is short."

Barlow looked up, outraged. "How can you be so unfeeling? I'm a human being like—"

The Los Angeles-Chicago "rocket" thundered overhead and Barlow broke off in mid-complaint. "Beautiful!" he breathed, following it with his eyes. "Beautiful!"

He climbed out of the vault, too interested to be pained by its roughness against his infantile skin. "After all," he said briskly, "this should have its sunny side. I never was much for reading, but this is just like one of those stories. And I ought to make some money out of it, shouldn't I?" He gave Hawkins a shrewd glance.

"You want money?" asked the potter. "Here." He handed over a fistful of change and bills. "You'd better put my shoes on. It'll be about a quarter mile. Oh, and you're—uh, modest?—yes, that was the word. Here." Hawkins gave him his pants, but Barlow was excitedly counting the money.

"Eighty-five, eighty-six—and it's dollars, too! I thought it'd be credits or whatever they call them. 'E Pluribus Unum' and 'Liberty'—just different faces. Say, is there a catch to this? Are these real, genuine, honest twenty-two-cent dollars like we had or just wallpaper?"

"They're quite all right, I assure you," said the potter. "I wish you'd come along. I'm in a hurry."

The man babbled as they stumped toward the shop. "Where are we going—The Council of Scientists, the World Coordinator or something like that?"

"Who? Oh, no. We call them 'President' and 'Congress.' No, that wouldn't do any good at all. I'm just taking you to see some people."

"I ought to make plenty out of this. *Plenty!* I could write books. Get some smart young fellow to put it into words for me and I'll bet I could turn out a best seller. What's the setup on things like that?"

"It's about like that. Smart young fellows. But there aren't any best sellers any more. People don't read much nowadays. We'll find something equally profitable for you to do."

Back in the shop, Hawkins gave Barlow a suit of clothes, deposited him in the waiting room and called Central in Chicago. "Take him away," he pleaded. "I have time for one more firing and he blathers and blathers. I haven't told him anything. Perhaps we should just turn him loose and let him find his own level, but there's a chance—"

"The Problem," agreed Central. "Yes, there's a chance."

The potter delighted Barlow by making him a cup of coffee with a cube that not only dissolved in cold water but heated the water to boiling point. Killing time, Hawkins chatted about the "rocket" Barlow had admired and had to haul himself up short; he had almost told the real estate man what its top speed really was—almost, indeed, revealed that it was not a rocket.

He regretted, too, that he had so casually handed Barlow a couple of hundred dollars. The man seemed obsessed with fear that they were worthless since Hawkins refused to take a note or I.O.U. or even a definite promise of repayment. But Hawkins couldn't go into details, and was very glad when a stranger arrived from Central.

"Tinny-Peete, from Algeciras," the stranger told him swiftly as the two of them met at the door. "Psychist for Poprob. Polassigned special overtake Barlow."

"Thank Heaven," said Hawkins. "Barlow," he told the man from the past, "this is Tinny-Peete. He's going to take care of you and help you make lots of money."

The psychist stayed for a cup of the coffee whose preparation had delighted Barlow, and then conducted the real estate man down the corduroy road to his car, leaving the potter to speculate on whether he could at last crack his kilns.

Hawkins, abruptly dismissing Barlow and the Problem, happily picked the chinking from around the door of the number two kiln, prying it open a trifle. A blast of heat and the heady, smoky scent of the reduction fire delighted him. He peered and saw a corner of a shelf glowing cherry red, becoming obscured by wavering black areas as it lost heat through the opened door. He slipped a charred wood paddle under a mug on the shelf and pulled it out as a sample, the hairs on the back of his hand curling and scorching. The mug crackled and pinged and Hawkins sighed happily.

The bismuth resinate luster had fired to perfection, a haunting film of silvery-black metal with strange bluish lights in it as it turned before the eyes, and the Problem of Population seemed very far away to Hawkins then.

Barlow and Tinny-Peete arrived at the concrete highway where the psychist's car was parked in a safety bay.

"What—a—*boat!*" gasped the man from the past.

"Boat? No, that's my car."

Barlow surveyed it with awe. Swept-back lines, deep-drawn compound curves, kilograms of chrome. He ran his hands over the door—or was it the door?—in a futile search for a handle, and asked respectfully, "How fast does it go?"

The psychist gave him a keen look and said slowly, "Two hundred and fifty. You can tell by the speedometer."

"Wow! My old Chevvy could hit a hundred on a straightaway, but you're out of my class, mister!"

Tinny-Peete somehow got a huge, low door open and Barlow descended three steps into immense cushions, floundering over to the right. He was too fascinated to pay serious attention to his flayed dermis. The dashboard was a lovely wilderness of dials, plugs, indicators, lights, scales and switches.

The psychist climbed down into the driver's seat and did something with his feet. The motor started like lighting a blowtorch as big as a silo.

Wallowing around in the cushions, Barlow saw through a rear-view mirror a tremendous exhaust filled with brilliant white sparkles.

"Do you like it?" yelled the psychist.

"It's terrific!" Barlow yelled back. "It's—"

He was shut up as the car pulled out from the bay into the road with a great *voo-ooo-ooom!* A gale roared past Barlow's head, though the windows seemed to be closed; the impression of speed was terrific. He located the speedometer on the dashboard and saw it climb past 90, 100, 150, 200.

"Fast enough for me," yelled the psychist, noting that Barlow's face fell in response. "Radio?"

He passed over a surprisingly light object like a football helmet, with no trailing wires, and pointed to a row of buttons. Barlow put on the helmet, glad to have the roar of air stilled, and pushed a pushbutton. It lit up satisfyingly, and Barlow settled back even farther for a sample of the brave new world's supermodern taste in ingenious entertainment.

"TAKE IT AND STICK IT!" a voice roared in his ears.

He snatched off the helmet and gave the psychist an injured look. Tinny-Peete grinned and turned a dial associated with the pushbutton layout. The man from the past donned the helmet again and found the voice had lowered to normal.

"The show of shows! The supershow! The super-duper show! The quiz of quizzes! *Take It and Stick It!*"

There were shrieks of laughter in the background.

"Here we got the contes-tants all ready to go. You know how we work it. I hand a contes-tant a triangle-shaped cutout and like that down the line. Now we got these here boards, they got cutout places the same shape as the triangles and things, only they're all different shapes, and the first contes-tant that sticks the cutouts into the boards, he wins.

"Now I'm gonna innaview the first contes-tant. Right here, honey. What's your name?"

"Name? Uh—"

"Hoddaya like that, folks? She don't remember her name! Hah? *Would you buy that for a quarter?*" The question was spoken with arch significance, and the audience shrieked, howled and whistled its appreciation.

It was dull listening when you didn't know the punch lines and catch lines. Barlow pushed another button, with his free hand ready at the volume control.

"—latest from Washington. It's about Senator Hull-Mendoza. He is still attacking the Bureau of Fisheries. The North California Syndicalist says he got affydavits that John Kingsley-Schultz is a bluenose from way back. He didn't publistat the affydavits, but he says they say that Kingsley-Schultz was saw at bluenose meetings in Oregon State College and later at Florida University. Kingsley-Schultz says he gotta confess he did major in fly casting at Oregon and got his Ph.D. in game-fish at Florida.

"And here is a quote from Kingsley-Schultz: 'Hull-Mendoza don't know what he's talking about. He should drop dead.' Unquote. Hull-Mendoza says he won't publistat the affydavits to pertect his sources. He says they was sworn by three former employes of the Bureau which was fired for in-competence and in-com-pat-ibility by Kingsley-Schultz.

"Elsewhere they was the usual run of traffic accidents. A three-way pileup of cars on Route 66 going outta Chicago took twelve lives. The Chicago-Los Angeles morning rocket crashed and exploded in the Mohave—Mo-javvy—whatever-you-call-it Desert. All the 94 people aboard got killed. A Civil Aeronautics Authority investigator on the scene says that the pilot was buzzing herds of sheep and didn't pull out in time.

"Hey! Here's a hot one from New York! A diesel tug run wild in the harbor while the crew was below and shoved in the port bow of the luckshury liner *S. S. Placentia.* It says the ship filled and sank taking the lives of an es-ti-mated 180 passengers and 50 crew members. Six divers was sent down to study the wreckage, but they died, too, when their suits turned out to be fulla little holes.

"And here is a bulletin I just got from Denver. It seems—"

Barlow took off the headset uncomprehendingly. "He seemed so callous," he yelled at the driver. "I was listening to a newscast—"

Tinny-Peete shook his head and pointed at his ears. The roar of air was deafening. Barlow frowned baffledly and stared out of the window.

A glowing sign said:

MOOGS!
WOULD YOU BUY IT
FOR A QUARTER?

He didn't know what Moogs was or were; the illustration showed an incredibly proportioned girl, 99.9 percent naked, writhing passionately in animated full color.

The roadside jingle was still with him, but with a new feature. Radar or something spotted the car and alerted the lines of the jingle. Each in turn sped along a roadside track, even with the car, so it could be read before the next line was alerted.

IF THERE'S A GIRL
YOU WANT TO GET
DEFLOCCULIZE
UNROMANTIC SWEAT.

"A*R*M*P*I*T*T*O"

Another animated job, in two panels, the familiar "Before and After." The first said, "Just Any Cigar?" and was illustrated with a two-person domestic tragedy of a wife holding her nose while her coarse and red-faced husband puffed a slimy-looking rope. The second panel glowed, "Or a VUELTA ABAJO?" and was illustrated with—

Barlow blushed and looked at his feet until they had passed the sign.

"Coming into Chicago!" bawled Tinny-Peete.

Other cars were showing up, all of them dreamboats.

Watching them, Barlow began to wonder if he knew what a kilometer was, exactly. They seemed to be traveling so slowly, if you ignored the roaring air past your ears and didn't let the speedy lines of the dreamboats fool you. He would have sworn they were really crawling along at twenty-five, with occasional spurts up to thirty. How much was a kilometer, anyway?

The city loomed ahead, and it was just what it ought to be: towering skyscrapers, overhead ramps, landing platforms for helicopters—

He clutched at the cushions. Those two copters. They were going to—they were going to—they—

He didn't see what happened because their apparent collision courses took them behind a giant building.

Screamingly sweet blasts of sound surrounded them as they stopped for a red light. "What the hell is going on here?" said Barlow in a shrill, frightened voice, because the braking time was just about zero, and he wasn't hurled against the dashboard. "Who's kidding who?"

"Why, what's the matter?" demanded the driver.

The light changed to green and he started the pickup. Barlow stiffened as he realized that the rush of air past his ears began just a brief, unreal split second before the car was actually moving. He grabbed for the door handle on his side.

The city grew on them slowly: scattered buildings, denser buildings, taller buildings, and a red light ahead. The car rolled to a stop in zero braking time, the rush of air cut off an instant after it stopped, and Barlow was out of the car and running frenziedly down a sidewalk one instant after that.

They'll track me down, he thought, panting. *It's a secret police thing. They'll get you—mind-reading machines, television eyes everywhere, afraid you'll tell their slaves about freedom and stuff. They don't let anybody cross them, like that story I once read.*

Winded, he slowed to a walk and congratulated himself that he had guts enough not to turn around. That was what they always watched for. Walking, he was just another business-suited back among hundreds. He would be safe, he would be safe—

A hand gripped his shoulder and words tumbled from a large, coarse, handsome face thrust close to his: "Wassamatta bumpinninna people likeya owna sidewalk gotta miner slamya inna mushya bassar!" It was neither the mad potter nor the mad driver.

"Excuse me," said Barlow. "What did you say?"

"Oh, yeah?" yelled the stranger dangerously, and waited for an answer.

Barlow, with the feeling that he had somehow been suckered into the short end of an intricate land-title deal, heard himself reply belligerently, "Yeah!"

The stranger let go of his shoulder and snarled, "Oh, yeah?"

"Yeah!" said Barlow, yanking his jacket back into shape.

"Aaah!" snarled the stranger, with more contempt and disgust than ferocity. He added an obscenity current in Barlow's time, a standard but physiologically impossible directive, and strutted off hulking his shoulders and balling his fists.

Barlow walked on, trembling. Evidently he had handled it well enough. He stopped at a red light while the long, low dreamboats roared before him and pedestrians in the sidewalk flow with him threaded their ways through the stream of cars. Brakes screamed, fenders clanged and dented, hoarse cries flew back and forth between drivers and walkers. He leaped backward frantically as one car swerved over an arc of sidewalk to miss another.

The signal changed to green; the cars kept on coming for about thirty seconds and then dwindled to an occasional light runner. Barlow crossed warily and leaned against a vending machine, blowing big breaths.

Look natural, he told himself. *Do something normal. Buy something from the machine.* He fumbled out some change, got a newspaper for a dime, a handkerchief for a quarter and a candy bar for another quarter.

The faint chocolate smell made him ravenous suddenly. He clawed at the glassy wrapper printed "*Crigglies*" quite futilely for a few seconds, and then it divided neatly by itself. The bar made three good bites, and he bought two more and gobbled them down.

Thirsty, he drew a carbonated orange drink in another one of the glassy wrappers from the machine for another dime. When he fumbled with it, it divided neatly and spilled all over his knees. Barlow decided he had been there long enough and walked on.

The shop windows were—shop windows. People still wore and bought clothes, still smoked and bought tobacco, still ate and bought food. And they still went to the movies, he saw with pleased surprise as he passed and then returned to a glittering place whose sign said it was THE BIJOU.

The place seemed to be showing a triple feature, *Babies Are Terrible, Don't Have Children*, and *The Canali Kid.*

It was irresistible; he paid a dollar and went in.

He caught the tail end of *The Canali Kid* in three-dimensional, full-color, full-scent production. It appeared to be an interplanetary saga winding up with a chase scene and a reconciliation between estranged hero and heroine. *Babies Are Terrible* and *Don't Have Children* were fantastic arguments against parenthood—the grotesquely exaggerated dangers of painfully graphic childbirth, vicious children, old parents beaten and starved by their sadistic offspring. The audience, Barlow astoundedly noted, was placidly chomping sweets and showing no particular signs of revulsion.

The *Coming Attractions* drove him into the lobby. The fanfares were shattering, the blazing colors blinding, and the added scents stomach heaving.

When his eyes again became accustomed to the moderate lighting of the lobby, he groped his way to a bench and opened the newspaper he had bought. It turned out to be *The Racing Sheet*, which afflicted him with a crushing sense of loss. The familiar boxed index in the lower-left-hand corner of the front page showed almost unbearably that Churchill Downs and Empire City were still in business—

Blinking back tears, he turned to the Past Performance at Churchill. They weren't using abbreviations any more, and the pages because of that were single-column instead of double. But it was all the same—or was it?

He squinted at the first race, a three-quarter-mile maiden claimer for thirteen hundred dollars. Incredibly, the track record was two minutes, ten and three-fifths seconds. Any beetle in his time could have knocked off the three-quarter in one-fifteen. It was the same for the other distances, much worse for route events.

What the hell had happened to everything?

He studied the form of a five-year-old brown mare in the second and couldn't make head or tail of it. She'd won and lost and placed and showed and lost and placed without rhyme or reason. She looked like a front runner for a couple of races and then she looked like a no-good pig and then she looked like a mudder but the next time it rained she wasn't and then she was a stayer and then she was a pig again. In a good five-thousand-dollar allowances event, too!

Barlow looked at the other entries and it slowly dawned on him that they were all like the five-year-old brown mare. Not a single damned horse running had even the slightest trace of class.

Somebody sat down beside him and said, "That's the story."

Barlow whirled to his feet and saw it was Tinny-Peete, his driver.

"I was in doubts about telling you," said the psychist, "but I see you have some growing suspicions of the truth. Please don't get excited. It's all right, I tell you."

"So you've got me," said Barlow.

"*Got* you?"

"Don't pretend. I can put two and two together. You're the secret police. You and the rest of the aristocrats live in luxury on the sweat of these oppressed slaves. You're afraid of me because you have to keep them ignorant."

There was a bellow of bright laughter from the psychist that got them blank looks from other patrons of the lobby. The laughter didn't sound at all sinister.

"Let's get out of here," said Tinny-Peete, still chuckling. "You couldn't possibly have it more wrong." He engaged Barlow's arm and led him to the street. "The actual truth is that the millions of workers live in luxury on the sweat of the handful of aristocrats. I shall probably die before my time of overwork unless—" He gave Barlow a speculative look. "You may be able to help us."

"I know that gag," sneered Barlow. "I made money in my time and to make money you have to get people on your side. Go ahead and shoot me if you want, but you're not going to make a fool out of me."

"You nasty little ingrate!" snapped the psychist, with a kaleidoscopic change of mood. "This damned mess is all your fault and the fault of people like you! Now come along and no more of your nonsense."

He yanked Barlow into an office building lobby and an elevator that, disconcertingly, went *whoosh* loudly as it rose. The real estate man's knees were wobbly as the psychist pushed him from the elevator, down a corridor and into an office.

A hawk-faced man rose from a plain chair as the door closed behind them. After an angry look at Barlow, he asked the psychist, "Was I called from the Pole to inspect this—this—?"

"Unget updandered. I've deeprobed etfind quasichance exhim Poprobattackline," said the psychist soothingly.

"Doubt," grunted the hawk-faced man.

"Try," suggested Tinny-Peete.

"Very well. Mr. Barlow, I understand you and your lamented had no children."

"What of it?"

"This of it. You were a blind, selfish stupid ass to tolerate economic and social conditions which penalized childbearing by the prudent and foresighted. You made us what we are today, and I want you to know that we are far from satisfied. Damn-fool rockets! Damn-fool automobiles! Damn-fool cities with overhead ramps!"

"As far as I can see," said Barlow, "you're running down the best features of your time. Are you crazy?"

"The rockets aren't rockets. They're turbojets—good turbojets, but the fancy shell around them makes for a bad drag. The automobiles have a top speed of one hundred kilometers per hour—a kilometer is, if I recall my paleolinguistics, three-fifths of a mile—and the speedometers are all rigged accordingly so the drivers will think they're going two hundred and fifty. The cities are ridiculous, expensive, unsanitary, wasteful conglomerations of people who'd be better off and more productive if they were spread over the countryside.

"We need the rockets and trick speedometers and cities because, while you and your kind were being prudent and foresighted and not having children, the migrant workers, slum dwellers and tenant farmers were shiftlessly and shortsightedly having children—breeding, breeding. My God, how they bred!"

"Wait a minute," objected Barlow. "There were lots of people in our crowd who had two or three children."

"The attrition of accidents, illness, wars and such took care of that. Your intelligence was bred out. It is gone. Children that should have been born never were. The just-average, they'll-get-along majority took over the population. The average IQ now is 45."

"But that's far in the future—"

"So are you," grunted the hawk-faced man sourly.

"But who are *you* people?"

"Just people—real people. Some generations ago, the geneticists realized at last that nobody was going to pay any attention to what they said, so they abandoned words for deeds. Specifically, they formed and recruited for a closed corporation intended to maintain and improve the breed. We are their descendants, about three million of us. There are five billion of the others, so we are their slaves.

"During the past couple of years I've designed a skyscraper, kept Billings Memorial Hospital here in Chicago running, headed off war with Mexico and directed traffic at LaGuardia Field in New York."

"I don't understand! Why don't you let them go to hell in their own way?"

The man grimaced. "We tried it once for three months. We holed up at the South Pole and waited. They didn't notice it. Some drafting room people were missing, some chief nurses didn't show up, minor government people on the nonpolicy level couldn't be located. It didn't seem to matter.

"In a week there was hunger. In two weeks there were famine and plague, in three weeks war and anarchy. We called off the experiment; it took us most of the next generation to get things squared away again."

"But why *didn't* you let them kill each other off?"

"Five billion corpses mean about five hundred million tons of rotting flesh."

Barlow had another idea. "Why don't you sterilize them?"

"Two and one-half billion operations is a lot of operations. Because they breed continuously, the job would never be done."

"I see. Like the marching Chinese!"

"Who the devil are they?"

"It was a—uh—paradox of my time. Somebody figured out that if all the Chinese in the world were to line up four abreast, I think it was, and start marching past a given point, they'd never stop because of the babies that would be born and grow up before they passed the point."

"That's right. Only instead of 'a given point,' make it 'the largest conceivable number of operating rooms that we could build and staff.' There could never be enough."

"Say!" said Barlow. "Those movies about babies—was that your propaganda?"

"It was. It doesn't seem to mean a thing to them. We have abandoned the idea of attempting propaganda contrary to a biological drive."

"So if you work *with* a biological drive—?"

"I know of none which is consistent with inhibition of fertility."

Barlow's face went poker blank, the result of years of careful discipline. "You don't, huh? You're the great brains and you can't think of any?"

"Why, no," said the psychist innocently. "Can you?"

"That depends. I sold ten thousand acres of Siberian tundra—through a dummy firm, of course—after the partition of Russia. The buyers thought they were getting improved building lots on the outskirts of Kiev. I'd say that was a lot tougher than this job."

"How so?" asked the hawk-faced man.

"Those were normal, suspicious customers and these are morons, born suckers. You just figure out a con they'll fall for; they won't know enough to do any smart checking."

The psychist and the hawk-faced man had also had training; they kept themselves from looking with sudden hope at each other.

"You seem to have something in mind," said the psychist.

Barlow's poker face went blanker still. "Maybe I have. I haven't heard any offer yet."

"There's the satisfaction of knowing that you've prevented Earth's resources from being so plundered," the hawk-faced man pointed out, "that the race will soon become extinct."

"I don't know that," Barlow said bluntly. "All I have is your word."

"If you really have a method, I don't think any price would be too great," the psychist offered.

"Money," said Barlow.

"All you want."

"More than you want," the hawk-faced man corrected.

"Prestige," added Barlow. "Plenty of publicity. My picture and my name in the papers and over TV every day, statues to me, parks and cities and streets and other things named after me. A whole chapter in the history books."

The psychist made a facial sign to the hawk-faced man that meant, "Oh, brother!"

The hawk-faced man signaled back, "Steady, boy!"

"It's not too much to ask," the psychist agreed.

Barlow, sensing a seller's market, said, "Power!"

"Power?" the hawk-faced man repeated puzzledly. "Your own hydro station or nuclear pile?"

"I mean a world dictatorship with me as dictator!"

"Well, now—" said the psychist, but the hawk-faced man interrupted, "It would take a special emergency act of Congress but the situation warrants it. I think that can be guaranteed."

"Could you give us some indication of your plan?" the psychist asked.

"Ever hear of lemmings?"

"No."

"They are—were, I guess, since you haven't heard of them—little animals in Norway, and every few years they'd swarm to the coast and swim out to sea until they drowned. I figure on putting some lemming urge into the population."

"How?"

"I'll save that till I get the right signatures on the deal."

The hawk-faced man said, "Id like to work with you on it, Barlow. My name's Ryan-Ngana." He put out his hand.

Barlow looked closely at the hand, then at the man's face. "Ryan what?"

"Ngana."

"That sounds like an African name."

"It is. My mother's father was a Watusi."

Barlow didn't take the hand. "I thought you looked pretty dark. I don't want to hurt your feelings, but I don't think I'd be at my best working with you. There must be somebody else just as well qualified, I'm sure."

The psychist made a facial sign to Ryan-Ngana that meant, "Steady *yourself*, boy!"

"Very well," Ryan-Ngana told Barlow. "We'll see what arrangement can be made."

"It's not that I'm prejudiced, you understand. Some of my best friends—"

"Mr. Barlow, don't give it another thought. Anybody who could pick on the lemming analogy is going to be useful to us."

And so he would, thought Ryan-Ngana, alone in the office after Tinny-Peete had taken Barlow up to the helicopter stage. So he would. Poprob had exhausted every rational attempt and the new Poprobattack-lines would have to be irrational or subrational. This creature from the past with his lemming legends and his improved building lots would be a fountain of precious vicious self-interest.

Ryan-Ngana sighed and stretched. He had to go and run the San Francisco subway. Summoned early from the Pole to study Barlow, he'd left unfinished a nice little theorem. Between interruptions, he was slowly constructing an n-dimensional geometry whose foundations and superstructure owed no debt whatsoever to intuition.

Upstairs, waiting for a helicopter, Barlow was explaining to Tinny-Peete that he had nothing against Negroes, and Tinny-Peete wished he had some of Ryan-Ngana's imperturbability and humor for the ordeal.

The helicopter took them to International Airport where, Tinny-Peete explained, Barlow would leave for the Pole.

The man from the past wasn't sure he'd like a dreary waste of ice and cold.

"It's all right," said the psychist. "A civilized layout. Warm, pleasant. You'll be able to work more efficiently there. All the facts at your fingertips, a good secretary—"

"I'll need a pretty big staff," said Barlow, who had learned from thousands of deals never to take the first offer.

"I meant a private, confidential one," said Tinny-Peete readily, "but you can have as many as you want. You'll naturally have top-primary-top priority if you really have a workable plan."

"Let's not forget this dictatorship angle," said Barlow.

He didn't know that the psychist would just as readily have promised him deification to get him happily on the "rocket" for the Pole. Tinny-Peete had no wish to be torn limb from limb; he knew very well that it would end that way if the population learned from this anachronism that there was a small elite which considered itself head, shoulders, trunk and groin above the rest. The fact that this assumption was perfectly true and the fact that the elite was condemned by its superiority to a life of the most grinding toil would not be considered; the difference would.

The psychist finally put Barlow aboard the "rocket" with some thirty people—real people—headed for the Pole.

Barlow was airsick all the way because of a posthypnotic suggestion Tinny-Peete had planted in him. One idea was to make him as averse as possible to a return trip, and another idea was to spare the other passengers from his aggressive, talkative company.

Barlow during the first day at the Pole was reminded of his first day in the Army. It was the same now-where-the-hell-are-we-going-to-put-*you?* business until he took a firm line with them. Then instead of acting like supply sergeants they acted like hotel clerks.

It was a wonderful, wonderfully calculated buildup, and one that he failed to suspect. After all, in his time a visitor from the past would have been lionized.

At day's end he reclined in a snug underground billet with the sixty-mile gales roaring yards overhead and tried to put two and two together.

It was like old times, he thought—like a coup in real estate where you had the competition by the throat, like a fifty-percent rent boost when you knew damned well there was no place for the tenants to move, like smiling when you read over the breakfast orange juice that the city council had decided to build a school on the ground you had acquired by a deal with the city council. And it was simple. He would just sell tundra building lots to eagerly suicidal lemmings, and that was absolutely all there was to solving The Problem that had these double-domes spinning.

They'd have to work out most of the details, naturally, but what the hell, that was what subordinates were for. He'd need specialists in advertising, engineering, communications—did they know anything about hypnotism? That might be helpful. If not, there'd have to be a lot of bribery done, but he'd make sure—damned sure—there were unlimited funds.

Just selling building lots to lemmings . . .

He wished, as he fell asleep, that poor Verna could have been in on this. It was his biggest, most stupendous deal. Verna—that sharp shyster Sam Immerman must have swindled her . . .

It began the next day with people coming to visit him. He knew the approach. They merely wanted to be helpful to their illustrious visitor from the past and would he help fill them in about his era, which unfortunately was somewhat obscure historically, and what did he think could be done about The Problem? He told them he was too old to be roped any more, and they wouldn't get any information out of him until he got a letter of intent from at least the Polar President and a session of the Polar Congress empowered to make him dictator.

He got the letter and the session. He presented his program, was asked whether his conscience didn't revolt at its callousness, explained succinctly that a deal was a deal and anybody who wasn't smart enough to protect himself didn't deserve protection—"Caveat emptor," he threw in for scholarship, and had to translate it to "Let the buyer beware." He didn't, he stated, give a damn about either the morons or their intelligent slaves; he'd told them his price and that was all he was interested in.

Would they meet it or wouldn't they?

The Polar President offered to resign in his favor, with certain temporary emergency powers that the Polar Congress would vote him if he thought them necessary. Barlow demanded the title of World Dictator, complete control of world finances, salary to be decided by himself, and the publicity campaign and historical writeup to begin at once.

"As for the emergency powers," he added, "they are neither to be temporary nor limited."

Somebody wanted the floor to discuss the matter, with the declared hope that perhaps Barlow would modify his demands.

"You've got the proposition," Barlow said. "I'm not knocking off even ten percent."

"But what if the Congress refuses, sir?" the President asked.

"Then you can stay up here at the Pole and try to work it out yourselves. I'll get what I want from the morons. A shrewd operator like me doesn't have to compromise; I haven't got a single competitor in this whole cockeyed moronic era."

Congress waived debate and voted by show of hands. Barlow won unanimously.

"You don't know how close you came to losing me," he said in his first official address to the joint Houses. "I'm not the boy to haggle; either I get what I ask, or I go elsewhere. The first thing I want is to see designs for a new palace for me—nothing *un*-ostentatious, either—and your best painters and sculptors to start working on my portraits and statues. Meanwhile, I'll get my staff together."

He dismissed the Polar President and the Polar Congress, telling them that he'd let them know when the next meeting would be.

A week later, the program started with North America the first target.

Mrs. Garvy was resting after dinner before the ordeal of turning on the dishwasher. The TV, of course, was on and it said, "Oooh!"—long, shuddery and ecstatic, the cue for the *Parfum Assault Criminale* spot commercial. "Girls," said the announcer hoarsely, "do you want your man? It's easy to get him—easy as a trip to Venus."

"Huh?" said Mrs. Garvy.

"Wassamatter?" snorted her husband, starting out of a doze.

"Ja hear that?"

"Wha'?"

"He said 'easy like a trip to Venus.' "

"So?"

"Well, I thought ya couldn't get to Venus. I thought they just had that one rocket thing that crashed on the Moon."

"Aah, women don't keep up with the news," said Garvy righteously, subsiding again.

"Oh," said his wife uncertainly.

And the next day, on *Henry's Other Mistress,* there was a new character who had just breezed in: Buzz Rentshaw, Master Rocket Pilot of the Venus run. On *Henry's Other Mistress,* "the broadcast drama about you and your neighbors, *folksy* people, *ordinary* people, *real* people!" Mrs. Garvy listened with amazement over a cooling cup of coffee as Buzz made hay of her hazy convictions.

MONA: Darling, it's so good to see you again!

BUZZ: You don't know how I've missed you on that dreary Venus run.

SOUND: *Venetian blind run down, key turned in lock.*

MONA: Was it *very* dull, dearest?

BUZZ: Let's not talk about my humdrum job, darling. Let's talk about us.

SOUND: *Creaking bed.*

Well, the program was back to normal at last. That evening Mrs. Garvy tried to ask again whether her husband was sure about those rockets, but he was dozing right through *Take It and Stick It,* so she watched the screen and forgot the puzzle.

She was still rocking with laughter at the gag line, "Would you buy it for a quarter?" when the commercial went on for the detergent powder she always faithfully loaded her dishwasher with on the first of every month.

The announcer displayed mountains of suds from a tiny piece of the stuff and coyly added, "Of course, Cleano don't lay around for you to pick up like the soap root on Venus, but it's pretty cheap and it's almost pretty near just as good. So for us plain folks who ain't lucky enough to live up there on Venus, Cleano is the real cleaning stuff!"

Then the chorus went into their "Cleano-is-the-stuff" jingle, but Mrs. Garvy didn't hear it. She was a stubborn woman, but it occurred to her that she was very sick indeed. She didn't want to worry her husband. The next day she quietly made an appointment with her family freud.

In the waiting room she picked up a fresh new copy of *Readers Pablum* and put it down with a faint palpitation. The lead article, according to the table of contents on the cover, was titled "The Most Memorable Venusian I Ever Met."

"The freud will see you now," said the nurse, and Mrs. Garvy tottered into his office.

His traditional glasses and whiskers were reassuring. She choked out the ritual. "Freud, forgive me, for I have neuroses."

He chanted the antiphonal, "Tut, my dear girl, what seems to be the trouble?"

"I got like a hole in the head," she quavered. "I seem to forget all kinds of things. Things like everybody seems to know and I don't."

"Well, that happens to everybody occasionally, my dear. I suggest a vacation on Venus."

The freud stared, openmouthed, at the empty chair. His nurse came in and demanded, "Hey, you see how she scrammed? What was the matter with *her?*"

He took off his glasses and whiskers meditatively. "You can search me. I told her she should maybe try a vacation on Venus." A momentary bafflement came into his face and he dug through his desk drawers until he found a copy of the four-color, profusely illustrated journal of his profession. It had come that morning and he had lip-read it, though looking mostly at the pictures. He leafed to the article "Advantages of the Planet Venus in Rest Cures."

"It's right there," he said.

The nurse looked. "It sure is," she agreed. "Why shouldn't it be?"

"The trouble with these here neurotics," decided the freud, "is that they all the time got to fight reality. Show in the next twitch."

He put on his glasses and whiskers again and forgot Mrs. Garvy and her strange behavior.

"Freud, forgive me, for I have neuroses."

"Tut, my dear girl, what seems to be the trouble?"

Like many cures of mental disorders, Mrs. Garvy's was achieved largely by self-treatment. She disciplined herself sternly out of the crazy notion that there had been only one rocket ship and that one a failure. She could join without wincing, eventually, in any conversation on the desirability of Venus as a place to retire, on its fabulous floral profusion. Finally she went to Venus.

All her friends were trying to book passage with the Evening Star Travel and Real Estate Corporation, but naturally the demand was crushing. She considered herself lucky to get a seat at last for the two-week summer cruise. The spaceship took off from a place called Los Alamos, New Mexico. It looked just like all the spaceships on television and in the picture magazines but was more comfortable than you would expect.

Mrs. Garvy was delighted with the fifty or so fellow-passengers assembled before takeoff. They were from all over the country and she had a distinct impression that they were on the brainy side. The captain, a tall, hawk-faced, impressive fellow named Ryan Something-or-other, welcomed them aboard and trusted that their trip would be a memorable one. He regretted that there would be nothing to see because, "due to the meteorite season," the ports would be dogged down. It was disappointing, yet reassuring that the line was taking no chances.

There was the expected momentary discomfort at takeoff and then two monotonous days of droning travel through space to be whiled away in the lounge at cards or craps. The landing was a routine bump and the voyagers were issued tablets to swallow to immunize them against any minor ailments.

When the tablets took effect, the lock was opened, and Venus was theirs.

It looked much like a tropical island on Earth, except for a blanket of cloud overhead. But it had a heady, otherworldly quality that was intoxicating and glamorous.

The ten days of the vacation were suffused with a hazy magic. The soap root, as advertised, was free and sudsy. The fruits, mostly tropical varieties transplanted from Earth, were delightful. The simple shelters provided by the travel company were more than adequate for the balmy days and nights.

It was with sincere regret that the voyagers filed again into the ship and swallowed more tablets doled out to counteract and sterilize any Venus illnesses they might unwittingly communicate to Earth.

Vacationing was one thing. Power politics was another.

At the Pole, a small man was in a soundproof room, his face deathly pale and his body limp in a straight chair.

In the American Senate Chamber, Senator Hull-Mendoza (Synd., N. Cal.) was saying, "Mr. President and gentlemen, I would be remiss in my duty as a legislature if'n I didn't bring to the attention of the au-gust body I see here a perilous situation which is fraught with peril. As is well known to members of this au-gust body, the perfection of space flight has brought with it a situation I can only describe as fraught with peril. Mr. President and gentlemen, now that swift American rockets now traverse the trackless void of space between this planet and our nearest planetarial neighbor in space—and, gentlemen, I refer to Venus, the star of dawn, the brightest jewel in fair Vulcan's diadome—now, I say, I want to inquire what steps are being taken to colonize Venus with a vanguard of patriotic citizens like those minutemen of yore.

"Mr. President and gentlemen! There are in this world nations, envious nations—I do not name Mexico—who by fair means or foul may seek to wrest from Columbia's grasp the torch of freedom of space; nations whose low living standards and innate depravity give them an unfair advantage over the citizens of our fair republic.

"This is my program: I suggest that a city of more than 100,000 population be selected by lot. The citizens of the fortunate city are to be awarded choice lands on Venus free and clear, to have and to hold and convey to their descendants. And the national government shall provide free transportation to Venus for these citizens. And this program shall continue, city by city, until there has been deposited on Venus a sufficient vanguard of citizens to protect our manifest rights in that planet.

"Objections will be raised, for carping critics we have always with us. They will say there isn't enough steel. They will call it a cheap giveaway. I say there *is* enough steel for *one* city's population to be transferred to Venus, and that is all that is needed. For when the time comes for the second city to be transferred, the first, emptied city can be wrecked for the needed steel! And is it a giveaway? Yes! It is the most glorious giveaway in the history of mankind! Mr. President and gentlemen, there is no time to waste—Venus must be American!"

Black-Kupperman, at the Pole, opened his eyes and said feebly, "The style was a little uneven. Do you think anybody'll notice?"

"You did fine, boy; just fine," Barlow reassured him.

Hull-Mendoza's bill became law.

Drafting machines at the South Pole were busy around the clock and the Pittsburgh steel mills spewed millions of plates into the Los Alamos spaceport of the Evening Star Travel and Real Estate Corporation. It was going to be Los Angeles, for logistic reasons, and the three most accomplished psychokineticists went to Washington and mingled in the crowd at the drawing to make certain that the Los Angeles capsule slithered into the fingers of the blindfolded Senator.

Los Angeles loved the idea and a forest of spaceships began to blossom in the desert. They weren't very good spaceships, but they didn't have to be.

A team at the Pole worked at Barlow's direction on a mail setup. There would have to be letters to and from Venus to keep the slightest taint of suspicion from arising. Luckily Barlow remembered that the problem had been solved once before—by Hitler. Relatives of persons incinerated in the furnaces of Lublin or Majdanek continued to get cheery postal cards.

The Los Angeles flight went off on schedule, under tremendous press, newsreel and television coverage. The world cheered the gallant Angelenos who were setting off on their patriotic voyage to the land of milk and honey. The forest of spaceships thundered up, and up, and out of sight without untoward incident. Billions envied the Angelenos, cramped and on short rations though they were.

Wreckers from San Francisco, whose capsule came up second, moved immediately into the city of the angels for the scrap steel their own flight would require. Senator Hull-Mendoza's constituents could do no less.

The president of Mexico, hypnotically alarmed at this extension of *yanqui imperialismo* beyond the stratosphere, launched his own Venus-colony program.

Across the water it was England versus Ireland, France versus Germany, China versus Russia, India versus Indonesia. Ancient hatreds grew into the flames that were rocket ships assailing the air by hundreds daily.

> Dear Ed, how are you? Sam and I are fine and hope you are fine. Is it nice up there like they say with food and close grone on trees? I drove by Springfield yesterday and it sure looked funny all the buildings down but of coarse it is worth it we have to keep the greasers in their place. Do you have any trouble with them on Venus? Drop me a line some time. Your loving sister, Alma.

> Dear Alma, I am fine and hope you are fine. It is a fine place here fine climate and easy living. The doctor told me today that I seem to be ten years younger. He thinks there is something in the air here keeps people young. We do not have much trouble with the greasers here they keep to theirselves it is just a question of us outnumbering them and staking out the best places for the Americans. In South Bay I know a nice little island that I have been saving for you and Sam with lots of blanket trees

and ham bushes. Hoping to see you and Sam soon, your loving brother, Ed.

Sam and Alma were on their way shortly.

Poprob got a dividend in every nation after the emigration had passed the halfway mark. The lonesome stay-at-homes were unable to bear the melancholy of a low population density; their conditioning had been to swarms of their kin. After that point it was possible to foist off the crudest stripped-down accommodations on would-be emigrants; they didn't care.

Black-Kupperman did a final job on President Hull-Mendoza, the last job that genius of hypnotics would ever do on any moron, important or otherwise.

Hull-Mendoza, panic stricken by his presidency over an emptying nation, joined his constituents. The *Independence*, aboard which traveled the national government of America, was the most elaborate of all the spaceships—bigger, more comfortable, with a lounge that was handsome, though cramped, and cloakrooms for Senators and Representatives. It went, however, to the same place as the others and Black-Kupperman killed himself, leaving a note that stated he "couldn't live with my conscience."

The day after the American President departed, Barlow flew into a rage. Across his specially built desk were supposed to flow all Poprob high-level documents, and this thing—this outrageous thing—called Poprob*term* apparently had got into the executive stage before he had even had a glimpse of it!

He buzzed for Rogge-Smith, his statistician. Rogge-Smith seemed to be at the bottom of it. Poprobterm seemed to be about first and second and third derivatives, whatever they were. Barlow had a deep distrust of anything more complex than what he called an "average."

While Rogge-Smith was still at the door, Barlow snapped, "What's the meaning of this? Why haven't I been consulted? How far have you people got and why have you been working on something I haven't authorized?"

"Didn't want to bother you, Chief," said Rogge-Smith. "It was really a technical matter, kind of a final cleanup. Want to come and see the work?"

Mollified, Barlow followed his statistician down the corridor.

"You still shouldn't have gone ahead without my okay," he grumbled. "Where the hell would you people have been without me?"

"That's right, Chief. We couldn't have swung it ourselves; our minds just don't work that way. And all that stuff you knew from Hitler—it wouldn't have occurred to us. Like poor Black-Kupperman."

They were in a fair-sized machine shop at the end of a slight upward incline. It was cold. Rogge-Smith pushed a button that started a motor, and a flood of arctic light poured in as the roof parted slowly. It showed a small spaceship with the door open.

Barlow gaped as Rogge-Smith took him by the elbow and his other boys appeared: Swenson-Swenson, the engineer; Tsutsugimushi-Duncan, his propellants man; Kalb-French, advertising.

"In you go, Chief," said Tsutsugimushi-Duncan. "This is Poprobterm."

"But I'm the world Dictator!"

"You bet, Chief. You'll be in history, all right—but this is necessary, I'm afraid."

The door was closed. Acceleration slammed Barlow cruelly to the metal floor. Something broke, and warm, wet stuff, salty tasting, ran from his mouth to his chin. Arctic sunlight through a port suddenly became a fierce lancet stabbing at his eyes; he was out of the atmosphere.

Lying twisted and broken under the acceleration, Barlow realized that some things had not changed, that Jack Ketch was never asked to dinner however many shillings you paid him to do your dirty work, that murder will out, that crime pays only temporarily.

The last thing he learned was that death is the end of pain.

QUESTIONS

1. Could the basic premise of the story be called bigoted? Why?
2. Is the lack of morality in this story justified?
3. Does John Barlow have any redeeming characteristics?
4. Mrs. Garvy is the most sympathetic figure in the story. Why is this so? Discuss characterization and its implications in "The Marching Morons."
5. The "aristocrats" seem more intelligent than some of today's geniuses. Why might this be so? Why, then, could they not solve the population problem themselves?
6. Would people fall for the "Lemming Scheme"? What is involved in subliminal advertising?
7. Is an IQ of 45 functional enough to make the story believable? Explain.
8. Discuss the story in relation to the selection from *The Limits to Growth* in Part I.
9. In science fiction, does the message, the moralizing, and the propaganda value of the story satisfactorily substitute for theme?

The Forever People

Jack Kirby

Science fiction is a form of popular literature and as such links up with the other media of pop culture, such as comic books, film, and television. Frequently these more visual media borrow their story lines and characterizations from the more verbal medium and in the process bring about a transformation. For example, there are comics in which previously published SF stories such as Frederic Brown's "Arena," are illustrated and given surprising new dimensions. There are also comics in which a single character or set of characters based on an original work of fiction undergo a series of adventures more or less in keeping with the original author's work. The award-winning comic Conan *is a prime example. Finally, and perhaps most interesting, are those comics in which their creators invent their own SF heroes. Superman was a first. The Forever People are in comic book limbo, publication having been indefinitely suspended, but they are an indication of the creative imaginations available in the second golden age of comics. Jack Kirby is an almost legendary figure of the comic book industry.*

THE FOREVER PEOPLE
OF SUPER TOWN
DC THE FOREVER PEOPLE
15¢
MAR. NO. 1
APPROVED BY THE COMICS CODE AUTHORITY
THEY BELONG TO SUNRISE-- THEY'RE HERE IN MID-DAY-- TO STOP THE DARK SPREAD OF NIGHT!
WAIT! THIS IS MY ONLY CHANCE TO FIND MY OWN KIND! YOU MUST TELL ME HOW TO REACH SUPERTOWN!
TRY THE BOOM TUBE-- IF YOU DARE!
BEAUTIFUL DREAMER
ALSO, A BIG BONUS GUEST STAR-- SUPERMAN!

THE FOREVER PEOPLE, No. 1, Feb.-March, 1971. Published bi-monthly by NATIONAL PERIODICAL PUBLICATIONS, INC., 2nd & Dickey Sts., Sparta, Ill. 62286. EDITORIAL, EXECUTIVE OFFICES 909 THIRD AVENUE, NEW YORK, N.Y. 10022. Jack Kirby, Editor. Carmine Infantino, Editorial Director. So. Harrison, Production Manager. Second Class Postage Entry Pending at Sparta, Ill. No subscriptions. For advertising rates address Richard A. Feldon & Co., 41 E. 42nd St., New York, N.Y. 10017.

The FOREVER
THEY'RE FROM A PLACE THAT MEN HAVE SOUGHT, BUT NEVER FOUND-- WE'VE SEEN THEIR LIKE BEFORE-- IN DIFFERENT AGES-- IN DIFFERENT GUISE-- BUT NEVER LIKE THIS-- YET, ALWAYS LIKE THIS-- WHEN MAN'S CIVILIZATION FACES DESTRUCTION...
BOOOM
RARRR

PEOPLE!
IN SEARCH OF A DREAM!
EDITED, DRAWN AND WRITTEN by JACK KIRBY (OUR MAN IN THE BOOM TUBE)
INKED BY: VINCE COLLETTA
GUEST-STARRING THE IMMORTAL SUPERMAN

WE'RE THROUGH THE BOOM TUBE! WE'RE HERE!
EEEEEHHAAAAAA
BIG BEAR GOT YOU HERE, VYKIN! REMEMBER THAT!
YOU GIANT-SIZED GRANITE-BRAIN! YOU DIDN'T PLOT OUR COURSE WITH THE MOTHER BOX!
WE MAY HAVE EMERGED AT THE WRONG SPOT!
TRUE!
A CAR--COMING UP FAST! EYES FRONT, YOU HAIRY DING-A-LING! WE'RE GOING TO COLLIDE!
COOL IT, I KNOW WHAT BUTTONS TO PUSH!
GOOD LORD! THAT THING--IT POPPED OUT OF NOWHERE!
EMERGENCY PHASE OUT INITIATED! GET READY TO FADE, FRIENDS!
IT'S TOO LATE TO CUT AWAY! WE'RE GOING TO HIT!
AT THE MOMENT OF COLLISION--
THE SUPER-CYCLE WORKS LIKE A CHARM!
OUR ATOMS HAVE BEEN RE-SHIFTED SO WE CAN PASS THROUGH THE CAR LIKE GHOSTS!
4

BUT THE YOUNG OCCUPANTS OF THE CAR, TERRIFIED BY THE EXPERIENCE, LOSE CONTROL OF THEIR VEHICLE...
CAN'T HOLD, LAURIE! WE'RE GOING OFF THE CLIFF!
THEN FOLLOWS ANOTHER STARTLING EVENT!
WE'RE NOT FALLING!
I CAN'T BELIEVE IT, BOBBY! WE'VE HALTED IN MID-AIR!
THE CAR IS BEING HELD BY SOME INVISIBLE FORCE!
THAT FELLOW WITH THAT STRANGE BOX! HE'S DOING THIS!
WE'RE BEING DRAWN BACK TO SAFETY! THAT'S WHAT COUNTS!
11X250
THE MOTHER BOX PROTECTS US ALL!
ARE YOU HURT?
WE SHOULD BE DEAD! WHAT ARE YOU CATS? MAGICIANS?
I AM VYKIN THE BLACK-- LISTEN-- MOTHER BOX IS APOLOGIZING FOR THIS UNFORTUNATE INCIDENT!
ER, I AM MARK MOONRIDER--WHAT VYKIN MEANS IS THAT MOTHER BOX IS LIKE A-- COMPUTER--
PING PING PING
WRONG! MOTHER BOX LIVES! SHE TALKS TO US-- PROTECTS US!
WE SHALL NEED HER WHEN THE TIME COMES TO RESCUE BEAUTIFUL DREAMER!
--I-IS THAT RIGHT-- HOW ABOUT THAT--
5

SHE HAS BEEN TAKEN HERE BY EVIL DARKSEID HIMSELF! THAT'S WHY WE RISKED COMING HERE FROM SUPER-TOWN!
--ONLY, HOT PILOT, BIG BEAR, FOULED THINGS UP--AS USUAL!
WHERE DID YOU PARK THE SUPER-CYCLE?
ON A WHITE, FAT CLOUD! DOES THAT MAKE YOU NERVOUS?
HASN'T ANYONE GIVEN THOUGHT TO THE YOUNG LADY? THESE SHOULD CALM HER!
HEH-HEH-- YOUNG SERIFAN IS DOING HIS BIG HERO BIT!
SERIFAN TURNS ON WITH FANTASIES! HE'S A SENSITIVE! WE'LL NEED HIM IF WE
HERE, MISS-- I TRUST THESE WILL HELP--
EVER HOPE TO CONTACT BEAUTIFUL DREAMER!
WOW! IT'S LUCKY I HAD MY CAMERA IN THE CAR!
WOULD YOU FELLAS MIND IF I TAKE SOME SHOTS?
GO AHEAD, BUT MAKE IT FAST! OUR MISSION HERE IS URGENT!
WHY DON'T YOU JUST SMILE?
CONTINUED ON 2ND PAGE FOLLOWING.
6

THAT EERIE LIGHT! WHAT IS IT?
IT COMES FROM THE BOOM TUBE!
IT HASN'T DE-MATERIALIZED YET!
GROOVY! IF IT'S AS WEIRD AS YOU CHARACTERS, I'VE GOT A SCOOP FOR A GOOD FRIEND!
THE TUBE IS JUST DOWN THE ROAD--
JIMMY OLSEN WILL EAT THIS UP, BOBBY!
BUT DON'T DRIVE INTO IT--YOU'RE NOT READY FOR THE TRIP!
THEY'LL JUST HAVE TIME TO SNAP A PHOTO. THE TUBE IS DUE TO FADE OUT VERY SOON!
MOONRIDER! LOOK TO SERIFAN--HE'S SLUMPING TO THE GROUND!
MY HEAD--THOUGHTS FROM OUTSIDE--STREAMING INTO MY BRAIN--I-I--
HE'S MADE CONTACT--WITH BEAUTIFUL DREAMER!
WHEN SERIFAN WAKES--WE WILL KNOW HER MESSAGE!
THEN, IT'S ACTION! WE'LL DEFY DARKSEID AND ALL HIS EVIL MINIONS TO GET HER BACK!
7

FROM THE NEARBY VEGETATION, BUSHES RUSTLE AND DEATH LOOKS OUT...
THEY MAKE PERFECT TARGETS! WE COULD NAIL THEM NOW!
NO, YOU FOOL! NOT YET!
WE'RE SUPPOSED TO REPORT TO DARKSEID WHEN THEY'VE BEEN SPOTTED!
BUT THEY'RE AN EASY KILL!
NOT AS EASY AS YOU THINK! THEY'RE NOT LIKE US!
THEY'RE LIKE THAT CHICK WE'RE HOLDING FOR DARKSEID-- SHE GIVES ME THE WHIM-WHAMS!
INTER-GANG REPORTING TO DARKSEID! THE BIRDS ARE OUT IN THE OPEN! DO WE FIRE?
ARE THEY OF THE TYPE I DESCRIBED TO YOU?
THEY'RE YOUNG-- ONE OF THEM HAS BLACKED OUT-- IT'S MORE LIKE HE FELL ASLEEP!
NO, YOU OAF! HE'S MADE MENTAL CONTACT WITH THE GIRL!
WHEN HE WAKES, THE YOUNG ONES WILL LEAVE! FOLLOW THEM!
YOU HEARD HIM! HOLD YOUR FIRE AND-- WAIT--
TOO BAD... INTER-GANG LIKES TO DELIVER GOOD SERVICE!
CONTINUED ON 2nd PAGE FOLLOWING.
8

BUT OTHER EVENTS ARE STIRRING! IN HIS SMALL OFFICE AT THE DAILY PLANET, CLARK KENT FINISHES AN INTERVIEW WITH A FAMOUS SPORTS FIGURE...
THANKS FOR DROPPING IN, ROCKY. THIS WILL MAKE A GREAT HUMAN INTEREST FEATURE!
GLAD TO HELP, KENT!
THE BOYS AT THE SPORTS DESK RATE YOU AS AN OKAY GUY!
SAY! THAT'S QUITE A GRIP YOU'VE GOT!
EVER BEEN IN THE RING?
ER--NO--I JUST EAT THE RIGHT MORNING CEREALS!
ROCKY--ONE QUESTION BEFORE YOU LEAVE--
WHY ARE YOU UNHAPPY?
CAUGHT THAT IN YOUR NOTES, DID YOU?
BUT YOU'RE THE CHAMP!
THAT'S JUST WHAT'S BUGGING ME!
THE PUBLIC LOVES AND RESPECTS YOU!
WHAT HAVE I DONE--THAT SUPERMAN COULDN'T DO BETTER?
HE CAN PUT DOWN AN ARMY OF TITLE-HOLDERS!
WITH SUPERMAN IN THE PICTURE, THE FIGHT GAME IS A FARCE!
YES--I-I SEE YOUR VIEWPOINT, ROCKY--
IF ONLY I COULD MEET HIM ON HIS OWN TERMS--!
NO CHARGE, KENT!
BUT KEEP IT OFF THE RECORD. IT MIGHT HURT THE GATE RECEIPTS!
SURE, CHAMP...
POOR, ROCKY--
POOR SUPER-MAN!
9

DESPITE HIS POWERS, HE IS A MINORITY OF ONE IN A TEEMING WORLD OF BILLIONS!
WHAT DOES SUPERMAN MEAN TO YOU, DOWN THERE?
A STRANGER IN A STRANGE LAND...
DO THEY SECRETLY RESENT HIM? FEAR HIM--? HATE HIM?
FOR THE FIRST TIME IN MANY YEARS-- I FEEL THAT I'M ALONE-- ALONE!
SUDDENLY...
CLARK! YOU'VE GOT TO SEE THESE PHOTOS!
THEY'LL BLOW YOUR MIND!
OH-- COME IN, JIMMY! "FLYING SAUCER TIME" AGAIN, EH?
YOU MUST BE KIDDING! THAT STUFF IS DEFINITELY "OUT!" THIS IS "IN" MATERIAL!
WHERE IN THE WILD BLUE YONDER DID YOU GET HOLD OF THESE SHOTS?
FROM FRIENDS OF MINE! AND I KNOW THEY WERE NOT "PUTTING ME ON!"
YES-- STRANGE TYPES-- AND YET--
EVER SEE A MOTORCYCLE LIKE THAT?-- AND THOSE KIDS--
SUPER-KIDS FROM A PLACE CALLED SUPER TOWN! THEY CALL THEMSELVES THE FOREVER PEOPLE! AND--
HOLD IT, JIMMY!-- JUST ONE SECOND!
10

SO YOU'RE GRABBED BY THE BOOM TUBE, HUH? ISN'T IT THE WILDEST?
MY FRIEND, BOBBY, SHOT THIS LAST FRAME AS IT WAS FADING OUT!
THERE IS SOMETHING--
ALTHOUGH, CLARK KENT STUDIES THE PHOTO--IT IS SUPERMAN'S VISION THAT PROBES THE TUBE'S STRANGE DEPTHS--
--IN THAT TUBE--
A TINY MICRODOT IN ITS INFINITE CENTER IS ENLARGED BY MILLIONS--AND A FANTASTIC IMAGE IS REVEALED!
--AT THE OTHER END--GOOD LORD!
ISN'T THAT A GAS?
THAT'S HOW THE SUPERKIDS SAID THEY GOT HERE! THROUGH THAT TUBE!
--A CITY--SUPERTOWN EXISTS!
JIMMY--NOW GIVE ME THIS ENTIRE STORY--STEP BY STEP--
--FROM THE BEGINNING!
YOU BET!
EVEN AS A LIE--THIS YARN WOULD BE A WHOPPER!
AS CLARK KENT LISTENS--IT IS SUPERMAN WHO DARES TO DREAM--AND HOPE--
NOW GET THIS--BOBBY AND LAURIE HAD THIS DATE, SEE?...
11

WHEN JIMMY OLSEN IS DONE--
HE IS HURRIEDLY USHERED OUT OF THE OFFICE...
THEN YOU'LL FOLLOW UP THE STORY! TERRIFIC!
WE'LL SEE WHAT THE FACTS ARE!
--AND THAT'S JUST EXACTLY WHAT I AIM TO DO!--BUT NOT AS CLARK KENT!
THIS IS SUPERMAN'S WORK!--BECAUSE IT'S SUPERMAN'S DREAM!
--THE ONLY WAY TO FIND SUPERTOWN--
--IS TO FIND THOSE KIDS!
--THEY WERE HEADED FOR THE CITY--AND I DO KNOW FROM WHAT DIRECTION!
LIKE A SUPERSONIC MISSILE, SUPERMAN FLASHES ACROSS THE SKY IN PURSUIT OF WHAT COULD BE A WILL-O'-THE-WISP--OR THE END OF ALL YEARNING!
12

BUT AS SUPERMAN STREAKS ACROSS THE SKY, HE PAYS NO ATTENTION TO THE HELI-COPTER ON A SIMILAR COURSE...
LOOK!--OUT THERE...!
SUPERMAN! I CAN'T THINK OF A MORE UNWELCOME SIGHT!
HE COULD BE A THREAT TO OUR MISSION--
BUT HE DOESN'T SEEM TO SUSPECT!
INTER-GANG TO DARKSEID! WE HAVE UNEXPECTED COMPANY-- SUPERMAN!
HE IS A DANGER! USE YOUR WEAPONS!
I DON'T WANT HIM MEDDLING!
BUT CAN THESE SIGMA-GUNS DO THE JOB--? YOU KNOW OF HIS POWERS!
STUN HIM, IF YOU CAN! THAT WILL BE ENOUGH! NOW, DISTURB ME NO FURTHER!
WHEN DARKSEID GIVES AN ORDER, IT MUST BE OBEYED! INTER-GANG IS ONLY SMALL APPLES IN THE CRIME EMPIRE HE'S BUILDING!
THERE'S MORE TO DARKSEID THAN THAT! HE MAKES ME BELIEVE THAT DRACULA IS ALIVE AND WELL IN TRANSYLVANIA!
SUPERMAN HAS SPOTTED THE KIDS!
THIS IS IT! ZERO IN ON HIM-- AND DON'T MISS!
13

MEANWHILE, SUPERMAN IS TOTALLY ABSORBED IN HIS SEARCH...
THERE--IN THAT ABANDONED LUMBER MILL IN THE DISTANCE--
IT COULD BE THEM!
I CAN SEE THEIR COSTUMES-- THAT STRANGE VEHICLE--JUST AS THEY WERE IN THOSE PHOTOS--
I'VE FOUND THEM!
HEADS UP, FRIENDS! WE'VE GOT ANOTHER VOLUNTEER FROM SUPERTOWN!
HE MAY BE A VOLUNTEER FOR DARKSEID!
WE'LL SOON FIND OUT!
SUDDENLY--!
ZZAP
SUPERMAN IS STRUCK HARD BY A SERIES OF SIGMA-BLASTS, AND ROLLS TO AVOID CONTACT WITH THIS UNKNOWN EXPLOSIVE!
ZZZARRAAP
IT WOULDN'T BE POLITE TO IGNORE A GREETING FROM SECRET ADMIRERS!
14

THIS HAS NEVER BEEN PART OF ANY OLYMPIC EVENT-- BUT IT COULD HAVE POSSIBILITIES!
SCRATCH ONE HELICOPTER AND MOTLEY CREW!
JUMP! OUR MISSION HAS FAILED!
ZOWK
THEY'RE LANDING AND SCATTERING LIKE RABBITS!
GOOD WORK, FRIEND!
WELCOME, SUPERTOWNER! JOINING UP AGAINST DARKSEID?
WHA--?
--ER-- I'M NOT FROM SUPERTOWN, BUT--
BUT HOW CAN THAT BE?
NO ONE LIVING HERE COULD SURVIVE A SIGMA-BLAST!
THIS IS NO TIME FOR SPOOFING, FRIEND--
DON'T WASTE TIME ON HIM, MOONRIDER! WE'VE GOT TO FIND BEAUTIFUL DREAMER!
MOTHER BOX SAYS SHE'S HERE--
PING PING PING
BUT WHEN HER SIGNALS PROBE FOR THE RIGHT LOCATION--THEY ARE SCATTERED BY A COUNTER-FORCE!
I MUST GAIN THE CONFIDENCE OF THESE SUPER-KIDS-- IF I EVER HOPE TO ACHIEVE WHAT I CAME FOR!
15

NOW WHAT, CLOWN? IS THIS A NEW ACT?
PERHAPS MY X-RAY VISION IS WHAT'S NEEDED!
MOTHER BOX WON'T LIKE THIS! BUT WE'LL RISK HER SONIC SCOLDING IF YOUR TRICK WORKS!
THERE! BENEATH THAT SHRUB--A SORT OF STRANGE METAL VALVE!
WAIT! BE CAREFUL--!
I'M THINKING OF BEAUTIFUL DREAMER! LET'S GO!
WE'RE WITH YOU, BIG BEAR!
THE VALVE HAS OPENED--! TRIGGERED BY OUR APPROACH!
IT'S RELEASING-- VAPOR!
MOTHER BOX SAYS TOXI-CLOUD!
POOOFF
WE'VE ONLY GOT SECONDS TO LIVE!
THAT'S ALL I'LL NEED! BUT I HOPE SECONDS WILL BE ENOUGH!
USE--MOTHER BOX-- SHE'LL PROTECT--
NO USE-- SHE CAN'T FUNCTION IN THIS AREA--
THE GROUND MUST BE CRAWLING WITH DARKSEID'S EVIL MACHINES!
16

WITH SUPERSONIC SPEED, SUPERMAN CREATES A MINIATURE TORNADO WHICH INSTANTANEOUSLY DISSIPATES THE POISON GAS...
THIS MAY CAUSE SOME SLIGHT DAMAGE--BUT IT WILL SAVE LIVES!
BUT THERE ARE NEW SURPRISES WAITING!
HANDS!--REACHING FOR ME!--I'M MOVING TOO FAST TO ESCAPE THEM!
WE'LL TEACH YOU NOT TO DEFY DARKSEID!
THE MOST FAITHFUL TO DARKSEID ARE HIS GRAVI-GUARDS!
VYKIN--WE'RE ALIVE--BUT STILL IN TROUBLE!
I SEE THEM, TOO!
SEIZE THE YOUNG ONES! THIS ONE HAS THE MIGHT TO MOVE A MOUNTAIN--
BUT IT SHALL NOT AVAIL HIM! DARKSEID CHOSE US WELL!
WE TRANSMIT GRAVITY WAVES FROM HEAVY MASS GALAXIES--WE CAN HOLD ANY SUPER-BEING!
IT'S TRUE--THERE IS INCREDIBLE, CRUSHING WEIGHT BEING CHANNELED INTO MY BODY!
17

HANG ON, SUPERMAN! THERE'S A WAY TO BEAT THESE BOULDER-SHOULDERED KNOT-HEADS!
THEY MOVE WITH THE SPEED OF GLUE! IT'S GIVEN US TIME TO SHAKE OFF THE EFFECTS OF THE VAPOR!
--AND RELEASE THE ONE WHO LIVES OUTSIDE OF ALL THINGS FINITE!
QUICK! --ASK MOTHER FOR THE RITUAL!
RISE, MOTHER BOX-- UNITE US AS ONE--
YOU BRATS ARE FINISHED!
SEND HIM YOUR SIGNAL, MOTHER BOX! MAKE US THE DOOR FOR HIM TO ENTER--
PREPARE FOR THE WORD, MOTHER BOX!
LET YOUR CIRCUITS CARRY THE WORD-- LET IT GROW LOUD-- UNTIL IT REACHES THE WINDS OF INFINITY!
TARRU!
I HAVE HEARD! I AM HERE! I AM THE INFINITY MAN!
18

W-WHERE DID HE COME FROM?
WHERE ALL OF NATURAL LAW SHIFTS, AND BENDS, AND CHANGES--
WHERE THE ANSWER TO GRAVITY IS ANTI-GRAVITY-- AND SIMPLY DONE!
POWER KNOWS NO PREJUDICE! THE SAVAGE WIELDS IT AS WELL AS THE CIVILIZED MAN!
NEVER HAVE I SEEN SUCH RESISTANCE!
THIS ONE KNOWS NO DEFEAT!
WITH ALMOST EFFORTLESS EASE, THE INFINITY MAN DISPATCHES THE REMAINING GRAVI-GUARD!
YOUR RULES DON'T APPLY TO ME, EVIL ONE!
19

WHAT RULES DO YOU OPERATE FROM, MISTER?
WHERE ARE THE BOYS?
THEY ARE SAFE-- FOR THE PRESENT-- LIKE ALL THINGS NOW LIVING WITH THE GREAT PERIL!
THIS GREAT PERIL COULDN'T BE NAMED-- DARKSEID-- COULD IT!
HOLOCAUST AND DEATH IS WHAT HE SERVES! THAT IS WHY HE ABDUCTED THE GIRL--
SHE IS ONE OF THE FEW WHOSE MIND CAN FATHOM THE ANTI-LIFE EQUATION! THE ULTIMATE WEAPON!
RELEASE HER, DARKSEID! I KNOW YOU CAN HEAR ME! YOU ARE NEVER FAR FROM YOUR TRAPS!
RELEASE THE GIRL! HER MIND WILL RESIST ENSLAVEMENT BY YOUR MACHINES!
DON'T SHOUT-- I AM HERE! YOU ARE RIGHT! THE GIRL'S MIND IS UNIQUE! IT WILL NOT INTERPRET THE EQUATION!
ALL OF MY ATTEMPTS AT FORCE HAVE FAILED!
IF YOU'VE HARMED HER, YOU SHALL PAY, DARKSEID!
NONSENSE! I HAVE NO FURTHER NEED OF HER! THERE! SHE RISES!
CONTINUED ON 2ND PAGE FOLLOWING.
20

I RELEASE HER TO YOUR CUSTODY--
ONE OF THEM SHALL YIELD TO ME!
THERE ARE OTHERS WHO CAN SOLVE THE EQUATION!
--AND WHEN THE SECRET IS MINE, I SHALL TEST IT HERE! --SNUFF OUT ALL LIFE ON EARTH--WITH A WORD!
NOW, FAREWELL! I LEAVE AS I CAME-- WITH THE POWER TO VANISH AS QUICKLY AS I APPEARED!
H-HE'S GONE!
WAIT! THOSE TANKS BENEATH THE TABLE--
RADION BOMBS! DARKSEID'S OWN FORMULA! IF WE MOVE THE GIRL, THE BOMBS WILL GO OFF!
HE MEANT TO DESTROY US ALL!
THIS CALLS FOR PERFECT TIMING!
WHA--!
THE TRICK IS TO OUT-SPEED THE BOMBS' IGNITION--AND I THINK I CAN DO IT!
INCREASING TO LIGHTSPEED, SUPERMAN IS OUT OF RANGE WHEN THE EXPLOSION COMES...
MADE IT!--AND NONE TO SOON!
21

DARKSEID'S UNDERGROUND COMPLEX MUST HAVE BEEN DESTROYED!
YOUR LIGHTNING POWERS HAVE SERVED US WELL!
THIS GAME IS STILL A MYSTERY TO ME! BUT I KNOW THIS--IT'S A DANGEROUS--DEADLY GAME!
IT IS BIGGER THAN YOU REALIZE! UNTIL I AM NEEDED AGAIN--I DEPART!
HEY! HOLD ON! I'VE GOT A MILLION QUESTIONS!
TAARU!
YOU CAN PUT YOUR QUESTIONS TO US, MISTER! YOU'RE A FRIEND!
THE BOYS--THEY'RE BACK--!
WE'VE GOT AN ARRANGEMENT WITH THE INFINITY MAN!
BEAUTIFUL DREAMER IS SAFE, THANKS TO YOU!
WHAT CAN WE DO TO SHOW OUR GRATITUDE?
ASK ANYTHING!
ALRIGHT, I WILL! HELP ME TO REACH SUPERTOWN!
THAT'S EASY! BUT WHY DO YOU WANT TO GO THERE NOW?
I-I NEED TO KNOW MORE! I'VE GOT TO SEE SUPERTOWN--
DARKSEID IS HERE! HE MUST BE STOPPED!
CONTINUED ON 2ND PAGE FOLLOWING.
22

I TELL YOU THE ACTION IS HERE! --AND YOU, AND ALL OF EARTH ARE INVOLVED!
IF THERE IS DANGER--I'LL BE BACK!
NOW, WILL YOU DO AS I ASK?
BUT IF DARKSEID CONQUERS--THERE WILL BE NOTHING--NOT EVEN SUPERTOWN!
HE WANTS TO GO, BIG BEAR. AND THAT'S ALL IT TAKES--A DEEP DESIRE!
--AND THE BOOM TUBE!
YES--I HEAR SOMETHING--
LISTEN--IT'S COMING THROUGH NOW!
IT'S HERE, FRIEND! AND YOU'VE EARNED THE TRIP!
BUT I HOPE YOU CAN LIVE WITH YOUR CONSCIENCE--LATER!
DON'T, BIG BEAR! DON'T SPOIL HIS DREAM--NOW THAT IT IS A REALITY!
I--I SEE IT!
LET'S GO! WE'LL CARRY ON WITHOUT HIM!
IT WILL BE A HARD FIGHT! DARKSEID AND HIS EVIL MINIONS WILL BE EVERYWHERE! BUT WE'LL DO OUR JOB!
BOOM
SUPERMAN DOES NOT HEAR THE YOUNGSTERS DEPART--HE CAN ONLY SEE THE WONDER BEFORE HIM!
THE BOOM TUBE IS FANTASTIC! BUT IT'S REAL, ALRIGHT!
IT'S A DIMENSIONAL BRIDGE--AND I'M CROSSING IT!--
RIGHT NOW!
23

BUT DEEP WITHIN, SUPERMAN FEELS THE STING OF APPREHENSION...
DOES THE ANSWER REALLY LIE AHEAD OF ME? DARKSEID AND HIS HIDDEN TERRORS--THE ANTI-LIFE EQUATION-- THE DANGER TO MANKIND--
AM I GOING THE WRONG WAY? IS EARTH THE BATTLEGROUND FOR SOME STRANGE SUPER-WAR?
IT COULD BE AS REAL AS THE BOOM TUBE!--AND I MAY BE DESERTING MANKIND WHEN IT NEEDS ME MOST!
I CAN'T GO ON! I CAN'T--
BOOOOM
THERE IS A LOUD THUNDERCLAP--AND SUPERMAN FINDS HIMSELF BACK ON EARTH!
AND AS THE BOOM TUBE FADES, SUPERMAN CATCHES A GLIMPSE OF DISTANT, GLEAMING TOWERS...
THEN, LIKE A DREAM, THEY TOO FADE, AND ARE GONE!
IT WAS THE WRONG TIME TO GO--
PERHAPS, SOMEDAY, I'LL TRY AGAIN... BUT THE TIME IS NOT NOW--NOT YET--
IN THE NEXT ISSUE... THE MYSTERY SURROUNDING the FOREVER PEOPLE BEGINS TO UNFOLD in:
SUPER-WAR!

QUESTIONS

1. Do you think the symbolism of "boom tube" and "mother box" would be lost on young readers?

2. Are the Forever People outdated? Do they still function as credible would-be saviors in the context of the 1970s?

3. What does Darkseid symbolize?

4. What does the Infinity Man symbolize?

5. Is Superman a tragic figure? Why?

6. Use this comic as a starting point for discussing the relationships between science fiction and mass culture.

7. Are the comic book pictures in "The Forever People" similar to ones you create in your mind as you read an unillustrated science fiction story? In what ways are they similar, if indeed they are? If not, how are they dissimilar?

The Star-Splitter

Robert Frost

This poem by Robert Frost expresses both a yearning for literal contact with the universal mystery and wonder at humankind's ultimate ignorance. If this poem was instead a science fiction story, the central character could well be the lonely inventor-dreamer sacrificing comfort for vision. Most of Frost's poetry is concerned with the ways in which people try to adjust in a time which, as he said in his poem "Directive," was "now too much for us."

"You know Orion always comes up sideways.
Throwing a leg up over our fence of mountains,
And rising on his hands, he looks in on me
Busy outdoors by lantern-light with something
I should have done by daylight, and indeed,
After the ground is frozen, I should have done
Before it froze, and a gust flings a handful
Of waste leaves at my smoky lantern chimney
To make fun of my way of doing things,
Or else fun of Orion's having caught me. 10
Has a man, I should like to ask, no rights
These forces are obliged to pay respect to?"
So Brad McLaughlin mingled reckless talk
Of heavenly stars with hugger-mugger farming,
Till having failed at hugger-mugger farming
He burned his house down for the fire insurance
And spent the proceeds on a telescope
To satisfy a lifelong curiosity
About our place among the infinities.

"What do you want with one of those blame things?" 20
I asked him well beforehand. "Don't you get one!"
"Don't call it blamed; there isn't anything
More blameless in the sense of being less
A weapon in our human fight," he said.
"I'll have one if I sell my farm to buy it."

There where he moved the rocks to plow the ground
And plowed between the rocks he couldn't move,
Few farms changed hands; so rather than spend years
Trying to sell his farm and then not selling,
He burned his house down for the fire insurance 30
And bought the telescope with what it came to.
He had been heard to say by several:
"The best thing that we're put here for's to see;
The strongest thing that's given us to see with's
A telescope. Someone in every town
Seems to me owes it to the town to keep one.
In Littleton it may as well be me."
After such loose talk it was no surprise
When he did what he did and burned his house down.

Mean laughter went about the town that day 40
To let him know we weren't the least imposed on,
And he could wait—we'd see to him tomorrow.
But the first thing next morning we reflected
If one by one we counted people out
For the least sin, it wouldn't take us long
To get so we had no one left to live with.
For to be social is to be forgiving.
Our thief, the one who does our stealing from us,
We don't cut off from coming to church suppers,
But what we miss we go to him and ask for. 50
He promptly gives it back, that is if still
Uneaten, unworn out, or undisposed of.
It wouldn't do to be too hard on Brad
About his telescope. Beyond the age
Of being given one for Christmas gift,
He had to take the best way he knew how
To find himself in one. Well, all we said was
He took a strange thing to be roguish over.
Some sympathy was wasted on the house,
A good old-timer dating back along; 60
But a house isn't sentient; the house
Didn't feel anything. And if it did,
Why not regard it as a sacrifice,
And an old-fashioned sacrifice by fire,
Instead of a new-fashioned one at auction?

Out of a house and so out of a farm
At one stroke (of a match), Brad had to turn
To earn a living on the Concord railroad,
As under-ticket-agent at a station
Where his job, when he wasn't selling tickets, 70
Was setting out, up track and down, not plants
As on a farm, but planets, evening stars
That varied in their hue from red to green.

He got a good glass for six hundred dollars.
His new job gave him leisure for stargazing.
Often he bid me come and have a look
Up the brass barrel, velvet black inside,
At a star quaking in the other end.
I recollect a night of broken clouds
And underfoot snow melted down to ice, 80
And melting further in the wind to mud.
Bradford and I had out the telescope.
We spread our two legs as we spread its three,
Pointed our thoughts the way we pointed it,
And standing at our leisure till the day broke,
Said some of the best things we ever said.
That telescope was christened the Star-Splitter,
Because it didn't do a thing but split
A star in two or three, the way you split
A globule of quicksilver in your hand 90
With one stroke of your finger in the middle.
It's a star-splitter if there ever was one,
And ought to do some good if splitting stars
'Sa thing to be compared with splitting wood.

We've looked and looked, but after all where are we?
Do we know any better where we are,
And how it stands between the night tonight
And a man with a smoky lantern chimney?
How different from the way it ever stood?

QUESTIONS

1. Both Brad McLaughlin and the narrator have ambivalent feelings about the stars. What are they? Find and discuss other ambivalences in the poem. What is the central paradox of the poem?

2. Did Brad commit an immoral act by burning down his house for the insurance? Are you satisfied with the way his action is justified here? Explain the townspeople's reaction.

3. What does the poem reveal about the narrator? What sort of person would you say he is?

4. Compare Brad McLaughlin to Owen Warland in Hawthorne's tale. Both characters are eccentric. In what does their eccentricity lie? How does the reaction of society to each of them differ?

5. Does "The Star-Splitter" answer any of the questions in the final stanza? Is it necessary that it do so?

6. Why is the poem written in narrative rather than lyric form? Could the story of Brad be told in a lyric? Describe the difference between a narrative and a lyric.

7. Do the style and tone of the poem convey a feeling that it is filled with "common sense" or "wisdom"? How do diction, imagery, and rhythm contribute to style and tone?

part 3

Breaking Outward

If our current problems of population and scarcity are eventually solved, humankind will doubtless continue to explore outer space. First we will visit planets that are near us, then ones that are farther away. Finally, when a way is discovered to travel either close to the speed of light or beyond it, the rest of our own galaxy and then other galaxies will come within reach of Earth's ships.

Stories of space travel are staples of the genre. On their most elementary level, they are called "space operas": traditional adventure stories with the space setting substituted for the open sea or the American plains; stories and novels with little characterization and much melodrama. At their best, stories of space travel—which are always tales of the Future, whether set in space or on alien planets—present many of the possible futures in which humans may find themselves. Incredible possibilities lie before us. In the future imagined by SF writers, we see the best and the worst of what may befall our distant descendants.

The section begins with questions raised about the value of future space exploration. Richard Eberhart's poem cautions us against the danger of going outward before we have settled our own psychological problems. His poem is similar to a number of SF works in which our planet is put in quarantine, humans perceived by other beings in the universe as the most aggressive and vicious, even evil, things in that universe. In contrast, the next selection, "The Far Look," presents a happier possibility. The story shows how the experience of moon-desolation, then rearrival on Earth could change humans into something close to "homo superior."

Vonda McIntyre's setting for "Of Mist, and Grass, and Sand" may be on some future Earth, or in an alternate dimension; but for the purposes of this unit we have taken the setting as located on another planet. Here, then, is an award-winning story of what it might be like to be in a different cultural pattern, with sexual roles slightly changed so as to bring out the fullest dimensions of a woman of the future, confronting a problem of the future. It is a mixture of the strange and the beautiful, of the exceptional and the normal. These people are different from us and yet like us, their characters and powers subtly shaped by their world.

Still other future possibilities present themselves for consideration. In Damon Knight's "Stranger Station" an "alien encounter" takes place. This is not the conventional "shootout" we see in so many other stories using the motif. Rather, the story suggests that humans will have to adapt to other beings, even the most inconceivable, if they are to derive benefit from the universe. Almost surely, the human race is not alone in the universe. But problems of future adaptation will take other forms than adjustment to strange species, as can be seen in "The Ship Who Sang," in which the central character is the highly trained brain of a woman. Helva is a "cyborg"; she is useful and brilliant, but she must learn to love and to mourn before she can completely fulfill her role. The woman-machine evokes our compassion as she painfully adjusts to her universe.

The universe has changed and we have moved farther into the future with the last selection of "Breaking Outward." Eons have gone by and much of humanity's past has been lost, even the planet Earth no longer has reality. Only vague memories and what at first appear to be human superstitions remain on what is finally recognized to be an outer space colony of Earth. This work, as do the others in this section, suggests some of the myriad possibilities that lie beyond our planet and our own time. All the selections stress change—perhaps that one element most characteristic of human life—and the adaptation to it. It may be that we shall never again know a time without "future shock." Perhaps, finally, we should never *choose* to know such a time.

On Shooting Particles Beyond the World

Richard Eberhart

Perhaps we have done enough; perhaps we are only making a mess of the heavens as an excuse for avoiding the mess on Earth. It could be that the real frontier of the future is "inner space": maybe we should stop going "out" and start learning to live "within."

The following poem, by Pulitzer Prize winning poet Richard Eberhart, was written even before the first Sputnik was shot into space. It presents an alternative to those who feel continued space exploration is necessary for humanity.

> "White Sands, N. M., Dec. 18 (UP). '*We first throw a little something into the skies,' Zwicky said. 'Then a little more, then a shipload of instruments—then ourselves.'* "

On this day man's disgust is known
Incipient before but now full blown
With minor wars of major consequence,
Duly building empirical delusions.

Now this little creature in a rage
Like new-born infant screaming compleat angler
Objects to the whole globe itself
And with a vicious lunge he throws

Metal particles beyond the orbit of mankind.
Beethoven shaking his fist at death, 10
A giant dignity in human terms,
Is nothing to this imbecile metal fury.

The world is too much for him. The green
Of earth is not enough, love's deities.
Peaceful intercourse, happiness of nations,
The wild animal dazzled on the desert.

If the maniac would only realize
The comforts of his padded cell

He would have penetrated the
Impenetrability of the spiritual. 20

It is not intelligent to go too far.
How he frets that he can't go too!
But his particles would maim a star,
His free-floating bombards rock the moon.

Good Boy! We pat the baby to eructate,
We pat him then for eructation.
Good Boy Man! Your innards are put out,
From now all space will be your vomitorium.

The atom bomb accepted this world,
Its hatred of man blew death in his face. 30
But not content, he'll send slugs beyond,
His particles of intellect will spit on the sun.

Not God he'll catch, in the mystery of space.
He flaunts his own out-cast state
As he throws his imperfections outward bound
And his shout that gives a hissing sound.

QUESTIONS

1. Do you feel that the actuality of space travel has confirmed Eberhart's judgment?

2. Explore the use of allusions in the poem.

3. Discuss the use of irony in this poem. Is it overwhelmed by indignation?

4. What are the most highly charged words in the poem?

5. Discuss the imagery used to describe man. To what different things is man compared by use of this imagery?

6. Is the poem misanthropic?

7. What questions does the poem raise about the value of our space program?

The Far Look

Theodore L. Thomas

Yesterday's SF visions frequently become today's scientific facts. It is difficult to predict tomorrow's technology; it is far more important to determine the effects of that technology on humanity. Theodore L. Thomas is an ex-military man who in this story displays great faith in his astronauts' potential. He seems to share an almost mystical belief with Arthur C. Clarke, whose repeated theme is that to become something more than homo sapiens, men must go to the stars, and the stars may turn them into gods.

This selection presents an alternate view to that suggested by Richard Eberhart's "On Shooting Particles Beyond the World." As such, it can provide a good basis for the argument that humanity is salvageable.

The ship appeared first as a dot low on the horizon. The television cameras immediately picked it up. At first the ship did not give the impression of motion; it seemed to hover motionless and swell in size. Then in a few seconds it passed the first television station, the screaming roar of its passage rocking the camera slightly.

Thirty miles beyond, its bellyskids touched the packed New Mexican sand. An immense dust cloud stirred into life at the rear of the ship and spread slowly across the desert.

As soon as the ship touched, the three helicopters took off to meet it. The helicopters were ten miles away when the ship halted and lay motionless. The dust began to dissipate rearward. The late afternoon sun distorted the flowing lines of the ship and made it look like some outlandish beast of prey crouched on the desert.

As the lead helicopter drew within a mile of the ship, its television camera caught the ship clearly for the first time. Telephoto lenses brought it in close, and viewers once again watched closely. They could see the pilot's head as he checked over his equipment. They looked admiringly at the stubby swept-back wings and at the gaping opening at the rear from which poured the fires of hell itself. But most of all they looked to the area amidship where the door was.

And as they watched, the door swung open. The sun slanted in and showed two figures standing there. The figures moved to a point just inside the door and stopped. They stood there looking out, motionless, for what seemed an interminable period. Then the two figures looked at each other, nodded, and jumped out of the door.

Though the sand was only four feet below the sill of the door, both men fell to their knees. They quickly arose, knocked the dust from their clothes, and started walking to where the helicopters were waiting. And all over the country people watched that now-familiar moon walk—the rocking of the body from side to side to get too-heavy feet off the ground, the relaxed muscles on the down step where the foot just seemed to plop against the ground.

But the cameras did not focus on the general appearance or action of the men. The zoom lenses went to work and a close-up of the faces of the two men side by side flashed across the country.

The faces even at first glance seemed different. And as the cameras lingered, it became apparent that there was something quite extraordinary there. These were men, but the eyes were different. There was an expression not found in human eyes. It was a level-eyed expression, undeviating. It was a penetrating, probing expression, yet one laden with compassion. There was a look in those eyes of things seen from deep inside, of things seen beyond the range of normal vision. It was a far look, a compelling look, a powerful look set in the eyes of normal men. And even when those eyes were closed, there was something different. A network of tiny creases laced out from the corners of each eye. The crinkled appearance of the eyes made each man appear older than he was, older and strangely wizened.

The cameras stayed on the men's faces as they awkwardly walked towards the helicopters. Even though several dignitaries hurried forward to greet the men, the camera remained on the faces, transmitting that strange look for all to see. A nation crammed forward to watch.

In Macon, Georgia, Mary Sinderman touched a wetted finger to the bottom of the iron. She heard it pop as she stared across her ironing board at the television screen with the faces of two men on it.

"Charlie. Oh, Charlie," she called. "Here they are."

A dark squat man in an undershirt came into the room and looked at the picture. "Yeah," he grunted. "They got it all right. Both of 'em."

"Aren't they handsome?" she said.

He threw a black look at her and said, "No, they ain't." And he went out of the door he had come in.

In Stanford, Connecticut, Walter Dwyer lowered his newspaper and peered over the top of it at the faces of two men on the television screen. "Look at that, honey," he said.

His wife looked up from her section of the paper and nodded silently. He said, "Two more, dear. If this keeps up, we'll all be able to retire and let them run things." She chuckled, and nodded and continued to watch the screen.

In Boise, Idaho, the Tankard Saloon was doing a moderate business.

The television set was on up over one end of the bar. The faces of two men flashed on the screen. Slowly a silence fell over the saloon as one person after another stopped what he was doing to watch. One man sitting in close under the screen raised his drink high in tribute to the two faces on the screen. And every man in the place followed suit.

In a long low building on the New Mexican flats, the wall TV set was on. A thin, earnest-faced young man wearing heavy glasses sat stiffly erect on a folding chair in front of the screen watching the two faces. He glanced briefly aside with a faint air of disapproval at the pipe being contentedly puffed on by an older man who stood near. He turned back to the screen and his disapproval vanished. "Dr. Scott," he said, "they both have the look."

The older man nodded wordlessly. They watched the awkwardness of the two men, apparent even from a view confined to their faces.

The young man said, "How long will it be before they arrive here, doctor?"

"About half to three-quarters of an hour. They've got to get the red plush carpet laid out for them first."

"Dr. Scott, do you think you'll be able to find out anything this time?"

A slight urge to tell this young man to keep his big fat mouth shut rose up in Dr. Scott. He noted the urge and catalogued it neatly in the niche filled with the urges of older, experienced men towards young naïve men who believe everything they learned at college, and no more.

But Dr. Scott answered gently, "I don't know, Dr. Webb, I don't know. We've examined sixteen of these fellows without finding out anything. I don't know why we should now."

"Have you no theories to explain it?"

"No. I have no theories. Once I had theories, but I haven't any any more." And Scott brought out a match, struck it, and began ejecting great sheets of flame and smoke from his pipe.

Webb quietly watched the scene on the screen. He saw the two men shake hands with an impressive assortment of generals, defence officials, air officials, space officials, and the assorted lot that clusters around such dignitaries.

Webb said, "Have you isolated all the factors resulting from your choice of men?"

Scott pulled reflectively on his pipe a time or two, and said, "As far as we've been able, yes."

"And you found nothing, even though you've been highly selective in picking the men?"

Again the reflective puffs of smoke; then, "Well, I'm not sure I know what you mean when you say 'highly selective.' We look for a combination of qualities, not any one or two or three qualities." More smoke. "Suppose you had to choose a man who was a good electrical engineer and who was also a good mule skinner. You'd find that the best man you could get would not be the best electrical engineeer, nor would he be the best mule skinner. Well, that's our problem, only ten times worse. We look for men with the combination of technological and psychological qualities that we know best equips the men for survival on the moon. But as soon as you try to isolate any one of the various qualities, you'll find there are thousands of other men that outshine ours in that particular quality. It's the combination that counts."

Webb hadn't taken his eyes off the handshaking and speech-making on the screen, but he had been listening to Scott.

Webb said, "Well, isn't it the combination that does it then? The good all-around men?"

"It might be," said Scott, "except for one thing. When we started this project we didn't know as much as we know now. The first ten men were not selected the way we select them now, yet the same ratio of them developed the far look. Two of them died on the Moon, and that helped teach us how to better select the ones that can survive. The point is that our selection system affects survival but doesn't seem to affect the far look."

Webb nodded. He watched the two men board a helicopter and saw it take off. The screen faded to a blare of martial music and then came to life on a toothy announcer praising the virtues of a hair shampoo. Webb snapped the set off, turned to Scott, and said, "Don't all these men go through some experience in common?"

Scott pulled hard at his pipe, but it was out. He reached in a side pocket and pulled out a match the size of a small pine tree. He struck it under the table, held it poised over the bowl, and said, "They go through a great many experiences in common. They go through two years of intensive training. They make a flight through space and land on the Moon. They spend twenty-eight days of hell reading instruments, making surveys, and collecting samples. They suffer loneliness such as no human being has ever known before. Their lives are in constant peril. Each pair has had at least one disaster during their stay. Then they get their replacements and come back to Earth. Yes, they have something in common all right. But a few come back without the far look. They've improved; they're better than most men here on Earth. But they are not on a par with the rest of these returning prodigies with crinkles around their eyes. Talk about *Homo superior.* We're making about two of them a month, and we haven't the foggiest idea of how we're doing it. *Ouch.*" And he flung the burnt-out pine tree into an ash tray.

Webb looked at him quizzically and then glanced at his watch. "Ten minutes," he said, "they'll be here in ten minutes." He walked to the window and looked out, listening to the hissing and bubbling of Scott's pipe going through the throes of being relighted. Webb said, "I suppose these two will become just as successful as the others. They've got 'the far look,' as you and the newspapers call it."

"Yes, they've got it. And they'll be as good as the others, too. I don't know whether they'll go into business or politics or science or art; but whatever it is, you can bet they'll be better at it than anybody else has ever been."

Webb continued to look out of the window for a while, trying to fit this latest information into his general background of knowledge. It would not fit. He shook his head and turned from the window and said, "We are missing something. Somewhere there is an element we are unaware of. These men must know what it is. They are keeping it from us, knowingly or unknowingly. All we have to do is dig out that missing element and I venture to say we will have the answer. It's as simple as that."

Scott looked at him. He puffed gently a time or two to slow the welling up of anger. He took the pipe from his mouth and said softly, "These men are concealing nothing, as far as our best efforts can show. We've pumped them full of half a dozen truth drugs. We've doped them and subjected them to hypnosis. On top of that they have all been completely frank and open with us. Maybe they're concealing something but I doubt it very much." And he put the pipe back in his mouth and clamped down on it hard.

Webb shook his head again. "I don't know. There's something missing here. I certainly mean to put these subjects through exhaustive tests. I'll dig something out of them."

The anger in Scott brought a flush to his face. He cupped the pipe bowl and studied the grey ashes while he considered whether a wrathful response would merely be a venting of his own anger or a real help to Webb. He decided that Webb might profit with a little cushioning against the shock he was due to receive in a very few minutes now. Scott pointed the stem of the pipe at Webb as he crossed the room towards him. He stopped in front of Webb and touched him on the lapel of the coat with the bit as he said, "Look here, young fella, these 'subjects' as you call them are like no subjects you ever had or conceived of. These men can twist you and me up into knots if they want to. They understand more about people than the entire profession of psychiatrics will learn in the next hundred years. These men are intellectual giants with a personality that can curl you up on the floor."

He put the pipe in his mouth and said, more gently, "You are in for a shock, Dr. Webb. I'm telling you this so you won't be quite as crushed when you meet these men. You've read about them, studied their histories, I know, but no mere description does justice to the force of their personalities. These two particular men are fresh from the Moon and do not yet fully realize the immense impact they have on people.

Now you'd best get yourself ready for quite an experience. You'll need all your strength to preserve an ounce of objectivity."

The murmur of approaching motors broke into the ensuing silence. Webb did not hear them at first; he stared at Scott, mouth slightly open. The murmur grew to a roar as the helicopters landed outside the building. Webb turned to look out of the window again, but the men dismounted on the far side of the plane and disappeared through a door in the building. In a moment footsteps sounded outside in the hall and the door crashed open.

Webb turned to see the two men with crinkles surrounding their eyes walk into the room. The taller of the two looked at Webb and Webb felt as if struck by a hot blast of wind. The level eyes were brilliant blue and seemed to reach into Webb and gently strum on the fibres of his nervous system. A sense of elation swept through him. He felt as he had once felt standing alone at dusk in a wind-tossed forest. He could not speak. His breath stopped. His muscles held rigid. And then the blue-eyed glance passed him and left him confused and restless and disappointed.

He dimly saw Scott cross the room and shake hands with the shorter man. Scott said, "How do you do. We are very glad for your safe return. Was everything in order when you left the Moon?"

The shorter man smiled as he shook Scott's hand. "Thank you, doctor. Yes, everything was in order. Our two replacements are off to a good start." He glanced at the taller man. They looked at each other, and smiled.

"Yes," said the taller man, "they are off to a good start. Fowler and McIntosh will do all right."

Don Fowler and Al McIntosh still had the shakes. After six days they still had the shakes whenever they remembered the first few moments of their landing on the Moon.

The ship had let down roughly. Fowler awkwardly climbed out through the lock first. He turned to make sure McIntosh was following him and then started to move around the ship to look for the two men they were to replace.

The ship lay near a crevice. A series of ripples in the rock marred the black shiny basalt surface that surrounded the crevice. The surface was washed clean of dust by the jets of the descending ship. As Fowler walked around the base of the ship his foot stepped into the trough of one of the ripples in the rock. It threw him off balance, tilted him towards the crevice. He struggled to right himself. Under Earth gravity he would simply have fallen, but under Lunar gravity he managed to retain his feet. But he staggered towards the crevice, stumbling in the ripples, unable to recover himself in the unaccustomed gravity. McIntosh grabbed for him. But with arms flailing, body twisting, feet groping, he disappeared down the crevice as if drawn into the maw of some hungry beast. McIntosh staggered behind him. His own feet skidded on the ripples in the hard, slick basalt. He, too, bobbled his way to the lip of the crevice and toppled in.

Thirty feet down the crevice narrowed to a point where the men could fall no farther. Both found themselves pinned firmly in place. Fowler was head down and four feet to McIntosh's left. They were unhurt but they began to worry when a few struggled showed them how firmly the slick rock gripped their spacesuits. The pilot of the spaceship, sealed in his tiny compartment, could not help them. The two men they were to replace might be miles away. The radios were useless for anything but line-of-sight work. So they hung there, waiting for something to happen.

Although they were completely helpless and hadn't the slightest idea of how to get out of their predicament, their training on Earth asserted itself. Fowler spoke first.

"Say, Mac. Did you get a chance to see what the Moon looks like before you joined me down here?"

"No. I had sort of hoped you'd noticed. Now we don't have a thing to talk about."

Silence, then,

"This is one for the books," said Fowler. "We spend ten seconds on the surface of the Moon and an undetermined period of time some odd feet beneath it. Can you see anything? All I can see is the bottom of this thing and all I can tell you about it is that it's black down there."

"No. I can't tilt my head back far enough to see out. I have a nice view of the wall, though. Dense, igneous, probably of basic plagioclose. Make a note of that, will you?"

"Can you reach me?"

"No. I can't even see you. Can you—"

"What are you fellows doing down there?" A new voice broke into the conversation. Neither Fowler nor McIntosh could think of an answer. "Stay right there," the voice continued, with something that sounded suspiciously like a chuckle in it. "We'll be down to get you out."

Both of the pinned men could hear a rock-scraping sound through their suits. Two pairs of hands rocked each man free of the walls and lifted him up to where he could bridge the crevice with knees and back. McIntosh was the first to be freed and he watched with close interest the easy freedom of movement of the two spacesuited figures as they released Fowler, turned him right side up, and lifted him up to where he could support himself in the crevice. All four then worked their way up the slick walls by sliding their backs up one wall while bracing their feet against the opposite wall.

It took Fowler and McIntosh appreciably longer to climb to the surface than the other two. There had been no words spoken in the crevice and there was little to say now. Fowler and McIntosh each solemnly shook hands with the other two. The clunk of the metallic-faced palms of the spacesuit and the gritty sound of the finger, wrist, and elbow joints made hand-shaking a noisy business in a spacesuit.

The two men led Folwer and McIntosh around to the other side of the spaceship and pointed westward across Mare Imbrium. One of them said, "About half a mile over there behind that rise you'll find the dome. About eight miles south of here you'll find the latest cargo rocket—came in two days ago. The terrain is pretty rough so you'd better wait a few days to get used to the gravity before you go after it. We left some hot tea for you at the dome. Watch yourselves now." And again there was their noisy business of shaking hands. Both Fowler and McIntosh tried to see the faces of the two men they were replacing, but they could not. It was daytime on the Moon and the faceplate filters were all in place. Their radio voices sounded the same as they had on Earth.

The two disappeared into the ship with a final wave of hands. Fowler and McIntosh turned and carefully and awkwardly moved westward away from the ship. A quarter of a mile away they turned to watch it and for the first time the men had the chance to see the actual moonscape.

Pictures are wonderful things and they are of great aid in conveying information. The two men were prepared for what they saw, yet they were deeply shocked. Words and pictures are often adequate to impart a complete understanding of a place or event. Yet where human emotions are intertwined with an experience mere words and pictures are inadequate.

And so Fowler and McIntosh reeled slightly as the garish barrenness of the moonscape impressed itself on their minds. It might well be that on Earth there existed similar wild wastelands, but they were limited, and human beings had crossed them, and human beings could stand out on them unprotected and feel the familiar heat of day and the cold of night. Here there was only death for the unarmoured man, swift death like nothing on Earth. And nowhere were there human beings, nor any possibility of human beings. Only the darker and lighter places, no colour, black sky, white spots for stars, and the moonscape itself nothing but brilliant grey shades of tones between the white stars and the black sky.

So Fowler and McIntosh, knowing in advance what it would be like, still had to struggle to fight down an urge to scream at finding themselves in a place where men did not exist. They stared out through the smoked filters, wide-eyed, panting, fine drops of perspiration beading their foreheads. Each could hear the harsh breath of the other in the earphones, and it helped a little to know they both felt the same.

A spot of fire caught their attention and they turned slightly to see. The spaceship stood ungainly and awkward with a network of pipework surrounding the base. The spot of fire turned into a column of fire and the ship trembled. The column produced a flat bed of fire on the surface of the Moon and the ship rose slowly. There was no dust. A small stream of fire reached out sideways as a balancing rocket sprang to life. The ship rose farther, faster now, and Fowler and McIntosh leaned back to watch it. Once it cleared the Moon's horizon it lost apparent motion; it seemed to hover merely, and to grow smaller. They watched it until the fire was indistinguishable with the stars, then they looked around again.

It was a little better this time, since they were prepared for an emotional response. But in another sense it was worse for they were truly alone now. The horror of utter aloneness again welled up inside them. And without knowing what they were doing they drew closer together until the spacesuits touched. The gentle thud registered in each consciousness and brought their attention in to themselves. They pressed together for a moment while they fought to organize their thoughts.

And then McIntosh drew a long deep breath and shook his head violently. Fowler could feel the relief it brought. They moved apart and looked around.

McIntosh said, "Let's go get that tea they mentioned."

"Right," said Fowler. "I could use some. That's the dome there." And he pointed west.

They headed for it. They could see the dome in every detail; and as they approached, the details grew larger. It was almost impossible to judge distances on the Moon. Everything stood out with brilliant clarity no matter how far away. The only effect of distance was to cause a shrinking in size.

The dome was startling in its familiarity. It was the precise duplicate to the last bolt of the dome they had lived in and operated for months in the hi-vac chambers on Earth.

The air lock was built to accommodate two men in a pinch. They folded back the antennas that projected up from their packs and they crawled into the lock together; neither suggested going in one at a time. They waited while the pump filled the lock with air from the inside; then they pushed into the dome itself and stood up and looked around.

Automatically their eyes flickered from one gauge to another, checking to make sure everything was right with the dome. They removed their helmets and checked more closely. Air pressure was a little high, eight pounds. Fowler reached out to throw the switch to bring it down when he remembered that a decision had been made just before they left Earth to carry the pressure a little higher than had been the practice in the past. A matter of sleeping comfort.

"How's the pottet?" asked McIntosh. His voice sounded different from the way it had on Earth.

Fowler noted the difference—a matter of the difference in air density—as he crossed the twenty-foot dome and squatted to look into a bin with a transparent side. The bin bore the label in raised letters, Potassium Tetraoxide.

On Earth, water is the first worry of those who travel to out-of-the-way places. Food is next, with comfort close behind depending on the climate. On the Moon, oxygen was first. The main source of oxygen was potassium tetraoxide, a wonderful compound that gave up oxygen when exposed to moisture and then combined with carbon dioxide and removed it from the atmosphere. And each man needed some one thousand pounds of the chemical to survive on the Moon for twenty-eight days. A cylinder, bulky and heavy, of liquid air mounted under the sled supplied the air make-up in the dome. And a tank of water, well insulated by means of a hollow shiny shell open to the Moon's atmosphere, gave them water and served in part as the agent to release oxygen from the pottet when needed.

The dome checked out and by common consent both men swung to the radio, hungry for the reassuring sound of another human voice. McIntosh tuned it and said into the mike, "Moon Station to Earth. Fowler and McIntosh checking in. Everything in order. Over."

About four seconds later the transmitter emitted what the two men waited to hear. "Pole Number One to Moon. Welcome to the network. How are you, boys? Everything shipshape? Over."

McIntosh glanced at Fowler and a vision of the crevice swam before them. McIntosh said, "Everything fine, Pole Number One. Dome in order. Men in good shape. All's well on the Moon. Over."

About three seconds' wait, then, "Good. We will now take up Schedule Charlie. Time, 0641. Next check-in, 0900. Out." McIntosh hung up the mike quickly, and hit the switches to save power.

The two men removed their spacesuits and sat down on a low bench and poured tea from the thermos.

McIntosh was a stocky man with blue eyes and sandy hair cut short. He was built like a rectangular block of granite, thick chest, thick waist, thick legs; even his fingers seemed square in cross section. His movements were deliberate and conveyed an air of relentlessness.

Fowler was slightly taller than McIntosh. His hair and eyes were black, his skin dark. He was lean and walked with a slight stoop. His waist seemed too small and his shoulders too wide. He moved in a flowing sinuous manner like a cat perpetually stalking its prey.

They sipped the hot liquid gratefully, inhaling the wet fragrance of it. They carried their cups to the edge of the dome and looked out of the double layer of transparent resin that served as one of the windows. The filter was in place and they pushed against it and looked out.

"Dreary-looking place, isn't it?" said Fowler.

McIntosh nodded and said, "Funny, you don't get the feel of the complete barrenness by looking at pictures."

"I noticed that, too."

They sipped their tea, holding it close under their noses when they weren't drinking, looking out at the moonscape, trying to grasp it, adjusting their minds to it, thinking of the days ahead, and sipping their tea.

They finished, and Fowler said, "Well, time to get to work. You all set?"

McIntosh nodded. They climbed into their spacesuits and passed through the lock, one at a time. They checked over the exterior of the dome and every piece of mechanism mounted on the sled. Fowler mounted an outside seat, cleared with McIntosh, and started the drive motor. The great sled, complete with dome, parabolic mirror, spherical boilers, batteries, antennas, and a complex of other equipment rolled slowly forward on great, sponge-filled tyres. McIntosh walked beside it. Fowler watched his odometer and when the sled had moved five hunded yards he brought it to a halt. He dismounted and the two of them continued the survey started months back by their predecessors.

They took samples, they read radiation levels, they ran the survey, they ate and slept, they took more samples. They kept a rigid routine, for that was the way to make time pass, that was the way to preserve sanity.

The days passed. The two men grew accustomed to the low gravitation, so they recovered the cargo rocket. Yet they moved about with more than the usual caution for Moon men; their experience of the first few seconds on the Moon loomed forbiddingly on their minds. They had learned earlier than the others that an insignificant and trivial bit of negligence can cost a man his life.

So the days passed. And as time went by they became aware of another phenomenon of life on the Moon. On Earth, in an uncomfortable and dangerous situation, you become accustomed to the surroundings and can achieve a measure of relaxation. Not on the Moon. The dismal bright and less-bright greys, the oppressive barrenness of the grey moonscape, the utter aloneness of two men in a grey wilderness, slowly took on the tone of a grey malevolence seeking an unguarded moment. And the longer they stayed the worse it became. So the men kept themselves busier than ever. They accomplished more and more work, driving themselves to exhaustion, sinking into restless sleep, and up to work some more. They made more frequent five-hundred-yard jumps; they expanded the survey; they sought frozen water or frozen air deep in crevices, but they found only frozen carbon dioxide. They kept a careful eye on the pottet, for hard-working men consume more oxygen, and the supply was limited. And every time they checked the remaining supply they remembered what had happened to Booker and Whitman.

A pipeline had frozen. Booker took a bucket of water and began to skirt the pottet bin. The bail of the bucket caught on the corner of the lid of the bin. Booker carelessly hoisted the bucket to free it. The lid pulled open and the canvas bucket struck a corner and emptied into the bin. Instantly the dome filled with oxygen and steam. The safety valves opened and bled off the steam and oxygen to the outside, where it froze and fell like snow and slowly evaporated. The bin ruptured from the heat and broke a line carrying hydraulic fluid. Twenty gallons of hydraulic fluid flooded the pottet, reacting with it, forming potassium salts with the silicone liquid, releasing some oxygen, irretrievably locking up the rest.

Booker's backward leap caromed him off the ceiling and out of harm's way. After a horrified moment, the two men assessed the damage and calmly radioed Earth that they had a seven-Earth-day supply of oxygen left. Whereupon they stocked one spacesuit with a full supply of salvaged pottet and lay down on their bunks. For six Earth days they lay motionless; activity consumes oxygen. They lay calm; panic makes the heart beat faster and a racing blood stream consumes oxygen.

Two men lay motionless on the Moon. For four days slightly more than two thousand men on Earth struggled to get an off-schedule rocket to the Moon. The already fantastic requirements of fuel and equipment needed to put two men and supplies on the Moon every month had to be increased. The tempo of round-the-clock schedules stepped up to inhuman heights; there were two men lying motionless on the Moon.

It lacked but a few hours of the seven days when Booker and Whitman felt the shudder that told them a rocket had crash-landed nearby. They sat up and looked at each other, and it was apparent that Whitman had the most strength left. So Booker climbed into the spacesuit while Whitman lay down again. And Booker went out to the crashed rocket feeling strong from the fresh oxygen in the spacesuit. He scraped up pottet along with the silica dust and carried it in a broken container back into the dome. Whitman was almost unconscious by the time Booker got back and put water into the pottet. The two men lived. And by the time their replacements arrived the dome was again in as perfect condition as it had been. Except there was a different type of cover on the pottet bin.

So Fowler and McIntosh worked endlessly, ranging far out from the dome on their survey. The tension built up in them, for the worst was yet to come. The long Lunar day was fast drawing to a close, and night was about to fall. The night was fourteen Earth-days long. A black night broken only by the faint harsh starlight, a night where the imagination does things that the eyes would not allow in daylight.

"Well, here it comes," said McIntosh on the twelfth Earth-day. He pointed west. Fowler climbed up on the hummock beside him and looked. He saw the bottom half of the sun masked by a distant mountain range and a broad band of shadow reaching out towards them. The shadow stretched as far north and south as he could see.

"Yes," said Fowler. "It won't be long now. We'd better get back."

They jumped down from the hummock and started for the dome,

samples forgotten. At first they walked, throwing glances back over their shoulder. The pace grew faster until they were travelling the peculiar ground-consuming lope of men in a hurry under light gravity.

They reached the dome and went in together. Inside they removed their helmets and McIntosh headed for the radio. Fowler dropped a hand on his shoulder and said, "Wait, Mac. We have half an hour before we're due to check in."

McIntosh picked up a cloth and wiped his wet forehead, running the cloth through his sandy hair. "Yes," he said. "You're right. If we check in too soon they'll worry. Let's make some tea."

They removed their suits and brewed two steaming cupfuls. They sat down and sipped the scalding fluid and slowly relaxed a little.

"You know," said Fowler, "it's right about now that I'm glad we have an independent water supply. Repurified stuff would begin to taste bad about now."

McIntosh nodded. "I noticed it a day or two ago. I think I'd have trouble if the water weren't fresh." And the two men fell silent thinking of Tilton and Beck.

Tilton and Beck had been the second pair of men on the Moon. Very little water was sent up in those days, only enough for make-up. Tiny stills and ion-exchange resins purified all body waste products and produced a pure clear water pre-eminently suitable for drinking. Tilton and Beck had lived on that water for weeks on Earth and they, along with dozens of others, had pronounced it as fit to drink as clean cool spring water.

Then they went to the Moon. Two Earth-days after night fell Beck thought the water tasted bad. Tilton did, too. They knew the water was sweet and clean, they knew it was their imagination that gave the water its taste, but they could not help it. They reached a point where the water wrenched at their inside; it tasted so foul they could not drink it. Then they radioed Earth for help, and began living off the make-up water. But Earth was not as experienced in emergency rocket send-offs in those days. The pleas for decent water for the men on the Moon grew weaker. The first rocket might have saved them, except its controls were erratic and it crash-landed five hundred miles from the dome. The second rocket carried the replacements, and when they entered the dome they found Tilton and Beck dead, cheeks sunken, skin parched, lips cracked and broken, dehydrated, dead of thirst. And within easy reach of the two dried-out bodies was twenty-five gallons of clear, pure—almost chemically pure—tasteless, odourless water, sparkling bright with dissolved oxygen.

Fowler and McIntosh finished their tea and radioed in at check time. They announced that night had overtaken them. A new schedule was set up, one with far more frequent radio contacts with Earth. And immediately they set about their new tasks. No more trips far from the dome, no surveying. They broke the telescope from its cover and set up the spectrometer. Inside the dome they converted part of the drafting table to a small but astonishingly complete analytical chemical laboratory.

The sun was gone completely now, but off to the east several mountain tops still glistened like the last flame that shoots up from an expiring fire. In an hour the gleam disappeared and night was completely come.

The planners of the Moon survey from the very beginning recognized that night on the Moon presented a difficult problem. So they scheduled replacements to arrive when the Moon day was about forty-eight hours old. Thus the replacements had twelve Earth-days of sunlight on the Moon to get themselves ready for the emotional ordeal of fourteen Earth-days of darkness. Then once the long night was ended, they had two Earth-days of sunlight before the next replacements arrived. Such a system insured that the spaceship landed on the Moon in daylight and also allowed optimum psychological adjustment for the Moon men. Shorter periods of residence on the Moon were not feasible, since the full twenty-eight days were needed to prepare for the shuttle flight from Earth to the space station, from the space station to the Moon, and return. Then, too, at least one supply rocket a month had to be crash-landed within easy walking distance of the dome. The effort and money expended by the United States to do these things were prodigious. But with the backing of the people, the project went ahead. Future property rights on the Moon might well go to the nation that continuously occupied it.

Fowler looked up from adjusting the telescope and said, "Look at that, Al." His arm pointed to the Earth brightly swimming in a sea of star-pointed blackness.

They saw the Western Hemisphere, white-dotted with clouds, and a brilliant blinding spot of white in the South Pacific off the coast of Peru where the ocean reflected the sun's light to them.

McIntosh said, "Beautiful, isn't it? I can just about see Florida. Good old Orlando. I'll bet the lemon blossoms smell good these days. You know, it looks even better at night than it does in day."

Fowler nodded inside his helmet as the two continued to watch the Earth. Fowler said, "You know, we've certainly gone and loused up a good old Earth tradition."

"What do you mean?"

"Well, picture it. A guy and his girl go out walking in the moonlight down there. They'd sigh and feel all choked up and gaze at the Moon and feel like the Moon was made for them alone. Now when they look up they know there's a couple of slobs sprinting around up here. It must take something away."

"I'll bet," chuckled McIntosh. "They must either get mad at us or feel very sorry for us."

Fowler dropped his gaze to the moonscape and looked around and said, "It sure looks different here at night."

They studied the eerie scene. As always, it showed nothing but varying shades of grey, but now the tones were dark and foreboding. The sharp, dim starlight and soft Earthshine threw no shadows but spread a ghostly luminescence over ridge and draw alike. It was impossible to tell just where the actual seeing left off and the imagination began.

Fowler muttered, almost under his breath, "The night is full of forms of fear."

"What?"

"The night is full of forms of fear. It's a line I read some place."

They looked around in silence, turning the ungainly spacesuits. McIntosh said, "It sure describes this place. Never saw such a weird sight."

They finally shrugged off the fascination of the moonscape and got to work.

Several Earth-days passed. The two men kept busy making astronomical observation and checking out some of the minerals collected during the long day. They made short trips out into the region around the dome but they took no samples; they let the scintillation counters built into their suits do the probing for hot spots as they simply walked around. They never got too far from the dome or from each other. And often while they were outside striding through the moondust on their separate paths, one of them would say, "How're things?" And the other would say, "O.K., how're things there?" The urge to hear a human voice rose powerful and often in the Moon night.

It was on one of these outside trips that their first real panic occurred. The two men were each about a hundred yards away from the dome and on opposite sides. McIntosh did not notice a telltale slight dip in the dust where a shallow crack lay almost filled with light flourlike particles. His foot went in. He twisted and fell on his back so that his caught leg would bend at the knee and not wrench the knee-joint of the suit. He hit with a jolt; his forward speed added to the normal speed of fall. The impact was not great but it clanged loudly inside the suit. McIntosh grunted, and said "damn," and sat up to free his foot. Fowler's voice sounded in his headphones. "You O.K., Mac?"

"Yeah," said McIntosh. "I fell down but I'm not hurt a bit. Things are fine."

"Mac," Fowler's voice was shrill. "You O.K.?"

"Yes. Not a thing wrong. Just took a—"

"For God's sake, Mac, answer me." Fowler's voice was a near scream, panic bubbling through it.

The fear was contagious. McIntosh yanked his foot out of the crevice, leaped to his feet, and ran for the dome shouting, "What is it, Walt? What's the matter? I'm coming. What is it?" And as he ran he could hear Fowler screaming now for Walt to answer.

McIntosh rounded the dome and almost collided with Fowler coming in the opposite direction. The two slipped and skidded to a halt, clouds of dust kicking up around their feet and settling as fast as they rose. Once stopped, the two men jumped towards each other and touched helmets.

"What is it, Walt?" shouted McIntosh.

"What happened to you?" came Fowler's voice, choked, gasping. McIntosh could hear it both through the helmet and through his headphones. It sounded hollow.

McIntosh shouted again. "I took a little spill, that's all. I told you I was all right over the set. Didn't you hear me?"

"No," Fowler was getting himself under control. "I kept calling you and getting no answer. Something must be wrong with the sets."

"Yeah. It's either your receiver or my transmitter. Let's go in and check them out."

They entered the dome together and removed their suits. They wiped the sweat from their faces and automatically started to make tea, but they stopped. Power was in short supply during the night and hot water had to be held to a minimum. So they checked the radios instead.

They went over McIntosh's transmitter first, since he had had the fall. They soon found the trouble. A tiny grain of silica shorted a condenser in the printed circuit. It was easily fixed and then the transmitter worked again. They put on the suits and went outside. But the shock they suffered was not so easily remedied. And thereafter when they were outside they were never out of sight of each other.

Time went by. The looming loneliness of the brooding moonscape closed ever more tightly around them. Their surroundings took on the stature of a living thing, menacing, waiting, lurking. Even the radio contacts with Earth lost much of their meaning; the voices were just voices, not really belonging to people, but emanating from some ominous creature poised just over the ridge. The loneliness grew.

On Earth a man can be deep in a trackless and impenetrable jungle, yet there is a chance a fellow human being will happen by. A man can be isolated on the remotest of desert islands and still maintain a reasonable hope that a ship, a canoe, or plane will carry another human being to him. A man sentenced to a life of solitary confinement knows for certain that there are people on the other side of the wall.

But on the Moon there is complete aloneness. There are no human beings and—what is worse—no possibility of any human beings. And never before had men, two men, found themselves in such a position.

The human mind, adaptable entity that it is, nevertheless had to reach beyond its boundaries to absorb the reality of perfect isolation.

The Lunar night wore on. Fowler and McIntosh were out spreading their dirty laundry for the usual three-hour exposure to Moon conditions before shaking the clothes out and packing them away till they were needed again.

Fowler straightened up and looked at the Earth for a moment, then said, "Mac, did you ever eat in a diner on a train?"

"Sure, many times."

"You remember how the headwaiter seated people?"

McIntosh thought for a moment then said, "I know what you mean. He keeps them apart. He seats individuals at empty tables until there are no more empty tables; then he begins to double them up."

"That's it. He preserves the illusion of isolation. I guess people don't know how much they need one another."

"I guess they don't. People are funny that way."

They grinned at each other through the faceplates, although it was too dark to see inside the spacesuits. They finished spreading the laundry and went into the dome together. Both of them had recently come to realize a striking thing. If one of them died, the other could not survive. It was difficult enough to preserve sanity with two. One alone could not last an Earth-day. The men on the Moon lived in pairs or they died in pairs. And if Fowler and McIntosh had thought to look at each other closely, they would have noticed a few incipient lines radiating from the eyes. Nothing abnormal, and certainly nothing as intense as the far look. Just the suggestion of a few lines around the eyes.

The night had only two Earth-days to run. Fowler and McIntosh for the first time began to turn their thoughts to the journey home, not with longing, not with anticipation, but as a possibility of something that might happen. The actuality of leaving the Moon seemed too unreal to be true. And the cold harsh fact was that the rocket might not come; it had happened before. So though they dimly realized that in a mere four Earth-days they might leave the grim greyness behind, they were not much concerned.

A series of observation ended. Fowler and McIntosh sipped hot tea, drawing the warmth into their chilled bodies. Fowler sat perched on one end of a bench. McIntosh cupped the teacup in his hands and stood looking out at the lowering moonscape, wishing he could pull his eyes from it, too fascinated by its awfulness to do so. There was complete silence in the dome.

"Don." The word came as a gasp, as though McIntosh had called the name before he had completely swallowed a mouthful of tea.

Fowler looked up, mildly curious. He saw McIntosh drop the teacup, saw it bounce off the floor. He saw McIntosh straining forward, taut, neck muscles standing out, mouth open, one hand against the clear plastic.

"Don. *I saw something move out there.*" The words were shrill, harsh, hysteria in every syllable.

Fowler landed beside him in a single leap and looked, not out of the window, but at his face. At the staring terror-filled eyes, the drawn mouth. Fowler threw his arms around McIntosh's chest and squeezed hard and said, "Easy, Mac, easy. Don't let the shadows get you. Things are all right."

"I tell you I saw something. A sudden movement. Near that hillock but at a greater range and to the right. Something moved, Don." And he inhaled a great shuddering gasp.

Fowler kept his arms around McIntosh and looked out. He saw only the jagged dim surface of the Moon. For a long moment he looked out, listening to McIntosh's gasping breath, a chill fear slowly rising inside him. He turned his head to look at McIntosh's face again, and as he did he caught a flicker of motion out of the corner of his eye. He dropped his arms and jerked his head back to look out as McIntosh screamed, "There, there it is again, but it's moved."

The two men, both panting, strained at the window. For a full minute they stood with every muscle pulled tight, gulping down air, perspiration prickling out of their scalps and running down over face and neck. Their eyes saw fantastic shapes in the sharp dim light but their minds told them it was imagination.

Then they saw it clearly. About one hundred yards straight out in front of the window a tiny fountain of moondust sprayed upwards and outwards from a glowing base that winked out as swiftly as it appeared. Like the blossoming of a death-coloured grey rose, the dust from a handspread of surface suddenly rose and spread outward in a circle and just as suddenly fell back to the surface.

"What is it?" hissed Fowler.

"I don't know."

They watched, the tension so great that they shuddered. They saw another one, bigger, out farther and to the left. They watched. Another, small, in much closer, the brief white base instantly flashing through shades of deeper reds and disappearing.

"Spacesuits," gasped Fowler. "Get into the spacesuits."

And he turned and jumped to the rack, McIntosh alongside him. They slipped into the cumbersome suits with the swift smoothness of long practice. They twisted the helmets on.

"Radio O.K.?" said McIntosh.

"Check. Let's look."

And the two jumped back to the window. The activity outside seemed to have stopped. They watched for six full minutes before they saw another of the dust fountains. After they saw it, they twisted their suits to look at each other. They were bringing themselves under control. They were rationally trying to reason out a cause for what they saw.

"Any ideas?" said McIntosh.

"No," said Fowler. "Let's look out of the other windows and see if we see anything."

They took up separate places at the two remaining windows.

"See anything?" said Fowler.

"Nothing. Just that hideous-looking terrain. I guess it's all on the other—Wait. There's one. Way out. I could just—"

"I've got one, too," said Fowler. "It's all around us. Let's call Earth."

They moved over to the radio. Fowler turned the volume high and McIntosh hit the On switch. Almost immediately they heard a voice, mounting swiftly in loudness. "Station Number One to Moon Station. Station Number One to Moon Station." Over and over it repeated the words.

McIntosh touched a microphone to his helmet, flipped the Transmit switch and said, "Moon Station to Station Number One. We hear you. Over."

"Thank God," came the voice. "Listen. The Leonid meteor swarm may hit you. Find cover. Find a cave or bridge and get out of the open. Repeat. Meteor swarm may hit you. Find cover. Over."

At the word "meteor" McIntosh swung to face Fowler. The two moved closer together to see into the faceplates. Each face broke into a smile of relief at the knowledge of what was happening.

McIntosh touched the microphone to his helmet and said, "We're already in it. There is no cave or other shelter within forty miles. How long do you expect the shower—"

There was a thunderous explosion and a brilliant flash of light that seared the eyeballs of both men. Something heavy dropped on them and gently clung to the spacesuits. They struggled futilely against the softness that enfolded them. McIntosh dropped the microphone and flailed his arms. Fowler sought to lift off the cloying substance; he dropped to one knee and fought it, but it would not give. Both men fought blind; the caressing enfolding material brought complete blackness.

McIntosh felt something grip his ankle and he lashed out with his foot. He felt it crash against something hard, but something that rolled with his kick and then bore back against his legs and knocked him over. His arms were still entangled in the material but he tried to flail the thing that crawled on top of him. With a superhuman effort he encircled the upper portion of the thing with layers of the soft material and began to squeeze. Through the thickness of the material he felt the familiar outline of a helmet with a short flexible antenna reaching up from the back. And he realized he was fighting Fowler.

He felt Fowler pull away the material that separated them. Then he heard Fowler's voice.

"Mac, it's me. The dome's punctured and fallen in on us. You hear me?"

"Yes," said McIntosh, gasping for air. "I don't know what happened. You all right?"

"Yes. Let's get out of here. Shoulder to shoulder till we find the lock. Let's go."

They crawled side by side, lifting the heavy leaded plastic in front of them. They bumped into the drafting table and oriented themselves. They passed out through the useless lock and stood up outside and looked at the dome.

It is a terrible thing when a man's home is destroyed. The agony of standing and looking at the ruins of all a man holds near and dear is a heavy burden on the human heart. But on Earth a man can go elsewhere; he has relatives, friends, to turn to. His heart may be heavy, but his life is not in peril.

But Fowler and McIntosh were on the Moon. They looked at their collapsed dome and doom itself froze around their hearts. There was no one to turn to, no place to go. They stood alone on a frozen, shadow-ridden, human-hating world. They stood hand in hand with death.

They looked at the collapsed dome and the way it lay over the equipment they knew so well, softening the sharp angles, filling in the hollow spaces in the interior. The equipment outside looked stark and awkward, standing high, silhouetted against the luminous greyness, looking forlorn. The antenna caught McIntosh's eye.

He swallowed heavily and said, "Let's radio Earth and give them the news. We were talking to them when we got hit."

Fowler dumbly followed him to a small box on the far side of the sled and watched him remove the mike and receiver from a small box. McIntosh faced out from the sled and held the receiver against one side of the helmet and the mike against the other. Fowler slipped behind him. They stood back to back, helmets touching, McIntosh doing the talking, Fowler operating the switches and listening to all that was said. The receiver was silent when Fowler turned it on. Earth was listening, waiting. He switched to Transmit and nudged McIntosh.

"Moon Station to Space Station Number One. Over."

In five seconds a voice came back. "Pole Station to Moon Station. Space Station Number One is out of line-of-sight. What happened? You all right?"

"Yes. Meteor punctured dome. We're outside. Over."

It was considerably more than five seconds before the voice came back, quieter but more intense. "Can you fix it?"

"We don't know. We'll go over the damage and talk to you soon. Out."

McIntosh dropped his hands and Fowler turned the switch off.

"Well," said McIntosh, "we'd better see how bad it is. They may want to call the whole thing off."

Fowler nodded. Getting the sled and dome and equipment to the Moon had called for prodigious effort and staggering cost. It could not be duplicated in a hurry. Their replacements were already on the way. The dome had to be operating if they were to stay. And the spaceship could only carry two men back.

"Let's look it over," said Fowler. As they turned to climb up on the sled a fountain of dust sprang up ten feet to their right. They looked out over the sullen moonscape; the meteors were still falling. But they didn't care. They climbed up on the sled and carefully picked their way on top of the collapsed material to where they had been standing when the meteor struck. They pulled out several folds and found the hole. They inspected it with growing excitement.

The hole was a foot in diameter, neatly round. Around the perimeter was a thick ridge charred slightly on the inner edge where the thermoplastic material had fused and rolled back. The ridge had strengthened the material and prevented it from splitting and tearing when the air in the dome rushed out. The hole in the inner layer measured about eighteen inches in diameter and the encircling ridge was even thicker.

Fowler held the hand-powered flashlight on the material surrounding the holes while he examined it carefully. "Mac," he said, "we can fix it. We've got enough scrap dome plastic to seal these holes. Let's see if the meteor went out the bottom."

They moved the holes around on the floor of the dome and found a four-inch hole through the plastic floor. Looking down it, they could see a small crater in the Moon's surface half-filled with a white solid.

McIntosh said, "It went through one of the batteries, but we won't miss it. We've got some scrap flooring plastic and some insulation around. We can fix this, too. Our make-up air is in good supply. Don," he stood up, "we're gonna make it."

"Yes," said Fowler, letting the light go out. "Let's radio Earth."

They went back to the set and Fowler reported their findings. They could hear the joy come back in the man's voice as he wished them luck and told them an extra rocket with make-up air would be on the way soon. Then the voice asked, "What about the meteor shower?"

Fowler and McIntosh looked around; they had forgotten the meteors again. The spurts of moondust still sprang up; they could see them clearly against the grey and black shadows.

"They're still falling," said Fowler. "Nothing to do but sweat them out. Call you later. Out." And he and McIntosh sat down. A nation sweat it out with them. An entire people felt fear strike at their hearts at the thought of two men sitting beside a collapsed dome amidst a shower of invisible cosmic motes travelling at unthinkable speed. But though the entire nation felt the horror of their position and wished them well with all its heart, it was not of the slightest aid to the two men on the Moon.

Quiet they sat and dumb. The meteors, forgotten for a moment, were to them now a part of the foreboding moonscape, challenging the presence of men in such a place. A mere light touch from a cosmic pebble, and a human life would snuff out. They sat quiet and dumb, looking at the moonscape grim as death. A touch on the hand, the foot, is enough; it would take so little. They were something apart from the human race, men, yet not men. For no man could be so alone as they, such a speck, a trifle, a nothing, so alone were they. Quiet they sat and dumb. But each man's heart beat thick and quick like a madman on a drum. And the meteors fell.

"Mac."

"Yes."

"Why do we sit here? Why don't we fix it?"

"Suppose it gets hit again?"

"Suppose it does. It'll be hit whether it's collapsed or full. At least we'll have these holes patched. Maybe it'll be easier for the next team. Let's patch the holes anyway and then see what's happening."

McIntosh stood up. "Of course," he said. "We can get that much done no matter what happens."

Fowler stood up and began to turn to the sled to climb up. A tiny spot of brightness suddenly appeared on McIntosh's left shoulder. With a feeling of blackness closing in on his body, Fowler flung himself at McIntosh and clamped a hand over the spot where the glow had been. The weight of his body knocked McIntosh down but Fowler clung to him, kept his hand pressed firmly against the spot where the meteor had hit.

"Mac," said Fowler with the taste of copper in his mouth. "Mac. Can you hear me?"

"I hear you fine. What's the matter with you? You like to scare me to death."

"You got hit. On the left shoulder. Your suit must be punctured. I've got my hand over it."

"Don, I didn't even feel it. There can't possibly be a hole there or I'd have felt the air go, or at least some of it. Take a look."

They got to their feet. Fowler kept his hand in place while he retrieved the flashlight. He got it going and quickly removed his hand and showed the light over the spot to look. At first he saw nothing, so he held his helmet closer. Then he saw it. A tiny crater so small as to amount to nothing beyond a slight disturbance of the shiny surface of the suit. Smaller than the head of a pin it was and not as deep as it was broad.

He let the light go out and said in a choked voice, "Must have been a small one, smaller than a grain of sand. No damage at all."

"Good. Let's get to work."

They cut out two four-foot squares of dome material and several chunks of flooring plastic. They filled the bottom of the hole in the floor with five inches of insulation. They plugged in a wedge-shaped soldering iron and melted the plastic and worked it in to the top three inches of flooring, making an undercut to seal the hole solidly. And the floor was fixed.

Fowler pulled over the squares of dome material while McIntosh adjusted the temperature of the iron to that just below the melting point of the material. Fowler placed the first square inside the hole in the inner layer. He ran the hot blade around the ridge of fused plastic. It sealed well; the thick, leaded, shiny, dome material stiffly flowed together and solidified. Fowler sealed the patches in place with a series of five fused circles concentric to the hole and spaced about three inches apart. The inner hole was hard to work with, for he had to reach through the outer hole, but he managed it. The outer hole went fast. And when they finished they were certain that the dome was as good as ever.

They stood up from their work and looked around. Out on to the moonscape they looked long and carefully. And nowhere could they see one of the dread dust fountains. Slowly and carefully they walked to the edge of the sled and dropped off. They sat down and looked some more, carefully preventing their imaginations from picturing things more fantastic than what was already there. After ten minutes there was no doubt about it, the meteor shower was over.

"Let's blow her up," said Fowler.

McIntosh checked the heated outlet from the air cylinder and then passed current through the coils that heated the cylinder itself. At his O.K., Fowler cracked the valve and air began to flow into the dome. They watched it carefully as it rose, looking for the tell-tale white streams that told of a leak. There were none detectable in either layer. And in half an hour the dome stood full and taut with a good five pounds pressure inside. They went in through the lock together.

McIntosh started the light tube while Fowler began a check of the gauges. In ten minutes it was apparent that things were in order. The dome was warming up too, so they took off their helmets, keeping a wary eye on the gauges. Soon they took off their suits.

The radio was still on, so Fowler called in to Earth that everything was in order. The voice was warm and friendly, congratulating them on their work and passing on the reassurances of men everywhere. They learned that their replacements were on schedule, so far. Fowler signed off.

The two men looked up at the patch on the ceiling, with its corners dangling downward. They looked at each other and Fowler started to make tea. McIntosh walked to a window and as he got there his feet started to slip out from under him. He caught himself and bent to see what he had slipped on. He found a thin sheet of ice on the floor.

"Where'd this come from?" he asked.

Fowler looked over and smiled and said, "That's from the cup of tea you dropped when you saw the first meteor. Remember?"

"Oooh, yes." And McIntosh chipped it up and put it in the waste pot to be purified and used on the pottet.

They had their tea, and they slept long and restlessly. They picked up their work schedule, and very soon they could see the brightness on the mountain tops to the west. The sun was coming back.

But it brought no joy. They were beyond any emotional response to night or day. Bright grey or dark grey, it did not matter. It was the Moon they were on and the lightness and darkness were all the same.

On the second Earth-day of sunlight they spoke to the approaching spaceship and made preparations to leave. The laundry was all done and ready for use. The dome was tidy. Their last job was to brew tea and put it in the thermos to keep it hot for their replacements; they would need it.

They donned their spacesuits for the last time on the Moon and went out of the lock together. They watched the little flame in the black sky grow larger.

The ship landed and the dust settled immediately. Fowler and McIntosh walked slowly towards the ship; they did not hurry. The door in the side opened, a ladder dropped out, and two suited figures climbed awkwardly to the Moon's surface.

Before they had a chance to look around, McIntosh called, "Over here. The dome is over here."

The four men came together and shook hands. Fowler said, "You can see the dome there." He pointed to it a half mile away. "We've left some hot tea for you there. The terrain is pretty rough so watch yourself moving around for a few days. Good luck." They shook hands. The replacements headed for the dome while Fowler and McIntosh went to the ship and climbed in without looking back. They dogged home the lock, removed their suits, stretched out on the acceleration bunks, and called "O.K.," into the intercom.

"Right," said the pilot from his compartment. "Welcome aboard and stand by."

In a moment they felt the acceleration, steadily mounting. But it soon eased off, and they slept. For most of the five-day journey they slept. And if they had thought to look at each other during their few waking hours, they would have seen nothing unusual—a few incipient, almost invisible lines around the eyes, nothing more. Neither Fowler nor McIntosh had the far look.

The ship reached the space station and tied to it. Fowler and McIntosh transferred to the shuttle and swiftly dropped towards Earth. They heard the air whistle as the air thickened.

The television cameras first picked up the ship as a small dot. People the world over craned forward to watch as the bellyskids touched the sand—people who did not know that the ship carried two Moon men who did not have the far look. The people watched the ship skid to a halt amidst a slowly settling cloud of dust.

And as they watched, the door amidships swung in. The sun slanted in through the door and showed two figures standing there. The figures moved to a point just inside the door and stopped. They stood there motionless, looking out for what seemed an interminable period.

As Fowler and McIntosh looked out of the door, they saw the shimmering sands of the New Mexico desert. But they saw more than that. They saw more than home. They saw the spawning place of the human race. In a roaring rush of recognition, they knew they had done more than simply return to Earth. They had rejoined the human race. They had been apart and were now once again with that brawling, pesky, restless race in which all were brothers, all were one. This was not a return to Earth. This was a return to the womb, to the womb that had nourished them and made them men. A flood of sympathy and heart-felt understanding poured through them as they stared out at the shimmering sands. The kinks and twists of personality fell away and left men of untrammelled mind.

Fowler and McIntosh looked at each other, nodded, and jumped out of the door. They fell to their knees in the unaccustomed gravity. They quickly arose, knocked the dust from their clothes, and started walking to where the helicopters were waiting.

The zoom lenses on the television cameras went to work and the faces of Fowler and McIntosh side by side flashed across the country.

And the eyes were different. A network of deep tiny creases laced out from the corners of each eye. The crinkled appearance of the eyes made each man appear older than he actually was. And there was a look in those eyes of things seen from deep inside. It was a far look, a compelling look, a powerful look set in the eyes of normal men.

QUESTIONS

1. Why do so many science fiction astronauts have blue eyes?

2. Why is there now a lack of public interest in the splashdown of American spaceships? In your opinion, was the space program worthwhile? Do you think it was a form of entertainment somewhat like the circuses of ancient Rome? Give reasons for your opinion.

3. Have "real-life" astronauts spoken of their loneliness? Why might they have chosen to do so or not to do so?

4. How would you describe the relationship between each pair of astronauts?

5. Is it possible to get "the far look" on Earth?

6. What does the cosmic awareness implied in the far look suggest?

7. In this story, the stay on the moon seems to have turned two ordinary "guys" into superheroes. Describe the "before" and "after" astronaut presented in "The Far Look."

8. Compare this story to Norman Mailer's description in the selection from *Of a Fire on the Moon.*

Of Mist, and Grass, and Sand

Vonda N. McIntyre

"Of Mist, and Grass, and Sand" is a multidimensioned, paradoxical story for the SF genre. Its scientist is supremely capable and a woman; its male lead plays a secondary role, but is not feminized; the harm committed out of ignorance is not irreparable. This 1974 Hugo winning story is an example of how fine characterization, style, and mood can be used in SF. Its author is gaining recognition as one of contemporary science fiction's outstanding writers.

Vonda McIntyre has a B.S. in biology—an invaluable asset for a science fiction writer. She is "coeditor of an anthology of original nonsexist SF stories, Aurora: Beyond Equality," *and has written the novel* The Clouds Return.

The little boy was frightened. Gently, Snake touched his hot forehead. Behind her, three adults stood close together, watching, suspicious, afraid to show their concern with more than narrow lines around their eyes. They feared Snake as much as they feared their only child's death. In the dimness of the tent, the flickering lamplights gave no reassurance.

The child watched with eyes so dark the pupils were not visible, so dull that Snake herself feared for his life. She stroked his hair. It was long and very pale, a striking color against his dark skin, dry and irregular for several inches near the scalp. Had Snake been with these people months ago, she would have known the child was growing ill.

"Bring my case, please," Snake said.

The child's parents started at her soft voice. Perhaps they had expected the screech of a bright jay, or the hissing of a shining serpent. This was the first time Snake had spoken in their presence. She had only watched, when the three of them had come to observe her from a distance and whisper about her occupation and her youth; she had only listened, and then nodded, when finally they came to ask her help. Perhaps they had thought she was mute.

The fair-haired younger man lifted her leather case. He held the satchel away from his body, leaning to hand it to her, breathing shallowly with nostrils flared against the faint smell of musk in the dry desert air. Snake had almost accustomed herself to the kind of uneasiness he showed; she had already seen it often.

When Snake reached out, the young man jerked back and dropped the case. Snake lunged and barely caught it, gently set it on the felt floor, and glanced at him with reproach. His husband and his wife came forward and touched him to ease his fear. "He was bitten once," the dark and handsome woman said. "He almost died." Her tone was not of apology, but of justification.

"I'm sorry," the younger man said. "It's—" He gestured toward her; he was trembling, and trying visibly to control the reactions of his fear. Snake glanced down, to her shoulder, where she had been unconsciously aware of the slight weight and movement. A tiny serpent, thin as the finger of a baby, slid himself around her neck to show his narrow head below her short black curls. He probed the air with his trident tongue in a leisurely manner, out, up and down, in, to savor the taste of the smells. "It's only Grass," Snake said. "He cannot harm you." If he were bigger, he might frighten; his color was pale green, but the scales around his mouth were red, as if he had just feasted as a mammal eats, by tearing. He was, in fact, much neater.

The child whimpered. He cut off the sound of pain; perhaps he had been told that Snake, too, would be offended by crying. She only felt sorry that his people refused themselves such a simple way of easing fear. She turned from the adults, regretting their terror of her but unwilling to spend the time it would take to convince them their reactions were unjustified. "It's all right," she said to the little boy. "Grass is smooth, and dry, and soft, and if I left him to guard you, even death could not reach your bedside." Grass poured himself into her narrow, dirty hand, and she extended him toward the child. "Gently." He reached out and touched the sleek scales with one fingertip. Snake could sense the effort of even such a simple motion, yet the boy almost smiled.

"What are you called?"

He looked quickly toward his parents, and finally they nodded. "Stavin," he whispered. He had no strength or breath for speaking.

"I am Snake, Stavin, and in a little while, in the morning, I must hurt you. You may feel a quick pain, and your body will ache for several days, but you will be better afterwards."

He stared at her solemnly. Snake saw that though he understood and feared what she might do, he was less afraid than if she had lied to him. The pain must have increased greatly as his illness became more apparent, but it seemed that others had only reassured him, and hoped the disease would disappear or kill him quickly.

Snake put Grass on the boy's pillow and pulled her case nearer. The lock opened at her touch. The adults still could only fear her; they had had neither time nor reason to discover any trust. The wife was old enough that they might never have another child, and Snake could tell by their eyes, their covert touching, their concern, that they loved this one very much. They must, to come to Snake in this country.

It was night, and cooling. Sluggish, Sand slid out of the case, moving his head, moving his tongue, smelling, tasting, detecting the warmths of bodies.

"Is that—?" The older husband's voice was low, and wise, but terrified, and Sand sensed the fear. He drew back into striking position and sounded his rattle softly. Snake spoke, moving her hand, and extended her arm. The pit viper relaxed and flowed around and around her slender wrist to form black and tan bracelets. "No," she said. "Your child is too ill for Sand to help. I know it is hard, but please try to be calm. This is a fearful thing for you, but it is all I can do."

She had to annoy Mist to make her come out. Snake rapped on the bag, and finally poked her twice. Snake felt the vibration of sliding scales, and suddenly the albino cobra flung herself into the tent. She moved quickly, yet there seemed to be no end to her. She reared back and up. Her breath rushed out in a hiss. Her head rose well over a meter above the floor. She flared her wide hood. Behind her, the adults gasped, as if physically assaulted by the gaze of the tan spectacle design on the back of Mist's hood. Snake ignored the people and spoke to the great cobra, focusing her attention by her words. "Ah, thou. Furious creature. Lie down; 'tis time for thee to earn thy dinner. Speak to this child, and touch him. He is called Stavin." Slowly, Mist relaxed her hood and allowed Snake to touch her. Snake grasped her firmly behind the head, and held her so she looked at Stavin. The cobra's silver eyes picked up the yellow of the lamplight. "Stavin," Snake said, "Mist will only meet you now. I promise that this time she will touch you gently."

Still, Stavin shivered when Mist touched his thin chest. Snake did not release the serpent's head, but allowed her body to slide against the boy's. The cobra was four times longer than Stavin was tall. She curved herself in stark white loops across his swollen abdomen, extending herself, forcing her head toward the boy's face, straining against Snake's hands. Mist met Stavin's frightened stare with the gaze of lidless eyes. Snake allowed her a little closer.

Mist flicked out her tongue to taste the child.

The younger husband made a small, cut-off, frightened sound. Stavin flinched at it, and Mist drew back, opening her mouth, exposing her fangs, audibly thrusting her breath through her throat. Snake sat back on her heels, letting out her own breath. Sometimes, in other places, the kinfolk could stay while she worked. "You must leave," she said gently. "It's dangerous to frighten Mist."

"I won't—"

"I'm sorry. You must wait outside."

Perhaps the younger husband, perhaps even the wife, would have made the indefensible objections and asked the answerable questions, but the older man turned them and took their hands and led them away.

"I need a small animal," Snake said as he lifted the tent-flap. "It must have fur, and it must be alive."

"One will be found," he said, and the three parents went into the glowing night. Snake could hear their footsteps in the sand outside.

Snake supported Mist in her lap and soothed her. The cobra wrapped herself around Snake's narrow waist, taking in her warmth. Hunger made the cobra even more nervous than usual, and she was hungry, as was Snake. Coming across the black sand desert, they had found sufficient water, but Snake's traps were unsuccessful. The season was summer, the weather was hot, and many of the furry tidbits Sand and Mist preferred were estivating. When the serpents missed their regular meal, Snake began a fast as well.

She saw with regret that Stavin was more frightened now. "I am sorry to send your parents away," she said. "They can come back soon."

His eyes glistened, but he held back the tears. "They said to do what you told me."

"I would have you cry, if you are able," Snake said. "It isn't such a terrible thing." But Stavin seemed not to understand, and Snake did not press him; she knew that his people taught themselves to resist a difficult land by refusing to cry, refusing to mourn, refusing to laugh. They denied themselves grief, and allowed themselves little joy, but they survived.

Mist had calmed to sullenness. Snake unwrapped her from her waist and placed her on the pallet next to Stavin. As the cobra moved, Snake guided her head, feeling the tension of the striking muscles. "She will touch you with her tongue," she told Stavin. "It might tickle, but it will not hurt. She smells with it, as you do with your nose."

"With her tongue?"

Snake nodded, smiling, and Mist flicked out her tongue to caress Stavin's cheek. Stavin did not flinch; he watched, his child's delight in knowledge briefly overcoming pain. He lay perfectly still as Mist's long tongue brushed his cheeks, his eyes, his mouth. "She tastes the sickness," Snake said. Mist stopped fighting the restraint of her grasp, and drew back her head. Snake sat on her heels and released the cobra, who spiraled up her arm and laid herself across her shoulders.

"Go to sleep, Stavin," Snake said. "Try to trust me, and try not to fear the morning."

Stavin gazed at her for a few seconds, searching for truth in Snake's pale eyes. "Will Grass watch?"

She was startled by the question, or, rather, by the acceptance behind the question. She brushed his hair from his forehead and smiled a smile that was tears just beneath the surface. "Of course." She picked Grass up. "Thou wilt watch this child, and guard him." The snake lay quiet in her hand, and his eyes glittered black. She laid him gently on Stavin's pillow.

"Now sleep."

Stavin closed his eyes, and the life seemed to flow out of him. The alteration was so great that Snake reached out to touch him, then saw that he was breathing, slowly, shallowly. She tucked a blanket around him and stood up. The abrupt change in position dizzied her; she staggered and caught herself. Across her shoulders, Mist tensed.

Snake's eyes stung and her vision was over-sharp, fever-clear. The sound she imagined she heard swooped in closer. She steadied herself against hunger and exhaustion, bent slowly, and picked up the leather case. Mist touched her cheek with the tip of her tongue.

She pushed aside the tent-flap and felt relief that it was still night. She could stand the heat, but the brightness of the sun curled through her, burning. The moon must be full; though the clouds obscured everything, they diffused the light so the sky appeared gray from horizon to horizon. Beyond the tents, groups of formless shadows projected from the ground. Here, near the edge of the desert, enough water existed so clumps and patches of bush grew, providing shelter and sustenance for all manner of creatures. The black sand, which sparkled and blinded in the sunlight, at night was like a layer of soft soot. Snake stepped out of the tent, and the illusion of softness disappeared; her boots slid crunching into the sharp hard grains.

Stavin's family waited, sitting close together between the dark tents that clustered in a patch of sand from which the bushes had been ripped and burned. They looked at her silently, hoping with their eyes, showing no expression in their faces. A woman somewhat younger than Stavin's mother sat with them. She was dressed, as they were, in a long loose robe, but she wore the only adornment Snake had seen among these people: a leader's circle, hanging around her neck on a leather thong. She and the older husband were marked close kin by their similarities: sharp-cut planes of face, high cheekbones, his hair white and hers graying early from deep black, their eyes the dark brown best suited for survival in the sun. On the ground by their feet a small black animal jerked sporadically against a net, and infrequently gave a shrill weak cry.

"Stavin is asleep," Snake said. "Do not disturb him, but go to him if he wakes."

The wife and young husband rose and went inside, but the older man stopped before her. "Can you help him?"

"I hope we may. The tumor is advanced, but it seems solid." Her own voice sounded removed, slightly hollow, as if she were lying. "Mist will be ready in the morning." She still felt the need to give him reassurance, but she could think of none.

"My sister wished to speak with you," he said, and left them alone, without introduction, without elevating himself by saying that the tall woman was the leader of this group. Snake glanced back, but the tent-flap fell shut. She was feeling her exhaustion more deeply, and across her shoulders Mist was, for the first time, a weight she thought heavy.

"Are you all right?"

Snake turned. The woman moved toward her with a natural elegance made slightly awkward by advanced pregnancy. Snake had to look up to meet her gaze. She had small fine lines at the corners of her eyes, as if she laughed, sometimes, in secret. She smiled, but with concern. "You seem very tired. Shall I have someone make you a bed?"

"Not now," Snake said, "not yet. I won't sleep until afterward."

The leader searched her face, and Snake felt a kinship with her in their shared responsibility.

"I understand, I think. Is there anything we can give you? Do you need aid with your preparations?"

Snake found herself having to deal with the questions as if they were complex problems. She turned them in her tired mind, examined them, dissected them, and finally grasped their meanings. "My pony needs food and water—"

"It is taken care of."

"And I need someone to help me with Mist. Someone strong. But it's more important that they aren't afraid."

The leader nodded. "I would help you," she said, and smiled again, a little. "But I am a bit clumsy of late. I will find someone."

"Thank you."

Somber again, the older woman inclined her head and moved slowly toward a small group of tents. Snake watched her go, admiring her grace. She felt small and young and grubby in comparison.

Sand began to unwrap himself from her wrist. Feeling the anticipatory slide of scales on her skin, she caught him before he could drop to the ground. Sand lifted the upper half of his body from her hands. He flicked out his tongue, peering toward the little animal, feeling its body heat, smelling its fear. "I know thou art hungry," Snake said, "but that creature is not for thee." She put Sand in the case, lifted Mist from her shoulder, and let her coil herself in her dark compartment.

The small animal shrieked and struggled again when Snake's diffuse shadow passed over it. She bent and picked it up. The rapid series of terrified cries slowed and diminished and finally stopped as she stroked it. Finally it lay still, breathing hard, exhausted, staring up at her with yellow eyes. It had long hind legs and wide pointed ears, and its nose twitched at the serpent smell. Its soft black fur was marked off in skewed squares by the cords of the net.

"I am sorry to take your life," Snake told it. "But there will be no more fear, and I will not hurt you." She closed her hand gently around it and, stroking it, grasped its spine at the base of its skull. She pulled, once, quickly. It seemed to struggle, briefly, but it was already dead. It convulsed; its legs drew up against its body, and its toes curled and quivered. It seemed to stare up at her, even now. She freed its body from the net.

Snake chose a small vial from her belt pouch, pried open the animal's clenched jaws, and let a single drop of the vial's cloudy preparation fall into its mouth. Quickly she opened the satchel again and called Mist out. The cobra came slowly, slipping over the edge, hood closed, sliding in the sharp-grained sand. Her milky scales caught the thin light. She smelled the animal, flowed to it, touched it with her tongue. For a moment Snake was afraid she would refuse dead meat, but the body was still warm, still twitching reflexively, and she was very hungry. "A tidbit for thee," Snake spoke to the cobra: a habit of solitude. "To whet thy appetite." Mist nosed the beast, reared back, and struck, sinking her short fixed fangs into the tiny body, biting again, pumping out her store of poison. She released it, took a better grip, and began to work her jaws around it; it would hardly distend her throat. When Mist lay quiet, digesting the small meal, Snake sat beside her and held her, waiting.

She heard footsteps in the coarse sand.

"I'm sent to help you."

He was a young man, despite a scatter of white in his black hair. He was taller than Snake, and not unattractive. His eyes were dark, and the sharp planes of his face were further hardened because his hair was pulled straight back and tied. His expression was neutral.

"Are you afraid?"

"I will do as you tell me."

Though his form was obscured by his robe, his long fine hands showed strength.

"Then hold her body, and don't let her surprise you." Mist was beginning to twitch from the effects of the drugs Snake had put in the small animal. The cobra's eyes stared, unseeing.

"If it bites—"

"Hold, quickly!"

The young man reached, but he had hesitated too long. Mist writhed, lashing out, striking him in the face with her tail. He staggered back, at least as surprised as hurt. Snake kept a close grip behind Mist's jaws, and struggled to catch the rest of her as well. Mist was no constrictor, but she was smooth and strong and fast. Thrashing, she forced out her breath in a long hiss. She would have bitten anything she could reach. As Snake fought with her, she managed to squeeze the poison glands and force out the last drops of venom. They hung from Mist's fangs for a moment, catching light as jewels would; the force of the serpent's convulsions flung them away into the darkness. Snake struggled with the cobra, aided for once by the sand, on which Mist could get no purchase. Snake felt the young man behind her, grabbing for Mist's body and tail. The seizure stopped abruptly, and Mist lay limp in their hands.

"I am sorry—"

"Hold her," Snake said. "We have the night to go."

During Mist's second convulsion, the young man held her firmly and was of some real help. Afterward, Snake answered his interrupted question. "If she were making poison and she bit you, you would probably die. Even now her bite would make you ill. But unless you do something foolish, if she manages to bite, she will bite me."

"You would benefit my cousin little, if you were dead or dying."

"You misunderstand. Mist cannot kill me." She held out her hand so he could see the white scars of slashes and punctures. He stared at them, and looked into her eyes for a long moment, then looked away.

The bright spot in the clouds from which the light radiated moved westward in the sky; they held the cobra like a child. Snake found herself half-dozing, but Mist moved her head, dully attempting to evade restraint, and Snake woke herself abruptly. "I must not sleep," she said to the young man. "Talk to me. What are you called?"

As Stavin had, the young man hesitated. He seemed afraid of her, or of something. "My people," he said, "think it unwise to speak our names to strangers."

"If you consider me a witch you should not have asked my aid. I know no magic, and I claim none."

"It's not a superstition," he said. "Not as you might think. We're not afraid of being bewitched."

"I can't learn all the customs of all the people on this earth, so I keep my own. My custom is to address those I work with by name." Watching him, Snake tried to decipher his expression in the dim light.

"Our families know our names, and we exchange names with those we would marry."

Snake considered that custom, and thought it would fit badly on her. "No one else? Ever?"

"Well . . . a friend might know one's name."

"Ah," Snake said. "I see. I am still a stranger, and perhaps an enemy."

"A *friend* would know my name," the young man said again. "I would not offend you, but now you misunderstand. An acquaintance is not a friend. We value friendship highly."

"In this land one should be able to tell quickly if a person is worth calling 'friend.' "

"We take friends seldom. Friendship is a great commitment."

"It sounds like something to be feared."

He considered that possibility. "Perhaps it's the betrayal of friendship we fear. That is a very painful thing."

"Has anyone ever betrayed you?"

He glanced at her sharply, as if she had exceeded the limits of propriety. "No," he said, and his voice was as hard as his face. "No friend. I have no one I call friend."

His reaction startled Snake. "That's very sad," she said, and grew silent, trying to comprehend the deep stresses that could close people off so far, comparing her loneliness of necessity and theirs of choice. "Call me Snake," she said finally, "if you can bring yourself to pronounce it. Saying my name binds you to nothing."

The young man seemed about to speak; perhaps he thought again that he had offended her, perhaps he felt he should further defend his customs. But Mist began to twist in their hands, and they had to hold her to keep her from injuring herself. The cobra was slender for her length, but powerful, and the convulsions she went through were more severe than any she had ever had before. She thrashed in Snake's grasp, and almost pulled away. She tried to spread her hood, but Snake held her too tightly. She opened her mouth and hissed, but no poison dripped from her fangs.

She wrapped her tail around the young man's waist. He began to pull her and turn, to extricate himself from her coils.

"She's not a constrictor," Snake said. "She won't hurt you. Leave her—"

But it was too late; Mist relaxed suddenly and the young man lost his balance. Mist whipped herself away and lashed figures in the sand. Snake wrestled with her alone while the young man tried to hold her, but she curled herself around Snake and used the grip for leverage. She started to pull herself from Snake's hands. Snake threw them both backward into the sand; Mist rose above her, open-mouthed, furious, hissing. The young man lunged and grabbed her just beneath her hood. Mist struck at him, but Snake, somehow, held her back. Together they deprived Mist of her hold and regained control of her. Snake struggled up, but Mist suddenly went quite still and lay almost rigid between them. They were both sweating; the young man was pale under his tan, and even Snake was trembling.

"We have a little while to rest," Snake said. She glanced at him and noticed the dark line on his cheek where, earlier, Mist's tail had slashed him. She reached up and touched it. "You'll have a bruise," she said. "But it will not scar."

"If it were true, that serpents sting with their tails, you would be restraining both the fangs and the stinger, and I'd be of little use."

"Tonight I'd need someone to keep me awake, whether or not they helped me with Mist." Fighting the cobra produced adrenalin, but now it ebbed, and her exhaustion and hunger were returning, stronger.

"Snake . . ."

"Yes?"

He smiled, quickly, half-embarrassed. "I was trying the pronunciation."

"Good enough."

"How long did it take you to cross the desert?"

"Not very long. Too long. Six days."

"How did you live?"

"There is water. We traveled at night, except yesterday, when I could find no shade."

"You carried all your food?"

She shrugged. "A little." And wished he would not speak of food.

"What's on the other side?"

"More sand, more bush, a little more water. A few groups of people, traders, the station I grew up and took my training in. And farther on, a mountain with a city inside."

"I would like to see a city. Someday."

"The desert can be crossed."

He said nothing, but Snake's memories of leaving home were recent enough that she could imagine his thoughts.

The next set of convulsions came, much sooner than Snake had expected. By their severity she gauged something of the stage of Stavin's illness, and wished it were morning. If she were to lose him, she would have it done, and grieve, and try to forget. The cobra would have battered herself to death against the sand if Snake and the young man had not been holding her. She suddenly went completely rigid, with her mouth clamped shut and her forked tongue dangling.

She stopped breathing.

"Hold her," Snake said. "Hold her head. Quickly, take her, and if she gets away, run. Take her! She won't strike at you now, she could only slash you by accident."

He hesitated only a moment, then grasped Mist behind the head. Snake ran, slipping in the deep sand, from the edge of the circle of tents to a place where bushes still grew. She broke off dry thorny branches that tore her scarred hands. Peripherally she noticed a mass of horned vipers, so ugly they seemed deformed, nesting beneath the clump of desiccated vegetation. They hissed at her; she ignored them. She found a narrow hollow stem and carried it back. Her hands bled from deep scratches.

Kneeling by Mist's head, she forced open the cobra's mouth and pushed the tube deep into her throat, through the air passage at the base of Mist's tongue. She bent close, took the tube in her mouth, and breathed gently into Mist's lungs.

She noticed: the young man's hands, holding the cobra as she had asked; his breathing, first a sharp gasp of surprise, then ragged; the sand scraping her elbows where she leaned; the cloying smell of the fluid seeping from Mist's fangs; her own dizziness, she thought from exhaustion, which she forced away by necessity and will.

Snake breathed, and breathed again, paused, and repeated, until Mist caught the rhythm and continued it unaided.

Snake sat back on her heels. "I think she'll be all right," she said. "I hope she will." She brushed the back of her hand across her forehead. The touch sparked pain: she jerked her hand down and agony slid along her bones, up her arm, across her shoulder, through her chest, enveloping her heart. Her balance turned on its edge. She fell, tried to catch herself but moved too slowly, fought nausea and vertigo and almost succeeded, until the pull of the earth seemed to slip away in pain and she was lost in darkness with nothing to take a bearing by.

She felt sand where it had scraped her cheek and her palms, but it was soft. "Snake, can I let go?" She thought the question must be for someone else, while at the same time she knew there was no one else to answer it, no one else to reply to her name. She felt hands on her, and they were gentle; she wanted to respond to them, but she was too tired. She needed sleep more, so she pushed them away. But they held her head and put dry leather to her lips and poured water into her throat. She coughed and choked and spat it out.

She pushed herself up on one elbow. As her sight cleared, she realized she was shaking. She felt as she had the first time she was snake-bit, before her immunities had completely developed. The young man knelt over her, his water flask in his hand. Mist, beyond him, crawled toward the darkness. Snake forgot the throbbing pain. "Mist!" She slapped the ground.

The young man flinched and turned, frightened; the serpent reared up, her head nearly at Snake's standing eye-level, her hood spread, swaying, watching, angry, ready to strike. She formed a wavering white line against black. Snake forced herself to rise, feeling as though she were fumbling with the control of some unfamiliar body. She almost fell again, but held herself steady. "Thou must not go to hunt now," she said. "There is work for thee to do." She held out her right hand to the side, a decoy, to draw Mist if she struck. Her hand was heavy with pain. Snake feared, not being bitten, but the loss of the contents of Mist's poison sacs. "Come here," she said. "Come here, and stay thy anger." She noticed blood flowing down between her fingers, and the fear she felt for Stavin was intensified. "Didst thou bite me, creature?" But the pain was wrong: poison would numb her, and the new serum only sting . . .

"No," the young man whispered from behind her.

Mist struck. The reflexes of long training took over. Snake's right hand jerked away, her left grabbed Mist as she brought her head back. The cobra writhed a moment, and relaxed. "Devious beast," Snake said. "For shame." She turned and let Mist crawl up her arm and over her shoulder, where she lay like the outline of an invisible cape and dragged her tail like the edge of a train.

"She did not bite me?"

"No," the young man said. His contained voice was touched with awe.

"You should be dying. You should be curled around the agony, and your arm swollen purple. When you came back—" He gestured toward her hand. "It must have been a bush viper."

Snake remembered the coil of reptiles beneath the branches, and touched the blood on her hand. She wiped it away, revealing the double puncture of a snakebite among the scratches of the thorns. The wound was slightly swollen. "It needs cleaning," she said. "I shame myself by falling to it." The pain of it washed in gentle waves up her arm, burning no longer. She stood looking at the young man, looking around her, watching the landscape shift and change as her tired eyes tried to cope with the low light of setting moon and false dawn. "You held Mist well, and bravely," she said to the young man. "I thank you."

He lowered his gaze, almost bowing to her. He rose, and approached her. Snake put her hand gently on Mist's neck so she would not be alarmed.

"I would be honored," the young man said, "if you would call me Arevin."

"I would be pleased to."

Snake knelt down and held the winding white loops as Mist crawled slowly into her compartment. In a little while, when Mist had stabilized, by dawn, they could go to Stavin.

The tip of Mist's white tail slid out of sight. Snake closed the case and would have risen, but she could not stand. She had not quite shaken off the effects of the new venom. The flesh around the wound was red and tender, but the hemorrhaging would not spread. She stayed where she was, slumped, staring at her hand, creeping slowly in her mind toward what she needed to do, this time for herself.

"Let me help you. Please."

He touched her shoulder and helped her stand. "I'm sorry," she said. "I'm so in need of rest . . ."

"Let me wash your hand," Arevin said. "And then you can sleep. Tell me when to awaken you—"

"I can't sleep yet." She collected herself, straightened, tossed the damp curls of her short hair off her forehead. "I'm all right now. Have you any water?"

Arevin loosened his outer robe. Beneath it he wore a loincloth and a leather belt that carried several leather flasks and pouches. His body was lean and well-built, his legs long and muscular. The color of his skin was slightly lighter than the sun-darkened brown of his face. He brought out his water flask and reached for Snake's hand.

"No, Arevin. If the poison gets in any small scratch you might have, it could infect."

She sat down and sluiced lukewarm water over her hand. The water dripped pink to the ground and disappeared, leaving not even a damp spot visible. The wound bled a little more, but now it only ached. The poison was almost inactivated.

"I don't understand," Arevin said, "how it is that you're unhurt. My younger sister was bitten by a bush viper." He could not speak as uncaringly as he might have wished. "We could do nothing to save her—nothing we have would even lessen her pain."

Snake gave him his flask and rubbed salve from a vial in her belt pouch across the closing punctures. "It's a part of our preparation," she said. "We work with many kinds of serpents, so we must be immune to as many as possible." She shrugged. "The process is tedious and somewhat painful." She clenched her fist; the film held, and she was steady. She leaned toward Arevin and touched his abraded cheek again. "Yes . . ." She spread a thin layer of the salve across it. "That will help it heal."

"If you cannot sleep," Arevin said, "can you at least rest?"

"Yes," she said. "For a little while."

Snake sat next to Arevin, leaning against him, and they watched the sun turn the clouds to gold and flame and amber. The simple physical contact with another human being gave Snake pleasure, though she found it unsatisfying. Another time, another place, she might do something more, but not here, not now.

When the lower edge of the sun's bright smear rose above the horizon, Snake rose and teased Mist out of the case. She came slowly, weakly, and crawled across Snake's shoulders. Snake picked up the satchel, and she and Arevin walked together back to the small group of tents.

Stavin's parents waited, watching for her, just outside the entrance of their tent. They stood in a tight, defensive, silent group. For a moment Snake thought they had decided to send her away. Then, with regret and fear like hot iron in her mouth, she asked if Stavin had died. They shook their heads, and allowed her to enter.

Stavin lay as she had left him, still asleep. The adults followed her with their stares, and she could smell fear. Mist flicked out her tongue, growing nervous from the implied danger.

"I know you would stay," Snake said. "I know you would help, if you could, but there is nothing to be done by any person but me. Please go back outside."

They glanced at each other, and at Arevin, and she thought for a moment that they would refuse. Snake wanted to fall into the silence and sleep. "Come, cousins," Arevin said. "We are in her hands." He opened the tent-flap and motioned them out. Snake thanked him with nothing more than a glance, and he might almost have smiled. She turned toward Stavin, and knelt beside him. "Stavin—" She touched his forehead; it was very hot. She noticed that her hand was less steady than before. The slight touch awakened the child. "It's time," Snake said.

He blinked, coming out of some child's dream, seeing her, slowly recognizing her. He did not look frightened. For that Snake was glad; for some other reason she could not identify she was uneasy.

"Will it hurt?"

"Does it hurt now?"

He hesitated, looked away, looked back. "Yes."

"It might hurt a little more. I hope not. Are you ready?"

"Can Grass stay?"

"Of course," she said.

And realized what was wrong.

"I'll come back in a moment." Her voice changed so much, she had pulled it so tight, that she could not help but frighten him. She left the tent, walking slowly, calmly, restraining herself. Outside, the parents told her by their faces what they feared.

"Where is Grass?" Arevin, his back to her, started at her tone. The younger husband made a small grieving sound, and could look at her no longer.

"We were afraid," the older husband said. "We thought it would bite the child."

"I thought it would. It was I. It crawled over his face, I could see its fangs—" The wife put her hands on the younger husband's shoulders, and he said no more.

"Where is he?" She wanted to scream; she did not.

They brought her a small open box. Snake took it and looked inside.

Grass lay cut almost in two, his entrails oozing from his body, half turned over, and as she watched, shaking, he writhed once, flicked his tongue out once, and in. Snake made some sound, too low in her throat to be a cry. She hoped his motions were only reflex, but she picked him up as gently as she could. She leaned down and touched her lips to the smooth green scales behind his head. She bit him quickly, sharply, at the base of the skull. His blood flowed cool and salty in her mouth. If he were not dead, she had killed him instantly.

She looked at the parents, and at Arevin; they were all pale, but she had no sympathy for their fear, and cared nothing for shared grief. "Such a small creature," she said. "Such a small creature, who could only give pleasure and dreams." She watched them for a moment more, then turned toward the tent again.

"Wait—" She heard the older husband move up close behind her. He touched her shoulder; she shrugged away his hand. "We will give you anything you want," he said, "but leave the child alone."

She spun on him in a fury. "Should I kill Stavin for your stupidity?" He seemed about to try to hold her back. She jammed her shoulder hard into his stomach, and flung herself past the tent-flap. Inside she kicked over the satchel. Abruptly awakened, and angry, Sand crawled out and coiled himself. When the younger husband and the wife tried to enter,

Sand hissed and rattled with a violence Snake had never heard him use before. She did not even bother to look behind her. She ducked her head and wiped her tears on her sleeve before Stavin could see them. She knelt beside him.

"What's the matter?" He could not help but hear the voices outside the tent, and the running.

"Nothing, Stavin," Snake said. "Did you know we came across the desert?"

"No," he said with wonder.

"It was very hot, and none of us had anything to eat. Grass is hunting now. He was very hungry. Will you forgive him and let me begin? I will be here all the time."

He seemed so tired; he was disappointed, but he had no strength for arguing. "All right." His voice rustled like sand slipping through the fingers.

Snake lifted Mist from her shoulders, and pulled the blanket from Stavin's small body. The tumor pressed up beneath his rib cage, distorting his form, squeezing his vital organs, sucking nourishment from him for its own growth, poisoning him with its wastes. Holding Mist's head, Snake let her flow across him, touching and tasting him. She had to restrain the cobra to keep her from striking; the excitement had agitated her. When Sand used his rattle, the vibrations made her flinch. Snake stroked her, soothing her; trained and bred-in responses began to return, overcoming the natural instincts. Mist paused when her tongue flicked the skin above the tumor, and Snake released her.

The cobra reared, and struck, and bit as cobras bite, sinking her fangs their short length once, releasing, instantly biting again for a better purchase, holding on, chewing at her prey. Stavin cried out, but he did not move against Snake's restraining hands.

Mist expended the contents of her venom sacs into the child, and released him. She reared up, peered around, folded her hood, and slid across the mats in a perfectly straight line toward her dark close compartment.

"It's done, Stavin."

"Will I die now?"

"No," Snake said. "Not now. Not for many years, I hope." She took a vial of powder from her belt pouch. "Open your mouth." He complied, and she sprinkled the powder across his tongue. "That will help the ache." She spread a pad of cloth across the series of shallow puncture wounds, without wiping off the blood.

She turned from him.

"Snake? Are you going away?"

"I will not leave without saying goodbye. I promise."

The child lay back, closed his eyes, and let the drug take him.

Sand coiled quiescently on the dark matting. Snake patted the floor to call him. He moved toward her, and suffered himself to be replaced in the satchel. Snake closed it, and lifted it, and it still felt empty. She heard noises outside the tent. Stavin's parents and the people who had come to help them pulled open the tent-flap and peered inside, thrusting sticks in even before they looked.

Snake set down her leather case. "It's done."

They entered. Arevin was with them too; only he was empty-handed. "Snake—" He spoke through grief, pity, confusion, and Snake could not tell what he believed. He looked back. Stavin's mother was just behind him. He took her by the shoulder. "He would have died without her. Whatever happens now, he would have died."

She shook his hand away. "He might have lived. It might have gone away. We—" She could speak no more for hiding tears.

Snake felt the people moving, surrounding her. Arevin took one step toward her and stopped, and she could see he wanted her to defend herself. "Can any of you cry?" she said. "Can any of you cry for me and my despair, or for them and their guilt, or for small things and their pain?" She felt tears slip down her cheeks.

They did not understand her; they were offended by her crying. They stood back, still afraid of her, but gathering themselves. She no longer needed the pose of calmness she had used to deceive the child. "Ah, you fools." Her voice sounded brittle. "Stavin—"

Light from the entrance struck them. "Let me pass." The people in front of Snake moved aside for their leader. She stopped in front of Snake, ignoring the satchel her foot almost touched. "Will Stavin live?" Her voice was quiet, calm, gentle.

"I cannot be certain," Snake said, "but I feel that he will."

"Leave us." The people understood Snake's words before they did their leader's; they looked around and lowered their weapons, and finally, one by one, they moved out of the tent. Arevin remained. Snake felt the strength that came from danger seeping from her. Her knees collapsed. She bent over the satchel with her face in her hands. The older woman knelt in front of her, before Snake could notice or prevent her. "Thank you," she said. "Thank you. I am so sorry . . ." She put her arms around Snake, and drew her toward her, and Arevin knelt beside them, and he embraced Snake too. Snake began to tremble again, and they held her while she cried.

Later she slept, exhausted, alone in the tent with Stavin, holding his hand. The people had caught small animals for Sand and Mist. They had given her food, and supplies, and sufficient water for her to bathe, though the last must have strained their resources.

When she awakened, Arevin lay sleeping nearby, his robe open in the heat, a sheen of sweat across his chest and stomach. The sternness in his expression vanished when he slept; he looked exhausted and vulnerable.

Snake almost woke him, but stopped, shook her head, and turned to Stavin.

She felt the tumor, and found that it had begun to dissolve and shrivel, dying, as Mist's changed poison affected it. Through her grief Snake felt a little joy. She smoothed Stavin's pale hair back from his face. "I would not lie to you again, little one," she whispered, "but I must leave soon. I cannot stay here." She wanted another three days' sleep, to finish fighting off the effects of the bush viper's poison, but she would sleep somewhere else. "Stavin?"

He half woke, slowly. "It doesn't hurt any more," he said.

"I am glad."

"Thank you . . ."

"Goodbye, Stavin. Will you remember later on that you woke up, and that I did stay to say goodbye?"

"Goodbye," he said, drifting off again. "Goodbye, Snake. Goodbye, Grass." He closed his eyes.

Snake picked up the satchel and stood gazing down at Arevin. He did not stir. Half grateful, half regretful, she left the tent.

Dusk approached with long, indistinct shadows; the camp was hot and quiet. She found her tiger-striped pony, tethered with food and water. New, full water-skins bulged on the ground next to the saddle, and desert robes lay across the pommel, though Snake had refused any payment. The tiger-pony whickered at her. She scratched his striped ears, saddled him, and strapped her gear on his back. Leading him, she started west, the way she had come.

"Snake—"

She took a breath, and turned back to Arevin. He was facing the sun; it turned his skin ruddy and his robe scarlet. His streaked hair flowed loose to his shoulders, gentling his face. "You must leave?"

"Yes."

"I hoped you would not leave before . . . I hoped you would stay, for a time . . ."

"If things were different, I might have stayed."

"They were frightened—"

"I told them Grass couldn't hurt them, but they saw his fangs and they didn't know he could only give dreams and ease dying."

"But can't you forgive them?"

"I can't face their guilt. What they did was my fault, Arevin. I didn't understand them until too late."

"You said it yourself, you can't know all the customs and all the fears."

"I'm crippled," she said. "Without Grass, if I can't heal a person, I cannot help at all. I must go home and face my teachers, and hope they'll forgive my stupidity. They seldom give the name I bear, but they gave it to me—and they'll be disappointed."

"Let me come with you."

She wanted to; she hesitated, and cursed herself for that weakness. "They may take Mist and Sand and cast me out, and you would be cast out too. Stay here, Arevin."

"It wouldn't matter."

"It would. After a while, we would hate each other. I don't know you, and you don't know me. We need calmness, and quiet, and time to understand each other well."

He came toward her, and put his arms around her, and they stood embracing for a moment. When he raised his head, there were tears on his cheeks. "Please come back," he said. "Whatever happens, please come back."

"I will try," Snake said. "Next spring, when the winds stop, look for me. The spring after that, if I do not come, forget me. Wherever I am, if I live, I will forget you."

"I will look for you," Arevin said, and he would promise no more.

Snake picked up her pony's lead, and started across the desert.

QUESTIONS

1. How is the heroine characterized? What devices are used to give her legendary qualities? Read up on the mythic figure of Asclepius and compare him to Snake. What were the two chief symbols of the Greek god of healing?

2. Where is the setting for the story? Earth? In the near or far future? On some other planet? In an alternate dimension? Discuss the role of setting and environment in the story.

3. There are several different kinds of love portrayed in this story. What are they? Discuss them in relation to the warm, affectionate bond established between Buddy and Lee in "Corona."

4. How do power and politics function in the story? What kind of society is depicted here? What role does trust play in the story?

5. Describe the style and pace of the story. How do these qualities contribute to the development of plot and theme?

Stranger Station

Damon Knight

When and if we get far enough "out there" we're bound to meet—many leading scientists feel—other beings. The "alien encounter" is one of the basic motifs of science fiction on which authors constantly play new variations. In "Stranger Station," Damon Knight, one of the masters of the genre, shows how fear and interdependence are universal. This story also depicts the bravery and suffering of nonhuman creatures, holding out hope for universal compassion and love. The human response is less ideal.

The clang of metal echoed hollowly down through the Station's many vaulted corridors and rooms. Paul Wesson stood listening for a moment as the rolling echoes died away. The maintenance rocket was gone, heading back to Home; they had left him alone in Stranger Station.

Stranger Station! The name itself quickened his imagination. Wesson knew that both orbital stations had been named a century ago by the then-British administration of the satellite service; "Home" because the larger, inner station handled the traffic of Earth and its colonies; "Stranger" because the outer station was designed specifically for dealings with foreigners—beings from outside the solar system. But even that could not diminish the wonder of Stranger Station, whirling out here alone in the dark—waiting for its once-in-two-decades visitor. . . .

One man, out of all Sol's billions, had the task and privilege of enduring the alien's presence when it came. The two races, according to Wesson's understanding of the subject, were so fundamentally different that it was painful for them to meet. Well, he had volunteered for the job, and he thought he could handle it—the rewards were big enough.

He had gone through all the tests, and against his own expectations he had been chosen. The maintenance crew had brought him up as dead weight, drugged in a survival hamper; they had kept him the same way while they did their work and then had brought him back to consciousness. Now they were gone. He was alone.

But not quite.

"Welcome to Stranger Station, Sergeant Wesson," said a pleasant voice. "This is your alpha network speaking. I'm here to protect and serve you in every way. If there's anything you want, just ask me." It was a neutral voice, with the kind of professional friendliness in it, like that of a good schoolteacher or rec supervisor.

Wesson had been warned, but he was still shocked at the human quality of it. The alpha networks were the last word in robot brains—computers, safety devices, personal servants, libraries, all wrapped up in one, with something so close to "personality" and "free will" that experts were still arguing the question. They were rare and fantastically expensive; Wesson had never met one before.

"Thanks," he said now, to the empty air. "Uh—what do I call you, by the way? I can't keep saying, 'Hey, alpha network.' "

"One of your recent predecessors called me Aunt Nettie," was the response.

Wesson grimaced. Alpha network—Aunt Nettie. He hated puns; that wouldn't do. "The aunt part is all right," he said. "Suppose I call you Aunt Jane. That was my mother's sister; you sound like her, a little bit."

"I am honored," said the invisible mechanism politely. "Can I serve you any refreshments now? Sandwiches? A drink?"

"Not just yet," said Wesson. "I think I'll look the place over first."

He turned away. That seemed to end the conversation as far as the network was concerned. A good thing; it was all right to have it for company, speaking when spoken to, but if it got talkative. . . .

The human part of the Station was in four segments: bedroom, living room, dining room, bath. The living room was comfortably large and pleasantly furnished in greens and tans; the only mechanical note in it was the big instrument console in one corner. The other rooms, arranged in a ring around the living room, were tiny; just space enough for Wesson, a narrow encircling corridor, and the mechanisms that would serve him. The whole place was spotlessly clean, gleaming and efficient in spite of its twenty-year layoff.

This is the gravy part of the run, Wesson told himself. The month before the alien came—good food, no work, and an alpha network for conversation. "Aunt Jane, I'll have a small steak now," he said to the network. "Medium rare, with hashed brown potatoes, onions and mushrooms, and a glass of lager. Call me when it's ready."

"Right," said the voice pleasantly. Out in the dining room, the autochef began to hum and cluck self-importantly. Wesson wandered over and inspected the instrument console. Air locks were sealed and tight, said the dials; the air was cycling. The station was in orbit and rotating on its axis with a force at the perimeter, where Wesson was, of one *g*. The internal temperature of this part of the Station was an even 73°.

The other side of the board told a different story; all the dials were dark and dead. Sector Two, occupying a volume some eighty-eight thousand times as great as this one, was not yet functioning.

Wesson had a vivid mental image of the Station, from photographs and diagrams—a five-hundred-foot Duralumin sphere, onto which the shallow thirty-foot disk of the human section had been stuck apparently as an afterthought. The whole cavity of the sphere, very nearly—except for a honeycomb of supply and maintenance rooms and the all-important, recently enlarged vats—was one cramped chamber for the alien. . . .

"Steak's ready!" said Aunt Jane.

The steak was good, bubbling crisp outside the way he liked it, tender and pink inside. "Aunt Jane," he said with his mouth full, "this is pretty soft, isn't it?"

"The steak?" asked the voice, with a faintly anxious note.

Wesson grinned. "Never mind," he said. "Listen, Aunt Jane, you've been through this routine—how many times? Were you installed with the Station, or what?"

"I was not installed with the Station," said Aunt Jane primly. "I have assisted at three contacts."

"Um. Cigarette," said Wesson, slapping his pockets. The autochef hummed for a moment, and popped a pack of G. I.'s out of a vent. Wesson lighted up. "All right," he said, "you've been through this three times. There are a lot of things you can tell me, right?"

"Oh, yes, certainly. What would you like to know?"

Wesson smoked, leaning back reflectively, green eyes narrowed. "First," he said, "read me the Pigeon report—you know, from the *Brief History.* I want to see if I remember it right."

"Chapter Two," said the voice promptly. "First contact with a non-Solar intelligence was made by Commander Ralph C. Pigeon on July 1, 1987, during an emergency landing on Titan. The following is an excerpt from his official report:

" 'While searching for a possible cause for our mental disturbance, we discovered what appeared to be a gigantic construction of metal on the far side of the ridge. Our distress grew stronger with the approach to this construction, which was polyhedral and approximately five times the length of the *Cologne.*

" 'Some of those present expressed a wish to retire, but Lt. Acuff and myself had a strong sense of being called or summoned in some indefinable way. Although our uneasiness was not lessened, we therefore agreed to go forward and keep radio contact with the rest of the party while they returned to the ship.

" 'We gained access to the alien construction by way of a large, irregular opening. . . . The internal temperature was minus seventy-five degrees Fahrenheit; the atmosphere appeared to consist of methane and ammonia. . . . Inside the second chamber, an alien creature was waiting for us. We felt the distress, which I have tried to describe, to a much greater degree than before, and also the sense of summoning or pleading.

. . . We observed that the creature was exuding a thick yellowish fluid from certain joints or pores in its surface. Though disgusted, I managed to collect a sample of this exudate, and it was later forwarded for analysis. . . .'

"The second contact was made ten years later by Commodore Crawford's famous Titan Expedition—"

"No, that's enough," said Wesson. "I just wanted the Pigeon quote." He smoked, brooding. "It seems kind of chopped off, doesn't it? Have you got a longer version in your memory banks anywhere?"

There was a pause. "No," said Aunt Jane.

"There was more to it when I was a kid," Wesson complained nervously. "I read that book when I was twelve, and I remember a long description of the alien—that is, I remember its being there." He swung around. "Listen, Aunt Jane—you're a sort of universal watchdog, that right? You've got cameras and mikes all over the Station?"

"Yes," said the network, sounding—was it Wesson's imagination?—faintly injured.

"Well, what about Sector Two? You must have cameras up there, too, isn't that so?"

"Yes."

"All right, then you can tell me. What do the aliens look like?"

There was a definite pause. "I'm sorry, I can't tell you that," said Aunt Jane.

"No," said Wesson, "I didn't think you could. You've got orders not to, I guess, for the same reason those history books have been cut since I was a kid. Now, what would the reason be? Have you got any idea, Aunt Jane?"

There was another pause. "Yes," the voice admitted.

"Well?"

"I'm sorry, I can't—"

"—tell you that," Wesson repeated along with it. "All right. At least we know where we stand."

"Yes, Sergeant. Would you like some dessert?"

"No dessert. One other thing. *What happens to Station watchmen, like me, after their tour of duty?*"

"They are upgraded to Class Seven, students with unlimited leisure, and receive outright gifts of seven thousand stellors, plus free Class One housing. . . ."

"Yeah, I know all that," said Wesson, licking his dry lips. "But here's what I'm asking you. The ones you know—what kind of shape were they in when they left here?"

"The usual human shape," said the voice brightly. "Why do you ask, Sergeant?"

Wesson made a discontented gesture. "Something I remember from a bull session at the Academy. I can't get it out of my head; I know it had something to do with the Station. Just a part of a sentence: '. . . blind as a bat and white bristles all over. . . .' Now, would that be a description of the alien—or the watchman when they came to take him away?"

Aunt Jane went into one of her heavy pauses. "All right, I'll save you the trouble," said Wesson. "You're sorry, you can't tell me that."

"I *am* sorry," said the robot sincerely.

As the slow days passed into weeks, Wesson grew aware of the Station almost as a living thing. He could feel its resilient metal ribs enclosing him, lightly bearing his weight with its own as it swung. He could feel the waiting emptiness "up there," and he sensed the alert electronic network that spread around him everywhere, watching and probing, trying to anticipate his needs.

Aunt Jane was a model companion. She had a record library of thousands of hours of music; she had films to show him, and micro-printed books that he could read on the scanner in the living room; or if he preferred, she would read to him. She controlled the Station's three telescopes, and on request would give him a view of Earth or the Moon or Home. . . .

But there was no news. Aunt Jane would obligingly turn on the radio receiver if he asked her, but nothing except static came out. That was the thing that weighed most heavily on Wesson, as time passed—the knowledge that radio silence was being imposed on all ships in transit, on the orbital stations, and on the planet-to-space transmitters. It was an enormous, almost a crippling handicap. Some information could be transmitted over relatively short distances by photophone, but ordinarily the whole complex traffic of the space lanes depended on radio.

But this coming alien contact was so delicate a thing that even a radio voice, out here where the Earth was only a tiny disk twice the size of the Moon, might upset it. It was so precarious a thing, Wesson thought, that only one man could be allowed in the Station while the alien was there, and to give that man the company that would keep him sane, they had to install an alpha network. . . .

"Aunt Jane?"

The voice answered promptly, "Yes, Paul."

"This distress that the books talk about—you wouldn't know what it is, would you?"

"No, Paul."

"Because robot brains don't feel it, right?"

"Right, Paul."

"So tell me this—why do they need a man here at all? Why can't they get along with just you?"

A pause. "I don't know, Paul." The voice sounded faintly wistful. Were those gradations of tone really in it, Wesson wondered, or was his imagination supplying them?

He got up from the living room couch and paced restlessly back and forth. "Let's have a look at Earth," he said. Obediently, the viewing screen on the console glowed into life: there was the blue Earth, swimming deep below him, in its first quarter, jewel bright. "Switch it off," Wesson said.

"A little music?" suggested the voice, and immediately began to play something soothing, full of woodwinds.

"No," said Wesson. The music stopped.

Wesson's hands were trembling; he had a caged and frustrated feeling.

The fitted suit was in its locker beside the air lock. Wesson had been topside in it once or twice; there was nothing to see up there, just darkness and cold. But he had to get out of this squirrel cage. He took the suit down and began to get into it.

"Paul," said Aunt Jane anxiously, "are you feeling nervous?"

"Yes," he snarled.

"Then don't go into Sector Two," said Aunt Jane.

"Don't tell me what to do, you hunk of tin!" said Wesson with sudden anger. He zipped up the front of his suit with a vicious motion.

Aunt Jane was silent.

Seething, Wesson finished his check-off and opened the lock door.

The air lock, an upright tube barely large enough for one man, was the only passage between Sector One and Sector Two. It was also the only exit from Sector One; to get here in the first place, Wesson had had to enter the big lock at the "south" pole of the sphere, and travel all the way down inside, by drop hole and catwalk. He had been drugged unconscious at the time, of course. When the time came, he would go out the same way; neither the maintenance rocket nor the tanker had any space, or time, to spare.

At the "north" pole, opposite, there was a third air lock, this one so huge it could easily have held an interplanet freighter. But that was nobody's business—no human being's.

In the beam of Wesson's helmet lamp, the enormous central cavity of the Station was an inky gulf that sent back only remote, mocking glimmers of light. The near walls sparkled with hoarfrost. Sector Two was not yet pressurized; there was only a diffuse vapor that had leaked through the airseal and had long since frozen into the powdery deposit that lined the walls. The metal rang cold under his shod feet; the vast emptiness of the chamber was the more depressing because it was airless, unwarmed and unlit. *Alone,* said his footsteps; alone. . . .

He was thirty yards up the catwalk when his anxiety suddenly grew stronger. Wesson stopped in spite of himself and turned clumsily, putting his back to the wall. The support of the solid wall was not enough. The catwalk seemed threatening to tilt underfoot, dropping him into the lightless gulf.

Wesson recognized this drained feeling, this metallic taste at the back of his tongue. It was fear.

The thought ticked through his head: *They want me to be afraid.* But why? Why now? Of what?

Equally suddenly, he knew. The nameless pressure tightened, like a great fist closing, and Wesson had the appalling sense of something so huge that it had no limits at all, descending, with a terrible endless swift slowness. . . .

It was time.

His first month was up.

The alien was coming.

As Wesson turned, gasping, the whole huge structure of the Station around him seemed to dwindle to the size of an ordinary room—and Wesson with it, so that he seemed to himself like a tiny insect, frantically scuttling down the walls toward safety.

Behind him as he ran, the Station *boomed.*

In the silent rooms, all the lights were burning dimly. Wesson lay still, looking at the ceiling. Up there his imagination formed a shifting, changing image of the alien—huge, shadowy, formlessly menacing.

Sweat had gathered in globules on his brow. He stared, unable to look away.

"That was why you didn't want me to go topside, huh, Aunt Jane?" he said hoarsely.

"Yes. The nervousness is the first sign. But you gave me a direct order, Paul."

"I know it," he said vaguely, still staring fixedly at the ceiling. "A funny thing . . . Aunt Jane?"

"Yes, Paul?"

"You won't tell me what it looks like, right?"

"No, Paul."

"I don't want to know. Lord, I don't *want* to know. . . . Funny thing, Aunt Jane, part of me is just pure funk—I'm so scared I'm nothing but a jelly."

"I know," said the voice gently.

"—And part is real cool and calm, as if it didn't matter. Crazy, the things you think about. You know?"

"What things, Paul?"

He tried to laugh. "I'm remembering a kids' party I went to twenty, twenty-five years ago. I was—let's see—I was nine. I remember, because that was the same year my father died.

"We were living in Dallas then, in a rented mobile house, and there was a family in the next tract with a bunch of redheaded kids. They were always throwing parties; nobody liked them much, but everybody always went."

"Tell me about the party, Paul."

He shifted on the couch. "This one—this one was a Halloween party. I remember the girls had on black and orange dresses, and the boys mostly wore spirit costumes. I was about the youngest kid there, and I felt kind of out of place. Then all of a sudden one of the redheads jumps up in a skull mask, hollering, 'C'mon, everybody get ready for hide-and-seek.' And he grabs *me*, and says, '*You* be it,' and before I can even move, he shoves me into a dark closet. And I hear that door lock behind me."

He moistened his lips. "And then—you know, in the darkness—I feel something hit my *face*. You know, cold and clammy, like—I don't know—something dead. . . .

"I just hunched up on the floor of that closet, waiting for that thing to touch me again. You know? That thing, cold and kind of gritty, hanging up there. You know what it was? A cloth glove, full of ice and bran cereal. A joke. Boy, that was one joke I never forgot. . . . Aunt Jane?"

"Yes, Paul."

"Hey, I'll bet you alpha networks made great psychs, huh? I could lie here and tell you anything, because you're just a machine—right?"

"Right, Paul," said the network sorrowfully.

"Aunt Jane, Aunt Jane . . . It's no use kidding myself along. I can *feel* that thing up there, just a couple of yards away."

"I know you can, Paul."

"I can't stand it, Aunt Jane."

"You can if you think you can, Paul."

He writhed on the couch. "It's—it's dirty, it's clammy. My God, is it going to be like that for *five* months? I can't, it'll kill me, Aunt Jane."

There was another thunderous boom, echoing down through the structural members of the Station. "What's that?" Wesson gasped. "The other ship—casting off?"

"Yes. Now he's alone, just as you are."

"Not like me. He can't be feeling what I'm feeling. Aunt Jane, you don't know. . . ."

Up there, separated from him only by a few yards of metal, the alien's enormous, monstrous body hung. It was that poised weight, as real as if he could touch it, that weighed down his chest.

Wesson had been a space dweller for most of his adult life and knew even in his bones that, if an orbital station ever collapsed, the "under" part would not be crushed but would be hurled away by its own angular momentum. This was not the oppressiveness of planetside buildings, where the looming mass above you seemed always threatening to fall. This was something else, completely distinct, and impossible to argue away.

It was the scent of danger, hanging unseen up there in the dark, waiting, cold and heavy. It was the recurrent nightmare of Wesson's childhood—the bloated unreal shape, no-color, no-size, that kept on hideously falling toward his face. . . . It was the dead puppy he had pulled out of the creek, that summer in Dakota—wet fur, limp head, cold, cold, *cold*. . . .

With an effort, Wesson rolled over on the couch and lifted himself to one elbow. The pressure was an insistent chill weight on his skull; the room seemed to dip and swing around him in slow, dizzy circles.

Wesson felt his jaw muscles contorting with the strain as he knelt, then stood erect. His back and legs tightened; his mouth hung painfully open. He took one step, then another, timing them to hit the floor as it came upright.

The right side of the console, the one that had been dark, was lighted. Pressure in Sector Two, according to the indicator, was about one and a third atmospheres. The air-lock indicator showed a slightly higher pressure of oxygen and argon; that was to keep any of the alien atmosphere from contaminating Sector One, but it also meant that the lock would no longer open from either side. Wesson found that irrationally comforting.

"Lemme see Earth," he gasped.

The screen lighted up as he stared into it. "It's a long way down," he said. A long, long way down to the bottom of that well. . . . He had spent ten featureless years as a servo tech in Home Station. Before that, he'd wanted to be a pilot, but had washed out the first year—couldn't take the math. But he had never once thought of going back to Earth.

Now, suddenly, after all these years, that tiny blue disk seemed infinitely desirable.

"Aunt Jane, Aunt Jane, it's beautiful," he mumbled.

Down there, he knew, it was spring; and in certain places, where the edge of darkness retreated, it was morning—a watery blue morning like the sea light caught in an agate, a morning with smoke and mist in it, a morning of stillness and promise. Down there, lost years and miles away, some tiny dot of a woman was opening her microscopic door to listen to an atom's song. Lost, lost, and packed away in cotton wool, like a specimen slide—one spring morning on Earth.

Black miles above, so far that sixty Earths could have been piled one on another to make a pole for his perch, Wesson swung in his endless circle within a circle. Yet, vast as the gulf beneath him was, all this—Earth, Moon, orbital stations, ships; yes, the Sun and all the rest of his planets, too—was the merest sniff of space, to be pinched up between thumb and finger.

Beyond—there was the true gulf. In that deep night, galaxies lay sprawled aglitter, piercing a distance that could only be named in a meaningless number, a cry of dismay: O . . . O . . . O . . .

Crawling and fighting, blasting with energies too big for them, men had come as far as Jupiter. But if a man had been tall enough to lie with his boots toasting in the Sun and his head freezing at Pluto, still he would have been too small for that overwhelming emptiness. Here, not at Pluto, was the outermost limit of man's empire; here the Outside funneled down to meet it, like the pinched waist of an hourglass; here, and only here, the two worlds came near enough to touch. Ours—and Theirs.

Down at the bottom of the board, now, the golden dials were faintly alight, the needles trembling ever so little on their pins.

Deep in the vats, the golden liquid was trickling down: "*Though disgusted, I took a sample of the exudate, and it was forwarded for analysis. . . .*"

Space-cold fluid, trickling down the bitter walls of the tubes, forming little pools in the cups of darkness; goldenly agleam there, half alive. The golden elixir. One drop of the concentrate would arrest aging for twenty years—keep your arteries soft, tonus good, eyes clear, hair pigmented, brain alert.

That was what the tests of Pigeon's sample had showed. That was the reason for the whole crazy history of the "alien trading post"—first a hut on Titan, then later, when people understood more about the problem, Stranger Station.

Once every twenty years, an alien would come down out of Somewhere, and sit in the tiny cage we had made for him, and make us rich beyond our dreams—rich with life—and still we did not know why.

Above him, Wesson imagined he could see that sensed body awallow in the glacial blackness, its bulk passively turning with the Station's spin, bleeding a chill gold into the lips of the tubes—drip . . . drop. . . .

Wesson held his head. The pressure inside made it hard to think; it felt as if his skull were about to fly apart. "Aunt Jane," he said.

"Yes, Paul." The kindly, comforting voice, like a nurse. The nurse who stands beside your cot while you have painful, necessary things done to you. Efficient, trained friendliness.

"Aunt Jane," said Wesson, "do you know why they keep coming back?"

"No," said the voice precisely. "It is a mystery."

Wesson nodded. "I had," he said, "an interview with Gower before I left Home. You know Gower? Chief of the Outerworld Bureau. Came up especially to see me."

"Yes?" said Aunt Jane encouragingly.

"Said to me, 'Wesson, you got to find out. Find out if we can count on them to keep up the supply. You know? There's fifty million more of us,' he says, 'than when you were born. We need more of the stuff, and we got to know if we can count on it. Because,' he says, 'you know what would happen if it stopped?' Do you know, Aunt Jane?"

"It would be," said the voice, "a catastrophe."

"That's right," Wesson said respectfully. "It would. Like, he says to me, 'What if the people in the Nefud area were cut off from the Jordan Valley Authority? Why, there'd be millions dying of thirst in a week.

" 'Or what if the freighters stopped coming to Moon Base? Why,' he says, 'there'd be thousands starving and smothering to death.'

"He says, 'Where the water is, where you can get food and air, people are going to settle and get married, you know? And have kids.'

"He says, 'If the so-called longevity serum stopped coming. . . .' Says, 'Every twentieth adult in the Sol family is due for his shot this year.' Says, 'Of those, almost twenty percent are one hundred fifteen or older.' Says, 'The deaths in that group in the first year would be at least three times what the actuarial tables call for.' " Wesson raised a strained face. "I'm thirty-four, you know?" he said. "That Gower, he made me feel like a baby."

Aunt Jane made a sympathetic noise.

"Drip, drip," said Wesson hysterically. The needles of the tall golden indicators were infinitesimally higher. "Every twenty years we need more of the stuff, so somebody like me has to come out and take it for five lousy months. And one of *them* has to come out and sit there, and *drip*. *Why*, Aunt Jane? What for? Why should it matter to them whether we live a long time or not? Why do they keep on coming back? What do they take *away* from here?"

But to these questions, Aunt Jane had no reply.

All day and every day, the lights burned cold and steady in the circular gray corridor around the rim of Sector One. The hard gray flooring had been deeply scuffed in that circular path before Wesson ever walked there—the corridor existed for that only, like a treadmill in a squirrel cage. It said "Walk," and Wesson walked. A man would go crazy if he sat still, with that squirming, indescribable pressure on his head; and so Wesson paced off the miles, all day and every day, until he dropped like a dead man in the bed at night.

He talked, too, sometimes to himself, sometimes to the listening alpha network; sometimes it was difficult to tell which. "Moss on a rock," he muttered, pacing. "Told him, wouldn't give twenty mills for any shell. . . . Little pebbles down there, all colors." He shuffled on in silence for a while. Abruptly: "I don't see *why* they couldn't have given me a cat."

Aunt Jane said nothing. After a moment Wesson went on, "Nearly everybody at Home has a cat, for God's sake, or a goldfish or something. You're all right, Aunt Jane, but I can't *see* you. My God, I mean if they couldn't send a man a woman for company—what I mean, my God, I never liked *cats*." He swung around the doorway into the bedroom, and absentmindedly slammed his fist into the bloody place on the wall.

"But a cat would have been *something*," he said.

Aunt Jane was still silent.

"Don't pretend your feelings are hurt. I know you, you're only a machine," said Wesson. "Listen, Aunt Jane, I remember a cereal package one time that had a horse and a cowboy on the side. There wasn't much room, so about all you saw was their faces. It used to strike me funny how much they looked alike. Two ears on the top with hair in the middle. Two eyes. Nose. Mouth with teeth in it. I was thinking, we're kind of distant cousins, aren't we, us and the horses. But compared to that thing up there—we're *brothers*. You know?"

"Yes," said Aunt Jane quietly.

"So I keep asking myself, why couldn't they have sent a horse or a cat *instead* of a man? But I guess the answer is because only a man could take what I'm taking. God, only a man. Right?"

"Right," said Aunt Jane with deep sorrow.

Wesson stopped at the bedroom doorway again and shuddered, holding onto the frame. "Aunt Jane," he said in a low, clear voice, "you take pictures of *him* up there, don't you?"

"Yes, Paul."

"And you take pictures of me. And then what happens? After it's all over, who looks at the pictures?"

"I don't know," said Aunt Jane humbly.

"You don't know. But whoever looks at 'em, it doesn't do any good. Right? We got to find out why, why, why. . . . And we never do find out, do we?"

"No," said Aunt Jane.

"But don't they figure that if the man who's going through it could see him, he might be able to tell something? That other people couldn't? Doesn't that make sense?"

"That's out of my hands, Paul."

He sniggered. "That's funny. Oh, that's funny." He chortled in his throat, reeling around the circuit.

"Yes, that's funny," said Aunt Jane.

"Aunt Jane, tell me what happens to the watchmen."

"I can't tell you that, Paul."

He lurched into the living room, sat down before the console, beat on its smooth, cold metal with his fists. "What are you, some kind of monster? Isn't there any blood in your veins, or oil or *anything*?"

"Please, Paul—"

"Don't you see, all I want to know, can they talk? Can they tell anything after their tour is over?"

"No, Paul."

He stood upright, clutching the console for balance. "They can't? No, I figured. And you know why?"

"No."

"Up there," said Wesson obscurely. "Moss on the rock."

"Paul, what?"

"We get changed," said Wesson, stumbling out of the room again. "We get changed. Like a piece of iron next to a magnet. Can't help it. You—nonmagnetic, I guess. Goes right through you, huh, Aunt Jane? You don't get changed. You stay here, wait for the next one."

"Yes," said Aunt Jane.

"You know," said Wesson, pacing, "I can tell how he's lying up there. Head *that* way, tail the other. Am I right?"

"Yes," said Aunt Jane.

Wesson stopped. "Yes," he said intently. "So you *can* tell me what you see up there, can't you, Aunt Jane?"

"No. Yes. It isn't allowed."

"Listen, Aunt Jane, *we'll die* unless we can find out what makes those aliens tick! Remember that." Wesson leaned against the corridor wall, gazing up. "He's turning now—around this way. Right?"

"Yes."

"Well, what else is he doing? Come on, Aunt Jane, tell me!"

A pause. "He is twitching his—"

"What?"

"I don't know the words."

"My God, my God," said Wesson, clutching his head, "of course there aren't any words." He ran into the living room, clutched the console, and stared at the blank screen. He pounded the metal with his fist. "You've got to show me, Aunt Jane, come on and show me—show me!"

"It isn't allowed," Aunt Jane protested.

"You've got to do it just the same, or we'll *die*, Aunt Jane—millions of us, billions, and it'll be your fault, get it? *Your fault*, Aunt Jane!"

"*Please*," said the voice. There was a pause. The screen flickered to life, for an instant only. Wesson had a glimpse of something massive and dark, but half transparent, like a magnified insect—a tangle of nameless limbs, whiplike filaments, claws, wings. . . .

He clutched the edge of the console.

"Was that all right?" Aunt Jane asked.

"Of course! What do you think, it'll kill me to look at it? Put it back, Aunt Jane, put it back!"

Reluctantly, the screen lighted again. Wesson stared and went on staring. He mumbled something.

"What?" said Aunt Jane.

"*Life of my love, I loathe thee*," said Wesson, staring. He roused himself after a moment and turned away. The image of the alien stayed with him as he went reeling into the corridor again; he was not surprised to find that it reminded him of all the loathsome, crawling, creeping things the Earth was full of. That explained why he was not supposed to see the alien, or even know what it looked like—because that fed his hate. And it was all right for him to be afraid of the alien, but he was not supposed to hate it. . . . Why not? Why not?

His fingers were shaking. He felt drained, steamed, dried up and withered. The one daily shower Aunt Jane allowed him was no longer enough. Twenty minutes after bathing the acid sweat dripped again from his armpits, the cold sweat was beaded on his forehead, the hot sweat was in his palms. Wesson felt as if there were a furnace inside him, out of control, all the dampers drawn. He knew that, under stress, something of the kind did happen to a man; the body's chemistry was altered—more adrenalin, more glycogen in the muscles, eyes brighter, digestion retarded. That was the trouble—he was burning himself up, unable to fight the thing that tormented him, nor run from it.

After another circuit, Wesson's steps faltered. He hesitated, and went into the living room. He leaned over the console, staring. From the screen, the alien stared blindly up into space. Down in the dark side, the golden indicators had climbed: the vats were more than two thirds filled.

To *fight* or *run*. . . .

Slowly Wesson sank down in front of the console. He sat hunched, head bent, hands squeezed tight between his knees, trying to hold onto the thought that had come to him.

If the alien felt a pain as great as Wesson's—or greater—

Stress might alter the alien's body chemistry, too.

Life of my love, I loathe thee.

Wesson pushed the irrelevant thought aside. He stared at the screen, trying to envisage the alien up there, wincing in pain and distress—sweating a golden sweat of horror. . . .

After a long time, he stood up and walked into the kitchen. He caught the table edge to keep his legs from carrying him on around the circuit. He sat down.

Humming fondly, the autochef slid out a tray of small glasses—water, orange juice, milk. Wesson put the water glass to his stiff lips; the water was cool and hurt his throat. Then the juice, but he could drink only a little of it; then he sipped the milk. Aunt Jane hummed approvingly.

Dehydrated. How long had it been since he had eaten or drunk? He looked at his hands. They were thin bundles of sticks, ropy-veined, with hard yellow claws. He could see the bones of his forearms under the skin, and his heart's beating stirred the cloth at his chest. The pale hairs on his arms and thighs—were they blond or white?

The blurred reflections in the metal trim of the dining room gave him no answers—only pale faceless smears of gray. Wesson felt light-headed and very weak, as if he had just ended a bout of fever. He fumbled over his ribs and shoulder bones. He was thin.

He sat in front of the autochef for a few minutes more, but no food came out. Evidently Aunt Jane did not think he was ready for it, and perhaps she was right. *Worse for them than for us,* he thought dizzily. *That's why the Station's so far out, why radio silence, and only one man aboard. They couldn't stand it at all, otherwise. . . .* Suddenly he could think of nothing but sleep—the bottomless pit, layer after layer of smothering velvet, numbing and soft. . . . His leg muscles quivered and twitched when he tried to walk, but he managed to get to the bedroom and fall on the mattress. The resilient block seemed to dissolve under him. His bones were melting.

He woke with a clear head, very weak, thinking cold and clear: *When two alien cultures meet, the stronger must transform the weaker with love or hate.* "Wesson's Law," he said aloud. He looked automatically for pencil and paper, but there was none, and he realized he would have to tell Aunt Jane, and let her remember it.

"I don't understand," she said.

"Never mind, remember it anyway. You're good at that, aren't you?"

"Yes, Paul."

"All right—I want some breakfast."

He thought about Aunt Jane, so nearly human, sitting up here in her metal prison, leading one man after another through the torments of hell—nursemaid, protector, torturer. They must have known that something would have to give. . . . But the alphas were comparatively new; nobody understood them very well. Perhaps they really thought that an absolute prohibition could never be broken.

. . . *the stronger must transform the weaker.* . . .

I'm the stronger, he thought. *And that's the way it's going to be.* He stopped at the console, and the screen was blank. He said angrily, "Aunt Jane!" And with a guilty start, the screen flickered into life.

Up there, the alien had rolled again in his pain. Now the great clustered eyes were staring directly into the camera; the coiled limbs threshed in pain; the eyes were staring, asking, pleading. . . .

"*No*," said Wesson, feeling his own pain like an iron cap, and he slammed his hand down on the manual control. The screen went dark. He looked up, sweating, and saw the floral picture over the console.

The thick stems were like antennae, the leaves thoraxes, the buds like blind insect eyes. The whole picture moved slightly, endlessly, in a slow waiting rhythm.

Wesson clutched the hard metal of the console and stared at the picture, with sweat cold on his brow, until it turned into a calm, meaningless arrangement of lines again. Then he went into the dining room, shaking, and sat down.

After a moment he said, "Aunt Jane, does it get worse?"

"No. From now on, it gets better."

"How long?" he asked vaguely.

"One month."

A month, getting "better"—that was the way it had always been, with the watchman swamped and drowned, his personality submerged. Wesson thought about the men who had gone before him—Class Seven citizenship, with unlimited leisure, and Class One housing. Yes, sure—in a sanatorium.

His lips peeled back from his teeth, and his fists clenched hard. *Not me!* he thought.

He spread his hands on the cool metal to study them. He said, "How much longer do they usually stay able to talk?"

"You are already talking longer than any of them. . . ."

Then there was a blank. Wesson was vaguely aware, in snatches, of the corridor walls moving past and the console glimpsed and of a thunderous cloud of ideas that swirled around his head in a beating of wings. The aliens—what did they want? And what happened to the watchmen in Stranger Station?

The haze receded a little, and he was in the dining room again, staring vacantly at the table. Something was wrong.

He ate a few spoonfuls of the gruel the autochef served him, then pushed it away; the stuff tasted faintly unpleasant. The machine hummed anxiously and thrust a poached egg at him, but Wesson got up from the table.

The Station was all but silent. The resting rhythm of the household machines throbbed in the walls, unheard. The blue-lighted living room was spread out before him like an empty stage setting, and Wesson stared as if he had never seen it before.

He lurched to the console and stared down at the pictured alien on the screen—heavy, heavy, asprawl with pain in the darkness. The needles of the golden indicators were high, the enlarged vats almost full. *It's too much for him,* Wesson thought with grim satisfaction. The peace that followed the pain had not descended as it was supposed to; no, not this time!

He glanced up at the painting over the console—heavy crustacean limbs that swayed gracefully in the sea. . . .

He shook his head violently. *I won't let it; I won't give in!* He held the back of one hand close to his eyes. He saw the dozens of tiny cuneiform wrinkles stamped into the skin over the knuckles, the pale hairs sprouting, the pink shiny flesh of recent scars. *I'm human,* he thought. But when he let his hand fall onto the console, the bony fingers seemed to crouch like crustaceans' legs, ready to scuttle.

Sweating, Wesson stared into the screen. Pictured there, the alien met his eyes, and it was as if they spoke to each other, mind to mind, an instantaneous communication that needed no words. There was a piercing sweetness to it, a melting, dissolving luxury of change into something that would no longer have any pain. . . . A pull, a calling.

Wesson straightened up slowly, carefully, as if he held some fragile thing in his mind that must not be handled roughly, or it would disintegrate. He said hoarsely, "Aunt Jane!"

She made some responsive noise.

He said, "Aunt Jane, I've got the answer! The whole thing! Listen, now wait—listen!" He paused a moment to collect his thoughts. "*When two alien cultures meet, the stronger must transform the weaker with love or hate.* Remember? You said you didn't understand what that meant. I'll *tell* you what it means. When these—monsters—met Pigeon a hundred years ago on Titan, *they knew* we'd have to meet again. They're spreading out, colonizing, and so are we. We haven't got interstellar flight yet, but give us another hundred years, we'll *get* it. *We'll wind up out there, where they are.* And they can't stop us. Because they're not killers, Aunt Jane, it isn't in them. They're *nicer* than us. See, they're like the missionaries, and we're the South Sea Islanders. *They* don't kill their enemies, oh, no—perish the thought!"

She was trying to say something, to interrupt him, but he rushed on. "Listen! The longevity serum—that was a lucky accident. But they played it for all it's worth. Slick and smooth. They come and give us the stuff free—they don't ask for a thing in return. Why not? Listen.

"They come here, and the shock of that first contact makes them sweat out that golden gook we need. Then, the last month or so, the pain always eases off. Why? Because the two minds, the human and alien, they stop fighting each other. Something gives way, it goes soft, and there's a mixing together. And that's where you get the human casualties of this operation—the bleary men that come out of here not even able to talk human language anymore. Oh, I suppose they're happy—happier than I am!—because they've got something big and wonderful inside 'em. Something that you and I can't even understand. But if you took them and put them together again with the aliens who spent time here, *they could all live together—they're adapted.*

"That's what they're aiming for!" He struck the console with his fist. "Not now—but a hundred, two hundred years from now! When we start expanding out to the stars—when we go a-conquering—we'll have already been conquered! Not by weapons, Aunt Jane, not by hate—by love! Yes, love! *Dirty, stinking, low-down, sneaking love!*"

Aunt Jane said something, a long sentence, in a high, anxious voice.

"What?" said Wesson irritably. He couldn't understand a word.

Aunt Jane was silent. "What, what?" Wesson demanded, pounding the console. "Have you got it through your tin head or not? *What?*"

Aunt Jane said something else, tonelessly. Once more, Wesson could not make out a single word.

He stood frozen. Warm tears started suddenly out of his eyes. "Aunt Jane—" he said. He remembered, *You are already talking longer than any of them.* Too late? Too late? He tensed, then whirled and sprang to the closet where the paper books were kept. He opened the first one his hand struck.

The black letters were alien squiggles on the page, little humped shapes, without meaning.

The tears were coming faster, he couldn't stop them—tears of weariness, tears of frustration, tears of hate. "*Aunt Jane!*" he roared.

But it was no good. The curtain of silence had come down over his head. He was one of the vanguard—the conquered men, the ones who would get along with their strange brothers, out among the alien stars.

The console was not working anymore; nothing worked when he wanted it. Wesson squatted in the shower stall, naked, with a soup bowl in his hands. Water droplets glistened on his hands and forearms; the pale short hairs were just springing up, drying.

The silvery skin of reflection in the bowl gave him back nothing but a silhouette, a shadow man's outline. He could not see his face.

He dropped the bowl and went across the living room, shuffling the pale drifts of paper underfoot. The black lines on the paper, when his eye happened to light on them, were worm shapes, crawling things, conveying nothing. He rolled slightly in his walk; his eyes were glazed. His head twitched, every now and then, sketching a useless motion to avoid pain.

Once the bureau chief, Gower, came to stand in his way. "You fool," he said, his face contorted in anger, "you were supposed to go on to the end, like the rest. Now look what you've done!"

"I found out, didn't I?" Wesson mumbled, and as he brushed the man aside like a cobweb, the pain suddenly grew more intense. Wesson clasped his head in his hands with a grunt, and rocked to and fro a moment, uselessly, before he straightened and went on. The pain was coming in waves now, so tall that at their peak his vision dimmed out, violet, then gray.

It couldn't go on much longer. Something had to burst.

He paused at the bloody place and slapped the metal with his palm, making the sound ring dully up into the frame of the Station: *rroom . . . rroom. . . .*

Faintly an echo came back: *boo-oom. . . .*

Wesson kept going, smiling a faint and meaningless smile. He was only marking time now, waiting. Something was about to happen.

The kitchen doorway sprouted a sudden sill and tripped him. He felt heavily, sliding on the floor, and lay without moving beneath the slick gleam of the autochef.

The pressure was too great—the autochef's clucking was swallowed up in the ringing pressure, and the tall gray walls buckled slowly in. . . .

The Station lurched.

Wesson felt it through his chest, palms, knees, and elbows: the floor was plucked away for an instant and then swung back.

The pain in his skull relaxed its grip a little. Wesson tried to get to his feet.

There was an electric silence in the Station. On the second try, he got up and leaned his back against a wall. *Cluck*, said the autochef suddenly, hysterically, and the vent popped open, but nothing came out.

He listened, straining to hear. What?

The Station bounced beneath him, making his feet jump like a puppet's; the wall slapped his back hard, shuddered, and was still; but far off through the metal cage came a long angry groan of metal, echoing, diminishing, dying. Then silence again.

The Station held its breath. All the myriad clickings and pulses in the walls were suspended; in the empty rooms the lights burned with a yellow glare, and the air hung stagnant and still. The console lights in the living room glowed like witch fires. Water in the dropped bowl, at the bottom of the shower stall, shone like quicksilver, waiting.

The third shock came. Wesson found himself on his hands and knees, the jolt still tingling in the bones of his body, staring at the floor. The sound that filled the room ebbed away slowly and ran down into the silences—a resonant metallic sound, shuddering away now along the girders and hull plates, rattling tinnily into bolts and fittings, diminishing, noiseless, gone. The silence pressed down again.

The floor leaped painfully under his body, one great resonant blow that shook him from head to foot.

A muted echo of that blow came a few seconds later, as if the shock had traveled across the Station and back.

The bed, Wesson thought, and scrambled on hands and knees through the doorway, along a floor curiously tilted, until he reached the rubbery block.

The room burst visibly upward around him, squeezing the block flat. It dropped back as violently, leaving Wesson bouncing helplessly on the mattress, his limbs flying. It came to rest, in a long reluctant groan of metal.

Wesson rolled up on one elbow, thinking incoherently, *Air, the air lock*. Another blow slammed him down into the mattress, pinched his lungs shut, while the room danced grotesquely over his head. Gasping for breath in the ringing silence, Wesson felt a slow icy chill rolling toward him across the room—and there was a pungent smell in the air. *Ammonia!* he thought, and the odorless, smothering methane with it.

His cell was breached. The burst membrane was fatal—the alien's atmosphere would kill him.

Wesson surged to his feet. The next shock caught him off balance, dashed him to the floor. He arose again, dazed and limping; he was still thinking confusedly, *The air lock—get out*.

When he was halfway to the door, all the ceiling lights went out at once. The darkness was like a blanket around his head. It was bitter cold now in the room, and the pungent smell was sharper. Coughing, Wesson hurried forward. The floor lurched under his feet.

Only the golden indicators burned now—full to the top, the deep vats brimming, golden-lipped, gravid, a month before the time. Wesson shuddered.

Water spurted in the bathroom, hissing steadily on the tiles, rattling in the plastic bowl at the bottom of the shower stall. The light winked on and off again. In the dining room, he heard the autochef clucking and sighing. The freezing wind blew harder; he was numb with cold to the hips. It seemed to Wesson abruptly that he was not at the top of the sky at all, but down, *down* at the bottom of the sea—trapped in this steel bubble, while the dark poured in.

The pain in his head was gone, as if it had never been there, and he understood what that meant: Up there, the great body was hanging like butcher's carrion in the darkness. Its death struggles were over, the damage done.

Wesson gathered a desperate breath, shouted, "Help me! The alien's dead! He kicked the Station apart—the methane's coming in! Get help, do you hear me? *Do you hear me?*"

Silence. In the smothering blackness, he remembered: *She can't understand me anymore. Even if she's alive.*

He turned, making an animal noise in his throat. He groped his way on around the room, past the second doorway. Behind the walls, something was dripping with a slow cold tinkle and splash, a forlorn night sound. Small, hard, floating things rapped against his legs. Then he touched a smooth curve of metal—the air lock.

Eagerly he pushed his feeble weight against the door. It didn't move. Cold air was rushing out around the door frame, a thin knife-cold stream, but the door itself was jammed tight.

The suit! He should have thought of that before. If he just had some pure air to breathe and a little warmth in his fingers. . . . But the door of the suit locker would not move, either. The ceiling must have buckled.

And that was the end, he thought, bewildered. There were no more ways out. But there *had* to be. . . . He pounded on the door until his arms would not lift anymore; it did not move. Leaning against the chill metal, he saw a single light blink on overhead.

The room was a wild place of black shadows and swimming shapes—the book leaves, fluttering and darting in the air stream. Schools of them beat wildly at the walls, curling over, baffled, trying again; others were swooping around the outer corridor, around and around; he could see them whirling past the doorways, dreamlike, a white drift of silent paper in the darkness.

The acrid smell was harsher in his nostrils. Wesson choked, groping his way to the console again. He pounded it with his open hand, crying weakly—he wanted to see Earth.

But when the little square of brightness leaped up, it was the dead body of the alien that Wesson saw.

It hung motionless in the cavity of the Station, limbs dangling stiff and still, eyes dull. The last turn of the screw had been too much for it. But Wesson had survived. . . .

For a few minutes.

The dead alien face mocked him; a whisper of memory floated into his mind: *We might have been brothers.* . . . All at once Wesson passionately wanted to believe it—wanted to give in, turn back. That passed. Wearily he let himself sag into the bitter *now,* thinking with thin defiance, *It's done—hate wins. You'll have to stop this big giveaway—can't risk this happening again. And we'll hate you for that—and when we get out to the stars—*

The world was swimming numbly away out of reach. He felt the last fit of coughing take his body, as if it were happening to someone else besides him.

The last fluttering leaves of paper came to rest. There was a long silence in the drowned room.

Then:

"Paul," said the voice of the mechanical woman brokenly; "Paul," it said again, with the hopelessness of lost, unknown, impossible love.

QUESTIONS

1. Why is the alpha network feminine? What is "her" primary function?

2. Why didn't Wesson have more psychological preparation for his mission than a month of rest and relaxation? What were the questions Wesson asked that the alpha network was not allowed to answer? Why wasn't she permitted to answer these questions?

3. Why is the alien's ooze yellow? Would not another color have been more disgusting?

4. In your view, is Wesson a sympathetic character? Can you empathize with his anxiety?

5. What does the creature stand for?

6. "When two alien cultures meet, the stronger must transform the weaker with love or hate." What was the nature of the interaction between Wesson and the alien? What did Wesson see as the major threat to human triumph? What did he give his life battling for?

7. Why is fear of the unknown greater than fear of the known, even if the known is the most terrible thing imaginable?

8. Is the ending an unhappy one? What does the ending seem to suggest?

The Ship Who Sang

Anne McCaffrey

Throughout history, and probably for eons before history, humans have anthropomorphized the world around them: in the beginning they spoke to animals, trees, the wind; today they talk with their machines—cars, boats, refrigerators. We have even given our machines more "human" attributes than we give ourselves. In the movie 2001 *the computer HAL appeared to numerous critics as the most sympathetic "character" in the film. During the Second World War many planes used in combat were dubbed with human names. In the following story, the strong ties between human and "machine"* (or *"cyborg"*) *are taken a step further.*

Anne McCaffrey lives in Ireland and has written a series of stories about the relationships of "machines" to humans, collected in a book for which this story provided the title. Her novella "Weyr Search" won a Hugo in 1968. "The Ship Who Sang" is a love story.

She was born a thing and as such would be condemned if she failed to pass the encephalograph test required of all newborn babies. There was always the possibility that though the limbs were twisted, the mind was not, that though the ears would hear only dimly, the eyes see vaguely, the mind behind them was receptive and alert.

The electro-encephalogram was entirely favorable, unexpectedly so, and the news was brought to the waiting, grieving parents. There was the final, harsh decision: to give their child euthanasia or permit it to become an encapsulated "brain," a guiding mechanism in any one of a number of curious professions. As such, their offspring would suffer no pain, live a comfortable existence in a metal shell for several centuries, performing unusual service to Central Worlds.

She lived and was given a name, Helva. For her first 3 vegetable months she waved her crabbed claws, kicked weakly with her clubbed feet, and enjoyed the usual routine of the infant. She was not alone, for there were three other such children in the big city's special nursery. Soon they all were removed to Central Laboratory School, where their delicate transformation began.

One of the babies died in the initial transferral, but of Helva's 'class,' 17 thrived in the metal shells. Instead of kicking feet, Helva's neural responses started her wheels; instead of grabbing with hands, she manipulated mechanical extensions. As she matured, more and more neural synapses would be adjusted to operate other mechanisms that went into the maintenance and running of a space ship. For Helva was destined to be the "brain" half of a scout ship, partnered with a man or a woman, whichever she chose, as the mobile half. She would be among the elite of her kind. Her initial intelligence tests registered above normal and her adaptation index was unusually high. As long as her development within her shell lived up to expectations, and there were no side-effects from the pituitary tinkering, Helva would live a rewarding, rich and unusual life, a far cry from what she would have faced as an ordinary, "normal" being.

However, no diagram of her brain patterns, no early I.Q. tests recorded certain essential facts about Helva that Central must eventually learn. They would have to bide their official time and see, trusting that the massive doses of shell-psychology would suffice her, too, as the necessary bulwark against her unusual confinement and the pressures of her profession. A ship run by a human brain could not run rogue or insane with the power and resources Central had to build into their scout ships. Brain ships were, of course, long past the experimental stages. Most babies survived the perfected techniques of pituitary manipulation that kept their bodies small, eliminating the necessity of transfers from smaller to larger shells. And very, very few were lost when the final connection was made to the control panels of ship or industrial combine. Shell-people resembled mature dwarfs in size whatever their natal deformities were, but the well-oriented brain would not have changed places with the most perfect body in the Universe.

So, for happy years, Helva scooted around in her shell with her classmates, playing such games as Stall, Power-Seek, studying her lessons in trajectory, propulsion techniques, computation, logistics, mental hygiene, basic alien psychology, philology, space history, law, traffic, codes: all the et ceteras that eventually became compounded into a reasoning, logical, informed citizen. Not so obvious to her, but of more importance to her teachers, Helva ingested the precepts of her conditioning as easily as she absorbed her nutrient fluid. She would one day be grateful to the patient drone of the subconscious-level instruction.

Helva's civilization was not without busy, do-good associations, exploring possible inhumanities to terrestrial as well as extraterrestrial citizens. One such group—Society for the Preservation of the Rights of Intelligent Minorities—got all incensed over shelled "children" when Helva was just turning 14. When they were forced to, Central Worlds shrugged its shoulders, arranged a tour of the Laboratory Schools and set the tour off to a big start by showing the members case histories, complete with photographs. Very few committees ever looked past the first few photos. Most of their original objections about "shells" were overriden by the relief that these hideous (to them) bodies *were* mercifully concealed.

Helva's class was doing fine arts, a selective subject in her crowded program. She had activated one of her microscopic tools which she would later use for minute repairs to various parts of her control panel. Her subject was large—a copy of the Last Supper—and her canvas, small—the head of a tiny screw. She had tuned her sight to the proper degree. As she worked she absentmindedly crooned, producing a curious sound. Shell-people used their own vocal chords and diaphragms, but sound issued through microphones rather than mouths. Helva's hum, then, had a curious vibrancy, a warm, dulcet quality even in its aimless chromatic wanderings.

"Why, what a lovely voice you have," said one of the female visitors.

Helva "looked" up and caught a fascinating panorama of regular, dirty craters on a flaky pink surface. Her hum became a gurgle of surprise. She instinctively regulated her "sight" until the skin lost its cratered look and the pores assumed normal proportions.

"Yes, we have quite a few years of voice training, madam," remarked Helva calmly. "Vocal peculiarities often become excessively irritating during prolonged intrastellar distances and must be eliminated. I enjoyed my lessons."

Although this was the first time that Helva had seen unshelled people, she took this experience calmly. Any other reaction would have been reported instantly.

"I meant that you have a nice singing voice . . . dear," the lady said.

"Thank you. Would you like to see my work?" Helva asked, politely. She instinctively sheered away from personal discussions, but she filed the comment away for further meditation.

"Work?" asked the lady.

"I am currently reproducing the Last Supper on the head of a screw."

"O, I say," the lady twittered.

Helva turned her vision back to magnification and surveyed her copy critically.

"Of course, some of my color values do not match the old Master's and the perspective is faulty, but I believe it to be a fair copy."

The lady's eyes, unmagnified, bugged out.

"Oh, I forget," and Helva's voice was really contrite. If she could have blushed, she would have. "You people don't have adjustable vision."

The monitor of this discourse grinned with pride and amusement as Helva's tone indicated pity for the unfortunate.

"Here, this will help," said Helva, substituting a magnifying device in one extension and holding it over the picture.

In a kind of shock, the ladies and gentlemen of the committee bent to observe the incredibly copied and brilliantly executed Last Supper on the head of a screw.

"Well," remarked one gentleman who had been forced to accompany his wife, "the good Lord can eat where angels fear to tread."

"Are you referring, sir," asked Helva politely, "to the Dark Age discussions of the number of angels who could stand on the head of a pin?"

"I had that in mind."

"If you substitute 'atom' for 'angel,' the problem is not insoluble, given the metallic content of the pin in question."

"Which you are programmed to compute?"

"Of course."

"Did they remember to program a sense of humor, as well, young lady?"

"We are directed to develop a sense of proportion, sir, which contributes the same effect."

The good man chortled appreciatively and decided the trip was worth his time.

If the investigation committee spent months digesting the thoughtful food served them at the Laboratory School, they left Helva with a morsel as well.

"Singing," as applicable to herself required research. She had, of course, been exposed to and enjoyed a music appreciation course that had included the better known classical works such as "Tristan und Isolde," "Candide," "Oklahoma," and "Nozze di Figaro," along with the atomic age singers, Birgit Nilsson, Bob Dylan, and Geraldine Todd, as well as the curious rhythmic progressions of the Venusians, Capellan visual chromatics, the sonic concerti of the Altairians, and Reticulan croons. But "singing" for any shell-person posed considerable technical difficulties. Shell-people were schooled to examine every aspect of a problem or situation before making a prognosis. Balanced properly between optimism and practicality, the nondefeatist attitude of the shell-people led them to extricate themselves, their ships, and personnel, from bizarre situations. Therefore to Helva, the problem that she couldn't open her mouth to sing, among other restrictions, did not bother her. She would work out a method, bypassing her limitations, whereby she could sing.

She approached the problem by investigating the methods of sound reproduction through the centuries, human and instrumental. Her own sound production equipment was essentially more instrumental than vocal. Breath control and the proper enunciation of vowel sounds within the oral cavity appeared to require the most development and practice. Shell-people did not, strictly speaking, breathe. For their purposes, oxygen and other gases were not drawn from the surrounding atmosphere through the medium of lungs but sustained artificially by solution in their shells. After experimentation, Helva discovered that she could manipulate her diaphragmic unit to sustain tone. By relaxing the throat muscles and expanding the oral cavity well into the frontal sinuses, she could direct the vowel sounds into the most felicitous position for proper reproduction through her throat microphone. She compared the results with tape recordings of modern singers and was not unpleased, although her own tapes had a peculiar quality about them, not at all unharmonious, merely unique. Acquiring a repertoire from the Laboratory library was no problem to one trained to perfect recall. She found herself able to sing any role and any song which struck her fancy. It would not have occurred to her that it was curious for a female to sing bass, baritone, tenor, mezzo, soprano, and coloratura as she pleased. It was, to Helva, only a matter of the correct reproduction and diaphragmic control required by the music attempted.

If the authorities remarked on her curious avocation, they did so among themselves. Shell-people were encouraged to develop a hobby so long as they maintained proficiency in their technical work.

On the anniversary of her 16th year, Helva was unconditionally graduated and installed in her ship, the XH-834. Her permanent titanium shell was recessed behind an even more indestructible barrier in the central shaft of the scout ship. The neural, audio, visual, and sensory connections were made and sealed. Her extendibles were diverted, connected or augmented and the final, delicate-beyond-description brain taps were completed while Helva remained anesthetically unaware of the proceedings. When she woke, she *was* the ship. Her brain and intelligence controlled every function from navigation to such loading as a scout ship of her class needed. She could take care of herself and her ambulatory half, in any situation already recorded in the annals of Central Worlds and any situation its most fertile minds could imagine.

Her first actual flight, for she and her kind had made mock flights on dummy panels since she was 8, showed her to be a complete master of the techniques of her profession. She was ready for her great adventures and the arrival of her mobile partner.

There were nine qualified scouts sitting around collecting base pay the day Helva reported for active duty. There were several missions that demanded instant attention, but Helva had been of interest to several department heads in Central for some time and each bureau chief was determined to have her assigned to *his* section. No one had remembered to introduce Helva to the prospective partners. The ship always chose its own partner. Had there been another "brain" ship at the base at the moment, Helva would have been guided to make the first move. As it was, while Central wrangled among itself, Robert Tanner sneaked out of the pilots' barracks, out to the field and over to Helva's slim metal hull.

"Hello, anyone at home?" Tanner said.

"Of course," replied Helva, activating her outside scanners. "Are you my partner?" she asked hopefully, as she recognized the Scout Service uniform.

"All you have to do is ask," he retorted in a wistful tone.

"No one has come. I thought perhaps there was no partners available and I've had no directive from Central."

Even to herself Helva sounded a little self-pitying, but the truth was she was lonely, sitting on the darkened field. She had always had the company of other shells and more recently, technicians by the score. The sudden solitude had lost its momentary charm and become oppressive.

"No directives from Central is scarcely a cause for regret, but there happen to be eight other guys biting their fingernails to the quick just waiting for an invitation to board you, you beautiful thing."

Tanner was inside the central cabin as he said this, running appreciative fingers over her panel, the scout's gravity-chair, poking his head into the cabins, the galley, the head, the pressured-storage compartments.

"Now, if you want to goose Central and do *us* a favor all in one, call up the barracks and let's have a ship-warming–partner-picking party. Hmmmm?"

Helva chuckled to herself. He was so completely different from the occasional visitors or the various Laboratory technicians she had encountered. He was so gay, so assured, and she was delighted by his suggestion of a partner-picking party. Certainly it was not against anything in her understanding of regulations.

"Cencom, this is XH-834. Connect me with Pilot Barracks."

"Visual?"

"Please."

A picture of lounging men in various attitudes of boredom came on her screen.

"This is XH-834. Would the unassigned scouts do me the favor of coming aboard?"

Eight figures galvanized into action, grabbing pieces of wearing apparel, disengaging tape mechanisms, disentangling themselves from bedsheets and towels.

Helva dissolved the connection while Tanner chuckled gleefully and settled down to await their arrival.

Helva was engulfed in an unshell-like flurry of anticipation. No actress on her opening night could have been more apprehensive, fearful or breathless. Unlike the actress, she could throw no hysterics, china objets d'art, or grease-paint to relieve her tension. She could, of course, check her stores for edibles and drinks, which she did, serving Tanner from the virgin selection of her commissary.

Scouts were colloquially known as "brawns" as opposed to their ship "brains." They had to pass as rigorous a training program as the brains and only the top 1 percent of each contributory world's highest scholars were admitted to Central Worlds Scout Training Program. Consequently the eight young men who came pounding up the gantry into Helva's hospitable lock were unusually fine-looking, intelligent, well-coordinated and adjusted young men, looking forward to a slightly drunken evening, Helva permitting, and all quite willing to do each other dirt to get possession of her.

Such a human invasion left Helva mentally breathless, a luxury she thoroughly enjoyed for the brief time she felt she should permit it.

She sorted out the young men. Tanner's opportunism amused but did not specifically attract her; the blond Nordsen seemed too simple; dark-haired Al-atpay had a kind of obstinacy with which she felt no compassion; Mir-Ahnin's bitterness hinted an inner darkness she did not wish to lighten, although he made the biggest outward play for her attention. Hers was a curious courtship—this would be only the first of several marriages for her, for brawns retired after 75 years of service, or earlier if they were unlucky. Brains, their bodies safe from any deterioration, were indestructible. In theory, once a shell-person had paid off the massive debt of early care, surgical adaptation and maintenance charges, he or she was free to seek employment elsewhere. In practice, shell-people remained in the service until they chose to self-destruct or died in line of duty. Helva had actually spoken to one shell-person 322 years old. She had been so awed by the contact she hadn't presumed to ask the personal questions she had wanted to.

Her choice of a brawn did not stand out from the others until Tanner started to sing a scout ditty, recounting the misadventures of the bold, dense, painfully inept Billy Brawn. An attempt at harmony resulted in cacophony and Tanner wagged his arms wildly for silence.

"What we need is a roaring good lead tenor. Jennan, besides palming aces, what do you sing?"

"Sharp," Jennan replied with easy good humor.

"If a tenor is absolutely necessary, I'll attempt it," Helva volunteered.

"My good *woman*," Tanner protested.

"Sound your 'A'," laughed Jennan.

Into the stunned silence that followed the rich, clear, high "A,' Jennan remarked quietly, "Such an A Caruso would have given the rest of his notes to sing."

It did not take them long to discover her full range.

"All Tanner asked for was one roaring good lead tenor," Jennan said jokingly, "and our sweet mistress supplied us an entire repertory company. The boy who gets this ship will go far, far, far."

"To the Horsehead Nebula?" asked Nordsen, quoting an old Central saw.

"To the Horsehead Nebula and back, we shall make beautiful music," said Helva, chuckling.

"Together," Jennan said. "Only you'd better make the music and, with my voice, I'd better listen."

"I rather imagined it would be I who listened," suggested Helva.

Jennan executed a stately bow with an intricate flourish of his crush-brimmed hat. He directed his bow toward the central control pillar where Helva *was.* Her own personal preference crystallized at that precise moment and for that particular reason: Jennan, alone of the men, had addressed his remarks directly at her physical presence, regardless of the fact that he knew she could pick up his image wherever he was in the ship and regardless of the fact that her body was behind massive metal walls. Throughout their partnership, Jennan never failed to turn his head in her direction no matter where he was in relation to her. In response to this personalization, Helva at that moment and from then on always spoke to Jennan only through her central mike, even though that was not always the most efficient method.

Helva didn't know that she fell in love with Jennan that evening. As she had never been exposed to love or affection, only the drier cousins, respect and admiration, she could scarcely have recognized her reaction to the warmth of his personality and thoughtfulness. As a shell-person, she considered herself remote from emotions largely connected with physical desires.

"Well, Helva, it's been swell meeting you," said Tanner suddenly as she and Jennan were arguing about the baroque quality of "Come All Ye Sons of Art." "See you in space some time, you lucky dog, Jennan. Thanks for the party, Helva."

"You don't have to go so soon?" asked Helva, realizing belatedly that she and Jennan had been excluding the others from this discussion.

"Best man won," Tanner said, wryly. "Guess I'd better go get a tape on love ditties. Might need 'em for the next ship, if there're any more at home like you."

Helva and Jennan watched them leave, both a little confused.

"Perhaps Tanner's jumping to conclusions?" Jennan asked.

Helva regarded him as he slouched against the console, facing her shell directly. His arms were crossed on his chest and the glass he held had been empty for some time. He was handsome, they all were; but his watchful eyes were unwary, his mouth assumed a smile easily, his voice (to which Helva was particularly drawn) was resonant, deep, and without unpleasant overtones or accent.

"Sleep on it, at any rate, Helva. Call me in the morning if it's your opt."

She called him at breakfast, after she had checked her choice through Central. Jennan moved his things aboard, received their joint commission, had his personality and experience file locked into her reviewer, gave her the coordinates of their first mission. The XH-834 officially became the JH-834.

Their first mission was a dull but necessary crash priority (Medical got Helva), rushing a vaccine to a distant system plagued with a virulent spore disease. They had only to get to Spica as fast as possible.

After the initial, thrilling forward surge at her maximum speed, Helva realized her muscles were to be given less of a workout than her brawn on this tedious mission. But they did have plenty of time for exploring each other's personalities. Jennan, of course, knew what Helva was capable of as a ship and partner, just as she knew what she could expect from him. But these were only facts and Helva looked forward eagerly to learning that human side of her partner which could not be reduced to a series of symbols. Nor could the give and take of two personalities be learned from a book. It had to be experienced.

"My father was a scout, too, or is that programmed?" began Jennan their third day out.

"Naturally."

"Unfair, you know. You've got all my family history and I don't know one blamed thing about yours."

"I've never known either," Helva said. "Until I read yours, it hadn't occurred to me I must have one, too, someplace in Central's files."

Jennan snorted. "Shell-psychology!"

Helva laughed. "Yes, and I'm even programmed against curiosity about it. You'd better be, too."

Jennan ordered a drink, slouched into the gravity couch opposite her, put his feet on the bumpers, turning himself idly from side to side on the gimbals.

"Helva—a made-up name . . ."

"With a Scandinavian sound."

"You aren't blonde," Jennan said positively.

"Well, then, there're dark Swedes."

"And blonde Turks and this one's harem is limited to one."

"Your woman in purdah, yes, but you can comb the pleasure houses—" Helva found herself aghast at the edge to her carefully trained voice.

"You know," Jennan interrupted her, deep in some thought of his own, "my father gave me the impression he was a lot more married to his ship, the Silvia, than to my mother. I know I used to think Silvia was my grandmother. She was a low number so she must have been a great-great-grandmother at least. I used to talk to her for hours."

"Her registry?" asked Helva, unwittingly jealous of everyone and anyone who had shared his hours.

"422. I think she's TS now. I ran into Tom Burgess once."

Jennan's father had died of a planetary disease, the vaccine for which his ship had used up in curing the local citizens.

"Tom said she'd got mighty tough and salty. You lose your sweetness and I'll come back and haunt you, girl," Jennan threatened.

Helva laughed. He startled her by stamping up to the column panel, touching it with light, tender fingers.

"I *wonder* what you look like," he said softly, wistfully.

Helva had been briefed about this natural curiosity of scouts. She didn't know anything about herself and neither of them ever would or could.

"Pick any form, shape, and shade and I'll be yours obliging," she countered, as training suggested.

"Iron Maiden, I fancy blondes with long tresses," and Jennan pantomined Lady Godiva-like tresses. "Since you're immolated in titanium, I'll call you Brunehilde, my dear," and he made his bow.

With a chortle, Helva launched into the appropriate aria just as Spica made contact.

"What'n'ell's that yelling about? Who are you? And unless you're Central Worlds Medical go away. We've got a plague. No visiting privileges."

"My ship is singing, we're the JH-834 of Worlds and we've got your vaccine. What are our landing coordinates?"

"Your *ship* is singing?"

"The greatest S.A.T.B. in organized space. Any request?"

The JH-834 delivered the vaccine but no more arias and received immediate orders to proceed to Leviticus IV. By the time they got there, Jennan found a reputation awaiting him and was forced to defend the 834's virgin honor.

"I'll stop singing," murmured Helva contritely as she ordered up poultices for this third black eye in a week.

"You will not," Jennan said through gritted teeth. "If I have to black eyes from here to the Horsehead to keep the snicker out of the title, we'll be the ship who sings."

After the "ship who sings" tangled with a minor but vicious narcotic ring in the Lesser Magellanics, the title became definitely respectful. Central was aware of each episode and punched out a "special interest" key on JH-834's file. A first-rate team was shaking down well.

Jennan and Helva considered themselves a first-rate team, too, after their tidy arrest.

"Of all the vices in the universe, I *hate* drug addiction," Jennan remarked as they headed back to Central Base. "People can go to hell quick enough without that kind of help."

"Is that why you volunteered for Scout Service? To redirect traffic?"

"I'll bet my official answer's on your review."

"In far too flowery wording. 'Carrying on the traditions of my family, which has been proud of four generations in Service,' if I may quote you your own words."

Jennan groaned. "I was *very* young when I wrote that. I certainly hadn't been through Final Training. And once I was in Final Training, my pride wouldn't let me fail. . . .

"As I mentioned, I used to visit Dad on board the Silvia and I've a very good idea she might have had her eye on me as a replacement for my father because I had had massive doses of scout-oriented propaganda. It took. From the time I was 7, I was going to be a scout or else." He shrugged as if deprecating a youthful determination that had taken a great deal of mature application to bring to fruition.

"Ah, so? Scout Sahir Silan on the JS-422 penetrating into the Horsehead Nebulae?"

Jennan chose to ignore her sarcasm.

"With *you*, I may even get that far. But even with Silvia's nudging *I* never day-dreamed myself *that* kind of glory in my wildest flights of fancy. I'll leave the whoppers to your agile brain henceforth. I have in mind a smaller contribution to space history."

"So modest?"

"No. Practical. We also serve, et cetera." He placed a dramatic hand on his heart.

"Glory hound!" scoffed Helva.

"Look who's talking, my Nebula-bound friend. At least I'm not greedy. There'll only be one hero like my dad at Parsaea, but I *would* like to be remembered for some kudo. Everyone does. Why else do or die?"

"Your father died on his way back from Parsaea, if I may point out a few cogent facts. So he could never have known he was a hero for damming the flood with his ship. Which kept Parsaean colony from being abandoned. Which gave them a chance to discover the antiparalytic qualities of Parsaea. Which *he* never knew."

"I know," said Jennan softly.

Helva was immediately sorry for the tone of her rebuttal. She knew very well how deep Jennan's attachment to his father had been. On his review a note was made that he had rationalized his father's loss with the unexpected and welcome outcome of the Affair at Parsaea.

"Facts are not human, Helva. My father was and so am I. And *basically*, so are you. Check over your dial, 834. Amid all the wires attached to you is a heart, an underdeveloped human heart. Obviously!"

"I apologize, Jennan," she said.

Jennan hesitated a moment, threw out his hands in acceptance and then tapped her shell affectionately.

"If they ever take us off the milkruns, we'll make a stab at the Nebula, huh?"

As so frequently happened in the Scout Service, within the next hour they had orders to change course, not to the Nebula, but to a recently colonized system with two habitable planets, one tropical, one glacial. The sun, named Ravel, had become unstable; the spectrum was that of a rapidly expanding shell, with absorption lines rapidly displacing toward violet. The augmented heat of the primary had already forced evacuation of the nearer world, Daphnis. The pattern of spectral emissions gave indication that the sun would sear Chloe as well. All ships in the immediate spatial vicinity were to report to Disaster Headquarters on Chloe to effect removal of the remaining colonists.

The JH-834 obediently presented itself and was sent to outlying areas on Chloe to pick up scattered settlers who did not appear to appreciate the urgency of the situation. Chloe, indeed, was enjoying the first temperatures above freezing since it had been flung out of its parent. Since many of the colonists were religious fanatics who had settled on rigorous Chloe to fit themselves for a life of pious reflection, Chloe's abrupt thaw was attributed to sources other than a rampaging sun.

Jennan had to spend so much time countering specious arguments that he and Helva were behind schedule on their way to the fourth and last settlement.

Helva jumped over the high range of jagged peaks that surrounded and sheltered the valley from the former raging snows as well as the present heat. The violent sun with its flaring corona was just beginning to brighten the deep valley as Helva dropped down to a landing.

"They'd better grab their toothbrushes and hop aboard," Helva said. "HQ says speed it up."

"All women," remarked Jennan in surprise as he walked down to meet them. "Unless the men on Chloe wear furred skirts."

"Charm 'em but pare the routine to the bare essentials. And turn on your two-way private."

Jennan advanced smiling, but his explanation of his mission was met with absolute incredulity and considerable doubt as to his authenticity. He groaned inwardly as the matriarch paraphrased previous explanations of the warming sun.

"Revered mother, there's been an overload on that prayer circuit and the sun is blowing itself up in one obliging burst. I'm here to take you to the spaceport at Rosary—"

"That Sodom?" The worthy woman glowered and shuddered disdainfully at his suggestion. "We thank you for your warning but we have no wish to leave our cloister for the rude world. We must go about our morning meditation which has been interrupted—"

"It'll be permanently interrupted when that sun starts broiling you. You must come now," Jennan said firmly.

"Madame," said Helva, realizing that perhaps a female voice might carry more weight in this instance than Jennan's very masculine charm.

"Who spoke?" cried the nun, startled by the bodiless voice.

"I, Helva, the ship. Under my protection you and your sisters-in-faith may enter safely and be unprofaned by association with a male. I will guard you and take you safely to a place prepared for you."

The matriarch peered cautiously into the ship's open port.

"Since only Central Worlds is permitted the use of such ships, I acknowledge that you are not trifling with us, young man. However, we are in no danger here."

"The temperature at Rosary is now 99°," said Helva. "As soon as the sun's rays penetrate directly into this valley, it will also be 99°, and it is due to climb to approximately 180° today. I notice your buildings are made of wood with moss chinking. Dry moss. It should fire around noontime."

The sunlight was beginning to slant into the valley through the peaks and the fierce rays warmed the restless group behind the matriarch. Several opened the throats of their furry parkas.

"Jennan," said Helva privately to him, "our time is very short."

"I can't leave them, Helva. Some of those girls are barely out of their teens."

"Pretty, too. No wonder the matriarch doesn't want to get in."

"Helva."

"It will be the Lord's will," said the matriarch stoutly and turned her back squarely on rescue.

"To burn to death?" shouted Jennan as she threaded her way through her murmuring disciples.

"They want to be martyrs? Their opt, Jennan," said Helva dispassionately, "We must leave and that is no longer a matter of option."

"How can I leave, Helva?"

"Parsaea?" Helva asked tauntingly as he stepped forward to grab one of the women. "You can't drag them *all* aboard and we don't have time to fight it out. Get on board, Jennan, or I'll have you on report."

"They'll die," muttered Jennan dejectedly as he reluctantly turned to climb on board.

"You can risk only so much," Helva said sympathetically. "As it is we'll just have time to make a rendezvous. Lab reports a critical speedup in spectral evolution."

Jennan was already in the airlock when one of the younger women, screaming, rushed to squeeze in the closing port. Her action set off the others. They stampeded through the narrow-opening. Even crammed back to breast, there was not enough room inside for all the women. Jennan broke out spacesuits to the three who would have to remain with him in the airlock. He wasted valuable time explaining to the matriarch that she must put on the suit because the airlock had no independent oxygen or cooling units.

"We'll be caught," said Helva in a grim tone to Jennan on their private connection. "We've lost 18 minutes in this last-minute rush. I am now overloaded for maximum speed and I must attain maximum speed to outrun the heat wave."

"Can you lift? We're suited."

"Lift? Yes," she said, doing so. "Run? I stagger."

Jennan, bracing himself and the women, could feel her sluggishness as she blasted upward. Heartlessly, Helva applied thrust as long as she could, despite the fact that the gravitational force mashed her cabin passengers brutally and crushed two fatally. It was a question of saving as many as possible. The only one for whom she had any concern was Jennan and she was in desperate terror about his safety. Airless and uncooled, protected by only one layer of metal, not three, the airlock was not going to be safe for the four trapped there, despite their spacesuits. These were only the standard models, not built to withstand the excessive heat to which the ship would be subjected.

Helva ran as fast as she could but the incredible wave of heat from the explosive sun caught them halfway to cold safety.

She paid no heed to the cries, moans, pleas, and prayers in her cabin. She listened only to Jennan's tortured breathing, to the missing throb in his suit's purifying system and the sucking of the overloaded cooling unit. Helpless, she heard the hysterical screams of his three companions as they writhed in the awful heat. Vainly, Jennan tried to calm them, tried to explain they would soon be safe and cool if they could be still and endure the heat. Undisciplined by their terror and torment, they tried to strike out at him despite the close quarters. One flailing arm became entangled in the leads to his power pack and the damage was quickly done. A connection, weakened by heat and the dead weight of the arm, broke.

For all the power at her disposal, Helva was helpless. She watched as Jennan fought for his breath, as he turned his head beseechingly toward *her*, and died.

Only the iron conditioning of her training prevented Helva from swinging around and plunging back into the cleansing heart of the exploding sun. Numbly she made rendezvous with the refugee convoy. She obediently transferred her burned, heat-prostrated passengers to the assigned transport.

"I will retain the body of my scout and proceed to the nearest base for burial," she informed Central dully.

"You will be provided escort," was the reply.

"I have no need of escort."

"Escort is provided, XH-834," she was told curtly. The shock of hearing Jennan's initial severed from her call number cut off her half-formed protest. Stunned, she waited by the transport until her screens showed the arrival of two other slim brain ships. The cortege proceeded homeward at unfunereal speeds.

"834? The ship who sings?"

"I have no more songs."

"Your scout was Jennan."

"I do not wish to communicate."

"I'm 422."

"Silvia?"

"Silvia died a long time ago. I'm 422. Currently MS," the ship rejoined curtly. "AH-640 is our other friend, but Henry's not listening in. Just as well—he wouldn't understand it if you wanted to turn rogue. But I'd stop *him* if he tried to deter you."

"Rogue?" The term snapped Helva out of her apathy.

"Sure. You're young. You've got power for years. Skip. Others have done it. 732 went rogue 20 years ago after she lost her scout on a mission to that white dwarf. Hasn't been seen since."

"I never heard about rogues."

"As it's exactly the thing we're conditioned against, you sure wouldn't hear about it in school, my dear," 422 said.

"Break conditioning?" cried Helva, anguished, thinking longingly of the white, white furious hot heart of the sun she had just left.

"For you I don't think it would be hard at the moment," 422 said quietly, her voice devoid of her earlier cynicism. "The stars are out there, winking."

"Alone?" cried Helva from her heart.

"Alone!" 422 confirmed bleakly.

Alone with all of space and time. Even the Horsehead Nebula would not be far enough away to daunt her. Alone with a hundred years to live with her memories and nothing . . . nothing more.

"Was Parsaea worth it?" she asked 422 softly.

"Parsaea?" 422 repeated, surprised. "With his father? Yes. We were there, at Parsaea when we were needed. Just as you . . . and his son . . . were at Chloe. When you were needed. The crime is not knowing where need is and not being there."

"But *I* need *him*. Who will supply my need?" said Helva bitterly. . . .

"834," said 422 after a day's silent speeding, "Central wishes your report. A replacement awaits your opt at Regulus Base. Change course accordingly."

"A replacement?" That was certainly not what she needed . . . a reminder inadequately filling the void Jennan left. Why, her hull was barely cool of Chloe's heat. Atavistically, Helva wanted time to mourn Jennan.

"Oh, none of them are impossible if *you're* a good ship," 422 remarked philosophically. "And it is just what you need. The sooner the better."

"You told them I wouldn't go rogue, didn't you?" Helva said.

"The moment passed you even as it passed me after Parsaea, and before that, after Glen Arthur, and Betelgeuse."

"We're conditioned to go on, aren't we? We *can't* go rogue. You were testing."

"Had to. Orders. Not even Psych knows why a rogue occurs. Central's very worried, and so, daughter, are your sister ships. I asked to be your escort. I . . . don't want to lose you both."

In her emotional nadir, Helva could feel a flood of gratitude for Silvia's rough sympathy.

"We've all known this grief, Helva. It's no consolation, but if we couldn't feel with our scouts, we'd only be machines wired for sound."

Helva looked at Jennan's still form stretched before her in its shroud and heard the echo of his rich voice in the quiet cabin.

"Silvia! I *couldn't* help him," she cried from her soul.

"Yes, dear, I know," 422 murmured gently and then was quiet.

The three ships sped on, wordless, to the great Central Worlds base at Regulus. Helva broke silence to acknowledge landing instructions and the officially tendered regrets.

The three ships set down simultaneously at the wooded edge where Regulus' gigantic blue trees stood sentinel over the sleeping dead in the small Service cemetery. The entire Base complement approached with measured step and formed an aisle from Helva to the burial ground. The honor detail, out of step, walked slowly into her cabin. Reverently they placed the body of her dead love on the wheeled bier, covered it honorably with the deep blue, star-splashed flag of the Service. She watched as it was driven slowly down the living aisle which closed in behind the bier in last escort.

Then, as the simple words of interment were spoken, as the atmosphere planes dipped in tribute over the open grave, Helva found voice for her lonely farewell.

Softly, barely audible at first, the strains of the ancient song of evening and requiem swelled to the final poignant measure until black space itself echoed back the sound of the song the ship sang.

QUESTIONS

1. Was the scientific alteration of the infant Helva inhumane? Would euthanasia or a handicapped life be kinder alternatives?

2. What kind of society is suggested by the story?

3. How does Helva act like a typical teenager?

4. Can you get a clear picture of Helva's appearance? If yes, how would you describe that appearance? If no, why not?

5. In what year does the story take place? On what planet does it begin? Would the story have been strengthened if these two aspects of the setting were more definite than they are?

6. Did Jennan want to die? Explain your answer.

7. What significance does the rogue ship have?

8. Does Helva mourn as though a lover had died? What attitude toward death is implied by her fast recovery? If Helva were merely a "normal" human being, how would she have reacted differently? If she were merely a computer, what would her "reactions" have been?

The Last True God

Lester del Rey

Classic science fiction is a genre that often deals with a mixture of legend and religion, as in Frank Herbert's Dune *and Robert Heinlein's* Stranger in a Strange Land. *The following story combines the common "search for God" and "lost history" motifs of SF, among others. Lester del Rey is one of the "classic" SF writers, perhaps most honored for his* Nerves, *a hopefully nonprophetic story about an accident in an atomic energy plant. He writes "classic" or "hard core" science fiction without apology, and asks that other nonfantasists do the same.*

> *Religion is the sometime legitimate bastard of superstition, and superstition is most often based on some remote reality. Amid the ashes of a ruined world a mute and hollow god awaits the call to service. He is . . .*

THE LAST TRUE GOD

Keir Soth lifted his eyes wearily from the tattered fragment of a book he was trying to read as he heard the gritty cycle of the airlock. He sighed and rose to his feet to stare through the left vision port at the alien landscape beyond the ship.

Melok was a harsh world. Even at sunset it showed no softening of the raw desert that ran directly to the ugly brick towers of the city to Keir's right. The sky was dull with a thin overcast of dust and haze. Three miles away most of the red sun was hidden by the immense pyramid that was the native temple. Already there was a yellow wash of light glowing from an opening in the fane.

Por Dain came into the control room to stand beside him. The scientist was older than Keir and slightly shorter but they might have been brothers from their looks. Both were normally dark of complexion and abnormally lean and sharp of features. Por Dain had removed his protective garment but sand and grit still clung to the creases around his eyes. Fatigue from the double gravity of Melok showed in the droop of his shoulders.

"Five thousand light-years of searching space in this can," he muttered. "Then, less than thirty parsecs from home we find—this. By Earth, I'm tired of all these superstitious savages and their tin god!"

Keir Soth winced at the oath, reaching out to touch the tiny emblem that represented a hemisphere of lost Earth. He was not, of course, superstitious. But childhood habits were hard to break.

Por Dain snorted. "Can't you get it through your head there's no truth to the legend, Keir? How could any planet wrap itself in a silver haze and then just disappear—supposedly into some mystic higher dimension—to leave its colonies stranded? Tommyrot!"

"But we found the picture of just such a happening on that world in the third quadrant," the captain protested.

"A world that had been barren of human life for at least twenty thousand years," Por Dain reminded him. "Do you think our legend would have lasted that long?"

Keir Soth shook his head reluctantly. There were legends of some great war in the heavens that had blasted civilizations back some fifteen hundred years—and those were probably true. There was even evidence that Melok itself might have been the enemy world, since it had been rendered almost lethally radioactive at the same time. Its atmosphere still contained more radiation than Keir found comfortable to think of. But a legend older than twenty millennia . . . ?

And there were other puzzles. If men had been colonizing worlds so long ago, why were there no ancient and advanced worlds? Did every planet rise to spew out colonies and then die in some new holocaust of war with those colonies? Was life so stupid?

Lyssa the Novitiate came into the cabin then, bringing broth and platters of rations for them. She was quite typical of her kind—blond as no other women were, slight, resembling a porcelain doll. The girls who served Earth were carefully bred to look alike.

Surprisingly, Por Dain made room for her on his seat. The old agnostic usually avoided her, bitter at the law forcing all ships to carry at least one Novitiate. She smiled her usual pleasant and empty smile at him as she began the evening invocation in the ancient speech.

" '*F I forget thee Ozine* . . ."

"She did fine today," Por Dain admitted when he saw Keir's questioning look. "She talked that high priest Shaggoth into letting her up by that Earth-damned tin god of theirs and she planted three pickups."

She made the circle of Earth but the blasphemy didn't seem to bother her.

"Shaggoth calls it the last true god," Lyssa said.

She had been uncomplaining throughout the voyage. After finding the pieces of books on the ancient planet, she had even begun teaching them the ancient tongue. That had proved fortunate, since the natives of Melok also used it for their ritual and Shaggoth spoke it enough like

Lyssa's version to be understood. She'd proved helpful enough on the voyage. Besides, men needed a woman on a long trip.

Why Shaggoth seemed to accept her was another puzzle about this dratted world. He had been rough enough on Por and Keir, forbidding them to come within three hundred feet of his fane. And he had refused to let even the girl see his sacred books, though he made no secret of their existence. The scholars back on Homeworld would give a dozen fortunes for the legends of any alien world, too!

It was dark outside—except for the red light of Melok's four visible moons—when Por Dain finished his food and stood up to try the tricky outside receptors. The old man's hands shook with fatigue as he tuned them. Then he grunted with pleasure and surprise. He had been tinkering with the receptors for weeks—and now at last one seemed to be working properly. It showed the inside of the temple clearly. Shaggoth was fussing about with bits of wire, making happy sounds. The high priest was a dark, hairy man, grotesquely short and ugly. There was something indecent about his expression and his chuckling.

Then the focus cleared for depth. For the first time, the two men saw the god worshiped on Melok.

"A robot!" Keir exclaimed. "A robot like the legends in the books from the ruined planet."

Por Dain nodded slowly. "Looks like it. I knew it was metal—yet how can it be? Metal would have gone to pieces by now. It must be some kind of statue shaped of tin and made to look like the robots their legends described. These savages are worshipping a machine."

It was an ancient piece in any event. Dust and grime had been polished from it but there was an unmistakable patina of centuries. It was vaguely manlike, though its face gained the touch of nobility without any definite features.

"Maybe it is the wreck of a real robot," Por decided. "If the ancients before the bombing here had some of our alloys—it could be. Now there's religion for you, Keir. A race of men blindly worshipping something they made for a servant."

Lyssa touched the Earth emblem but her smile remained unchanged. She no longer protested Por's remarks. Instead she pointed to Shaggoth, who was blowing out the torch and turning down the gas mantles.

"He's coming here," she said.

In that she was right. The pickup showed him moving across the sand toward them, badly distorted but recognizable.

Por had turned the gain up enough to see by the dim temple lights. He caught Keir's attention and began tracing the thing Shaggoth had been working on.

It was a weirdly wired mess of coils and blocks of some kind, seemingly directed toward their ship. Por pointed out where the wires led from it and were either stuck on the robot body or somehow plugged in.

"Must be a mockup of some machine from the legends," Keir guessed. "Ritual magic—similarity principle. But does he think some kind of god power is still generated in that creature?"

"There's always power in the god," Lyssa informed them. "Shaggoth has bragged of it. He makes miracle fires with it."

Any power in those batteries had been dead for millennia, Keir realized. But a clever priest could fake something to convince his followers.

"Maybe he's coming here to warn us he's making big medicine and we're in his power," Por guessed.

Lyssa shook her head, her smile deepening slightly. "He's coming to see me. He asked me today. I think he wants to be converted to the blessed lost-Earth faith."

"You're not going out, Lyssa," Keir told her sharply. "And you're not letting him in." He flipped a toggle to cut in the hull pickups. Around the ship were some fifty partly concealed figures waiting patiently, as they had waited every night. "That's an order, Lyssa. Stay away from the airlock until morning."

She nodded faintly, then more firmly at his expression. "All right," she agreed softly, though her smile was almost gone. "Good night, then. I'll sleep now."

They heard her sounds of final prayers and the faint noise of her body sinking into the hammock in her tiny room. After a while Por Dain also retired.

Keir sat watching the high priest. Shaggoth reached the ship and knocked softly. Then he squatted down in the sand, motionless and patient. Keir waited but nothing else happened. And finally he released his control seat and sank onto it. The last sounds he heard were the heavy breathing of Por Dain and Lyssa's faintly adenoidal snores.

A heavy hand on his shoulder shook him back to consciousness. Por Dain stood over him, scowling and swearing.

"She's gone! The Earth-damned crusading little fool—she pulled a sneak and they're all gone."

Keir snapped out of his stupor. By the clock, six hours of the long Melok night had passed since he fell asleep. He saw that the outside hull pickups were on, showing no sign of the natives or of Shaggoth.

"We've got to get out and rescue her," he muttered thickly, reaching for the caffein tablets.

"No chance. Holy Earth, look at them!"

Por Dain had turned the pickups toward the temple and the distorted one showed an enormous crowd of Melok natives streaming from the city and mounting toward their fane.

Then the one good pickup caught Shaggoth as the priest moved into view. Gas jets were now casting a half-light over the temple, and the priest was again busy with his wired contraption.

"Damn him," Por growled. "He isn't as ignorant as I thought. That savage is tuning a circuit, looks like. Ah!"

As he spoke, the contraption seemed to come to life. A blue glow ran over the coils and turned white. It seemed to spread like a spark climbing a Jacob's ladder. Then it was a faint glow of spherical shape that stretched and grew too thin to see.

Then acolytes appeared, bearing Lyssa. She was trussed firmly but seemed unharmed. She made no sound but her smile was gone. Her eyes, wide and round with fear, were centered on Shaggoth.

A chanting began as the acolytes laid her on a stone block before their last true god. Shaggoth approached her, holding two wands from which wires led to the robot's body.

Keir Soth found himself blaspheming heavily as he reached for the weapons in a drawer of the control panel.

But Por Dain held him back. "Don't be a fool, Captain. It's a bluff. He wants us to come out to rescue her. That's his whole plan. Then he'll have the ship. There must be a horde of the savages waiting below the hull where we can't pick them up."

"Then we'll take the ship there."

"No." Anger mingled with reluctant respect in Por Dain's expression. "I recognize that field he's generating now from the layout of parts. We've got one like it on Homeworld—only no bigger than a pea yet at maximum. You can't get through. It would damp the engines half a mile before we reached the pyramid."

No wonder the priest had refused to let them see the ancient books. He must have a technical library there—and somehow the old faker comprehended what was in them, however little he used them for the good of his followers.

Shaggoth was staring directly into the pickup, as if aware that they could see him. Now he brought the wands into contact with Lyssa's body, smiling thickly as she screamed.

Keir began warming the engines. "I'll take the ship in as close as we dare," he said. "Then we get out and kill as many as we can trying to reach her."

Por Dain began loading the weapons as the engines warmed.

Again Shaggoth brought the insulated wands against the Novitiate's body. Her muscles tensed in a wild spasm but the savage chant rose to cover any cries she made.

The ship was just beginning to respond, rising sluggishly. Keir grinned thinly, hoping a horde of Melok natives were caught under that pressure field. The ship couldn't yet operate well but power was building up.

Again Melok brought down the wands. And this time the chant quieted.

"Help me—" Hers was a cry that should have torn the heart from a brazen idol. "For the love of Earth, help me—"

And help came.

The robot figure moved. A metal arm swung down to tear the wires free from its body. Slowly, ponderously, the figure straightened. There was a creaking sound as the limbs moved, and dirt and scale chipped away. Then it was erect.

In two strides the metal figure had caught the frozen priest and broken him like a thin stick across one knee. Shaggoth was flung back into the mob of screaming, fleeing worshippers.

For a moment the robot halted, staring toward Lyssa. It sank to one knee. A bass voice sounded over the pickup, using an oddly pure-sounding form of the ancient tongue.

"Saintly One, I—"

The words cut off as the robot bent closer. Then something like a sigh came from it. It stood up quietly, moving to snap the bindings away from Lyssa's limbs. She lay limp. The metal arms reached under her to lift her.

The robot turned then, facing away from the pickup for a long minute, its head up as if listening. Again there was a sigh.

"The field is too strong," the even bass voice said in the ancient tongue. The figure turned, searching until it located the pickup.

"I go by another way," the robot said slowly and carefully. "Your lady is safe but you who are in the ship must wait until I appear again."

It turned quickly toward the throne on which it had sat. A foot reached out to kick the massive structure aside, while a hand made a pass through the air. Almost instantly, an opening appeared in what had seemed solid rock. The robot stepped into it, carrying the Novitiate, and disappeared. Immediately after it was gone the rock closed tightly. A small explosion seemed to take place inside.

Keir had the ship up but now there was no place to go. "Wait until he appears where?" he asked bitterly. "Or until he can get safely hidden away with her in some hole in the ground?"

"Try cruising slowly toward the pyramid," Por Dain suggested. "Maybe there's a secret shaft out to the bottom and he'll show up there."

"He'd better."

Before the ship was in full motion, however, they saw the robot again. This time he was only a dot on their screen until Por raised the magnification of the hull pickup. He stood three miles from the pyramid on a narrow ledge of the most ancient of the brick structures. Lyssa was still unconscious in his arms. Somehow he had traveled that distance in less than five minutes. Now he stood staring into space, as if listening to a voice from the stars.

Then his head dropped. "So long?" he asked. "Fiften hundred years from the radiation that paralyzed my mind until the right words could waken me?" He sighed again and seemed to listen once more. He nodded slightly and turned to face the ship. From the receiver of the now useless temple pickup a softer and warmer voice spoke, using standard Homeworld speech. "Bring your ship close to me and open your airlock. I will leap across. And do not fear. I shall be the Watcher for Homeworld now, since these people have forfeited all right to one."

Keir Soth manipulated the ship very delicately across the small distance while Por Dain went down to the airlock. It was tricky maneuvering but Keir had time enough to see a series of small explosions running like a mole's trail from the pyramid across the desert to the big brick building. Whatever secret way the robot had known was destroyed now.

The metal figure leaped when the ship was fifty feet away. Keir flinched and held his breath. Then he heard the lock cycling to full space closure and the robot came into the control room, with Lyssa conscious and smiling her pleasant and empty smile beside him. Por Dain stood in the doorway as the robot glanced around at the controls.

"I have brought the few books from here that you can use," the robot said, pointing to a small sack Por Dain was holding. "There is no need to wait here longer."

He slipped confidently into the captain's chair, reaching for the controls. With unerring accuracy he plotted the course toward Homeworld and the ship began its gradual acceleration into the red sky and toward space.

Keir Soth shook his head, benumbed by wonder. "How could Melok have lost any war if they could create robots like you?"

The Watcher looked back at the three humans and his voice was soft but filled with immense pride. "I was never created on Melok," he said. "I came from Earth!"

There was only the soft drone of the ship's engines as Lyssa and Keir Soth slipped to their knees, to be followed a moment later by a former agnostic, Por Dain.

QUESTIONS

1. Use the story to discuss the relationships and differences between religion and legend.

2. What is the explanation for the dislike felt by Por Dain toward Lyssa? What does each character represent?

3. Why was one Novitiate included on every ship? What might have been the origin of this requirement?

4. What legendary rather than religious values does the robot represent? What historical "facts" serve as the basis for legend and religion in this story?

5. Use this story to discuss suspense in science fiction. Do most SF authors have rather standard ways of creating suspense, of keeping their readers moving quickly through their stories? What are these ways?

part 4

Aftermath

Science fiction that stressed a "doomsday" view reached a high point of popularity in the late 1960s. Its warnings of the end of civilization or the end of the world itself found a ready audience among people who were increasingly aware of ecological problems. In one way or another, the doomsday motif compels the reader to stand at a far remove from our common experience; to judge humanity in perspective, from a distance that can make minor current problems seem massive and reduce apparently major current difficulties to insignificance.

Kurt Vonnegut's "Tomorrow and Tomorrow and Tomorrow" is a story centering on overpopulation. But unlike "The Marching Morons" in Part II, it contains no final solution to a dilemma that has catastrophically affected humanity's patterns of living. Although we may laugh—the story is certainly comic—we also realize that the social and physical amenities that make life tolerable are seriously threatened by our increased scientific knowledge, particularly our ability to prolong life. Science also threatens our way of life in James Tiptree, Jr.'s "The Man Who Walked Home." A scientific accident has started a chain reaction that blew the present civilization apart. Some people survive, but "hardscience" is outlawed. In this story we gain an awareness of the enormously destructive potential of a "minor accident" caused by our advanced technology. Tiptree's story moves toward a hopeful conclusion, however. In contrast, "The Year of the Jackpot" portrays our worst dreams coming true. Strange events flourish; two humans are caught in the breakdown of world normality. Heinlein's story takes us step by step toward doomsday, predicting how collapse will take place almost daily.

The view of the end of the world isn't always gloomy, sometimes it is amusing. "A Vision of Judgment" is humorous, ironic, and optimistic. In Wells's story we are all hopeless creatures, petty, with an exaggerated notion of our importance. In our pride we may think we deserve either damnation or exaltation, but all we will receive is mercy from a god that has a sense of humor and will offer us another chance. We are often given another chance in the doomsday vision. For example, not all humanity, but only the present civilization is destroyed in "The Horses." As in previous selections, some people survive the cataclysmic end. Mercy is again offered and a new civilization—hopefully a better civilization—is seen at the point at which it begins.

All doomsday stories share one characteristic, at least. They reveal the SF writer's capacity for projecting the present far forward. Perhaps the most disturbing aspect of these stories is that so many writers sense the destructive path humanity appears to have taken. The hopeful element of doomsday stories lies in the compassion expressed by their writers. Often these writers suggest the belief—against great odds—that somehow, despite the horrors we may inflict on ourselves, we will find or invent a better way after "The End." Even if the imagined end is final, some "good" human actions make the race appear as if its existence had meaning, showed some capability for a redeeming love.

Tomorrow and Tomorrow and Tomorrow

Kurt Vonnegut, Jr.

In 1974, Rona and Laurence Cherry wrote, in The New York Times, *"By 2005, when the generation of the postwar baby boom reaches retirement age, some experts estimate [that] almost a quarter of the population will be 65 years and over." The best-selling novelist Kurt Vonnegut, Jr., author of such works as* The Sirens of Titan, Slaughterhouse Five, *and* Breakfast of Champions, *here explores, with black humor, some of the consequences of overpopulation, thus bringing to life a future that is already the present in some teeming sections of the world.*

The year was 2158 A.D., and Lou and Emerald Schwartz were whispering on the balcony outside Lou's family's apartment on the seventy-sixth floor of Building 257 in Alden Village, a New York housing development that covered what had once been known as Southern Connecticut. When Lou and Emerald had married, Em's parents had tearfully described the marriage as being between May and December; but now, with Lou one hundred and twelve and Em ninety-three, Em's parents had to admit that the match had worked out well.

But Em and Lou weren't without their troubles, and they were out in the nippy air of the balcony because of them.

"Sometimes I get so mad, I feel like just up and diluting his anti-gerasone," said Em.

"That'd be against Nature, Em," said Lou, "it'd be murder. Besides, if he caught us tinkering with his anti-gerasone, not only would he disinherit us, he'd bust my neck. Just because he's one hundred and seventy-two doesn't mean Gramps isn't strong as a bull."

"Against Nature," said Em. "Who knows what Nature's like anymore? Ohhhhh—I don't guess I could ever bring myself to dilute his anti-gerasone or anything like that, but, gosh, Lou, a body can't help thinking Gramps is never going to leave if somebody doesn't help him along a little. Golly—we're so crowded a person can hardly turn around, and

Verna's dying for a baby, and Melissa's gone thirty years without one." She stamped her feet. "I get so sick of seeing his wrinkled old face, watching him take the only private room and the best chair and the best food, and getting to pick out what to watch on TV, and running everybody's life by changing his will all the time."

"Well, after all," said Lou bleakly, "Gramps *is* head of the family. And he can't help being wrinkled like he is. He was seventy before anti-gerasone was invented. He's going to leave, Em. Just give him time. It's his business. I know he's tough to live with, but be patient. It wouldn't do to do anything that'd rile him. After all, we've got it better'n anybody else, there on the daybed."

"How much longer do you think we'll get to sleep on the daybed before he picks another pet? The world's record's two months, isn't it?"

"Mom and Pop had it that long once, I guess."

"When *is* he going to leave, Lou?" said Emerald.

"Well, he's talking about giving up anti-gerasone right after the Five-Hundred-Mile Speedway Race."

"Yes—and before that it was the Olympics, and before that the World's Series, and before that the Presidential Elections, and before that I-don't-know-what. It's been just one excuse after another for fifty years now. I don't think we're ever going to get a room to ourselves or an egg or anything."

"All right—call me a failure!" said Lou. "What can I do? I work hard and make good money, but the whole thing, practically, is taxed away for defense and old age pensions. And if it wasn't taxed away, where you think we'd find a vacant room to rent? Iowa, maybe? Well, who wants to live on the outskirts of Chicago?"

Em put her arms around his neck. "Lou, hon, I'm not calling you a failure. The Lord knows you're not. You just haven't had a chance to be anything or have anything because Gramps and the rest of his generation won't leave and let somebody else take over."

"Yeah, yeah," said Lou gloomily. "You can't exactly blame 'em, though, can you? I mean, I wonder how quick we'll knock off the anti-gerasone when we get Gramps' age."

"Sometimes I wish there wasn't any such thing as anti-gerasone!" said Emerald passionately. "Or I wish it was made out of something real expensive and hard-to-get instead of mud and dandelions. Sometimes I wish folks just up and died regular as clockwork, without anything to say about it, instead of deciding themselves how long they're going to stay around. There ought to be a law against selling the stuff to anybody over one hundred and fifty."

"Fat chance of that," said Lou, "with all the money and votes the old people've got." He looked at her closely. "You ready to up and die, Em?"

"Well, for heaven's sakes, what a thing to say to your wife. Hon! I'm not even one hundred yet." She ran her hands lightly over her firm, youthful figure, as though for confirmation. "The best years of my life are still ahead of me. But you can bet that when one hundred and fifty rolls around, old Em's going to pour her anti-gerasone down the sink, and quit taking up room, and she'll do it smiling."

"Sure, sure," said Lou, "you bet. That's what they all say. How many you heard of doing it?"

"There was that man in Delaware."

"Aren't you getting kind of tired of talking about him, Em? That was five months ago."

"All right, then—Gramma Winkler, right here in the same building."

"She got smeared by a subway."

"That's just the way she picked to go," said Em.

"Then what was she doing carrying a six-pack of anti-gerasone when she got it?"

Emerald shook her head wearily and covered her eyes. "I dunno, I dunno, I dunno. All I know is, something's just got to be done." She sighed. "Sometimes I wish they'd left a couple of diseases kicking around somewhere, so I could get one and go to bed for a little while. Too many people!" she cried, and her words cackled and gabbled and died in a thousand asphalt-paved, skyscraper-walled courtyards.

Lou laid his hand on her shoulder tenderly. "Aw, hon, I hate to see you down in the dumps like this."

"If we just had a car, like the folks used to in the old days," said Em, "we could go for a drive, and get from people for a little while. Gee—if *those* weren't the days!"

"Yeah," said Lou, "before they'd used up all the metal."

"We'd hop in, and Pop'd drive up to a filling station and say, 'Fillerup!' "

"That *was* the nuts, wasn't it—before they'd used up all the gasoline."

"And we'd go for a carefree ride in the country."

"Yeah—all seems like a fairyland now, doesn't it, Em? Hard to believe there really used to be all that space between cities."

"And when we got hungry," said Em, "we'd find ourselves a restaurant, and walk in, big as you please and say, 'I'll have a steak and French-fries, I believe,' or, 'How are the pork chops today?' " She licked her lips, and her eyes glistened.

"Yeah man!" growled Lou. "How'd you like a hamburger with the works, Em?"

"Mmmmmmmm."

"If anybody'd offered us processed seaweed in those days, we would have spit right in his eye, huh, Em?"

"Or processed sawdust," said Em.

Doggedly, Lou tried to find the cheery side of the situation.

"Well, anyway, they've got the stuff so it tastes a lot less like seaweed and sawdust than it did at first; and they say it's actually better for us than what we used to eat."

"I felt fine!" said Em fiercely.

Lou shrugged. "Well, you've got to realize, the world wouldn't be able to support twelve billion people if it wasn't for processed seaweed and sawdust. I mean, it's a wonderful thing, really. I guess. That's what they say."

"They say the first thing that pops into their heads," said Em. She closed her eyes. "Golly—remember shopping, Lou? Remember how the stores used to fight to get our folks to buy something? You didn't have to wait for somebody to die to get a bed or chairs or a stove or anything like that. Just went in—bing!—and bought whatever you wanted. Gee whiz that was nice, before they used up all the raw materials. I was just a little kid then, but I can remember so plain."

Depressed, Lou walked listlessly to the balcony's edge, and looked up at the clean, cold, bright stars against the black velvet of infinity. "Remember when we used to be bugs on science fiction, Em? Flight seventeen, leaving for Mars, launching ramp twelve. 'Board! All non-technical personnel kindly remain in bunkers. Ten seconds . . . nine . . . eight . . . seven . . . six . . . five . . . four . . . three . . . two . . . *one! Main Stage! Barrrrrroooom!*"

"Why worry about what was going on on Earth?" said Em, looking up at the stars with him. "In another few years, we'd all be shooting through space to start life all over again on a new planet."

Lou sighed. "Only it turns out you need something about twice the size of the Empire State Building to get one lousy colonist to Mars. And for another couple of trillion bucks he could take his wife and dog. *That's* the way to lick overpopulation—*emigrate!*"

"Lou—?"

"Hmmm?"

"When's the Five-Hundred-Mile Speedway Race?"

"Uh—Memorial Day, May thirtieth."

She bit her lip. "Was that awful of me to ask?"

"Not very, I guess. Everybody in the apartment's looked it up to make sure."

"I don't want to be awful," said Em, "but you've just got to talk over these things now and then, and get them out of your system."

"Sure you do. Feel better?"

"Yes—and I'm not going to lose my temper anymore, and I'm going to be just as nice to him as I know how."

"That's my Em."

They squared their shoulders, smiled bravely, and went back inside.

Gramps Schwartz, his chin resting on his hands, his hands on the crook of his cane, was staring irascibly at the five-foot television screen that dominated the room. On the screen, a news commentator was summarizing the day's happenings. Every thirty seconds or so, Gramps would jab the floor with his cane-tip and shout, "Hell! We did that a hundred years ago!"

Emerald and Lou, coming in from the balcony, were obliged to take seats in the back row, behind Lou's father and mother, brother and sister-in-law, son and daughter-in-law, grandson and wife, granddaughter and husband, great-grandson and wife, nephew and wife, grandnephew and wife, great-grandniece and husband, great-grandnephew and wife, and, of course, Gramps, who was in front of everybody. All, save Gramps, who was somewhat withered and bent, seemed by pre-anti-gerasone standards, to be about the same age—to be somewhere in their late twenties or early thirties.

"*Meanwhile,*" the commentator was saying, "*Council Bluffs, Iowa, was still threatened by stark tragedy. But two hundred weary rescue workers have refused to give up hope, and continue to dig in an effort to save Elbert Haggedorn, one hundred and eighty-three, who has been wedged for two days in a . . .*"

"I wish he'd get something more cheerful," Emerald whispered to Lou.

"Silence!" cried Gramps. "Next one shoots off his big bazoo while the TV's on is gonna find hisself cut off without a dollar—" and here his voice suddenly softened and sweetened "when they wave that checkered flag at the Indianapolis Speedway, and old Gramps gets ready for the Big Trip Up Yonder." He sniffed sentimentally, while his heirs concentrated desperately on not making the slightest sound. For them, the poignancy of the prospective Big Trip had been dulled somewhat by its having been mentioned by Gramps about once a day for fifty years.

"*Dr. Brainard Keyes Bullard,*" said the commentator, "*President of Wyandotte College, said in an address tonight that most of the world's ills can be traced to the fact that Man's knowledge of himself has not kept pace with his knowledge of the physical world.*"

"Hell!" said Gramps. "We said that a hundred years ago!"

"*In Chicago tonight,*" said the commentator, "*a special celebration is taking place in the Chicago Lying-in Hospital. The guest of honor is Lowell W. Hitz, age zero. Hitz, born this morning, is the twenty-five-millionth child to be born in the hospital.*" The commentator faded, and was replaced on the screen by young Hitz, who squalled furiously.

"Hell," whispered Lou to Emerald, "we said that a hundred years ago."

"I heard that!" shouted Gramps. He snapped off the television set, and his petrified descendants stared silently at the screen. "You, there, boy—"

"I didn't mean anything by it, sir," said Lou.

"Get me my will. You know where it is. You kids *all* know where it is. Fetch, boy!"

Lou nodded dully, and found himself going down the hall, picking his way over bedding to Gramps' room, the only private room in the Schwartz apartment. The other rooms were the bathroom, the living room, and the wide, windowless hallway, which was originally intended to serve as a dining area, and which had a kitchenette in one end. Six mattresses and four sleeping bags were dispersed in the hallway and living room, and the daybed, in the living room, accommodated the eleventh couple, the favorites of the moment.

On Gramps' bureau was his will, smeared, dog-eared, perforated, and blotched with hundreds of additions, deletions, accusations, conditions, warnings, advice, and homely philosophy. The document was, Lou reflected, a fifty-year diary, all jammed onto two sheets—a garbled, illegible log of day after day of strife. This day, Lou would be disinherited for the eleventh time, and it would take him perhaps six months of impeccable behavior to regain the promise of a share in the estate.

"Boy!" called Gramps.

"Coming, sir." Lou hurried back into the living room, and handed Gramps the will.

"Pen!" said Gramps.

He was instantly offered eleven pens, one from each couple.

"Not *that* leaky thing," he said, brushing Lou's pen aside. "Ah, there's a nice one. Good boy, Willy." He accepted Willy's pen. That was the tip they'd all been waiting for. Willy, then, Lou's father, was the new favorite.

Willy, who looked almost as young as Lou, though one hundred and forty-two, did a poor job of concealing his pleasure. He glanced shyly at the daybed, which would become his, and from which Lou and Emerald would have to move back into the hall, back to the worst spot of all by the bathroom door.

Gramps missed none of the high drama he'd authored, and he gave his own familiar role everything he had. Frowning and running his finger along each line, as though he were seeing the will for the first time, he read aloud in a deep, portentous monotone, like a bass tone on a cathedral organ:

"I, Harold D. Schwartz, residing in Building 257 of Alden Village, New York City, do hereby make, publish, and declare this to be my last Will and Testament, hereby revoking any and all former wills and codicils by me at any time heretofore made." He blew his nose importantly, and went on, not missing a word, and repeating many for emphasis—repeating in particular his ever-more-elaborate specifications for a funeral.

At the end of these specifications, Gramps was so choked with emotion that Lou thought he might forget why he'd gotten out the will in the first place. But Gramps heroically brought his powerful emotions under control, and, after erasing for a full minute, he began to write and speak at the same time. Lou could have spoken his lines for him, he'd heard them so often.

"I have had many heartbreaks ere leaving this vale of tears for a better land," Gramps said and wrote. "But the deepest hurt of all has been dealt me by—" He looked around the group, trying to remember who the malefactor was.

Everyone looked helpfully at Lou, who held up his hand resignedly.

Gramps nodded, remembering, and completed the sentence: "my great-grandson, Louis J. Schwartz."

"Grandson, sir," said Lou.

"Don't quibble. You're in deep enough now, young man," said Gramps, but he changed the trifle. And from there he went without a misstep through the phrasing of the disinheritance, causes for which were disrespectfulness and quibbling.

In the paragraph following, the paragraph that had belonged to everyone in the room at one time or another, Lou's name was scratched out and Willy's substituted as heir to the apartment and, the biggest plum of all, the double bed in the private bedroom. "So!" said Gramps, beaming. He erased the date at the foot of the will, and substituted a new one, including the time of day. "Well—time to watch the McGarvey Family." The McGarvey Family was a television serial that Gramps had been following since he was sixty, or for one hundred and twelve years. "I can't wait to see what's going to happen next," he said.

Lou detached himself from the group and lay down on his bed of pain by the bathroom door. He wished Em would join him, and he wondered where she was.

He dozed for a few moments, until he was disturbed by someone's stepping over him to get into the bathroom. A moment later, he heard a faint gurgling sound, as though something were being poured down the washbasin drain. Suddenly, it entered his mind that Em had cracked up, and that she was in there doing something drastic about Gramps.

"Em—!" he whispered through the panel. There was no reply, and Lou pressed against the door. The worn lock, whose bolt barely engaged its socket, held for a second, then let the door swing inward.

"Morty!" gasped Lou.

Lou's great-grandnephew, Mortimer, who had just married and brought his wife home to the Schwartz menage, looked at Lou with consternation and surprise. Morty kicked the door shut, but not before Lou had glimpsed what was in his hand—Gramps' enormous economy-size bottle of anti-gerasone, which had been half-emptied, and which Morty was refilling to the top with tap water.

A moment later, Morty came out, glared defiantly at Lou, and brushed past him wordlessly to rejoin his pretty bride.

Shocked, Lou didn't know what on earth to do. He couldn't let Gramps take the mousetrapped anti-gerasone; but if he warned Gramps about it, Gramps would certainly make life in the apartment, which was merely insufferable now, harrowing.

Lou glanced into the living room, and saw that the Schwartzes, Emerald among them, were momentarily at rest, relishing the botches that McGarveys had made of *their* lives. Stealthily, he went into the bathroom, locked the door as well as he could, and began to pour the contents of Gramps' bottle down the drain. He was going to refill it with full-strength anti-gerasone from the twenty-two smaller bottles on the shelf. The bottle contained a half-gallon, and its neck was small, so it seemed to Lou that the emptying would take forever. And the almost imperceptible smell of anti-gerasone, like Worcestershire sauce, now seemed to Lou, in his nervousness, to be pouring out into the rest of the apartment through the keyhole and under the door.

"*Gloog-gloog-gloog-gloog-*," went the bottle monotonously. Suddenly, up came the sound of music from the living room, and there were murmurs and the scraping of chair legs on the floor. "*Thus ends*," said the television announcer, "*the 29,121st chapter in the life of your neighbors and mine, the McGarveys.*" Footsteps were coming down the hall. There was a knock on the bathroom door.

"Just a sec," called Lou cheerily. Desperately, he shook the big bottle, trying to speed up the flow. His palms slipped on the wet glass, and the heavy bottle smashed to splinters on the tile floor.

The door sprung open, and Gramps, dumfounded, stared at the mess.

Lou grinned engagingly through his nausea, and, for want of anything remotely resembling a thought, he waited for Gramps to speak.

"Well, boy," said Gramps at last, "looks like you've got a little tidying up to do."

And that was all he said. He turned around, elbowed his way through the crowd, and locked himself in his bedroom.

The Schwartzes contemplated Lou in incredulous silence for a moment longer, and then hurried back to the living room, as though some of his horrible guilt would taint them, too, if they looked too long. Morty stayed behind long enough to give Lou a quizzical, annoyed glance. Then he, too, went into the living room, leaving only Emerald standing in the doorway.

Tears streamed over her cheeks. "Oh, you poor lamb—please don't look so awful. It was my fault. I put you up to this."

"No," said Lou, finding his voice, "really you didn't. Honest, Em, I was just—"

"You don't have to explain anything to me, hon. I'm on your side no matter what." She kissed him on his cheek, and whispered in his ear. "It wouldn't have been murder, hon. It wouldn't have killed him. It wasn't such a terrible thing to do. It just would have fixed him up so he'd be able to go any time God decided He wanted him."

"What's gonna happen next, Em?" said Lou hollowly. "What's he gonna do?"

Lou and Emerald stayed fearfully awake almost all night, waiting to see what Gramps was going to do. But not a sound came from the sacred bedroom. At two hours before dawn, the pair dropped off to sleep.

At six o'clock they arose again, for it was time for their generation to eat breakfast in the kitchenette. No one spoke to them. They had twenty minutes in which to eat, but their reflexes were so dulled by the bad night that they had hardly swallowed two mouthfuls of egg-type processed seaweed before it was time to surrender their places to their son's generation.

Then, as was the custom for whomever had been most recently disinherited, they began preparing Gramps' breakfast, which would presently be served to him in bed, on a tray. They tried to be cheerful about it. The toughest part of the job was having to handle the honest-to-God eggs and bacon and oleomargarine on which Gramps spent almost all of the income from his fortune.

"Well," said Emerald, "I'm not going to get all panicky until I'm sure there's something to be panicky about."

"Maybe he doesn't know what it was I busted," said Lou hopefully.

"Probably thinks it was your watch crystal," said Eddie, their son, who was toying apathetically with his buckwheat-type processed sawdust cakes.

"Don't get sarcastic with your father," said Em, "and don't talk with your mouth full, either."

"I'd like to see anybody take a mouthful of this stuff and *not* say something," said Eddie, who was seventy-three. He glanced at the clock. "It's time to take Gramps his breakfast, you know."

"Yeah, it is, isn't it," said Lou weakly. He shrugged. "Let's have the tray, Em."

"We'll both go."

Walking slowly, smiling bravely, they found a large semicircle of long-faced Schwartzes standing around the bedroom door.

Em knocked. "Gramps," she said brightly, "break-fast is rea-dy."

There was no reply, and she knocked again, harder.

The door swing open before her fist. In the middle of the room, the soft, deep, wide, canopied bed, the symbol of the sweet by-and-by to every Schwartz, was empty.

A sense of death, as unfamiliar to the Schwartzes as Zoroastrianism or the causes of the Sepoy Mutiny, stilled every voice and slowed every heart. Awed, the heirs began to search gingerly under the furniture and behind the drapes for all that was mortal of Gramps, father of the race.

But Gramps had left not his earthly husk but a note, which Lou finally found on the dresser, under a paperweight which was a treasured souvenir from the 2000 World's Fair. Unsteadily, Lou read it aloud:

" 'Somebody who I have sheltered and protected and taught the best I know how all these years last night turned on me like a mad dog and diluted my anti-gerasone, or tried to. I am no longer a young man. I can no longer bear the crushing burden of life as I once could. So, after last night's bitter experience, I say goodbye. The cares of this world will soon drop away like a cloak of thorns, and I shall know peace. By the time you find this, I will be gone.' "

"Gosh," said Willy brokenly, "he didn't even get to see how the Five-Hundred-Mile Speedway Race was going to come out."

"Or the World's Series," said Eddie.

"Or whether Mrs. McGarvey got her eyesight back," said Morty.

"There's more," said Lou, and he began reading aloud again: " 'I, Harold D. Schwartz . . . do hereby make, publish and declare this to be my last Will and Testament, hereby revoking any and all former will and codicils by me at any time heretofore made.' "

"No!" cried Willy. "Not another one!"

" 'I do stipulate' " read Lou, " 'that all of my property, of whatsoever kind and nature, not be divided, but do devise and bequeath it to be held in common by my issue, without regard for generation, equally, share, and share alike.' "

"Issue?" said Emerald.

Lou included the multitude in a sweep of his hand. "It means we all own the whole damn shootin' match."

All eyes turned instantly to the bed.

"Share and share alike?" said Morty.

"Actually," said Willy, who was the oldest person present, "it's just like the old system, where the oldest people head up things with their headquarters in here, and—"

"I like *that!*" said Em. "Lou owns as much of it as you do, and I say it ought to be for the oldest one who's still working. You can snooze around here all day, waiting for your pension check, and poor Lou stumbles in here after work, all tuckered out, and—"

"How about letting somebody who's never had any privacy get a little crack at it?" said Eddie hotly. "Hell, you old people had plenty of privacy back when you were kids. I was born and raised in the middle of the goddam barracks in the hall! How about—"

"Yeah?" said Morty. "Sure, you've all had it pretty tough, and my heart bleeds for you. But try honeymooning in the hall for a real kick."

"Silence!" shouted Willy imperiously. "The next person who opens his mouth spends the next six months by the bathroom. Now clear out of my room. I want to think."

A vase shattered against the wall, inches above his head. In the next moment, a free-for-all was underway, with each couple battling to eject every other couple from the room. Fighting coalitions formed and dissolved with the lightning changes of the tactical situation. Em and Lou were thrown into the hall, where they organized others in the same situation, and stormed back into the room.

After two hours of struggle, with nothing like a decision in sight, the cops broke in.

For the next half-hour, patrol wagons and ambulances hauled away Schwartzes, and then the apartment was still and spacious.

An hour later, films of the last stages of the riot were being televised to 500,000,000 delighted viewers on the Eastern Seaboard.

In the stillness of the three-room Schwartz apartment on the 76th floor of Building 257, the television set had been left on. Once more the air was filled with the cries and grunts and crashes of the fray, coming harmlessly now from the loudspeaker.

The battle also appeared on the screen of the television set in the police station, where the Schwartzes and their captors watched with professional interest.

Em and Lou were in adjacent four-by-eight cells, and were stretched out peacefully on their cots.

"Em—" called Lou through the partition, "you got a washbasin all your own too?"

"Sure. Washbasin, bed, light—the works. Ha! And we thought Gramps' room was something. How long's this been going on?" She held out her hand. "For the first time in forty years, hon, I haven't got the shakes."

"Cross your fingers," said Lou, "the lawyer's going to try to get us a year."

"Gee," said Em dreamily, "I wonder what kind of wires you'd have to pull to get solitary?"

"All right, pipe down," said the turnkey, "or I'll toss the whole kit and caboodle of you right out. And first one who lets on to anybody outside how good jail is ain't never getting back in!"

The prisoners instantly fell silent.

The living room of the Schwartz apartment darkened for a moment, as the riot scenes faded, and then the face of the announcer appeared, like the sun coming from behind a cloud. "*And now, friends,*" he said, "*I have a special message from the makers of anti-gerasone, a message for all you folks over one hundred and fifty. Are you hampered socially by wrinkles, by stiffness of joints and discoloration or loss of hair, all because these things came upon you before anti-gerasone was developed? Well, if you are, you need no longer suffer, need no longer feel different and out of things.*

"*After years of research, medical science has now developed* super-*anti-gerasone! In weeks, yes weeks, you can look, feel, and act as young as your great-great-grandchildren! Wouldn't you pay* $5,000 *to be indistinguishable from everybody else? Well, you don't have to. Safe, tested super-anti-gerasone costs you only dollars a day. The average cost of regaining all the sparkle and attractiveness of youth is less than fifty dollars.*

"*Write now for your free trial carton. Just put your name and address on a dollar postcard, and mail it to 'Super,' Box* 500,000, *Schenectady,* N. Y. *Have you got that? I'll repeat it.* 'Super.' *Box . . .*" Underlining the announcer's words was the scratching of Gramps' fountain-pen, the one Willy had given him the night before. He had come in a few minutes previous from the Idle Hour Tavern, which commanded a view of Building 257 across the square of asphalt known as the Alden Village Green. He had called a cleaning woman to come straighten the place up, and had hired the best lawyer in town to get his descendants a conviction. Gramps had then moved the daybed before the television screen so that he could watch from a reclining position. It was something he'd dreamed of doing for years.

"Schen-*ec*-ta-dy," mouthed Gramps. "Got it." His face had changed remarkably. His facial muscles seemed to have relaxed, revealing kindness and equanimity under what had been taut, bad-tempered lines. It was almost as though his trial package of *Super*-anti-gerasone had already arrived. When something amused him on television, he smiled easily, rather than barely managing to lengthen the thin line of his mouth a millimeter. Life was good. He could hardly wait to see what was going to happen next.

QUESTIONS

1. Discuss the desirability of perpetual youth, good health, and life. What effect would these conditions have on the quality of life here on Earth?

2. Given the invention of an antiaging, antidisease tonic, would the housing arrangements in this story be probable or would the break-up of the extended family continue? What conditions might cause the return of the extended family?

3. Does the story have a hero and a villain?

4. This story is a comedy. What elements make it comic? In answering this question consider the level of language, the situation, characterization, and especially the ending.

5. Traditionally, the happy ending of a comedy represents the reintegration, usually of rebellious youth, into society, usually represented by the family. How does the happy ending of "Tomorrow and Tomorrow and

Tomorrow" differ from the traditional one? What does prison usually represent?

6. This story touches on a number of critical ecological, demographic, and social problems facing us today. What are they?

7. Is this a characteristic Vonnegut story? Do you consider the author a "mainstream" or a "science fiction" writer? Give reasons for your choice.

The Man Who Walked Home

James Tiptree, Jr.

We have begun to conquer space—we have not yet learned to cope with time. Our forced submission to time feeds our fantasies and our nightmares, from the Connecticut Yankee who ruled King Arthur's court to Tithonus who lived eternally, aging all the while. Time travel—our symbolic battle with time—is, next to space travel, perhaps the most common motif of science fiction. "The Man Who Walked Home" contains the long chronological time span so often presenf in SF—allowing us to speculate about which forms of human behavior will have continuity and which will not. This story also allows readers to speculate about how myth and legend begin and grow. The story is particularly noteworthy for its prevailing sense of melancholy and dread.

James Tiptree, Jr., is one of the newer SF writers to have gained considerable recognition; his works have regularly appeared in "best of the year" anthologies.

—Transgression! Terror! And he thrust and lost there—punched into impossibility, abandoned, never to be known how, the wrong man in the most wrong of all wrong places in that unimaginable collapse of never-to-be-reimagined mechanism—he stranded, undone, his lifeline severed, he in that nanosecond knowing his only tether parting, going away, the longest line to life withdrawing, winking out, disappearing forever beyond his grasp—telescoping away from him into the closing vortex beyond which lay his home, his life, his only possibility of being; seeing it sucked back into the deepest maw, melting, leaving him orphaned on what never-to-be-known shore of total wrongness—of beauty beyond joy, perhaps? Of horror? Of nothingness? Of profound otherness only, certainly whatever it was, that place into which he transgressed, certainly it could not support his life there, his violent and violating aberrance; and he, fierce, brave, crazy—clenched into one total protest, one body-fist of utter repudiation of himself there in that place, forsaken there—what did he do? Rejected, exiled, hungering homeward more desperate than any lost beast driving for its unreachable home, his home, his HOME—and no way, no transport, no vehicle, means, machinery, no force but his intolerable resolve aimed homeward along that vanishing vector, that last and only lifeline—he did, what?

He walked.

Home.

Precisely what hashed up in the work of the major industrial lessee of the Bonneville Particle Acceleration Facility in Idaho was never known. Or rather, all those who might have been able to diagnose the original malfunction were themselves obliterated almost at once in the greater catastrophe which followed.

The nature of this second cataclysm was not at first understood either. All that was ever certain was that at 1153.6 of May 2, 1989 Old Style, the Bonneville laboratories and all their personnel were transformed into an intimately disrupted form of matter resembling a high-energy plasma, which became rapidly airborne to the accompaniment of radiating seismic and atmospheric events.

The disturbed area unfortunately included an operational MIRV Watchdog bomb.

In the confusions of the next hours the Earth's population was substantially reduced, the biosphere was altered, and the Earth itself was marked with numbers of more conventional craters. For some years thereafter the survivors were existentially preoccupied and the peculiar dust bowl at Bonneville was left to weather by itself in the changing climatic cycles.

It was not a large crater; just over a kilometer in width and lacking the usual displacement lip. Its surface was covered with a finely divided substance which dried into dust. Before the rains began it was almost perfectly flat. Only in certain lights, had anyone been there to inspect it, a small surface marking or abraded place could be detected almost exactly at the center.

Two decades after the disaster a party of short brown people appeared from the south, together with a flock of somewhat atypical sheep. The crater at this time appeared as a wide shallow basin in which the grass did not grow well, doubtless from the almost complete lack of soil microorganisms. Neither this nor the surrounding vigorous grass were found to harm the sheep. A few crude hogans went up at the southern edge and a faint path began to be traced across the crater itself, passing by the central bare spot.

One spring morning two children who had been driving sheep across the crater came screaming back to camp. A monster had burst out of the ground before them, a huge flat animal making a dreadful roar. It vanished in a flash and a shaking of the earth, leaving an evil smell. The sheep had run away.

Since this last was visibly true, some elders investigated. Finding no sign of the monster and no place in which it could hide, they settled for beating the children, who settled for making a detour around the monster-spot, and nothing more occurred for a while.

The following spring the episode was repeated. This time an older girl was present but she could add only that the monster seemed to be rushing flat out along the ground without moving at all. And there was a scraped place in the dirt. Again nothing was found; an evil-ward in a cleft stick was placed at the spot.

When the same thing happened for the third time a year later, the detour was extended and other charm wands were added. But since no harm seemed to come of it and the brown people had seen far worse, sheep-tending resumed as before. A few more instantaneous apparitions of the monster were noted, each time in the spring.

At the end of the third decade of the new era a tall old man limped down the hills from the south, pushing his pack upon a bicycle wheel. He camped on the far side of the crater, and soon found the monster-site. He attempted to question people about it, but no one understood him, so he traded a knife for some meat. Although he was obviously feeble, something about him dissuaded them from killing him, and this proved wise because he later assisted the women to treat several sick children.

He spent much time around the place of the apparition and was nearby when it made its next appearance. This excited him very much, and he did several inexplicable but apparently harmless things, including moving his camp into the crater by the trail. He stayed on for a full year watching the site and was close by for its next manifestation. After this he spent a few days making a charmstone for the spot and then left, northward, hobbling, as he had come.

More decades passed. The crater eroded and a rain-gully became an intermittent steamlet across one edge of the basin. The brown people and their sheep were attacked by a band of grizzled men, after which the survivors went away eastward. The winters of what had been Idaho were now frost-free; aspen and eucalyptus sprouted in the moist plain. Still the crater remained treeless, visible as a flat bowl of grass, and the bare place at the center remained. The skies cleared somewhat.

After another three decades a larger band of black people with ox-drawn carts appeared and stayed for a time, but left again when they too saw the thunderclap-monster. A few other vagrants straggled by.

Five decades later a small permanent settlement had grown up on the nearest range of hills, from which men riding on small ponies with dark stripes down their spines herded humped cattle near the crater. A herdsman's hut was built by the streamlet, which in time became the habitation of an olive-skinned, red-haired family. In due course one of this clan again observed the monster-flash, but these people did not depart. The stone the tall man had placed was noted and left undisturbed.

The homestead at the crater's edge grew into a group of three and was joined by others, and the trail across it became a cartroad with a log bridge over the stream. At the center of the still-faintly-discernible crater the cartroad made a bend, leaving a grassy place which bore on its center about a square meter of curiously impacted bare earth and a deeply-etched sandstone rock.

The apparition of the monster was now known to occur regularly each spring on a certain morning in this place, and the children of the community dared each other to approach the spot. It was referred to in a phrase that could be translated as "the Old Dragon." The Old Dragon's appearance was always the same: a brief, violent thunderburst which began and cut off abruptly, in the midst of which a dragon-like creature was seen apparently in furious motion on the earth although it never actually moved. Afterward there was a bad smell and the earth smoked. People who saw it from close by spoke of a shivering sensation.

Early in the second century two young men rode into town from the north. Their ponies were shaggier than the local breed and the equipment they carried included two boxlike objects which the young men set up at the monster-site. They stayed in the area a full year observing two materializations of the Old Dragon, and they provided much news and maps of roads and trading-towns in the cooler regions to the north. They built a windmill which was accepted by the community and offered to build a lighting machine, which was refused. Then they departed with their boxes after unsuccessfully attempting to persuade a local boy to learn to operate one.

In the course of the next decades other travelers stopped by and marveled at the monster, and there was sporadic fighting over the mountains to the south. One of the armed bands made a cattle-raid into the crater hamlet. It was repulsed, but the raiders left a spotted sickness which killed many. For all this time the bare place at the crater's center remained, and the monster made his regular appearances, observed or not.

The hill-town grew and changed and the crater hamlet grew to be a town. Roads widened and linked into networks. There were gray-green conifers in the hills now, spreading down into the plain, and chirruping lizards lived in their branches.

At century's end a shabby band of skin-clad squatters with stunted milk-beasts erupted out of the west and were eventually killed or driven away, but not before the local herds had contracted a vicious parasite. Veterinaries were fetched from the market-city up north, but little could be done. The families near the crater left, and for some decades the area was empty. Finally cattle of a new strain reappeared in the plain and the crater hamlet was reoccupied. Still the bare center continued annually to manifest the monster and he became an accepted phenomenon of the area. On several occasions parties came from the distant Northwest Authority to observe it.

The crater hamlet flourished and grew into the fields where cattle had grazed and part of the old crater became the town park. A small seasonal tourist industry based on the monster-site developed. The townspeople rented rooms for the appearances and many more-or-less authentic monster-relics were on display in the local taverns.

Several cults now grew up around the monster. Some held that it was a devil or damned soul forced to appear on Earth in torment to expiate the catastrophe of two centuries back. Others believed that it, or he, was some kind of messenger whose roar portended either doom or hope according to the believer. One very vocal sect taught that the apparition registered the moral conduct of the townspeople over the past year, and scrutinized the annual apparition for changes which could be interpreted for good or ill. It was considered lucky, or dangerous, to be touched by some of the dust raised by the monster. In every generation at least one small boy would try to hit the monster with a stick, usually acquiring a broken arm and a lifelong tavern tale. Pelting the monster with stones or other objects was a popular sport, and for some years people systematically flung prayers and flowers at it. Once a party tried to net it and were left with strings and vapor. The area itself had long since been fenced off at the center of the park.

Through all this the monster made his violently enigmatic annual appearance, sprawled furiously motionless, unreachably roaring.

Only as the fourth century of the new era went by was it apparent that the monster had been changing slightly. He was now no longer on the earth but had an arm and a leg thrust upward in a kicking or flailing gesture. As the years passed he began to change more quickly until at the end of the century he had risen to a contorted crouching pose, arms outflung as if frozen in gyration. His roar, too, seemed somewhat differently pitched and the earth after him smoked more and more.

It was then widely felt that the man-monster was about to do something, to make some definitive manifestation, and a series of natural disasters and marvels gave support to a vigorous cult teaching this doctrine. Several religious leaders journeyed to the town to observe the apparitions.

However, the decades passed and the man-monster did nothing more than turn slowly in place, so that he now appeared to be in the act of sliding or staggering while pushing himself backward like a creature blown before a gale. No wind, of course, could be felt, and presently the general climate quieted and nothing came of it all.

Early in the fifty century New Calendar three survey parties from the North Central Authority came through the area and stopped to observe the monster. A permanent recording device was set up at the site, after assurances to the townfolk that no hardscience was involved. A local boy was trained to operate it; he quit when his girl left him but another volunteered. At this time nearly everyone believed that the apparition was a man, or the ghost of one. The record-machine boy and a few others, including the school mechanics teacher, referred to him as The

Man John. In the next decades the roads were greatly improved; all forms of travel increased and there was talk of building a canal to what had been the Snake River.

One May morning at the end of Century Five a young couple in a smart green mule-trap came jogging up the highroad from the Sandreas Rift Range to the southwest. The girl was golden-skinned and chatted with her young husband in a language unlike that ever heard by the Man John either at the end or the beginning of his life. What she said to him has, however, been heard in every age and tongue.

"Oh Serli, I'm so glad we're taking this trip now! Next summer I'll be so busy with baby."

To which Serli replied as young husbands often have, and so they trotted up to the town's inn. Here they left trap and bags and went in search of her uncle who was expecting them there. The morrow was the day of the Man John's annual appearance, and her Uncle Laban had come from the MacKenzie History Museum to observe it and to make certain arrangements.

They found him with the town school instructor of mechanics, who was also the recorder at the monster-site. Presently Uncle Laban took them all with him to the town mayor's office to meet with various religious personages. The mayor was not unaware of tourist values, but he took Uncle Laban's part in securing the cultists' grudging assent to the MacKenzie authorities' secular interpretation of the "monster," which was made easier by the fact that they disagreed among themselves. Then, seeing how pretty the niece was, the mayor took them all home to dinner.

When they returned to the inn for the night it was abrawl with holiday makers.

"Whew," said Uncle Laban. "I've talked myself dry, sister's daughter. What a weight of holy nonsense is that Morsha female! Serli, my lad, I know you have questions. Let me hand you this to read; it's the guide book we're giving 'em to sell. Tomorrow I'll answer for it all." And he disappeared into the crowded tavern.

So Serli and his bride took the pamphlet upstairs to bed with them, but it was not until the next morning at breakfast that they found time to read it.

" 'All that is known of John Delgano,' " read Serli with his mouth full, " 'comes from two documents left by his brother Carl Delgano in the archives of the MacKenzie Group in the early years after the holocaust.' Put some honey on this cake, Mira my dove. 'Verbatim transcript follows; this is Carl Delgano speaking.

" 'I'm not an engineer or an astronaut like John. I ran an electronics repair shop in Salt Lake City. John was only trained as a spaceman, he never got to space, the slump wiped all that out. So he tied up with this commercial group who were leasing part of Bonneville. They wanted a man for some kind of hard vacuum tests; that's all I knew about it. John and his wife moved to Bonneville, but we all got together several times a year, our wives were like sisters. John had two kids, Clara and Paul.

" 'The tests were all supposed to be secret, but John told me confidentially they were trying for an anti-gravity chamber. I don't know if it ever worked. That was the year before.

" 'Then that winter they came down for Christmas and John said they had something new. He was really excited. A temporal displacement, he called it; some kind of time effect. He said the chief honcho was like a real mad scientist. Big ideas. He kept adding more angles every time some other project would quit and leave equipment he could lease. No, I don't know who the top company was—maybe an insurance conglomerate, they had all the cash, didn't they? I guess they'd pay to catch a look at the future; that figures. Anyway, John was go, go, go. Katharine was scared; that's natural. She pictured him like, you know, H. G. Wells—walking around in some future world. John told her it wasn't like that at all. All they'd get would be this kind of flicker, like a second or two. All kinds of complications'—Yes, yes, my greedy piglet, some brew for me too. This is thirsty work!

"So . . . 'I remember I asked him, what about the Earth moving? I mean, you could come back in a different place, right? He said they had that all figured. A spatial trajectory. Katherine was so scared we dropped it. John told her, don't worry, I'll come home. But he didn't. Not that it makes any difference, of course; everything was wiped out. Salt Lake too. The only reason I'm here is that I went up by Calgary to see Mom, April twenty-ninth. May second it all blew. I didn't find you folks at MacKenzie until July. I guess I may as well stay. That's all I know about John, except that he was an all-right guy. If that accident started all this it wasn't his fault.

" 'The second document'—In the name of love, little mother, do I have to read all this! Oh very well; but you will kiss me first, madam. Must you look so ineffable? . . . 'The second document. Dated in the year eighteen, New Style, written by Carl'—see the old handwriting, my plump pigeon. Oh, very well, very well.

" 'Written at Bonneville Crater. I have seen my brother John Delgano. When I knew I had the rad sickness I came down here to look around. Salt Lake's still hot. So I hiked up here by Bonneville. You can see the crater where the labs were; it's grassed over. It's different, it's not radioactive, my film's OK. There's a bare place in the middle. Some Indios here told me a monster shows up here every year in the spring. I saw it myself a couple of days after I got here but I was too far away to see much, except I was sure it's a man. In a vacuum suit. There was a lot of noise and dust, took me by surprise. It was all over in a second. I figured it's pretty close to the day, I mean, May second, old.

" 'So I hung around a year and he showed up again yesterday. I was on the face side and I could see his face through the faceplate. It's John all right. He's hurt. I saw blood on his mouth and his suit is frayed some. He's lying on the ground. He didn't move while I could see him but the dust boiled up, like a man sliding onto base without moving. His eyes are open like he was looking. I don't understand it anyway, but I know it's John, not a ghost. He was in exactly the same position each time and there's a loud crack like thunder and another sound like a siren, very fast. And an ozone smell, and smoke. I felt a kind of shudder.

" 'I know it's John there and I think he's alive. I have to leave here now to take this back while I can still walk. I think somebody should come here and see. Maybe you can help John. Signed, Carl Delgano.

" 'These records were kept by the MacKenzie Group but it was not for several years—' Etcetera, first light-print, etcetera, archives, analysts, etcetera—very good! Now it is time to meet your uncle, my edible one, after we go upstairs for just a moment."

"No, Serli, I will wait for you downstairs," said Mira prudently.

When they came into the town park Uncle Laban was directing the installation of a large durite slab in front of the enclosure around the Man John's appearance-spot. The slab was wrapped in a curtain to await the official unveiling. Townspeople and tourists and children thronged the walks and a Ride-For-Good choir was singing in the bandshell. The morning was warming up fast. Vendors hawked ices and straw toys of the monster and flowers and good-luck confetti to throw at him. Another religious group stood by in dark robes; they belonged to the Repentance church beyond the park. Their pastor was directing somber glares at the crowd in general and Mira's uncle in particular.

Three official-looking strangers who had been at the inn came up and introduced themselves to Uncle Laban as observers from Alberta Central. They went on into the tent which had been erected over the enclosure, carrying with them several pieces of equipment which the town-folk eyed suspiciously.

The mechanics teacher finished organizing a squad of students to protect the slab's curtain, and Mira and Serli and Laban went on into the tent. It was much hotter inside. Benches were set in rings around a railed enclosure about twenty feet in diameter. Inside the railing the earth was bare and scuffed. Several bunches of flowers and blooming poinciana branches leaned against the rail. The only thing inside the rail was a rough sandstone rock with markings etched on it.

Just as they came in a small girl raced across the open center and was yelled at by everybody. The officials from Alberta were busy at one side of the rail, where the light-print box was mounted.

"Oh, no," muttered Mira's uncle, as one of the officials leaned over to set up a tripod stand inside the rails. He adjusted it and a huge horsetail of fine feathery filaments blossomed out and eddied through the center of the space.

"Oh *no*," Laban said again. "Why can't they let it be?"

"They're trying to pick up dust from his suit, is that right?" Serli asked.

"Yes, insane. Did you get time to read?"

"Oh yes," said Serli.

"Sort of," added Mira.

"Then you know. He's falling. Trying to check his—well, call it velocity. Trying to slow down. He must have slipped or stumbled. We're getting pretty close to when he lost his footing and started to fall. What did it? Did somebody trip him?" Laban looked from Mira to Serli, dead serious now. "How would you like to be the one who made John Delgano fall?"

"Ooh," said Mira in quick sympathy. Then she said, "Oh."

"You mean," asked Serli, "whoever made him fall caused all the, caused—"

"Possible," said Laban.

"Wait a minute," Serli frowned. "He did fall. So somebody had to do it—I mean, he has to trip or whatever. If he doesn't fall the past would all be changed, wouldn't it? No war, no—"

"Possible," Laban repeated. "God knows. All *I* know is that John Delgano and the space around him is the most unstable, improbable, highly charged area ever known on Earth and I'm damned if I think anybody should go poking sticks in it."

"Oh come now, Laban!" One of the Alberta men joined them, smiling. "Our dust-mop couldn't trip a gnat. It's just vitreous monofilaments."

"Dust from the future," grumbled Laban. "What's it going to tell you? That the future has dust in it?"

"If we could only get a trace from that thing in his hand."

"In his hand?" asked Mira. Serli started leafing hurriedly through the pamphlet.

"We've had a recording analyzer aimed at it," the Albertan lowered his voice, glancing around. "A spectroscope. We know there's something there, or was. Can't get a decent reading. It's severely deteriorated."

"People poking at him, grabbing at him," Laban muttered. "You—"

"*Ten minutes!*" shouted a man with a megaphone. "Take your places, friends and strangers."

The Repentance people were filing in at one side, intoning an ancient incantation, "mi-seri-cordia, ora pro nobis!"

The atmosphere suddenly took on tension. It was now very close and hot in the big tent. A boy from the mayor's office wiggled through the crowd, beckoning Laban's party to come and sit in the guest chairs on the second level on the "face" side. In front of them at the rail one of the Repentance ministers was arguing with an Albertan official over his right to occupy the space taken by a recorder, it being his special duty to look into the Man John's eyes.

"Can he really see us?" Mira asked her uncle.

"Blink your eyes," Laban told her. "A new scene every blink, that's what he sees. Phantasmagoria. Blink-blink-blink—for god knows how long."

"Mi-sere-re, pec-cavi," chanted the penitentials. A soprano neighed. "May the red of sin pa-aa-ass from us!"

"They believe his oxygen tab went red because of the state of their souls." Laban chuckled. "Their souls are going to have to stay damned a while; John Delgano has been on oxygen reserve for five centuries—or rather, he *will be* low for five centuries more. At a half-second per year his time, that's fifteen minutes. We know from the audio trace he's still breathing more or less normally and the reserve was good for twenty minutes. So they should have their salvation about the year seven hundred, if they last that long."

"*Five minutes!* Take your seats, folks. Please sit down so everyone can see. Sit down, folks."

"It says we'll hear his voice through his suit speaker," Serli whispered. "Do you know what he's saying?"

"You get mostly a twenty-cycle howl," Laban whispered back. "The recorders have spliced up something like *ayt*, part of an old word. Take centuries to get enough to translate."

"Is it a message?"

"Who knows? Could be his word for 'date' or 'hate.' 'Too late,' maybe. Anything."

The tent was quieting. A fat child by the railing started to cry and was pulled back onto a lap. There was a subdued mumble of praying. The Holy Joy faction on the far side rustled their flowers.

"Why don't we set our clocks by him?"

"It's changing. He's on sidereal time."

"*One minute.*"

In the hush the praying voices rose slightly. From outside a chicken cackled. The bare center space looked absolutely ordinary. Over it the recorder's silvery filaments eddied gently in the breath from a hundred lungs. Another recorder could be heard ticking faintly.

For long seconds nothing happened.

The air developed a tiny hum. At the same moment Mira caught a movement at the railing on her left.

The hum developed a beat and vanished into a peculiar silence and suddenly everything happened at once.

Sound burst on them, raced shockingly up the audible scale. The air cracked as something rolled and tumbled in the space. There was a grinding, wailing roar and—

He was there.

Solid, huge—a huge man in a monster suit, his head was a dull bronze transparent globe holding a human face, dark smear of open mouth. His position was impossible, legs strained forward thrusting himself back, his arms frozen in a whirlwind swing. Although he seemed to be in a frantic forward motion nothing moved, only one of his legs buckled or sagged slightly—

—And then he was gone, utterly and completely gone in a thunderclap, leaving only the incredible afterimage in a hundred pairs of staring eyes. Air boomed, shuddering, dust roiled out mixed with smoke.

"Oh, oh my God," gasped Mira, unheard, clinging to Serli. Voices were crying out, choking. "He saw me, he saw me!" a woman shrieked. A few people dazedly threw their confetti into the empty dust-cloud; most had failed to throw at all. Children began to howl. "He *saw* me!" the woman screamed hysterically. "Red, Oh Lord have mercy!" a deep male voice intoned.

Mira heard Laban swearing furiously and looked again into the space. As the dust settled she could see that the recorder's tripod had tipped over into the center. There was a dusty mound lying against it—flowers. Most of the end of the stand seemed to have disappeared or been melted. Of the filaments nothing could be seen.

"Some damn fool pitched flowers into it. Come on, let's get out."

"Was it under, did it trip him?" asked Mira, squeezed in the crowd.

"It was still red, his oxygen thing," Serli said over her head. "No mercy this trip, eh, Laban?"

"Shsh!" Mira caught the Repentance pastor's dark glance. They jostled through the enclosure gate and were out in the sunlit park, voices exclaiming, chattering loudly in excitement and relief.

"It was terrible," Mira cried softly. "Oh, I never thought it was a real live man. There he is, he's *there.* Why can't we help him? Did we trip him?"

"I don't know; I don't think so," her uncle grunted. They sat down near the new monument, fanning themselves. The curtain was still in place.

"Did we change the past?" Serli laughed, looked lovingly at his little wife. He wondered for a moment why she was wearing such odd earrings. Then he remembered he had given them to her at that Indian pueblo they'd passed.

"But it wasn't just those Alberta people," said Mira. She seemed obsessed with the idea. "It was the flowers really." She wiped at her forehead.

"Mechanics or superstition," chuckled Serli. "Which is the culprit, love or science?"

"Shsh." Mira looked about nervously. "The flowers were love, I guess

. . . I feel so strange. It's hot. Oh, thank you." Uncle Laban had succeeded in attracting the attention of the ice-drink vendor.

People were chatting normally now and the choir struck into a cheerful song. At one side of the park a line of people were waiting to sign their names in the visitors' book. The mayor appeared at the park gate, leading a party up the bougainvillea alley for the unveiling of the monument.

"What did it say on that stone by his foot?" Mira asked. Serli showed her the guidebook picture of Carl's rock with the inscription translated below: WELCOME HOME JOHN.

"I wonder if he can see it."

The mayor was about to begin his speech.

Much later when the crowd had gone away the monument stood alone in the dark, displaying to the moon the inscription in the language of that time and place:

ON THIS SPOT THERE APPEARS ANNUALLY THE FORM OF MAJOR JOHN DELGANO, THE FIRST AND ONLY MAN TO TRAVEL IN TIME.

MAJOR DELGANO WAS SENT INTO THE FUTURE SOME HOURS BEFORE THE HOLOCAUST OF DAY ZERO. ALL KNOWLEDGE OF THE MEANS BY WHICH HE WAS SENT IS LOST, PERHAPS FOREVER. IT IS BELIEVED THAT AN ACCIDENT OCCURRED WHICH SENT HIM MUCH FARTHER THAN WAS INTENDED. SOME ANALYSTS SPECULATE THAT HE MAY HAVE GONE AS FAR AS FIFTY THOUSAND YEARS AHEAD. HAVING REACHED THIS UNKNOWN POINT MAJOR DELGANO APPARENTLY WAS RECALLED, OR ATTEMPTED TO RETURN, ALONG THE COURSE IN SPACE AND TIME THROUGH WHICH HE WAS SENT. HIS TRAJECTORY IS THOUGHT TO START AT THE POINT WHICH OUR SOLAR SYSTEM WILL OCCUPY AT A FUTURE TIME AND IS TANGENT TO THE COMPLEX HELIX WHICH OUR EARTH DESCRIBES AROUND THE SUN.

HE APPEARS ON THIS SPOT IN THE ANNUAL INSTANTS IN WHICH HIS COURSE INTERSECTS OUR PLANET'S ORBIT AND HE IS APPARENTLY ABLE TO TOUCH THE GROUND IN THOSE INSTANTS. SINCE NO TRACE OF HIS PASSAGE INTO THE FUTURE HAS BEEN MANIFESTED, IT IS BELIEVED THAT HE IS RETURNING BY A DIFFERENT MEANS THAN HE WENT FORWARD. HE IS ALIVE IN OUR PRESENT. OUR PAST IS HIS FUTURE AND OUR FUTURE IS HIS PAST. THE TIME OF HIS APPEARANCES IS SHIFTING GRADUALLY IN SOLAR TIME TO CONVERGE ON THE MOMENT OF 1153.6 ON MAY 2ND 1989 OLD STYLE, OR DAY ZERO.

THE EXPLOSION WHICH ACCOMPANIED HIS RETURN TO HIS OWN TIME AND PLACE MAY HAVE OCCURRED WHEN SOME ELEMENTS OF THE PAST INSTANTS OF HIS COURSE WERE CARRIED WITH HIM INTO THEIR OWN PRIOR EXISTENCE. IT IS CERTAIN THAT THIS EXPLOSION PRECIPITATED THE WORLDWIDE HOLOCAUST WHICH ENDED FOREVER THE AGE OF HARDSCIENCE.

—He was falling, losing control, failing in his fight against the terrible

momentum he had gained, fighting with his human legs shaking in the inhuman stiffness of his armor, his soles charred, not gripping well now, not enough traction to brake, battling, thrusting as the flashes came, the punishing alternation of light, dark, light, dark, which he had borne so long, the claps of air thickening and thinning against his armor as he skidded through space which was time, desperately braking as the flickers of earth hammered against his feet—only his feet mattered now, only to slow and stay on course—and the pull, the beacon was getting slacker; as he came near home it was fanning out, hard to stay centered; he was becoming, he supposed, more probable; the wound he had punched in time was healing itself. In the beginning it had been so tight—a single ray in a closing tunnel—he had hurled himself after it like an electron flying to the anode, aimed surely along that exquisitely complex single vector of possibility of life, shot and been shot like a squeezed pip into the last chink in that rejecting and rejected nowhere through which he, John Delgano, could conceivably continue to exist, the hole leading to home—and pounded down it across time, across space, pumping with his human legs as the real Earth of that unreal time came under him, his course as certain as the twisting dash of an animal down its burrow, he a cosmic mouse on an interstellar, intertemporal race for his nest with the wrongness of everything closing round the rightness of that one course, the atoms of his heart, his blood, his every well crying Home—HOME! —as he drove himself after that fading breath-hole, each step faster, surer, stronger, until he raced with invincible momentum upon the rolling flickers of Earth as a man might race a rolling log in a torrent! Only the stars stayed constant around him from flash to flash, he looked down past his feet at a million strobes of Crux, of Triangulum; once at the height of his stride he had risked a century's glance upward and seen the Bears weirdly strung out from Polaris—But a Polaris not the Pole Star now, he realized, jerking his eyes back to his racing feet, thinking, I am walking home to Polaris, home! to the strobing beat. He had ceased to remember where he had been, the beings, people or aliens or things he had glimpsed in the impossible moment of being where he could not be; had ceased to see the flashes of worlds around him, each flash different, the jumble of bodies, walls, landscapes, shapes, and colors beyond deciphering–some lasting a breath, some changing pell-mell—the faces, limbs, things poking at him; the nights he had pounded through, dark or lit by strange lamps; roofed or unroofed; the days flashing sunlight, gales, dust, snow, interiors innumerable, strobe after strobe into night again; he was in daylight now, a hall of some kind; I am getting closer at last, he thought, the feel is changing—but he had to slow down, to check; and that stone near his feet, it had stayed there some time now, he wanted to risk a look but he did not dare, he was so tired, and he was sliding, was going out of control, fighting to kill the merciless velocity that would not let him slow down; he was hurt, too, something had hit him back there, they had done something, he didn't know what back somewhere in the kaleidoscope of faces, arms, hooks, beams, centuries of creatures grabbing at him—and his oxygen was going, never mind, it would last—it had to last, he was going home, home! And he had forgotten now the message he had tried to shout, hoping it could be picked up somehow, the important thing he had repeated; and the thing he had carried, it was gone now, his camera was gone too, something had torn it away—but he was coming home! Home! If only he could kill this momentum, could stay on the failing course, could slip, scramble, slide, somehow ride this avalanche down to home, to home—and his throat said Home!—said Kate, Kate! And his heart shouted, his lungs almost gone now, as his legs fought, fought and failed, as his feet gripped and skidded and held and slid, as he pitched, flailed, pushed, strove in the gale of timerush across space, across time, at the end of the longest path ever: the path of John Delgano, coming home.

QUESTIONS

1. Describe the different uses of language in the story. How is language used in the opening exposition and the final conclusion? In what way does the language used in these sections differ from the language used in the rest of the story? What is the effect of this different usage?

2. Are the characters in the story stereotypes? Describe how the characterizations strengthen the story.

3. What devices does the author use to indicate a change of time?

4. What modern views of time are reflected in this story?

5. How do the names the apparition was known by reflect the general beliefs of the times in which he appeared? Describe those beliefs.

6. What probably made John Delgano start to fall?

7. After the holocaust, "hardscience" was outlawed. How do we know this? By the end of the story, is "hardscience" making a comeback? What indications are there in the story to support your answer? What modern views of time are reflected in this story?

8. Is a complete understanding of the "science" in this story necessary for the reader to enjoy it or to follow its logic? Is a knowledge of history necessary to the enjoyment of this story?

The Year of the Jackpot

Robert Heinlein

In a time of crisis, of doomsday predictions becoming commonplace realities, of future shock, of increasing eccentricity, it is no wonder that we seek a logical explanation for what is befalling us. Certainly, statistics can be used to prove almost anything, but what if, this time, *the pattern discerned is the true one? Perhaps the most frightening thing about this story by the acknowledged dean of science fiction writers is that "the year of the jackpot" could come about for other reasons than the sun's changes. It makes us wonder how we would prepare, what we would do, if* this *were the year, or even if this were the decade in which all was about to end.*

At first Potiphar Breen did not notice the girl who was undressing.

She was standing at a bus stop only ten feet away. He was indoors but that would not have kept him from noticing; he was seated in a drugstore booth adjacent to the bus stop; there was nothing between Potiphar and the young lady but plate glass and an occasional pedestrian.

Nevertheless he did not look up when she began to peel. Propped up in front of him was a Los Angeles *Times*; beside it, still unopened, were the *Herald-Express* and the *Daily News.* He was scanning the newspaper carefully but the headline stories got only a passing glance. He noted the maximum and minimum temperatures in Brownsville, Texas and entered them in a neat black notebook; he did the same with the closing prices of three blue chips and two dogs on the New York Exchange, as well as the total number of shares. He then began a rapid sifting of minor news stories, from time to time entering briefs of them in his little book; the items he recorded seemed randomly unrelated—among them a publicity release in which Miss National Cottage Cheese Week announced that she intended to marry and have twelve children by a man who could prove that he had been a life-long vegetarian, a circumstantial but wildly unlikely flying saucer report, and a call for prayers for rain throughout Southern California.

Potiphar had just written down the names and addresses of three residents of Watts, California who had been miraculously healed at a tent meeting of the God-is-All First Truth Brethren by the Reverend

Dickie Bottomley, the eight-year-old evangelist, and was preparing to tackle the *Herald-Express,* when he glanced over his reading glasses and saw the amateur ecdysiast on the street corner outside. He stood up, placed his glasses in their case, folded the newspapers and put them carefully in his right coat pocket, counted out the exact amount of his check and added twenty-five cents. He then took his raincoat from a hook, placed it over his arm, and went outside.

By now the girl was practically down to the buff. It seemed to Potiphar Breen that she had quite a lot of buff. Nevertheless she had not pulled much of a house. The corner newsboy had stopped hawking his disasters and was grinning at her, and a mixed pair of transvestites who were apparently waiting for the bus had their eyes on her. None of the passers-by stopped. They glanced at her, then with the self-conscious indifference to the unusual of the true Southern Californian, they went on their various ways. The transvestites were frankly staring. The male member of the team wore a frilly feminine blouse but his skirt was a conservative Scottish kilt—his female companion wore a business suit and Homburg hat; she stared with lively interest.

As Breen approached the girl hung a scrap of nylon on the bus stop bench, then reached for her shoes. A police officer, looking hot and unhappy, crossed with the lights and came up to them. "Okay," he said in a tired voice, "that'll be all, lady. Get them duds back on and clear out of here."

The female transvestite took a cigar out of her mouth. "Just," she said, "what business is it of yours, officer?"

The cop turned to her. "Keep out of this!" He ran his eyes over her get up, that of her companion. "I ought to run both of you in, too."

The transvestite raised her eyebrows. "Arrest us for being clothed, arrest her for not being. I think I'm going to like this." She turned to the girl, who was standing still and saying nothing, as if she were puzzled by what was going on. "I'm a lawyer, dear." She pulled a card from her vest pocket. "If this uniformed Neanderthal persists in annoying you, I'll be delighted to handle him."

The man in the kilt said, "Grace! Please!"

She shook him off. "Quiet, Norman—this *is* our business." She went on to the policeman, "Well? Call the wagon. In the meantime my client will answer no questions."

The official looked unhappy enough to cry and his face was getting dangerously red. Breen quietly stepped forward and slipped his raincoat around the shoulders of the girl. She looked startled and spoke for the first time. "Uh—thanks." She pulled the coat about her, cape fashion.

The female attorney glanced at Breen then back to the cop. "Well, officer? Ready to arrest us?"

He shoved his face close to hers. "I ain't going to give you the satisfaction!" He sighed and added, "Thanks, Mr. Breen—you know this lady?"

"I'll take care of her. You can forget it, Kawonski."

"I sure hope so. If she's with you, I'll do just that. But get her out of here, Mr. Breen—please!"

The lawyer interrupted. "Just a moment—you're interfering with my client."

Kawonski said, "Shut up, you! You heard Mr. Breen—she's with him. Right, Mr. Breen?"

"Well—yes. I'm a friend. I'll take care of her."

The transvestite said suspiciously, "I didn't hear *her* say that."

Her companion said, "Grace—please! There's our bus."

"And I didn't hear her say she was your client," the cop retorted. "You look like a—" His words were drowned out by the bus's brakes. "—and besides that, if you don't climb on that bus and get off my territory, I'll . . . I'll . . ."

"You'll what?"

"Grace! We'll miss our bus."

"Just a moment, Norman. Dear, is this man really a friend of yours? Are you with him?"

The girl looked uncertainly at Breen, then said in a slow voice, "Uh, yes. That's right."

"Well . . ." The lawyer's companion pulled at her arm. She shoved her card into Breen's hand and got on the bus; it pulled away.

Breen pocketed the card. Kawonski wiped his forehead. "Why did you do it, lady?" he said peevishly.

The girl looked puzzled. "I . . . I don't know."

"You hear that, Mr. Breen? That's what they all say. And if you pull 'em in, there's six more the next day. The Chief said—" He sighed. "The Chief said—well, if I had arrested her like that female shyster wanted me to, I'd be out at a hundred and ninety-sixth and Ploughed Ground tomorrow morning, thinking about retirement. So get her out of here, will you?"

The girl said, "But—"

"No 'buts,' lady. Just be glad a real gentleman like Mr. Breen is willing to help you." He gathered up her clothes, handed them to her. When she reached for them she again exposed an uncustomary amount of skin; Kawonski hastily gave them to Breen instead, who crowded them into his coat pockets.

She let Breen lead her to where his car was parked, got in and tucked the raincoat around her so that she was rather more dressed than a girl usually is. She looked at him.

She saw a medium-sized and undistinguished man who was slipping down the wrong side of thirty-five and looked older. His eyes had that mild and slightly naked look of the habitual spectacles wearer who is not at the moment with glasses; his hair was gray at the temples and thin on top. His herringbone suit, black shoes, white shirt, and neat tie smacked more of the East than of California.

He saw a face which he classified as "pretty" and "wholesome" rather than "beautiful" and "glamorous." It was topped by a healthy mop of light brown hair. He set her age at twenty-five, give or take eighteen months. He smiled gently, climbed in without speaking and started his car.

He turned up Doheny Drive and east on Sunset. Near La Cienega he slowed down. "Feeling better?"

"Uh, I guess so Mr.—'Breen'?"

"Call me Potiphar. What's your name? Don't tell me if you don't want to."

"Me? I'm . . . I'm Meade Barstow."

"Thank you, Meade. Where do you want to go? Home?"

"I suppose so. I—Oh my no! I can't go home like *this*." She clutched the coat tightly to her.

"Parents?"

"No. My landlady. She'd be shocked to death."

"Where, then?"

She thought. "Maybe we could stop at a filling station and I could sneak into the ladies' room."

"Mmm. . . . maybe. See here, Meade—my house is six blocks from here and has a garage entrance. You could get inside without being seen." He looked at her.

She stared back. "Potiphar—you don't *look* like a wolf?"

"Oh, but I am! The worst sort." He whistled and gnashed his teeth. "See? But Wednesday is my day off from it."

She looked at him and dimpled. "Oh, well! I'd rather wrestle with you than with Mrs. Megeath. Let's go."

He turned up into the hills. His bachelor diggings were one of the many little frame houses clinging like fungus to the brown slopes of the Santa Monica Mountains. The garage was notched into this hill; the house sat on it. He drove in, cut the ignition, and led her up a teetery inside stairway into the living room. "In there," he said, pointing. "Help yourself." He pulled her clothes out of his coat pockets and handed them to her.

She blushed and took them, disappeared into his bedroom. He heard her turn the key in the lock. He settled down in his easy chair, took out his notebook, and opened the *Herald-Express*.

He was finishing the *Daily News* and had added several notes to his collection when she came out. Her hair was neatly rolled; her face was restored; she had brushed most of the wrinkles out of her skirt. Her sweater was neither too tight nor deep cut, but it was pleasantly filled. She reminded him of well water and farm breakfasts.

He took his raincoat from her, hung it up, and said, "Sit down, Meade."

She said uncertainly, "I had better go."

"Go if you must—but I had hoped to talk with you."

"Well—" She sat down on the edge of his couch and looked around. The room was small but as neat as his necktie, clean as his collar. The fireplace was swept; the floor was bare and polished. Books crowded bookshelves in every possible space. One corner was filled by an elderly flat-top desk; the papers on it were neatly in order. Near it, on its own stand, was a small electric calculator. To her right, French windows gave out on a tiny porch over the garage. Beyond it she could see the sprawling city; a few neon signs were already blinking.

She sat back a little. "This is a nice room—Potiphar. It looks like you."

"I take that as a compliment. Thank you." She did not answer; he went on, "Would you like a drink?"

"Oh, would I!" She shivered. "I guess I've got the jitters."

He got up. "Not surprising. What'll it be?"

She took Scotch and water, no ice; he was a Bourbon-and-ginger-ale man. She had soaked up half her highball in silence, then put it down, squared her shoulders and said, "Potiphar?"

"Yes, Meade?"

"Look—if you brought me here to make a pass, I wish you'd go ahead and make it. It won't do you a bit of good, but it makes me nervous to wait for it."

He said nothing and did not change his expression. She went on uneasily, "Not that I'd blame you for trying—under the circumstances. And I *am* grateful. But . . . well—it's just that I don't—"

He came over and took both her hands. "My dear, I haven't the slightest thought of making a pass at you. Nor need you feel grateful. I butted in because I was interested in your case."

"My case? Are you a doctor? A psychiatrist?"

He shook his head. "I'm a mathematician. A statistician, to be precise."

"Huh? I don't get it."

"Don't worry about it. But I would like to ask some questions. May I?"

"Uh, sure, sure! I owe you that much—and then some."

"You owe me nothing. Want your drink sweetened?"

She gulped it and handed him her glass, then followed him out into the kitchen. He did an exact job of measuring and gave it back. "Now tell me why you took your clothes off?"

She frowned. "I don't know. I *don't* know. I don't *know.* I guess I just went crazy." She added round-eyed, "But I don't feel crazy. Could I go off my rocker and not know it?"

"You're not crazy . . . not more so that the rest of us," he amended. "Tell me—where did you see someone else do this?"

"Huh? But I never have."

"Where did you read about it?"

"But I haven't. Wait a minute—those people up in Canada. Dooka-somethings."

"Doukhobors. That's all? No bareskin swimming parties? No strip poker?"

She shook her head. "No. You may not believe it but I was the kind of a little girl who undressed under her nightie." She colored and added, "I still do—unless I remember to tell myself it's silly."

"I believe it. No news stories?"

"No. Yes, there was too! About two weeks ago, I think it was. Some girl in a theater, in the audience, I mean. But I thought it was just publicity. You know the stunts they pull here."

He shook his head. "It wasn't. February 3rd, the Grand Theater, Mrs. Alvin Copley. Charges dismissed."

"Huh? How did *you* know?"

"Excuse me." He went to his desk, dialed the City News Bureau. "Alf? This is Pot Breen. They still sitting on that story? . . . yes, yes, the Gypsy Rose file. Any new ones today?" He waited; Meade thought that she could make out swearing. "Take it easy, Alf—this hot weather can't last forever. Nine, eh? Well, add another—Santa Monica Boulevard, late this afternoon. No arrest." He added, "Nope, nobody got her name—a middle-aged woman with a cast in one eye. I happened to see it . . . who, me? Why would I want to get mixed up? But it's rounding up into a very, very interesting picture." He put the phone down.

Meade said, "Cast in one eye, indeed!"

"Shall I call him back and give him your name?"

"Oh, no!"

"Very well. Now, Meade, we seemed to have located the point of contagion in your case—Mrs. Copley. What I'd like to know next is how you felt, what you were thinking about, when you did it?"

She was frowning intently. "Wait a minute, Potiphar—do I understand that *nine other* girls have pulled the stunt I pulled?"

"Oh, no—nine others *today*. You are—" He paused briefly. "—the three hundred and nineteenth case in Los Angeles county since the first of the year. I don't have figures on the rest of the country, but the suggestion to clamp down on the stories came from the eastern news services when the papers here put our first cases on the wire. That proves that it's a problem elsewhere, too."

"You mean that women all over the country are peeling off their clothes in public? Why, how shocking!"

He said nothing. She blushed again and insisted, "Well, it is shocking, even if it was me, this time."

"No, Meade. One case is shocking; over three hundred makes it scientifically interesting. That's why I want to know how it felt. Tell me about it."

"But— All right, I'll try. I told you I don't know why I did it; I still don't. I—"

"You remember it?"

"Oh, yes! I remember getting up off the bench and pulling up my sweater. I remember unzipping my skirt. I remember thinking I would have to hurry as I could see my bus stopped two blocks down the street. I remember how *good* it felt when I finally, uh—" She paused and looked puzzled. "But I still don't know why."

"What were you thinking about just before you stood up?"

"I don't remember."

"Visualize the street. What was passing by? Where were your hands? Were your legs crossed or uncrossed? Was there anybody near you? What were you thinking about?"

"Uh . . . nobody was on the bench with me. I had my hands in my lap. Those characters in the mixed-up clothes were standing near by, but I wasn't paying attention. I wasn't thinking much except that my feet hurt and I wanted to get home—and how unbearably hot and sultry it was. Then—" Her eyes became distant. "—suddenly I knew what I had to do and it was very urgent that I do it. So I stood up and I . . . and I—" Her voice became shrill.

"Take it easy!" he said. "Don't do it again."

"Huh? Why, Mr. Breen! I wouldn't do anything like that."

"Of course not. Then what?"

"Why, you put your raincoat around me and you know the rest." She faced him. "Say, Potiphar, what were you doing with a raincoat? It hasn't rained in weeks—this is the driest, hottest rainy season in years."

"In sixty-eight years, to be exact."

"Huh?"

"I carry a raincoat anyhow. Uh, just a notion of mine, but I feel that when it does rain, it's going to rain awfully hard." He added, "Forty days and forty nights, maybe."

She decided that he was being humorous and laughed. He went on, "Can you remember how you got the idea?"

She swirled her glass and thought. "I simply don't know."

He nodded. "That's what I expected."

"I don't understand you—unless you think I'm crazy. Do you?"

"No. I think you had to do it and could not help it and don't know why and can't know why."

"But *you* know." She said it accusingly.

"Maybe. At least I have some figures. Ever take any interest in statistics, Meade?"

She shook her head. "Figures confuse me. Never mind statistics—*I want to know why I did what I did!*"

He looked at her very soberly. "I think we're lemmings, Meade."

She looked puzzled, then horrified. "You mean those little furry mouselike creatures? The ones that—"

"Yes. The ones that periodically make a death migration, until millions, hundreds of millions of them drown themselves in the sea. Ask a lemming why he does it. If you could get him to slow up his rush toward death, even money says he would rationalize his answer as well as any college graduate. But he does it because he has to—and so do we."

"That's a horrid idea, Potiphar."

"Maybe. Come here, Meade. I'll show you figures that confuse me, too." He went to his desk and opened a drawer, took out a packet of cards. "Here's one. Two weeks ago—a man sues an entire state legislature for alienation of his wife's affection—and the judge lets the suit be tried. Or this one—a patent application for a device to lay the globe over on its side and warm up the arctic regions. Patent denied, but the inventor took in over three hundred thousand dollars in down payments on South Pole real estate before the postal authorities stepped in. Now he's fighting the case and it looks as if he might win. And here—prominent bishop proposes applied courses in the so-called facts of life in high schools." He put the card away hastily. "Here's a dilly: a bill introduced in the Alabama lower house to repeal the laws of atomic energy—not the present statutes, but the natural laws concerning nuclear physics; the wording makes that plain." He shrugged. "How silly can you get?"

"They're crazy."

"No, Meade. One such is crazy; a lot of them is a lemming death march. No, don't object—I've plotted them on a curve. The last time we had anything like this was the so-called Era of Wonderful Nonsense. But this one is much worse." He delved into a lower drawer, hauled out a graph. "The amplitude is more than twice as great and we haven't reached peak. What the peak will be I don't dare guess—three separate rhythms, reinforcing."

She peered at the curves. "You mean that the laddy with the arctic real estate deal is somewhere on this line?"

"He adds to it. And back here on the last crest are the flagpole sitters and the goldfish swallowers and the Ponzi hoax and the marathon dancers and the man who pushed a peanut up Pikes Peak with his nose. You're on the new crest—or you will be when I add you in."

She made a face. "I don't like it."

"Neither do I. But it's as clear as a bank statement. This year the human race is letting down its hair, flipping its lip with a finger, and saying, '*Wubba, wubba, wubba.*' "

She shivered. "Do you suppose I could have another drink? Then I'll go."

"I have a better idea. I owe you a dinner for answering questions. Pick a place and we'll have a cocktail before."

She chewed her lip. "You don't owe me anything. And I don't feel up to facing a restaurant crowd. I might . . . I might—"

"No, you wouldn't," he said sharply. "It doesn't hit twice."

"You're sure? Anyhow, I don't want to face a crowd." She glanced at his kitchen door. "Have you anything to eat in there? I can cook."

"Um, breakfast things. And there's a pound of ground round in the freezer compartment and some rolls. I sometimes make hamburgers when I don't want to go out."

She headed for the kitchen. "Drunk or sober, fully dressed or—naked, I can cook. You'll see."

He did see. Open-faced sandwiches with the meat married to toasted buns and the flavor garnished rather than suppressed by scraped Bermuda onion and thin-sliced dill, a salad made from things she had scrounged out of his refrigerator, potatoes crisp but not vulcanized. They ate it on the tiny balcony, sopping it down with cold beer.

He sighed and wiped his mouth. "Yes, Meade, you can cook."

"Some day I'll arrive with proper materials and pay you back. Then I'll prove it."

"You've already proved it. Nevertheless I accept. But I tell you three times, you owe me nothing."

"No? If you hadn't been a Boy Scout, I'd be in jail."

Breen shook his head. "The police have orders to keep it quiet at all costs—to keep it from growing. You saw that. And, my dear, you weren't a person to me at the time. I didn't even see your face; I—"

"You saw plenty else!"

"Truthfully, I didn't look. You were just a—a statistic."

She toyed with her knife and said slowly, "I'm not sure, but I think I've just been insulted. In all the twenty-five years that I've fought men off, more or less successfully, I've been called a lot of names—but a 'statistic'—why I ought to take your slide rule and beat you to death with it."

"My dear young lady—"

"I'm not a lady, that's for sure. But I'm *not* a statistic."

"My dear Meade, then. I wanted to tell you, before you did anything hasty, that in college I wrestled varsity middleweight."

She grinned and dimpled. "That's more the talk a girl likes to hear. I was beginning to be afraid you had been assembled in an adding machine factory. Potty, you're rather a dear."

"If that is a diminutive of my given name, I like it. But if it refers to my waist line, I resent it."

She reached across and patted his stomach. "I like your waist line; lean and hungry men are difficult. If I were cooking for you regularly, I'd really pad it."

"Is that a proposal?"

"Let it lie, let it lie—Potty, do you really think the whole country is losing its buttons?"

He sobered at once. "It's worse than that."

"Huh?"

"Come inside. I'll show you." They gathered up dishes and dumped them in the sink, Breen talking all the while. "As a kid I was fascinated by numbers. Numbers are pretty things and they combine in such interesting configurations. I took my degree in math, of course, and got a job as a junior actuary with Midwestern Mutual—the insurance outfit. That was fun—no way on earth to tell when a particular man is going to die, but an absolute certainty that so many men of a certain age group would die before a certain date. The curves were so lovely—and they always worked out. Always. You didn't have to know *why;* you could predict with dead certainty and never know why. The equations worked; the curves were right.

"I was interested in astronomy too; it was the one science where individual figures worked out neatly, completely, and accurately, down to the last decimal point the instruments were good for. Compared with astronomy the other sciences were mere carpentry and kitchen chemistry.

"I found there were nooks and crannies in astronomy where individual numbers won't do, where you have to go over to statistics, and I became even more interested. I joined the Variable Star Association and I might have gone into astronomy professionally, instead of what I'm in now—business consultation—if I hadn't gotten interested in something else."

" 'Business consultation'?" repeated Meade. "Income tax work?"

"Oh, no—that's too elementary. I'm the numbers boy for a firm of industrial engineers. I can tell a rancher exactly how many of his Hereford bull calves will be sterile. Or I tell a motion picture producer how much rain insurance to carry on location. Or maybe how big a company in a particular line must be to carry its own risk in industrial accidents. And I'm right. I'm always right."

"Wait a minute. Seems to be a big company would *have* to have insurance."

"Contrariwise. A really big corporation begins to resemble a statistical universe."

"Huh?"

"Never mind. I got interested in something else—cycles. Cycles are everything, Meade. And everywhere. The tides. The seasons. Wars. Love. Everybody knows that in the spring the young man's fancy lightly turns to what the girls never stopped thinking about, but did you know that it runs in an eighteen-year-plus cycle as well? And that a girl born at the wrong swing of the curve doesn't stand nearly as good a chance as her older or younger sister?"

"What? Is *that* why I'm a doddering old maid?"

"You're twenty-five?" He pondered. "Maybe—but your chances are picking up again; the curve is swinging up. Anyhow, remember you are just one statistic; the curve applies to the group. Some girls get married every year anyhow."

"Don't call me a statistic."

"Sorry. And marriages match up with acreage planted to wheat, with wheat cresting ahead. You could almost say that planting wheat makes people get married."

"Sounds silly."

"It *is* silly. The whole notion of cause-and-effect is probably superstition. But the same cycle shows a peak in house building right after a peak in marriages, every time."

"Now that makes sense."

"Does it? How many newlyweds do you know who can afford to build a house? You might as well blame it on wheat acreage. We don't know *why;* it just *is.*"

"Sun spots, maybe?"

"You can correlate sun spots with stock prices, or Columbia River salmon, or women's skirts. And you are just as much justified in blaming short skirts for sun spots as you are in blaming sun spots for salmon. We don't know. But the curves go on just the same."

"But there has to be some *reason* behind it."

"Does there? That's mere assumption. A fact has no 'why.' There it stands, self-demonstrating. Why did you take your clothes off today?"

She frowned. "That's not fair."

"Maybe not. But I want to show you why I'm worried." He went into the bedroom, came out with a large roll of tracing paper. "We'll spread it on the floor. Here they are, all of them. The 54-year cycle—see the Civil War there? See how it matches in? The 18 & ⅓ year cycle, the 9-plus cycle, the 41-month shorty, the three rhythms of sun spots—everything, all combined in one grand chart. Mississippi River floods, fur catches in Canada, stock market prices, marriages, epidemics, freight-car loadings, bank clearings, locust plagues, divorces, tree growth, wars, rainfall, earth magnetism, building construction patents applied for, murders—you name it; I've got it there."

She stared at the bewildering array of wavy lines. "But, Potty, what does it mean?"

"It means that these things all happen, in regular rhythm, whether we like it or not. It means that when skirts are due to go up, all the stylists in Paris can't make 'em go down. It means that when prices are going down, all the controls and supports and government planning can't make 'em go up." He pointed to a curve. "Take a look at the grocery ads. Then turn to the financial page and read how the Big Brains try to double-talk their way out of it. It means that when an epidemic is due, it happens, despite all the public health efforts. It means we're lemmings."

She pulled her lip. "I don't like it. 'I am the master of my fate,' and so forth. I've got free will, Potty. I know I have—I can feel it."

"I imagine every little neutron in an atom bomb feels the same way. He can go *spung!* or he can sit still, just as he pleases. But statistical mechanics work out anyhow. And the bomb goes off—which is what I'm leading up to. See anything odd there, Meade?"

She studied the chart, trying not to let the curving lines confuse her. "They sort of bunch up over at the right end."

"You're dern tootin' they do! See that dotted vertical line? That's right now—and things are bad enough. But take a look at that solid vertical; that's about six months from now—and that's when we get it. Look at the cycles—the long ones, the short ones, all of them. Every single last one of them reaches either a trough or a crest exactly on—or almost on—that line."

"That's bad?"

"What do you think? Three of the big ones troughed in 1929 and the depression almost ruined us . . . even with the big 54-year cycle supporting things. Now we've got the big one troughing—and the few crests are not things that help. I mean to say, tent caterpillars and influenza don't do us any good. Meade, if statistics mean anything, this tired old planet hasn't seen a jackpot like this since Eve went into the apple business. I'm scared."

She searched his face. "Potty—you're not simply having fun with me? You know I can't check up on you."

"I wish to heaven I were. No, Meade, I can't fool about numbers; I wouldn't know how. This is it. The Year of the Jackpot."

She was very silent as he drove her home. As they approached West Los Angeles, she said, "Potty?"

"Yes, Meade?"

"What do we *do* about it?"

"What do you do about a hurricane? You pull in your ears. What can you do about an atom bomb? You try to out-guess it, not be there when it goes off. What else can you do?"

"Oh." She was silent for a few moments, then added, "Potty? Will you tell me which way to jump?"

"Huh? Oh, sure! If I can figure it out."

He took her to her door, turned to go. She said, "Potty!"

He faced her. "Yes, Meade?"

She grabbed his head, shook it—then kissed him fiercely on the mouth. "There—is that just a statistic?"

"Uh, no."

"It had better not be," she said dangerously. "Potty, I think I'm going to have to change your curve."

II

"RUSSIANS REJECT UN NOTE"
"MISSOURI FLOOD DAMAGE EXCEEDS 1951 RECORD"
"MISSISSIPPI MESSIAH DEFIES COURT"
"NUDIST CONVENTION STORMS BAILEY'S BEACH"
"BRITISH-IRAN TALKS STILL DEAD-LOCKED"
"FASTER-THAN-LIGHT WEAPON PROMISED"
"TYPHOON DOUBLING BACK ON MANILA"
"MARRIAGE SOLEMNIZED ON FLOOR OF HUDSON—New York, 13 July, *In a specially-constructed diving suit built for two, Merydith Smithe, café society headline girl, and Prince Augie Schleswieg of New York and the Riviera were united today by Bishop Dalton in a service televised with the aid of the Navy's ultra-new–*"

As the Year of the Jackpot progressed Breen took melanchloy pleasure in adding to the data which proved that the curve was sagging as predicted. The undeclared World War continued its bloody, blundering way at half a dozen spots around a tortured globe. Breen did not chart it; the headlines were there for anyone to read. He concentrated on the odd facts in the other pages of the papers, facts which, taken singly, meant nothing, but taken together showed a disastrous trend.

He listed stock market prices, rainfall, wheat futures, but it was the "silly season" items which fascinated him. To be sure, some humans were always doing silly things—but at what point had prime damfoolishness become commonplace? When, for example, had the zombie-like professional models become accepted ideals of American womanhood? What were the gradations between National Cancer Week and National Athlete's Foot Week? On what day had the American people finally taken leave of horse sense?

Take transvestism—male-and-female dress customs were arbitrary, but they had seemed to be deeply rooted in the culture. When did the breakdown start? With Marlene Dietrich's tailored suits? By the late forties there was no "male" article of clothing that a woman could not wear in public—but when had men started to slip over the line? Should he count the psychological cripples who had made the word "drag" a byword in Greenwich Village and Hollywood long before this outbreak? Or were they "wild shots" not belonging on the curve? Did it start with some unknown normal man attending a masquerade and there discovering that skirts actually were more comfortable and practical than trousers? Or had it started with the resurgence of Scottish nationalism reflected in the wearing of kilts by many Scottish-Americans?

Ask a lemming to state his motives! The outcome was in front of him, a news story. Transvestism by draft-dodgers had at last resulted in a mass arrest in Chicago which was to have ended in a giant joint trial—only to have the deputy prosecutor show up in a pinafore and defy the judge to submit to an examination to determine the judge's true sex. The judge suffered a stroke and died and the trial was postponed—postponed forever in Breen's opinion; he doubted that this particular blue law would ever again be enforced.

Or the laws about indecent exposure, for that matter. The attempt to limit the Gypsy-Rose syndrome by ignoring it had taken the starch out of enforcement; now here was a report about the All Souls Community Church of Springfield: the pastor had reinstituted ceremonial nudity. Probably the first time this thousand years, Breen thought, aside from some screwball cults in Los Angeles. The reverend gentleman claimed that the ceremony was identical with the "dance of the high priestess" in the ancient temple of Karnak.

Could be—but Breen had private information that the "priestess" had been working the burlesque & nightclub circuit before her present engagement. In any case the holy leader was packing them in and had not been arrested.

Two weeks later a hundred and nine churches in thirty-three states offered equivalent attractions. Breen entered them on his curves.

This queasy oddity seemed to him to have no relation to the startling rise in the dissident evangelical cults throughout the country. These churches were sincere, earnest and poor—but growing, ever since the War. Now they were mutliplying like yeast. It seemed a statistical cinch that the United States was about to become godstruck again. He correlated it with Transcendentalism and the trek of the Latter Day Saints—hmm . . . yes, it fitted. And the curve was pushing toward a crest.

Billions in war bonds were now falling due; wartime marriages were reflected in the swollen peak of the Los Angeles school population. The Colorado River was at a record low and the towers in Lake Mead stood high out of the water. But the Angelenos committed slow suicide by watering lawns as usual. The Metropolitan Water District commissioners tried to stop it—it fell between the stools of the police powers of fifty "sovereign" cities. The taps remained open, trickling away the life blood of the desert paradise.

The four regular party conventions—Dixiecrats, Regular Republicans, the other Regular Republicans, and the Democrats—attracted scant attention, as the Know-Nothings had not yet met. The fact that the "American Rally," as the Know-Nothings preferred to be called, claimed not to be a party but an educational society did not detract from their strength. But what was their strength? Their beginnings had been so obscure that Breen had had to go back and dig into the December 1951 files—but he had been approached twice this very week to join them, right inside his own office—once by his boss, once by the janitor.

He hadn't been able to chart the Know-Nothings. They gave him chills in his spine. He kept column-inches on them, found that their publicity was shrinking while their numbers were obviously zooming.

Krakatau blew up on July 18th. It provided the first important transPacific TV-cast; its effect on sunsets, on solar constant, on mean temperature, and on rainfall would not be felt until later in the year. The San Andreas fault, its stresses unrelieved since the Long Beach disaster of 1933, continued to build up imbalance—an unhealed wound running the full length of the West Coast. Pelée and Etna erupted; Mauna Loa was still quiet.

Flying saucers seemed to be landing daily in every state. No one had exhibited one on the ground—or had the Department of Defense sat on them? Breen was unsatisfied with the off-the-record reports he had been able to get; the alcoholic content of some of them had been high. But the sea serpent on Ventura Beach was real; he had seen it. The troglodyte in Tennessee he was not in a position to verify.

Thirty-one domestic air crashes the last week in July . . . was it sabotage? Or was it a sagging curve on a chart? And that neo-polio epidemic that skipped from Seattle to New York? Time for a big epidemic? Breen's chart said it was. But how about B.W.? Could a chart *know* that a Slav biochemist would perfect an efficient virus-and-vector at the right time? Nonsense!

But the curves, if they meant anything at all, included "free will"; they averaged in all the individual "wills" of a statistical universe—and came out as a smooth function. Every morning three million "free wills" flowed toward the center of the New York megapolis; every evening they flowed out again—all by "free will," and on a smooth and predictable curve.

Ask a lemming! Ask *all* the lemmings, dead and alive—let them take a vote on it! Breen tossed his notebook aside and called Meade. "Is this my favorite statistic?"

"Potty! I was thinking about you."

"Naturally. This is your night off."

"Yes, but another reason, too. Potiphar, have you ever taken a look at the Great Pyramid?"

"I haven't even been to Niagara Falls. I'm looking for a rich woman, so I can travel."

"Yes, yes, I'll let you know when I get my first million, but—"

"That's the first time you've proposed to me this week."

"Shut up. Have you ever looked into the prophecies they found inside the pyramid?"

"Huh? Look, Meade, that's in the same class with astrology—strictly for squirrels. Grow up."

"Yes, of course. But Potty, I thought you were interested in anything odd. This is odd."

"Oh. Sorry. If it's 'silly season' stuff, let's see it."

"All right. Am I cooking for you tonight?"

"It's Wednesday, isn't it?"

"How soon?"

He glanced at his watch. "Pick you up in eleven minutes." He felt his whiskers. "No, twelve and a half."

"I'll be ready. Mrs. Megeath says that these regular dates mean that you are going to marry me."

"Pay no attention to her. She's just a statistic. And I'm a wild datum."

"Oh, well, I've got two hundred and forty-seven dollars toward that million. 'Bye!"

Meade's prize was the usual Rosicrucian come-on, elaborately printed, and including a photograph (retouched, he was sure) of the much disputed line on the corridor wall which was alleged to prophesy, by its various discontinuities, the entire future. This one had an unusual time scale but the major events were all marked on it—the fall of Rome, the Norman Invasion, the Discovery of America, Napoleon, the World Wars.

What made it interesting was that it suddenly stopped—now.

"What about it, Potty?"

"I guess the stonecutter got tired. Or got fired. Or they got a new head priest with new ideas." He tucked it into his desk. "Thanks. I'll think about how to list it." But he got it out again, applied dividers and a magnifying glass. "It says here," he announced, "that the end comes late in August—unless that's a fly speck."

"Morning or afternoon? I have to know how to dress."

"Shoes will be worn. All God's chilluns got shoes." He put it away.

She was quiet for a moment, then said, "Potty, isn't it about time to jump?"

"Huh? Girl, don't let *that* thing affect you! That's 'silly season' stuff."

"Yes. But take a look at *your* chart."

Nevertheless he took the next afternoon off, spent it in the reference room of the main library, confirmed his opinion of soothsayers. Nostradamus was pretentiously silly, Mother Shippey was worse. In any of them you could find what you looked for.

He did find one item in Nostradamus that he liked: "The Oriental shall come forth from his seat . . . he shall pass through the sky, through the waters and the snow, and he shall strike each one with his weapon."

That sounded like what the Department of Defense expected the commies to try to do to the Western Allies.

But it was also a description of every invasion that had come out of the "heartland" in the memory of mankind. Nuts!

When he got home he found himself taking down his father's Bible and turning to Revelations. He could not find anything that he could understand but he got fascinated by the recurring use of precise numbers. Presently he thumbed through the Book at random; his eye lit on: "Boast not thyself of tomorrow; for thou knowest not what a day may bring forth." He put the Book away, feeling humbled but not cheered.

The rains started the next morning. The Master Plumbers elected Miss Star Morning "Miss Sanitary Engineering" on the same day that the morticians designated her as "The Body I would Like Best to Prepare," and her option was dropped by Fragrant Features. Congress voted $1.37 to compensate Thomas Jefferson Meeks for losses incurred while an emergency postman for the Christmas rush of 1936, approved the appointment of five lieutenant generals and one ambassador and adjourned in eight minutes. The fire extinguishers in a midwest orphanage turned out to be filled with air. The chancellor of the leading football institution sponsored a fund to send peace messages and vitamins to the Politburo. The stock market slumped nineteen points and the tickers ran two hours late. Wichita, Kansas, remained flooded while Phoenix, Arizona, cut off drinking water to areas outside city limits. And Potiphar Breen found that he had left his raincoat at Meade Barstow's rooming house.

He phoned her landlady, but Mrs. Megeath turned him over to Meade. "What are you doing home on a Friday?" he demanded.

"The theater manager laid me off. Now you'll have to marry me."

"You can't afford me. Meade—seriously, baby, what happened?"

"I was ready to leave the dump anyway. For the last six weeks the popcorn machine has been carrying the place. Today I sat through *I Was A Teen-Age Beatnik* twice. Nothing to do."

"I'll be along."

"Eleven minutes?"

"It's raining. Twenty—with luck."

It was more nearly sixty. Santa Monica Boulevard was a navigable stream; Sunset Boulevard was a subway jam. He tried to ford the streams leading to Mrs. Megeath's house and found . . . problems.

"Potty! You look like a drowned rat."

"I'll live." But presently he found himself wrapped in a blanket robe belonging to the late Mr. Megeath and sipping hot cocoa while Mrs. Megeath dried his clothing in the kitchen.

"Meade . . . I'm 'at liberty,' too."

"Huh? You quit your job?"

"Not exactly. Old Man Wiley and I have been having differences of opinion about my answers for months—too much 'Jackpot factor' in the figures I give him to turn over to clients. Not that I call it that, but he has felt that I was unduly pessimistic."

"But you were right!"

"Since when has being right endeared a man to his boss? But that wasn't why he fired me; that was just the excuse. He wants a man willing to back up the Know-Nothing program with scientific double-talk. And I wouldn't join." He went to the window. "It's raining harder."

"But they haven't got any program."

"I know that."

"Potty, you should have joined. It doesn't mean anything—I joined three months ago."

"The hell you did!"

She shrugged. "You pay your dollar and you turn up for two meetings and they leave you alone. It kept my job for another three months. What of it?"

"Uh, well—I'm sorry you did it; that's all. Forget it. Meade, the water is over the curbs out there."

"You had better stay here overnight."

"Mmm . . . I don't like to leave 'Entropy' parked out in this stuff all night. Meade?"

"Yes, Potty?"

"We're both out of jobs. How would you like to duck north into the Mojave and find a dry spot?"

"I'd love it. But look, Potty—is this a proposal, or just a proposition?"

"Don't pull that 'either-or' stuff on me. It's just a suggestion for a vacation. Do you want to take a chaperone?"

"No."

"Then pack a bag."

"Right away. But look, Potiphar—pack a bag *how?* Are you trying to tell me it's *time to jump?*"

He faced her, then looked back at the window. "I don't know," he said slowly, "but this rain might go on quite a while. Don't take anything you don't have to have—but don't leave anything behind you can't get along without."

He repossessed his clothing from Mrs. Megeath while Meade was upstairs. She came down dressed in slacks and carrying two large bags; under one arm was a battered and rakish Teddy bear. "This is Winnie."

"Winnie the Pooh?"

"No, Winnie Churchill. When I feel bad he promises me 'blood, toil, tears, and sweat'; then I feel better. You said to bring anything I couldn't do without?" She looked at him anxiously.

"Right." He took the bags. Mrs. Megeath had seemed satisfied with his explanation that they were going to visit his (mythical) aunt in

Bakersfield before looking for jobs; nevertheless she embarrassed him by kissing him good-by and telling him to "take care of my little girl."

Santa Monica Boulevard was blocked off from use. While stalled in traffic in Beverly Hills he fiddled with the car radio, getting squawks and crackling noises, then finally one station nearby: "—in effect," a harsh, high, staccato voice was saying, "the Kremlin has given us till sundown to get out of town. This is your New York Reporter, who thinks that in days like these every American must personally keep his powder dry. And now for a word from—" Breen switched it off and glanced at her face. "Don't worry," he said. "They've been talking that way for years."

"You think they are bluffing?"

"I didn't say that. I said, 'don't worry.' "

But his own packing, with her help, was clearly on a "Survival Kit" basis—canned goods, all his warm clothing, a sporting rifle he had not fired in over two years, a first-aid kit and the contents of his medicine chest. He dumped the stuff from his desk into a carton, shoved it into the back seat along with cans and books and coats and covered the plunder with all the blankets in the house. They went back up the rickety stairs for a last check.

"Potty—where's your chart?"

"Rolled up on the back seat shelf. I guess that's all—hey, wait a minute!" He went to a shelf over his desk and began taking down small, sober-looking magazines. "I dern near left behind my file of *The Western Astronomer* and of the *Proceedings of the Variable Star Association.*"

"Why take them?"

"Huh? I must be nearly a year behind on both of them. Now maybe I'll have time to read."

"Hmm . . . Potty, watching you read professional journals is not my notion of a vacation."

"Quiet, woman! You took Winnie; I take these."

She shut up and helped him. He cast a longing eye at his electric calculator but decided it was too much like the White Knight's mouse trap. He could get by with his slide rule.

As the car splashed out into the street she said, "Potty, how are you fixed for cash?"

"Huh? Okay, I guess."

"I mean, leaving while the banks are closed and everything." She held up her purse. "Here's my bank. It isn't much, but we can use it."

He smiled and patted her knee. "Stout fellow! I'm sitting on my bank; I started turning everything to cash about the first of the year."

"Oh. I closed out my bank account right after we met."

"You did? You must have taken my maunderings seriously."

"I always take you seriously."

Mint Canyon was a five-mile-an-hour nightmare, with visibility limited to the tail lights of the truck ahead. When they stopped for coffee at Halfway, they confirmed what seemed evident: Cajon Pass was closed and long-haul traffic for Route 66 was being detoured through the secondary pass. At long, long last they reached the Victorville cut-off and lost some of the traffic—a good thing, as the windshield wiper on his side had quit working and they were driving by the committee system. Just short of Lancaster she said suddenly, "Potty, is this buggy equipped with a snorkel?"

"Nope."

"Then we had better stop. But I see a light off the road."

The light was an auto court. Meade settled the matter of economy versus convention by signing the book herself; they were placed in one cabin. He saw that it had twin beds and let the matter ride. Meade went to bed with her Teddy bear without even asking to be kissed goodnight. It was already gray, wet dawn.

They got up in the late afternoon and decided to stay over one more night, then push north toward Bakersfield. A high pressure area was alleged to be moving south, crowding the warm, wet mass that smothered Southern California. They wanted to get into it. Breen had the wiper repaired and bought two new tires to replace his ruined spare, added some camping items to his cargo, and bought for Meade a .32 automatic, a lady's social-purposes gun; he gave it to her somewhat sheepishly.

"What's this for?"

"Well, you're carrying quite a bit of cash."

"Oh. I thought maybe I was to use it to fight you off."

"Now, Meade—"

"Never mind. Thanks, Potty."

They had finished supper and were packing the car with their afternoon's purchases when the quake struck. Five inches of rain in twenty-four hours, more than three billion tons of mass suddenly loaded on a fault already overstrained, all cut loose in one subsonic, stomach-twisting rumble.

Meade sat down on the wet ground very suddenly; Breen stayed upright by dancing like a logroller. When the ground quieted down somewhat, thirty seconds later, he helped her up. "You all right?"

"My slacks are soaked." She added pettishly, "But, Potty, it never quakes in wet weather. *Never.*"

"It did this time."

"But—"

"Keep quiet, can't you?" He opened the car door and switched on the radio, waited impatiently for it to warm up. Shortly he was searching the entire dial. "Not a confounded Los Angeles station on the air!"

"Maybe the shock busted one of your tubes?"

"Pipe down." He passed a squeal and dialed back to it:

"—your Sunshine Station in Riverside, California. Keep tuned to this station for the latest developments. It is as of now impossible to tell the size of the disaster. The Colorado River aqueduct is broken; nothing is known of the extent of the damage nor how long it will take to repair it. So far as we know the Owens River Valley aqueduct may be intact, but all persons in the Los Angeles area are advised to conserve water. My personal advice is to stick your washtubs out into this rain, it can't last forever. If we had time, we'd play *Cool Water*, just to give you the idea. I now read from the standard disaster instructions, quote: 'Boil all water. Remain quietly in your homes and do not panic. Stay off the highways. Cooperate with the police and render—' Joe! Joe! Catch that phone! '—render aid where necessary. Do not use the telephone except for—' Flash! an unconfirmed report from Long Beach states that the Wilmington and San Pedro waterfront is under five feet of water. I repeat, this is unconfirmed. Here's a message from the commanding general, March Field: 'official, all military personnel will report—' "

Breen switched it off. "Get in the car."

"Where are we going?"

"North."

"We've paid for the cabin. Should we—"

"Get in!"

He stopped in the town, managed to buy six five-gallon-tins and a jeep tank. He filled them with gasoline and packed them with blankets in the back seat, topping off the mess with a dozen cans of oil. Then they were rolling.

"What are we doing, Potiphar?"

"I want to get west on the valley highway."

"Any particular place west?"

"I think so. We'll see. You work the radio, but keep an eye on the road, too. That gas back there makes me nervous."

Through the town of Mojave and northwest on 466 into the Tehachapi Mountains—Reception was poor in the pass but what Meade could pick up confirmed the first impression—worse than the quake of '06, worse than San Francisco, Managua, and Long Beach taken together.

When they got down out of the mountains it was clearing locally; a few stars appeared. Breen swung left off the highway and ducked south of Bakersfield by the county road, reached the Route 99 superhighway just south of Greenfield. It was, as he had feared, already jammed with refugees; he was forced to go along with the flow for a couple of miles before he could cut west at Greenfield toward Taft. They stopped on the western outskirts of the town and ate at an all-night truckers' joint.

They were about to climb back into the car when there was suddenly "sunrise" due south. The rosy light swelled almost instantaneously, filled the sky, and died; where it had been a red-and-purple pillar of cloud was mounting, mounting—spreading to a mushroom top.

Breen stared at it, glanced at his watch, then said harshly, "Get in the car."

"Potty—that was . . . that was—"

"That was—that used to be—Los Angeles. Get in the car!"

He simply drove for several minutes. Meade seemed to be in a state of shock, unable to speak. When the sound reached them he again glanced at his watch. "Six minutes and nineteen seconds. That's about right."

"Potty—*we should have brought Mrs. Megeath.*"

"How was I to know?" he said angrily. "Anyhow, you can't transplant an old tree. If she got it, she never knew it."

"Oh, I hope so!"

"Forget it; straighten out and fly right. We're going to have all we can do to take care of ourselves. Take the flashlight and check the map. I want to turn north at Taft and over toward the coast."

"Yes, Potiphar."

"And try the radio."

She quieted down and did as she was told. The radio gave nothing, not even the Riverside station; the whole broadcast range was covered by a curious static, like rain on a window. He slowed down as they approached Taft, let her spot the turn north onto the state road, and turned into it. Almost at once a figure jumped out into the road in front of them, waved his arms violently. Breen tromped on the brake.

The man came up on the left side of the car, rapped on the window; Breen ran the glass down. Then he stared stupidly at the gun in the man's left hand. "Out of the car," the stranger said sharply. "I've got to have it." He reached inside with his right hand, groped for the door lever.

Meade reached across Breen, stuck her little lady's gun in the man's face, pulled the trigger. Breen could feel the flash on his own face, never noticed the report. The man looked puzzled, with a neat, not-yet-bloody hole in his upper lip—then slowly sagged away from the car.

"Drive on!" Meade said in a high voice.

Breen caught his breath. "Good girl—"

"Drive on! *Get rolling!*"

They followed the state road through Los Padres National Forest, stopping once to fill the tank from their cans. They turned off onto a dirt road. Meade kept trying the radio, got San Francisco once but it was too jammed with static to read. Then she got Salt Lake City, faint but clear: "—since there are no reports of anything passing our radar screen the Kansas City bomb must be assumed to have been planted rather than delivered. This is a tentative theory but—" They passed into a deep cut and lost the rest.

When the squawk box again came to life it was a new voice:

"Conelrad," said a crisp voice, "coming to you over the combined networks. The rumor that Los Angeles has been hit by an atom bomb is totally unfounded. It is true that the western metropolis has suffered a severe earthquake shock but that is all. Government officials and the Red Cross are on the spot to care for the victims, but—and I repeat—there has *been no atomic bombing*. So relax and stay in your homes. Such wild rumors can damage the United States quite as much as enemy's bombs. Stay off the highways and listen for—" Breen snapped it off.

"Somebody," he said bitterly, "has again decided that 'Mama knows best.' They won't tell us any bad news."

"Potiphar," Meade said sharply, "that *was* an atom bomb . . . wasn't it?"

"It was. And now we don't know whether it was just Los Angeles—and Kansas City—or all the big cities in the country. All we know is that they are lying to us."

"Maybe I can get another station?"

"The hell with it." He concentrated on driving. The road was very bad.

As it began to get light she said, "Potty—do you know where we're going? Are we just keeping out of cities?"

"I think I do. If I'm not lost." He stared around them. "Nope, it's all right. See that hill up forward with the triple gendarmes on its profile?"

"Gendarmes?"

"Big rock pillars. That's a sure landmark. I'm looking for a private road now. It leads to a hunting lodge belonging to two of my friends—an old ranch house actually, but as a ranch it didn't pay."

"Oh. They won't mind us using it?"

He shrugged. "If they show up, we'll ask them. If they show up. They lived in Los Angeles, Meade."

"Oh. Yes, I guess so."

The private road had once been a poor grade of wagon trail; now it was almost impassable. But they finally topped a hogback from which they could see almost to the Pacific, then dropped down into a sheltered bowl where the cabin was. "All out, girl. End of the line."

Meade sighed. "It looks heavenly."

"Think you can rustle breakfast while I unload? There's probably wood in the shed. Or can you manage a wood range?"

"Just try me."

Two hours later Breen was standing on the hogback, smoking a cigarette, and staring off down to the west. He wondered if that was a mushroom cloud up San Francisco way? Probably his imagination, he decided, in view of the distance. Certainly there was nothing to be seen to the south.

Meade came out of the cabin. "Potty!"

"Up here."

She joined him, took his hand, and smiled, then snitched his cigarette and took a deep drag. She expelled it and said, "I know it's sinful of me, but I feel more peaceful than I have in months and months."

"I know."

"Did you see the canned goods in that pantry? We could pull through a hard winter here."

"We might have to."

"I suppose. I wish we had a cow."

"What would you do with a cow?"

"I used to milk four cows before I caught the school bus, every morning. I can butcher a hog, too."

"I'll try to find one."

"You do and I'll manage to smoke it." She yawned. "I'm suddenly terribly sleepy."

"So am I. And small wonder."

"Let's go to bed."

"Uh, yes. Meade?"

"Yes, Potty?"

"We may be here quite a while. You know that, don't you?"

"Yes, Potty."

"In fact it might be smart to stay put until those curves all start turning up again. They will, you know."

"Yes, I had figured that out."

He hesitated, then went on, "Meade . . . will you marry me?"

"Yes." She moved up to him.

After a time he pushed her gently away and said, "My dear, my very dear, uh—we could drive down and find a minister in some little town?"

She looked at him steadily. "That wouldn't be very bright, would it? I mean, nobody knows we're here and that's the way we want it. And besides, your car might not make it back up that road."

"No, it wouldn't be very bright. But I want to do the right thing."

"It's all right, Potty. It's *all right*."

"Well, then . . . kneel down here with me. We'll say them together."

"Yes, Potiphar." She knelt and he took her hand. He closed his eyes and prayed wordlessly.

When he opened them he said, "What's the matter?"

"Uh, the gravel hurts my knees."

"We'll stand up, then."

"No. Look, Potty, why don't we just go in the house and say them there?"

"Huh? Hell's bells, woman, we might forget to say them entirely. Now repeat after me: I, Potiphar, take thee, Meade—"

"Yes, Potiphar. I, Meade, take thee, Potiphar—"

III

"OFFICIAL: STATIONS WITHIN RANGE RELAY TWICE. EXECUTIVE BULLETIN NUMBER NINE—ROAD LAWS PREVIOUSLY PUBLISHED HAVE BEEN IGNORED IN MANY INSTANCES. PATROLS ARE ORDERED TO SHOOT WITHOUT WARNING AND PROVOST MARSHALS ARE DIRECTED TO USE DEATH PENALTY FOR UNAUTHORIZED POSSESSION OF GASOLINE. B.W. AND RADIATION QUARANTINE REGULATIONS PREVIOUSLY ISSUED WILL BE RIGIDLY ENFORCED. LONG LIVE THE UNITED STATES! HARLEY J. NEAL, LIEUTENANT GENERAL, ACTING CHIEF OF GOVERNMENT. ALL STATIONS RELAY TWICE."

"THIS IS THE FREE RADIO AMERICA RELAY NETWORK. PASS THIS ALONG, BOYS! GOVERNOR BRANDLEY WAS SWORN IN TODAY AS PRESIDENT BY ACTING CHIEF JUSTICE ROBERTS UNDER THE RULE-OF-SUCCESSION. THE PRESIDENT NAMED THOMAS DEWEY AS SECRETARY OF STATE AND PAUL DOUGLAS AS SECRETARY OF DEFENSE. HIS SECOND OFFICIAL ACT WAS TO STRIP THE RENEGADE NEAL OF RANK AND TO DIRECT HIS ARREST BY ANY CITIZEN OR OFFICIAL. MORE LATER. PASS THE WORD ALONG.

"HELLO, CQ, CQ, CQ. THIS IS W5KMR, FREEPORT. QRR, QRR! ANYBODY READ ME? ANYBODY? WE'RE DYING LIKE FLIES DOWN HERE. WHAT'S HAPPENED? STARTS WITH FEVER AND A BURNING THIRST BUT YOU CAN'T SWALLOW. WE NEED HELP. ANYBODY READ ME? HELLO, CQ 75, CQ 75 THIS IS W5 KILO METRO ROMEO CALLING QRR AND CQ 75. BY FOR SOMEBODY. . . . ANYBODY!!!"

"THIS IS THE LORD'S TIME, SPONSORED BY SWAN'S ELIXIR, THE TONIC THAT MAKES WAITING FOR THE KINGDOM OF GOD WORTHWHILE. YOU ARE ABOUT TO HEAR A MESSAGE OF CHEER FROM JUDGE BROOMFIELD, ANOINTED VICAR OF THE KINGDOM ON EARTH, BUT FIRST A BULLETIN: SEND YOUR CONTRIBUTIONS TO 'MESSIAH,' CLINT, TEXAS. DON'T TRY TO MAIL THEM: SEND THEM BY A KINGDOM MESSENGER OR BY SOME PILGRIM JOURNEYING THIS WAY. AND NOW THE TABERNACLE CHOIR FOLLOWED BY THE VOICE OF THE VICAR ON EARTH—"

"—THE FIRST SYMPTOM IS LITTLE RED SPOTS IN THE ARMPITS. THEY ITCH. PUT 'EM TO BED AT ONCE AND KEEP 'EM COVERED UP WARM. THEN GO SCRUB YOURSELF AND WEAR A MASK: WE DON'T KNOW YET HOW YOU CATCH IT. PASS IT ALONG, ED."

"—NO NEW LANDINGS REPORTED ANYWHERE ON THIS CONTINENT. THE PARATROOPERS WHO ESCAPED THE ORIGINAL SLAUGHTER ARE THOUGHT TO BE HIDING OUT IN THE POCONOS. SHOOT—BUT BE CAREFUL; IT MIGHT BE AUNT TESSIE. OFF AND CLEAR, UNTIL NOON TOMORROW—"

The curves were turning up again. There was no longer doubt in Breen's mind about that. It might not even be necessary to stay up here in the Sierra Madres through the winter—though he rather thought they would. He had picked their spot to keep them west of the fallout; it would be silly to be mowed down by the tail of a dying epidemic, or be shot by a nervous vigilante, when a few months' wait would take care of everything.

Besides, he had chopped all that firewood. He looked at his calloused hands—he had done all that work and, by George, he was going to enjoy the benefits!

He was headed out to the hogback to wait for sunset and do an hour's reading; he glanced at his car as he passed it, thinking that he would like to try the radio. He suppressed the yen; two thirds of his reserve gasoline was gone already just from keeping the battery charged for the radio—and here it was only December. He really ought to cut it down to twice a week. But it meant a lot to catch the noon bulletin of Free America and then twiddle the dial a few minutes to see what else he could pick up.

But for the past three days Free America had not been on the air—solar static maybe, or perhaps just a power failure. But that rumor that President Brandley had been assassinated—while it hadn't come from the Free radio . . . and it hadn't been denied by them, either, which was a good sign. Still, it worried him.

And that other story that lost Atlantis had pushed up during the quake period and that the Azores were now a little continent—almost certainly a hang-over of the "silly season"—but it would be nice to hear a follow-up.

Rather sheepishly he let his feet carry him to the car. It wasn't fair to listen when Meade wasn't around. He warmed it up, slowly spun the dial, once around and back. Not a peep at full gain, nothing but a terrible amount of static. Served him right.

He climbed the hogback, sat down on the bench he had dragged up there—their "memorial bench," sacred to the memory of the time Meade had hurt her knees on the gravel—sat down and sighed. His lean belly was stuffed with venison and corn fritters; he lacked only tobacco to make him completely happy. The evening cloud colors were spectacularly beautiful and the weather was extremely balmy for December; both, he thought, caused by volcanic dust, with perhaps an assist from atom bombs.

Surprising how fast things went to pieces when they started to skid! And surprising how quickly they were going back together, judging by the signs. A curve reaches trough and then starts right back up. World War III was the shortest big war on record—forty cities gone, counting Moscow and the other slave cities as well as the American ones—and then *whoosh!* neither side fit to fight. Of course, the fact that both sides had thrown their ICBMs over the pole through the most freakish arctic weather since Peary invented the place had a lot to do with it, he supposed. It was amazing that any of the Russian paratroop transports had gotten through at all.

He sighed and pulled the November 1951 copy of the *Western Astronomer* out of his pocket. Where was he? Oh, yes, *Some Notes on the Stability of G-Type Stars with Especial Reference to Sol*, by A. G. M. Dynkowski, Lenin Institute, translated by Heinrich Ley, F. R. A. S. Good boy, Ski—sound mathematician. Very clever application of harmonic series and tightly reasoned. He started to thumb for his place when he noticed a footnote that he had missed. Dynkowski's own name carried down to it: "This monograph was denounced by *Pravda* as romantic reactionariism shortly after it was published. Professor Dynkowski has been unreported since and must be presumed to be liquidated."

The poor geek! Well, he probably would have been atomized by now anyway, along with the goons who did him in. He wondered if they really had gotten all the Russki paratroopers? Well, he had killed his quota; if he hadn't gotten that doe within a quarter mile of the cabin and headed right back, Meade would have had a bad time. He had shot them in the back, the swine! and buried them beyond the woodpile—and then it had seemed a shame to skin and eat an innocent deer while those lice got decent burial.

Aside from mathematics, just two things worth doing—kill a man and love a woman. He had done both; he was rich.

He settled down to some solid pleasure. Dynkowski was a treat. Of course, it was old stuff that a G-type star, such as the sun, was potentially unstable; a G-O star could explode, slide right off the Russell diagram, and end up as a white dwarf. But no one before Dynkowski had defined the exact conditions for such a catastrophe, nor had anyone else devised mathematical means of diagnosing the instability and describing its progress.

He looked up to rest his eyes from the fine print and saw that the sun was obscured by a thin low cloud—one of those unusual conditions where the filtering effect is just right to permit a man to view the sun clearly with the naked eye. Probably volcanic dust in the air, he decided, acting almost like smoked glass.

He looked again. Either he had spots before his eyes or that was one fancy big sun spot. He had heard of being able to see them with the naked eye, but it had never happened to him. He longed for a telescope.

He blinked. Yep, it was still there, upper right. A *big* spot—no wonder the car radio sounded like a Hitler speech.

He turned back and continued on to the end of the article, being anxious to finish before the light failed. At first his mood was sheerest intellectual pleasure at the man's tight mathematical reasoning. A 3%

imbalance in the solar constant—yes, that was standard stuff; the sun would *nova* with that much change. But Dynkowski went further; by means of a novel mathematical operator which he had dubbed "yokes" he bracketed the period in a star's history when this could happen and tied it down further with secondary, tertiary, and quaternary yokes, showing exactly the time of highest probability. Beautiful! Dynkowski even assigned dates to the extreme limit of his primary yoke, as a good statistician should.

But, as he went back and reviewed the equations, his mood changed from intellectual to personal. Dynkowski was not talking about just any G-O star; in the latter part he meant old Sol himself, Breen's personal sun, the big boy out there with the oversized freckle on his face.

That was one hell of a big freckle! It was a hole you could chuck Jupiter into and not make a splash. He could see it very clearly now.

Everybody talks about "when the stars grow old and the sun grows cold"—but it's an impersonal concept, like one's own death. Breen started thinking about it very personally. How long would it take, from the instant the imbalance was triggered until the expanding wave front engulfed earth? The mechanics couldn't be solved without a calculator even though they were implicit in the equations in front of him. Half an hour, for a horseback guess, from incitement until the earth went *phutt!*

It hit him with gentle melancholy. No more? Never again? Colorado on a cool morning . . . the Boston Post road with autumn wood smoke tanging the air . . . Bucks county bursting in the spring. The wet smells of the Fulton Fish Market—no, that was gone already. Coffee at the *Morning Call.* No more wild strawberries on a hillside in Jersey, hot and sweet as lips. Dawn in the South Pacific with the light airs cool velvet under your shirt and never a sound but the chuckling of the water against the sides of the old rust bucket—what was her name? That was a long time ago—the *S.S. Mary Brewster.*

No more moon if the earth was gone. Stars—but no one to look at them.

He looked back at the dates bracketing Dynkowski's probability yoke. "Thine Alabaster Cities gleam, undimmed by—"

He suddenly felt the need for Meade and stood up.

She was coming out to meet him. "Hello, Potty! Safe to come in now—I've finished the dishes."

"I should help."

"You do the man's work; I'll do the woman's work. That's fair." She shaded her eyes. "What a sunset! We ought to have volcanoes blowing their tops every year."

"Sit down and we'll watch it."

She sat beside him and he took her hand. "Notice the sun spot? You can see it with your naked eye."

She stared. "Is that a sun spot? It looks as if somebody had taken a bite out of it."

He squinted his eyes at it again. Damned if it didn't look bigger!

Meade shivered. "I'm chilly. Put your arm around me." He did so with his free arm, continuing to hold hands with the other. It *was* bigger—the thing was growing.

What good is the race of man? Monkeys, he thought, monkeys with a spot of poetry in them, cluttering and wasting a second-string planet near a third-string star. But sometimes they finish in style.

She snuggled to him. "Keep me warm."

"It will be warmer soon. I mean I'll keep you warm."

"Dear Potty."

She looked up. "Potty—something funny is happening to the sunset."

"No darling—to the sun."

"I'm frightened."

"I'm here, dear."

He glanced down at the journal, still open beside him. He did not need to add up the two figures and divide by two to reach the answer. Instead he clutched fiercely at her hand, knowing with an unexpected and overpowering burst of sorrow that this was

The End

QUESTIONS

1. What reason might Heinlein have had for choosing Meade and Potiphar as names for his characters?

2. Does the dialogue seem unrealistic in this story? Justify your answer.

3. Criticize Meade from the standpoint of women's lib.

4. List the social institutions and patterns of behavior of which Heinlein seems to disapprove.

5. Potiphar's car is named *Entropy*. Define the word and explain how it relates to the story.

6. Was Meade justified in killing the would-be car thief?

7. Discuss the story's sexual morality. Is it dated?

8. Why is there a short uplift of mood just before the end of the story? Does it add to or subtract from the sense of reality?

9. In this story there is an allusion to the tale of Noah in the Bible (Genesis 7:12). What is that allusion? What does it suggest in terms of "The Year of the Jackpot"? Compare this story to two other biblical tales, the stories of Lot, especially Genesis 19:23–24, and of the Seven Seals of the Apocalypse,

especially Revelation 6:12–17 and 8:5–13. Are there similarities between these three stories? What are they?

10. Compare the story to *The Limits to Growth* in Part I. Are the two selections complementary? Which is most convincing? Why?

A Vision of Judgment

H. G. Wells

The world can end in many ways. H. G. Wells, whose science fiction imagination may never be equaled, recounts the Day of Judgment and the infinite mercy, patience, and humor of the traditional monotheistic God.

1

Bru-a-a-a.

I listened, not understanding.

Wa-ra-ra-ra.

"Good Lord!" said I, still only half awake. "What an infernal shindy!"

"Ra-ra-ra-ra-ra-ra-ra-ra-ra Ta-ra-rra-ra.

"It's enough," said I, "to wake——" and stopped short. Where was I?

Ta-rra-rara—louder and louder.

"It's either some new invention——"

Toora-toora-toora! Deafening!

"No," said I, speaking loud in order to hear myself. "That's the Last Trump."

Tooo-rraa!

2

The last note jerked me out of my grave like a hooked minnow.

I saw my monument (rather a mean little affair, and I wished I knew who'd done it), and the old elm tree and the sea view vanished like a puff of steam, and then all about me—a multitude no man could number, nations, tongues, kingdoms, peoples—children of all ages, in an amphitheatral space as vast as the sky. And over against us, seated on a throne of dazzling white cloud, the Lord God and all the host of his angels. I recognised Azreal by his darkness and Michael by his sword, and the great angel who had blown the trumpet stood with the trumpet still half raised.

3

"Prompt," said the little man beside me. "Very prompt. Do you see the angel with the book?"

He was ducking and craning his head about to see over and under and between the souls that crowded round us. "Everybody's here," he said. "Everybody. And now we shall know——

"There's Darwin," he said, going off at a tangent. "*He'll* catch it! And there—you see?—that tall, important-looking man trying to catch the eye of the Lord God, that's the Duke. But there's a lot of people one doesn't know.

"Oh! there's Priggles, the publisher. I have always wondered about printers' overs. Priggles was a clever man. . . . But we shall know now—even about him.

"I shall hear all that. I shall get most of the fun before. . . . *My* letter's S."

He drew the air in between his teeth.

"Historical characters, too. See? That's Henry the Eighth. There'll be a good bit of evidence. Oh, damn! He's Tudor."

He lowered his voice. "Notice this chap, just in front of us, all covered with hair. Paleolithic, you know. And there again——"

But I did not heed him, because I was looking at the Lord God.

4

"Is this *all?*" asked the Lord God.

The angel at the book—it was one of countless volumes, like the British Museum Reading-room Catalogue, glanced at us and seemed to count us in the instant.

"That's all," he said, and added: "It was, O God, a very little planet."

The eyes of God surveyed us.

"Let us begin," said the Lord God.

5

The angel opened the book and read a name. It was a name full of A's, and the echoes of it came back out of the uttermost parts of space. I did not catch it clearly, because the little man beside me said, in a sharp jerk, "*What's* that?" It sounded like "Ahab" to me; but it could not have been the Ahab of Scripture.

Instantly a small black figure was lifted up to a puffy cloud at the very feet of God. It was a stiff little figure, dressed in rich outlandish robes and crowned, and it folded its arms and scowled.

"Well?" said God, looking down at him.

We were privileged to hear the reply, and indeed the acoustic properties of the place were marvellous.

"I plead guilty," said the little figure.

"Tell them what you have done," said the Lord God.

"I was a king," said the little figure, "a great king, and I was lustful and proud and cruel. I made wars, I devastated countries, I built palaces, and the mortar was the blood of men. Hear, O God, the witnesses against me, calling to you for vengeance. Hundreds and thousands of witnesses." He waved his hands towards us. "And worse! I took a prophet—one of your prophets——"

"One of my prophets," said the Lord God.

"And because he would not bow to me, I tortured him for four days and nights, and in the end he died. I did more, O God, I blasphemed. I robbed you of your honours——"

"Robbed me of my honours," said the Lord God.

"I caused myself to be worshipped in your stead. No evil was there but I practised it; no cruelty wherewith I did not stain my soul. And at last you smote me, O God!"

God raised his eyebrows slightly.

"And I was slain in battle. And so I stand before you, meet for your nethermost Hell! Out of your greatness daring no lies, daring no pleas, but telling the truth of my iniquities before all mankind."

He ceased. His face I saw distinctly, and it seemed to me white and terrible and proud and strangely noble. I thought of Milton's Satan.

"Most of that is from the Obelisk," said the Recording Angel, finger on page.

"It is," said the Tyrannous Man, with a faint touch of surprise.

Then suddenly God bent foward and took this man in his hand, and held him up on his palm as if to see him better. He was just a little dark stroke in the middle of God's palm.

"*Did* he do all this?" said the Lord God.

The Recording Angel flattened his book with his hand.

"In a way," said the Recording Angel, carelessly.

Now when I looked again at the little man his face had changed in a very curious manner. He was looking at the Recording Angel with a strange apprehension in his eyes, and one hand fluttered to his mouth. Just the movement of a muscle or so, and all that dignity of defiance was gone.

"Read," said the Lord God.

And the angel read, explaining very carefully and fully all the wickedness of the Wicked Man. It was quite an intellectual treat.—A little "daring" in places, I thought, but of course Heaven has its privileges. . . .

6

Everybody was laughing. Even the prophet of the Lord whom the Wicked Man had tortured had a smile on his face. The Wicked Man was really such a preposterous little fellow.

"And then," read the Recording Angel, with a smile that set us all agog, "one day, when he was a little irascible from over-eating, he——"

"Oh, not *that*," cried the Wicked Man, "nobody knew of *that*.

"It didn't happen," screamed the Wicked Man. "I was bad—I was really bad. Frequently bad, but there was nothing so silly—so absolutely silly——"

The angel went on reading.

"O God!" cried the Wicked Man. "Don't let them know that! I'll repent! I'll apologise. . . ."

The Wicked Man on God's hand began to dance and weep. Suddenly shame overcame him. He made a wild rush to jump off the ball of God's little finger, but God stopped him by a dexterous turn of the wrist. Then he made a rush for the gap between hand and thumb, but the thumb closed. And all the while the angel went on reading—reading. The Wicked Man rushed to and fro across God's palm, and then suddenly turned about and fled up the sleeve of God.

I expected God would turn him out, but the mercy of God is infinite.

The Recording Angel paused.

"Eh?" said the Recording Angel.

"Next," said God, and before the Recording Angel could call upon the name a hairy creature in filthy rags stood upon God's palm.

7

"Has God got Hell up his sleeve then?" said the little man beside me.

"Is there a Hell?" I asked.

"If you notice," he said—he peered between the feet of the great angels—"there's no particular indication of the Celestial City."

" 'Ssh!" said a little woman near us, scowling. "Hear this blessed Saint!"

8

"He was Lord of the Earth, but I was the prophet of the God of Heaven," cried the Saint, "and all the people marvelled at the sign. For

I, O God, knew of the glories of thy Paradise. No pain, no hardship, gashing with knives, splinters thrust under my nails, strips of flesh flayed off, all for the glory and honour of God."

God smiled.

"And at last I went, I in my rags and sores, smelling of my holy discomforts——"

Gabriel laughed abruptly.

"And lay outside his gates, as a sign, as a wonder——"

"As a perfect nuisance," said the Recording Angel, and began to read, heedless of the fact that the Saint was still speaking of the gloriously unpleasant things he had done that Paradise might be his.

And behold, in that book the record of the Saint also was a revelation, a marvel.

It seemed not ten seconds before the Saint also was rushing to and fro over the great palm of God. Not ten seconds! And at last he also shrieked beneath that pitiless and cynical exposition, and fled also, even as the Wicked Man had fled, into the shadow of the sleeve. And it was permitted us to see into the shadow of the sleeve. And the two sat side by side, stark of all delusions, in the shadow of the robe of God's charity, like brothers.

And thither also I fled in my turn.

9

"And now," said God, as he shook us out of his sleeve upon the planet he had given us to live upon, the planet that whirled about green Sirius for a sun, "now that you understand me and each other a little better, . . . try again."

Then he and his great angels turned themselves about and suddenly had vanished.

The Throne had vanished.

All about me was a beautiful land, more beautiful than any I had ever seen before—waste, austere, and wonderful; and all about me were the enlightened souls of men in new clean bodies. . . .

QUESTIONS

1. How does "A Vision of Judgment" treat the character of God? Is Wells's God a kind or cruel figure?

2. Should the story be longer? Would it have been more successful had the lives of more people than the Wicked Man and the Saint been shown?

3. Do you agree with Wells that good or bad, man succeeds mainly in making himself ridiculous? Explain your answer.

4. Does either God or man have any dignity in Wells's story?

5. Is this story an instance of "science fiction"?

6. Compare this story to the preceding one by Heinlein. Both stories deal with the "last judgment" and both draw on the Judeo-Christian tradition, but both are radically different in tone and theme. Describe this difference.

7. Discuss satire as a literary mode. What is Wells actually ridiculing?

The Horses

Edwin Muir

The best end-of-the-world stories carry with them a new beginning. Here the British poet and translator Edwin Muir provides such a story, in the form of poetry. We can envision "the end" in many ways, but sometimes a better way of life, a deeper and truer chance, is at hand. It is a world without *miracles that would be most unreal to humanity.*

Barely a twelvemonth after
The seven days war that put the world to sleep,
Late in the evening the strange horses came.
By then we had made our covenant with silence,
But in the first few days it was so still
We listened to our breathing and were afraid.
On the second day
The radios failed; we turned the knobs; no answer.
On the third day a warship passed us, heading north,
Dead bodies piled on the deck. On the sixth day 10
A plane plunged over us into the sea. Thereafter
Nothing. The radios dumb;
And still they stand in corners of our kitchens,
And stand, perhaps, turned on, in a million rooms
All over the world. But now if they should speak,
If on a sudden they should speak again,
If on the stroke of noon a voice should speak,
We would not listen, we would not let it bring
That old bad world that swallowed its children quick
At one great gulp. We would not have it again. 20
Sometimes we think of the nations lying asleep,
Curled blindly in impenetrable sorrow,
And then the thought confounds us with its strangeness.

The tractors lie about our fields; at evening
They look like dank sea-monsters couched and waiting.
We leave them where they are and let them rust:

"They'll moulder away and be like other loam."
We make our oxen drag our rusty ploughs,
Long laid aside. We have gone back
Far past our fathers' land.

And then, that evening 30
Late in the summer the strange horses came.
We heard a distant tapping on the road,
A deepening drumming; it stopped, went on again
And at the corner changed to hollow thunder.
We saw the heads
Like a wild wave charging and were afraid.
We had sold our horses in our fathers' time
To buy new tractors. Now they were strange to us
As fabulous steeds set on an ancient shield
Or illustrations in a book of knights. 40
We did not dare go near them. Yet they waited,
Stubborn and shy, as if they had been sent
By an old command to find our whereabouts
And that long-lost archaic companionship.
In the first moment we had never a thought
That they were creatures to be owned and used.
Among them were some half-a-dozen colts
Dropped in some wilderness of the broken world,
Yet new as if they had come from their own Eden.
Since then they have pulled our ploughs and borne our loads, 50
But that free servitude still can pierce our hearts.
Our life is changed; their coming our beginning.

QUESTIONS

1. What circumstances made it necessary to have a "covenant with silence"?

2. Do the alternations of time impede or aid the poem?

3. What do the horses symbolize? Have they any connection to the horses of the Apocalypse?

4. The speaker would not, under any circumstances, have modern conveniences exist again. How strong is this commitment? Although justifiable, is it desirable?

5. In what sense could this poem be called religious?

6. Why are we told nothing of the narrator's own personal identity?

7. Discuss sound repetition in the poem, as it contributes particularly to feelings of acceptance and resolution.

part 5

Theories

Science fiction is a form of literature particularly well suited to close the gap between the scientific and literary fields that C. P. Snow called "The Two Cultures." SF authors have always taken the most recent advances in science and technology as starting points for their stories. However, in the period following the Second World War, they have also drawn from the concepts of sociology, psychology, philosophy, and political science. Because so much attention has been paid to the popular arts, SF has found itself unexpectedly appreciated as revealing the directions in which "The Two Cultures" may merge.

At one extreme, science fiction is regarded in the same way "primitive" and "folk" paintings are: as a genre that is interesting because its lack of sophistication indicates so directly the primal concerns that motivate it. At the other extreme, it is regarded as the most vital, most meaningful literature written today: a genre that tries to make clear the expanded consciousness modern humanity has gained from its encounter with a rapidly changing technology and a continually new perception of the universe.

This section begins with Leslie Fiedler's "Cross the Border, Close the Gap," a controversial essay in which the novelist-critic makes a strong argument for the relevance of "popular" literature to our deepest contemporary concerns. It is followed by Sam Lundwall's "Utopia," a piece of popular history and criticism, which reflects directly the passionate concern with the modern condition seen in so many SF works. Here is criticism with little pretense to objectivity. What "Utopia" may lose because of its author's commitment we feel it gains because of its involvement with the subject matter. It is abundantly clear that Lundwall *cares*, that the concept of utopia is important to him, is not merely an abstract concept to be studied at a distance and regarded with constant scholarly caution. In "The Theory and Practice of Time Travel" Larry Niven shows how fact is merged with fantasy to present convincing possibilities within the limitations imposed by logic. The SF writer is shown in this work as simultaneously a thinker and an entertainer. Arthur C. Clarke's "The Obsolescence of Man" also shows the SF writer as a thinker and reflects a major contemporary concern often seen in science fiction: the human-machine relationship. As the essay traces the development of machine intelligence and predicts a further development that may put *humans* into eclipse, Clarke demonstrates a characteristic mode of SF speculation: the logical extension of present realities into the future.

Edward Edelson's final article on the implications of our present knowledge about the universe is a brief excursion into the new perception we referred to earlier. Here is the last argument for the "truth" of SF. It is difficult to believe that beyond this planet there is a vast, complex arrangement of matter very different from what we've known in the past. It is, perhaps, as hard to grasp this new cosmology as it was to realize the human depravity implicit in the atomic destruction and mass-killings described in Part I. Yet, ultimately, both perceptions—of the universe and our capacity for destruction—are part of the same exploding consciousness occurring in us all.

Cross the Border, Close the Gap

Leslie A. Fiedler

SF is one of the last literary genres to receive serious scholarly and critical attention. Obviously, much of it cannot measure up to the traditional literary standards applied to mainstream literature. But the failure may not be SF's. Mainstream criteria may be inadequate. Another way of looking at literature, as suggested by the brilliant and iconoclastic critic and novelist Leslie Fiedler, may be more appropriate. "Cross the Border, Close the Gap" explores this possibility, opening up other critical approaches to the art and in the process showing that "pop lit" is a significant form of expression deserving careful literary scrutiny.

Almost all today's readers and writers are aware that we are living through the death throes of literary modernism and the birth pangs of postmodernism. The kind of literature that had arrogated to itself the name modern (with the presumption that it represented the ultimate advance in sensibility and form, that beyond it newness was not possible), and whose moment of triumph lasted from just before World War One until just after World War Two, is *dead*; i.e., belongs to history, not actuality. In the field of the novel, this means that the age of Proust, Mann and Joyce is over, just as in verse, that of T. S. Eliot and Paul Valéry is done with.

Obviously, this fact has not remained secret and some critics have even been attempting to deal with its implications. But they have been trying to do so in a language and with methods that are singularly inappropriate, since both language and method were invented by the modernists themselves to apologize for their own work and the work of their literary ancestors (John Donne, for instance, or the *symbolistes*), and to educate an audience capable of responding to them. Naturally, this will not do at all; so the second- or third-generation new critics in America prove themselves imbeciles and naïfs when confronted by, say, a poem by Allen Ginsberg, a novel by John Barth.

Why not, then, invent a new new criticism, a postmodernist criticism appropriate to postmodernist fiction and verse? It sounds simple enough—quite as simple as imperative—but it is, in fact, much simpler to say than to do; for the question that arises immediately is whether there can be *any* criticism adequate to postmodernism. The age of T. S.

Eliot, after all, was the age of a literature essentially self-aware, a literature dedicated to analysis, rationality, anti-romantic dialectic—and, consequently, aimed at respectability, gentility, even academicism. Criticism is natural, even essential to such an age; and to no one's surprise (though, finally, there were some voices crying out in dismay), the period of early 20th Century modernism became an age of criticism—an age in which criticism first invaded the novel, verse and drama and ultimately threatened to swallow up all other forms of literature. Certainly, looking back from this point, it seems as if many of the best books of the period were books of criticism (by T. S. Eliot, Ezra Pound and I.A. Richards, by John Crowe Ransom, Kenneth Burke and R. P. Blackmur, to mention only a few names); and its second-best were novels and poems eminently suited to critical analysis, particularly in schools and universities: the works of Proust-Mann-Joyce, for instance, to evoke a trilogy that seems at the moment more the name of a single college course than a list of three authors.

We have, however, entered quite another time—apocalyptic, anti-rational, blatantly romantic and sentimental; an age dedicated to joyous misology and prophetic irresponsibility; one distrustful of self-protective irony and too-great self-awareness. If criticism is to survive, therefore, if it is to become or remain useful, viable and relevant, it must be radically altered, though not in the direction indicated by Marxist critics, however subtle and refined they may be. The Marxists are last-ditch defenders of rationality and the primacy of political fact; they are intrinsically hostile to an age of myth and passion, sentimentality and fantasy.

A new criticism certainly will not be primarily concerned with structure or diction or syntax, all of which assume that the work of art "really" exists on the page rather than in the reader's apprehension and response. Not words on the page but words in the world or, rather, words in the head, at the private juncture of a thousand contexts—social, psychological, historical, biographical, geographical—in the consciousness of the reader (delivered for an instant, but an instant only, from all those contexts by the *ekstasis* of reading): This will be the proper concern of the critics to come. Certain older ones have already begun to provide examples of this sort of criticism by turning their backs on their teachers and even their own earlier practices. Norman O. Brown, for instance, who began with scholarly, somewhat Marxian studies of classic literature, has moved on to metapsychology in *Life Against Death* and *Love's Body*; while Marshall McLuhan, who made his debut with formalist examinations of Joyce and Gerard Manley Hopkins, has shifted to metasociological analyses of the mass media in *Understanding Media* and, finally, to a kind of pictographic shorthand, half put-on and half serious emulation of advertising style, in *The Medium Is the Massage*.

The voice, as well as the approach, is important in each case, since in neither Brown nor McLuhan does one hear the rhythm and tone usual to "scientific" criticism. No, the pitch, the rhythms, the dynamics of both are mantic, magical, more than a little *mad* (a concept that one desiring to deal with contemporary literature must learn to regard as more honorific than pejorative). In McLuhan and Brown—as in D. H. Lawrence—criticism is literature or it is nothing. Not amateur philosophy nor objective analysis, it differs from other forms of literary art in that it starts with the world of art itself, not with the world in general; it uses one work of art as an occasion to make another.

There have been many such mediating works of art in the past, both fairly recent (Nietzsche's *Birth of Tragedy*) and quite remote (Longinus' *On the Sublime*), that make it clear that the authority of the critic is based not on his skills in research nor his collation of texts but on his ability to find words and rhythms and images appropriate to his ecstatic vision of, say, the plays of Euripides or the opening verses of *Genesis*. To evoke Longinus or even Nietzsche, however, is in a sense misleading, suggesting models too grandiose and solemn. The newest criticism must be aesthetic, poetic in form as well as in substance; but it must also be comical, irreverent and vulgar. Examples have appeared everywhere in recent years—as in the case of Angus Wilson, who began a review of *City of Night* by writing quite matter-of-factly, "Everyone knows John Rechy is a little shit." And all at once, we are out of the Eliotic church, whose dogmas, delivered ex cathedra, two generations of students were expected to learn by heart: "Honest criticism and sensitive appreciation are directed not upon the poet but upon the poetry. . . . The mind of the mature poet differs from that of the immature one not precisely on any valuation of personality, not by being necessarily more interesting, or having 'more to say,' but rather by being a more finely perfected medium in which," etc.

Unless criticism refuses to take itself quite so seriously or at least permits its readers not to, it will inevitably continue to reflect the finicky canons of the genteel tradition and the depressing pieties of the culture religion of modernism, from which Eliot thought he had escaped—but to which, in fact, he only succeeded in giving a High Anglican tone: "It is our business, as readers of literature, to know what we like. It is our business, as Christians, *as well as* readers of literature, to know what we ought to like." But not to know that such stuff is laughable is to be imprisoned in church, cut off from the liberating privilege of comic sacrilege. It is high time, however, for such sacrilege rather than for piety.

The kind of criticism the age demands is death-of-art criticism, which is most naturally practiced by those who have come of age since the death of the new poetry and the new criticism. It seems evident that writers not blessed enough to be under 30 (or 35, or whatever the critical age is these days) must be reborn in order to seem relevant to the moment and to those who inhabit it most comfortably: the young. But one hasn't even the hope of being reborn unless he knows first that he is dead. No novelist can be reborn unless he knows that insofar as he remains a novelist in the traditional sense, he is dead. What was until only a few years ago a diagnosis, a predication (made almost from the moment of the invention of the novel: first form of pop literature and, therefore, conscious that, as compared with classic forms such as epic or tragedy, its life span was necessarily short) is now a fact. As certainly as the old God is dead, so the old novel is dead. Certain writers (Saul Bellow, for instance, or John Updike, Mary McCarthy or James Baldwin) continue to write old novels and certain readers, often with a sense of being quite up to date, continue to read them. But so do preachers continue to preach in the old churches and congregations gather to hear them.

It is not a matter of assuming, as does Marshall McLuhan, that the printed book is about to disappear; only of realizing that in all of its forms—and most notably, perhaps, the novel—the printed book is being radically altered. No medium of communication disappears merely because a new and more efficient one is invented. One thinks, for instance, of the lecture, presumably supernannuated by the invention of movable type, yet flourishing still after more than five centuries of obsolescence. What is demanded of a medium of communication when it becomes obsolete is that it become a form of entertainment, as recent developments in radio (the disappearance, for instance, of all high-minded commentators and pretentious playwrights) sufficiently indicate. Students are well aware of this truth in regard to the university lecture, and woe to the man who does not know it!

Even as the serious lecture was doomed by the technology of the 15th Century and the serious church service by the philology of the 18th and 19th, so is the serious novel and serious criticism by the technology and philology of the 20th. Like the lecture and the Christian church service, the novel's self-awareness must now include the perception of its own absurdity, even impossibility. Since the serious novel of our time is the art novel as practiced by Proust, Mann and Joyce and imitated by their epigoni, it is that odd blend of poetry, psychology and documentation, whose real though not always avowed end was to make itself canonical, that we must disavow. Matthew Arnold may have been quite correct in foreseeing the emergence of literature as Scripture in a world that was forsaking the old-time religion; but the life of the new scripture and the new-time religion was briefer than he could have guessed.

Before the Bible ceased to be central to the concerns of men in Western society, it had become merely a book among others; and this may have misled the Arnoldians, who could not believe that a time might come when not merely *the* Book ceased to move men but even books in general. Such, however, is the case—certainly as far as all books that consider themselves art, i.e., Scripture once removed, are concerned; and for this reason, the truly new new novel must be anti-art as well as anti-serious. But this means that it must become more like what it was in the beginning, what it seemed when Samuel Richardson could not be taken quite seriously and what it remained in England until Henry James had justified himself as an artist against such self-declared "entertainers" as Charles Dickens and Robert Louis Stevenson: popular, not quite reputable, a little dangerous. The critical interchange on the nature of the novel to which James contributed *The Art of the Novel* and Stevenson *A Humble Remonstrance* memorializes their debate—which in the Thirties most readers believed had been won hands down by James' defense of the novel of art, but which in the dawning Seventies we are not sure about at all, having reached a time when *Treasure Island* seems to be more to the point and the heart's delight than *The Princess Casamassima*.

This popular tradition the French may have understood once (in the days when Diderot praised Richardson extravagantly and the Marquis de Sade emulated him in a dirtier book than the Englishman dared), but they lost sight of it long ago. And certainly the so-called *nouveau roman* is, in its deadly earnestness, almost the opposite of anything truly new, which is to say, anti-art.

Totally isolated on the recent French scene is Boris Vian. He is in many ways a prototype of the new novelist, though he has been dead for over a decade and his most characteristic work belongs to the years just after World War Two. He was, first of all, an imaginary American (as even writers born in the United States must be these days), who found himself in opposition to the politics of America at the very moment he was most completely immersed in its popular culture—actually writing a detective novel called *I'll Spit on Your Grave* under the pen name Vernon Sullivan but pretending that he was only its translator into French. By virtue of this peculiar brand of mythological Americanism, he managed to straddle the border, if not quite close the gap, between high culture and low, belles-lettres and pop art. On the one hand, he was a writer of pop songs and a jazz trumpeter much influenced by the New Orleans style; and, on the other, he was the author of novels in which thinly disguised French intellectuals such as Jean Paul Sartre and Simone de Beauvoir are satirized. But even in his fiction, which seems at first glance conventionally avant-garde, the characters move toward their fates through an imaginary city whose main thoroughfare is called Boulevard Louis Armstrong.

Only now has Vian won the audience he deserved all along, finding it first among the young of Paris, who, like their American counterparts, know that such a closing of the gap between elite and mass culture is precisely the function of the novel now. And though most of the younger American authors who follow a similar course follow it without ever having known him, he seems more like them than like such eminent American forerunners as Faulkner or Hemingway. Vian, unfortunately, turned to the pop novel only for the work of his left hand, to which he was not willing even to sign his own name.

The young Americans who have succeeded Vian, on the other hand, have abandoned all concealment; and when they are most themselves, nearest to their central concerns, turn frankly to pop forms—though not to the detective story, which has become hopelessly compromised by middle-brow condescension, an affectation of college professors and Presidents. The forms of the novel that they prefer are those that seem now what the hardboiled detective story once seemed to Vian: at the farthest possible remove from art and avant-garde, the greatest distance from inwardness, analysis and pretension and, therefore, immune to lyricism on the one hand and righteous social commentary on the other. It is not compromise by the market place they fear; on the contrary, they choose the genre most associated with exploitation by the mass media—notably, the Western, science fiction and pornography.

Most congenial of all is the Western, precisely because it has for many decades seemed to belong exclusively to pulp magazines, run-of-the-mill TV series and class-B movies—experienced almost purely as myth and entertainment rather than as literature—and its sentimentality has come to possess our minds so completely that it can now be mitigated without essential loss by parody, irony and even critical analysis. In a sense, our mythological innocence has been preserved in the Western, awaiting the day when, no longer believing ourselves innocent in fact, we could decently return to claim it in fantasy. Such a return of the Western represents, of course, a rejection of laureates of the loss of innocence such as Henry James and Nathaniel Hawthorne—those particular favorites of the Forties who, despite their real virtues, turn out to have been too committed to the notion of European high art to survive as major influences in an age of pop. And it implies as well momentarily turning aside from our beloved Herman Melville (compromised by his new critical admirers and the countless Ph.D. dissertations they prompted) and even from Mark Twain. To Hemingway, Twain could still seem central to a living tradition, the father of us all; but, being folk rather than pop in essence, he has become ever more remote from an urban, industrialized world. Folk art knows and accepts its place in a class-structured world that pop blows up, whatever its avowed intentions. What remains is only the possibility of something closer to travesty than emulation—such a grotesque neo-Huck as the foul-mouthed D. J. in Norman Mailer's *Why Are We in Vietnam?*, who, it is wickedly suggested, may really be a black joker in Harlem pretending to be the white refugee from respectability. And, quite recently, Twain's book itself has been rewritten to please and mock its exegetes in John Seelye's *Huck Finn for the Critics*, which lops off the silly-happy ending, the deliverance of Nigger Jim (in which Hemingway never believed), and puts back into the tale the cussing and sex presumably excised by the least authentic part of Samuel Clemens' mind, as well as the revelation, at long last, that what Huck and Jim were smoking on the raft was not tobacco but hemp, which is to say, marijuana. Despite all, however, Huck seems for the moment to belong not to the childhood we all continue to live but to the one we have left behind.

Natty Bumppo, on the other hand, who dreamed originally in the suburbs of New York City and in Paris, survives, along with his author. Contrary to what we long believed, it is James Fenimore Cooper who remains alive, or, rather, who has been reborn, perhaps not so much as he saw himself as in the form D. H. Lawrence reimagined him en route to America. Cooper understood that the dream that does not fade with the building of cities, but assumes in their concrete and steel environment the compelling vividness of a waking hallucination, is the encounter of Old World men and New in the wilderness, the meeting of the transplanted European and the red Indian. No wonder Lawrence spoke of himself as "kindled by Fenimore Cooper."

The return of the redskin to the center of our art and our deep imagination, as we have retraced Lawrence's trip to the mythical America, not only is based on the revival of the oldest and most authentic of American pop forms but also projects certain meanings of our lives in terms more metapolitical than political, valid as myth rather than as history. Writers of Westerns have traditionally taken sides for or against the Indians; and unlike the authors of the movies that set the kids to cheering at the Saturday matinees of the Twenties and Thirties, the new novelists have taken a clear stand with the red man. In this act of mythological renegadism, they have not only implicitly declared themselves enemies of the Christian humanism but also rejected the act of genocide with which our nation began—and whose latest reflection, perhaps, is to be found in the war in Vietnam.

It is impossible to write any Western that does not in some sense glorify violence; but the violence celebrated in the anti-white Western is guerrilla violence—the sneak attack on civilization as practiced first by Geronimo and Cochise and other Indian warrior chiefs and more latterly apologized for by Ché Guevara or the spokesman for North Vietnam. Warfare, however, is not the final vision implicit in the new Western, which is motivated on a deeper level by a nostalgia for the tribe—a social organization thought of as preferable to both the bourgeois family, from which its authors come, and the soulless out-of-human-scale bureaucratic state, into which they are initiated via schools and universities. In the end, both the dream of violence in the woods and the vision of tribal life seem juvenile, even infantile. But this is precisely the point; for what recommends the Western to the new novelist is pre-eminently its association with children and with the kind of books superciliously identified with their limited and special needs.

The legendary Indians have nothing to do with art in the traditional sense but everything to do with joining boy to man, immaturity to maturity. They preside over the closing of the gap that aristocratic conceptions of art have opened between what fulfills us at 10 or 12 and what satisfies us at 50 or 60.

In light of all this, it is time to look again at the much-discussed immaturity of American literature, at the notorious fact that our classic books are boys' books, our greatest novels at home in the children's section of libraries; in short, that they are all in some sense Westerns—accounts of an idyllic encounter between white man and nonwhite in some variety of wilderness setting. But suddenly this fact—once read as a flaw—seems evidence of a real advantage, a clue to why the gap we now want to close opened so late and so unconvincingly in American letters. Before Henry James, none of our novelists felt himself cut off from the world of magic and wonder; he had only to go to sea or, especially, to cross our own particular border, the frontier, to inhabit a region where adults and children, educated and uneducated shared a common enchantment.

How different the plight of mid-19th Century English writers, such as Lewis Carroll or Edward Lear or George Macdonald, who had to pretend that they were writing for the nursery in order to enter the deep wonderland of their own imaginations. It makes a difference, after all, whether one thinks of the world across the border as faery or frontier, fantasy or history. It has been so long since Europeans lived their deepest dreams, but only yesterday for us. And this is why even now, when we are at last sundered from those dreams, we can turn rotten-ripe without loss of essential innocence, be decadent children playing Indians—be imaginary Americans, all of us, whether native to this land or not. But to be an American is precisely to imagine a destiny rather than to inherit one, since we have always been, insofar as we are Americans at all, inhabitants of myth rather than of history—and have now come to know it.

In any case, our best writers have been able to take up the Western again—at once playfully and seriously, quite like their ancestors who began the Revolution that made us a country by playing Indians in deadly earnest and dumping all that English tea into the salt sea. There are many writers still under 40—among them, the most distinguished of their generation—who have written new Westerns that have found the hearts of the young. John Barth's *The Sot-Weed Factor* represents the beginning of the wave that has been cresting ever since 1960 and that has carried with it not only Barth's near contemporaries such as Thomas Berger (in *Little Big Man*), Ken Kesey (in *One Flew Over the Cuckoo's Nest* and *Sometimes a Great Notion*) and, most recently, Leonard Cohen (in his extraordinarily gross and elegant *Beautiful Losers*) but has won over older and more established writers such as Norman Mailer, whose newest novel, *Why Are We in Vietnam?*, is not a book about a war in the East as much as a book about the idea of the West. Even William Burroughs, expert in drug fantasies and homosexual paranoia, keeps promising to turn to the genre, though so far, he has contented himself with science fiction—another pop form, another way of escaping from personal to public or popular myth, of using dreams to close a gap.

Science fiction does not seem at first glance to have an appeal as universal as the Western's, at least in book form, though perhaps it is too soon to judge; for it is a very young genre, having found its real meaning and scope (after tentative beginnings by Jules Verne and H. G. Wells) only after World War Two. At that point, two things became clear: first, that the future was upon us, that the pace of technological advance had become so swift that a distinction between present and future would be harder and harder to maintain; and, second, that the end of man, by annihilation or mutation, was a real, even an immediate possibility. But these are the two proper subjects of science fiction: the present future and the end of man, not time travel nor the penetration of outer space, except as they symbolize the former.

Perhaps only in advanced technologies that also have a tradition of self-examination and analysis can science fiction really flourish. For only in America, England and the Soviet Union does the science-fiction novel or post-novel seem to thrive; though science-fiction cartoon strips and comic books, as well as science-fiction TV programs and films (where the basic imagery is blissfully wed to electronic music and words are kept to a minimum) penetrate everywhere. In England and America, the prestige and influence of the genre are sufficient not only to allure Burroughs (in *Nova Express*) but also to provide a model for William Golding (in *Lord of the Flies*), Anthony Burgess (in *The Clockwork Orange*) and John Barth (whose second major book, *Giles Goat-Boy*, abandoned the Indian in favor of the future).

Quite unlike the Western, which asserts the difference between England and America, science fiction reflects what makes the two mutually distrustful communities one; as testified by a joint effort (an English author, an American director) such as the movie *2001: A Space Odyssey*. If there is still a common Anglo-Saxon form, it is science fiction. Yet even here, the American case is a little different from the English; for only in the United States is there a writer of first rank whose preferred mode has been from the first science fiction in its unmitigated pop form. Kurt Vonnegut, Jr., did not begin by making some sort of traditional bid for literary fame and then shift to science fiction, but was so closely identified with that popular, not-quite-respectable form from the first that the established critics were still ignoring him completely at a time when younger readers, attuned to the new rhythm of events by Marshall McLuhan and Buckminster Fuller, had already made underground favorites of his *The Sirens of Titan* and *Cat's Cradle*. That

Vonnegut now, after years of neglect, teaches writing in a famous American university and is hailed in lead reviews in the popular press is a tribute not to the critics' acuity but to the powers of the young.

The revival of pornography is best understood in this context, also; for it, like the Western and science fiction, is a form of pop art. Since Victorian times, it has been the *essential* form of pop art—the most unredeemable of all kinds of subliterature, understood as a sort of entertainment closer to vice than to art. Many notable recent works of the genre have tended to conceal this fact, often because the authors themselves have not understood what they were after and have tried to disguise their work as earnest morality (Hubert Selby's *Last Exit to Brooklyn*) or as parody (Terry Southern's *Candy*). But whatever the author's intent, all those writers who have helped move porn from the underground to the foreground have, in fact, been working toward the liquidation of the very conception of pornography, since the end of art on one side means the end of porn on the other. And that end is now in sight, in films, pop songs and poetry, but especially in the novel, which seemed initially more congenial than later pop-art forms to the sort of private masturbatory reverie that is essential to pornography.

The standard forms of heterosexual copulation, standardly or "poetically" recorded, seem oddly old-fashioned, even a little ridiculous; it is fellatio, buggery, flagellation that we demand in order to be sure that we are reading not love stories but pornography. A special beneficiary of this trend has been Norman Mailer, whose first novel, *The Naked and the Dead*, emulated the dying tradition of the anti-war art novel, with occasional obscenities thrown in, presumably in the interest of verisimilitude. But more and more, Mailer has come to move the obscenity to the center and the social commentary to the periphery, ending in *Why Are We in Vietnam?* with an insistence on foul language and an obsession with scatology that are obviously ends in themselves, too unremitting to be felt as merely an assault on oldfashioned sensibility and taste. And even in his earlier pop novel, *An American Dream*, which marked his emergence from ten years in which he produced no major fiction, he had committed himself to porn as a way into the region to which his title alludes: the place where, in darkness and filth, all men are alike—the Harvard graduate and the reader of the *Daily News*, joined in fantasies of murdering their wives and buggering their maids. To talk of such books in terms of Dostoievsky, as certain baffled critics have felt obliged to do, is absurd; James Bond is more to the point. But to confess this would be to confess that the old distinctions are no longer valid and that critics will have to find a claim to authority more appropriate to our times than the outmoded ability to discriminate between high and low.

Even more disconcertingly than Mailer, Philip Roth has, with *Portnoy's Complaint*, raised the question of whether pornography, even what was called hardcore pornography, any longer exists. Explicit, vulgar, joyous, gross and pathetic, Roth has established himself not only as the laureate of masturbation and oral-genital lovemaking but also as a master of the "thin" novel, the novel with minimum inwardness—ironically presented, in *Portnoy*, as a confession to a psychiatrist. Without its sexual interest, the continual balancing of titillation and burlesque, his book has no more meaning than any other dirty joke, to which genre it quite clearly belongs. There is pathos, even terror in great plenty, but it is dependent upon, subservient to the dirty jokes about mothers, Jews, shrinks, potency and impotency; and Roth is, consequently, quite correct when he asserts that he is less like such solemn and pious Jewish-American writers as Saul Bellow and Bernard Malamud than he is like Tiny Tim (himself actually half Arab and half Jew).

"I am a Jew freak," Roth has insisted, "not a Jewish sage"—and one is reminded of Lenny Bruce, who was there first, occupying the dangerous DMZ between the world of the stand-up comedian and that of the proper maker of fictions. But Bruce made no claim to being a novelist and, therefore, neither disturbed the critics nor opened up new possibilities for prose narrative. Before *Portnoy's Complaint*, the Jewish-American novel had come to seem an especially egregious example of the death of belles-lettres, having become smug, established, repetitive and sterile. But *Portnoy* marks the passage into the new world of porn and pop, as Roth's booming sales (even in hard covers!) perhaps sufficiently attest.

It is, of course, the middle aged and well heeled who buy the hardcover editions of the book; yet their children apparently are picking it up, too, for once, not even waiting for the paperback edition. They know it is a subversive book, as their parents do not (convinced that a boy who loves his mother can't be all bad), and as Roth himself, perhaps, was not at first quite aware. Before its publication, he had been at least equivocal on the subject of frankly disruptive literature—full of distrust, for instance, of Norman Mailer—and he appears, therefore, to have become a pop rebel despite himself, driven less by principle than by a saving hunger for the great audience, quite like that which moved John Updike recently out of his elitist exile toward best-sellerdom and relevance in *Couples*.

There is no doubt in the minds of most other writers whom the young especially prize at the moment that their essential task is to destroy just such distinctions and discriminations once and for all—by parody or exaggeration or grotesque emulation of the classic past, as well as by the adaptation and camping of pop forms. But to turn high art into vaudeville and burlesque at the same moment that mass art is being irreverently introduced into museums and libraries is to perform an act that has political as well as aesthetic implications, an act that closes a class, as well as a generation gap. The notion of one art for the "cultured" and a subart for the "uncultured" represents the last survival in mass industrial societies of an invidious distinction proper only to a class-structured community. Precisely because it carries on, as it has carried on ever since the middle of the 18th Century, a war against that anachronistic survival, pop art is, whatever its overt politics, subversive—a threat to all hierarchies insofar as it is hostile to order. What the final intrusion of pop into the citadels of high art provides for the critic is the exhilarating new possibility of making judgments about the goodness and badness of art quite separated from distinctions between high and low, with their concealed class bias.

But the new audience has not waited for new critics to guide them in this direction. Reversing the process typical of modernism—under whose aegis an unwilling, aging elite audience was bullied and cajoled slowly into accepting the most vital art of its time—postmodernism provides an example of a young, mass audience urging certain aging, reluctant critics toward the abandonment of their former elite status, in return for a freedom the prospect of which more terrifies than elates them. Postmodernism implies the closing of the gap between critic and audience, also if by critic one understands leader of taste and by audience, follower. But most importantly, it implies the closing of the gap between artist and audience or, at any rate, between professional and amateur in the realm of art.

It all follows logically enough. On the one hand, a poet such as Ed Sanders or a novelist such as Leonard Cohen grows weary of his confinement in the realm of traditional high art; and the former organizes a musical pop group called the Fugs, while the latter makes recordings of his own pop songs to his own guitar accompaniment.

Even more surprisingly, some who had begun as mere entertainers, pop performers without loftier pretensions, were crossing the line. Frank Zappa, for example, has, in interviews and in a forthcoming book, insisted on being taken seriously as poet and satirist, suggesting that the music of his own group, The Mothers of Invention, has been more a deliberate parody of pop than an extension of it in psychedelic directions; while Bob Dylan, who began by abandoning folk music with left-wing protest overtones in favor of electronic rock 'n' roll, finally succeeded in creating a kind of pop surrealist poetry, passionate, mysterious and quite complex—complex enough, in fact, to prompt a score of scholarly articles on his "art." Most recently, he has returned to acoustic instruments and to the most naïve traditions of country music—apparently out of a sense that he had grown too arty and had once more to close the gap by backtracking across the border. It is a spectacular case of the new artist as double agent.

Even more spectacular, however, is the case of John Lennon, who, coming into view first as merely one of the Beatles, then just another rock group from Liverpool, has revealed himself stage by stage as novelist, playwright, moviemaker, guru, sculptor, etc. There is a special pathos in his example, since, though initially inspired by American models, he has tried to work out his essentially American strategies in English idioms and in growing isolation on the generally dismal English scene. He has refused to become the prisoner of his special talent as a musician, venturing into other realms, where he has as little authority as anyone else. He thus provides one more model for the young who, without any special gift or calling, in the name of mere possibility, insist on making tens of thousands of records, movies, collections of verse, paintings, junk sculptures, even novels in complete contempt of professional standards. Perhaps, though, the novel is the most unpromising form for an amateur age (it is easier to learn the guitar or make a two-minute eight-millimeter film) and it may be doomed to become less and less important, no matter how it is altered. But for the moment, at least, on the border between the world of art and that of nonart, it flourishes with special vigor as it realizes its transitional status and is willing to surrender the kind of realism and analysis it once thought its special province in quest of the marvelous and magical it began by disavowing.

Samuel Richardson may have believed that when he wrote *Pamela* and *Clarissa,* he was delivering prose fiction from that bondage to the *merveilleux* that characterized the old romances; but it is clear now that he was merely translating the marvelous into new terms, specifically, into bourgeois English. It is time to be through with pretenses; for to close the gap means also to cross the border between the marvelous and the probable, the real and the mythical, the world of the boudoir and the countinghouse and the realm of what used to be called faery but has for so long been designated mere madness. Certainly, the basic images of pop forms such as the Western, science fiction and pornography suggest mythological as well as political or metapolitical meanings. The passage into Indian territory, the flight into outer space, the ecstatic release into the fantasy world of the orgy—all these are analogs for what has traditionally been described as a journey or pilgrimage toward a transcendent goal, a moment of vision.

Pop art can no more abide a mythological vacuum than can high art; and into the space left vacant by the disappearance of the matter of Troy and the myths of the ancient Middle East has rushed, first of all, the matter of childhood—the stuff of traditional fairy tales out of the Black Forest, which seems to the present generation especially attractive, perhaps, because their progressive parents tended to distrust it. But something much more radically new has appeared as well: the matter of metropolis and the myths of the present future, in which the nonhuman world about us, hostile or benign, is rendered in the guise not of elves or dwarfs or witches or even gods but of machines quite as uncanny as any Olympian—and apparently as immortal. Machines and the mythological figures appropriate to the media mass-produced and mass-distributed by machines: the newsboy who, saying "Shazam!" in an abandoned subway tunnel, becomes Captain Marvel; the reporter (with glasses) who, shucking his civilian garb in a telephone booth, is revealed as Superman, immune to all but Kryptonite—these are the appropriate images of power and grace for an urban, industrial world busy manufacturing the future.

But the comic-book heroes do not stand alone. Out of the world of jazz and rock, of newspaper headlines and political cartoons, of old movies immortalized on TV and idiot talk shows carried on car radios, new anti-gods and anti-heroes arrive. In the heads of our new writers, they live a secondary life, begin to realize their immortality—not only Jean Harlow and Marilyn Monroe and Humphrey Bogart, Charlie Parker and Louis Armstrong and Lenny Bruce, Geronimo and Billy the Kid, the Lone Ranger and Fu Manchu and the Bride of Frankenstein but Hitler and Stalin, John F. Kennedy and Lee Oswald and Jack Ruby, as well. For the press mythologizes certain public figures, the actors of pop history, even before they are dead, making a doomed President one with Superman in the supermarket of pop culture, as Norman Mailer perceived so accurately and reported so movingly in an essay on John F. Kennedy.

But the secret he told was already known to scores of younger writers and recorded in the text and texture of their work. In the deep memory of Leonard Cohen writing *Beautiful Losers*, or Richard Fariña composing *Been Down So Long It Looks Like Up to Me*, or Ken Kesey making *Sometimes a Great Notion*, there stir to life not archetypal images out of books read in school or at the urging of parents but those out of comic books forbidden in schools or radio and TV programs banned or condescendingly endured by parents. In the newest writers mockery and condescension are absent; they are living in the only world in which they feel at home. They are able to recapture a certain rude magic in its authentic context, by seizing on myths not as stored in encyclopedias or preserved in certain beloved ancient works but as apprehended at their moment of making—at a moment when they are not yet labeled myths.

The present movement—not only in its quest for myths but also in its preference for sentimentality over irony, and especially in its dedication to the primitive—resembles the beginnings of romanticism, with its yearning for the naïve and its attempt to find authentic sources for poetry in folk forms such as the *Märchen* or the ballads. But the romantics turned exclusively toward the past, in the hope of renewal—to a dream of the past, which they knew they could only write, not actually live. And there persists in the postmodernists some of that old nostalgia for folkways and folk rhythms, curiously tempered by the realization that the folk songs of an electronic age are made not in rural loneliness nor in sylvan retreats but in superstudios by boys singing into the sensitive ear of machines. What recent writers have learned and are true enough children of the present future to find exhilarating is not only that the naïve can be machine produced but that dreams themselves can be manufactured, projected on TV or laser beams with all the vividness of the visions of saints. In pre-electronic romanticism, it took an act of faith on the part of Novalis to be able to say, "Life is not a dream, but it can be and probably should be made one."

The dream, the vision, *ekstasis:* These have again become the avowed goals of literature; for our latest poets realize in this time of endings what their remotest ancestors knew in the era of beginnings, that merely to instruct and delight is not enough. They are convinced that wonder and fantasy that deliver the mind from the body, the body from the mind, must be naturalized to a world of machines—subverted, perhaps, or even transformed, but certainly not destroyed or denied. The ending of Ken Kesey's *One Flew Over the Cuckoo's Nest* expresses that conviction metaphorically when the Indian, who is his second hero, breaks out of the insane asylum in which the system has kept him impotent and trapped—and flees to join his fellows who are building a fishing weir on a giant hydroelectric power dam. The dam and weir both are essential to postelectronic romanticism, which knows that the point is no longer to pursue some uncorrupted West over the next horizon, since there is no incorruption and all our horizons have been reached. It is, rather, to make a thousand little Wests in the interstices of a machine civilization on its steel and concrete back; to live the tribal life among and with the support of machines; to shelter new communes under domes constructed according to the technology of Buckminster Fuller; and to warm the nakedness of new primitives with advanced techniques of solar heating.

All this is less a matter of choice than of necessity; because, it has turned out, machine civilization tends inevitably to synthesize the primitive, and *ekstasis* is the unforeseen end of advanced technology, mysticism the by-product—no more nor no less accidental than penicillin—of scientific research. In the antiseptic laboratories of Switzerland, the psychedelic drug LSD was first developed, first tried by two white-coated experimenters; and even now, Dow Chemical, which manufactures napalm, also produces the even more powerful psychedelic agent STP. It is, in large part, thanks to machines—the supermachines that, unlike their simpler prototypes, insist on tending us rather than demanding we tend them—that we live in the midst of a great religious revival, scarcely noticed by the official spokesmen of established Christian churches, since it speaks quite another language. Yet many among us feel that they are able to live honestly only by what machines cannot do better than they—which is why certain poets and novelists, as well as pop singers and pornographic playwrights, are suggesting in print, on the air, everywhere, that not work but vision is the proper activity of men and that, therefore, the contemplative life may, after all, be preferable to the active one. In such an age, it is not surprising that the books that most move the young are essentially religious books, as, indeed, pop art is always religious.

In the immediate past, however, when an absolute distinction was made between high art and pop, works of the latter category tended to be the secret scriptures of a kind of shabby, storefront church—a religion as exclusive in its attempt to remain the humble possession of the unambitious and unlettered as the canonical works of high art in their claim to be an esoteric gospel of art itself, available only to a cultivated elite. But in a time of closing the gap, literature becomes again prophetic and universal—a continuing revelation appropriate to a permanent religious revolution, whose function is precisely to transform the secular crowd into a sacred community, one with each other and equally at home in the world of technology and the realm of wonder. Pledged like Isaiah to speaking the language of everyone, the prophets of the new dispensation can afford to be neither finicky nor genteel; and they echo, therefore, the desperate cry of the Hebrew prototype: "I am a man of unclean lips . . . in the midst of a people of unclean lips."

Let those to whom religion means security beware, for it is no new established church that is in the process of being founded; and its communicants are, therefore, less like the pillars of the Lutheran Church or Anglican gentlemen than they are like ranters, enthusiasts, Dionysiacs, Anabaptists: holy disturbers of the peace of the devout. Leonard Cohen, in a moment of vision that constitutes the climax of *Beautiful Losers*, aptly calls them new Jews; for he sees them as a saved remnant moving across deserts of boredom, out of that exile from our authentic selves that we all share, toward a salvation none of us can quite imagine. Such new Jews, Cohen (himself a Jew as well as a Canadian) adds, do not have to be Jewish, but probably do have to be Americans—by which he must surely mean imaginary Americans, since, as we have been observing all along, there were never any other kind.

QUESTIONS

1. Do you feel Leslie Fiedler overstates his case? Why? What, in summary form, is his case?

2. Would you say that Fiedler's style of writing is informal or formal? Explain your choice. Describe the difference between an informal and formal essay.

3. What is the approach of New Criticism? What does Fiedler say is replacing it? What reasons does he give for the change in critical approach?

4. What is the Marxist approach to literary criticism? Why does Fiedler reject it as inappropriate to "postmodernist" literature?

5. What are the significant differences between elite literature and pop

lit? Do you agree with Fiedler's descriptions of the pop genres? If yes, why, and if no, why not?

6. Does popularity have any relation to the merit of a literary work? Explain your answer.

7. What other reasons, aside from the literary ones mentioned in the essay, might there be for the need to "cross the border, close the gap"? Does Fiedler discuss these fully?

8. In discussing the triumph of pop literature, Fiedler mentions John Barth, Ken Kesey, Leonard Cohen, William Burroughs, and Kurt Vonnegut, Jr. among others. Do you think these writers are pop authors? Choose one and discuss his work in relation to pop lit forms.

9. Apply some of the ways of criticism suggested in "Cross the Border, Close the Gap" to *The Forever People* comic.

Utopia

Sam Lundwall

The desire for a harmonious, rational, problem-free life has been with humanity for a very long time. But this desire, expressed in what has come to be known as the "utopian vision," presents a large number of problems itself. The following selection from Sam J. Lundwall's Science Fiction: What It's All About *discusses these problems with much perception and insight. In a highly opinionated and controversial manner, Lundwall provides a brief history of the utopian vision and in doing so throws considerable light on the major concerns of science fiction, in which stories about utopias are an important subgenre.*

"Where do you want to partake of your dinner, madame? On the ground floor, in one of the big halls one, two or more storeys up? We have dining halls up to the eleventh floor. We also have private rooms, up to the fourteenth floor. Please make up your mind. The first elevator starts within one minute . . . My good ladies and gentlemen . . . Here we have the second elevator with octagonal parlours that hold fifty guests each. Here is the third elevator . . . Please step inside!"

It was one of the employees of the Central Hotel, an Escalator Major, who organized the ascendent to the dinner. The Central Hotel was situated in the old Humlegården, or rather in the place where this ancient park had been, and approximately on the spot where, five hundred years ago, a small building had been erected for the Royal Library, which was the name given to the government's rather insignificant collection of books during the days of the kingdom.

New guests arrived constantly, most of them by air-velocipedes, air-cabs and other flying vehicles. Only a small number, perhaps a couple of hundreds, let themselves be hoisted up from the ground floor. The others steered right into one of the upper floors, where the vehicles were received in a number of velocipede stables, checked and guarded . . .

When you entered one of the great dining-halls, you found that they were filled with bustling activity. Around the extensive buffets that lined the walls thronged the guests that didn't have time to sit down for a real meal, but instead quickly swallowed some of the universal-energy-extract pills that always were available and made it possible to eat in seconds the equivalent of two or three ordinary meals.

The guests that had more time on their hands sat at big or small tables, richly decorated by pieces of art made with the many newly discovered metals. At every table there were a certain number of buttons, similar to those that in ancient times were used for the so-called electric bell system, and on every button the name of a dish could be read. This was the menu of the time. You pressed a button, and immediately the desired dish appeared from the floor and was pushed over to the table. Waiters or waitresses were nowhere to be seen, but every time that a dish appeared on the table, an electric signal went to one of the cashiers by the entrance, where a machine immediately noted down the dish along with the number of the guest that had ordered it, and at the exit the guest must pay his bill before he walked out.

The Central Hotel was, like all other restaurants in Stockholm, amply supplied with eat- and drinkables from all parts of the world. One could have kangaroo-steak, tapir ham, peacock breast and other meat dishes from faraway places, everything fresh. The animal might have been killed the day before by one of the modern butchering- and hunting-machines and sent to the hotel by air freight . . .

"Look what we have won by putting science into the kitchen!" exclaimed Aromasia, as she brought her guests to a table in one of the big halls of the Central Hotel.

"But the poetry!" objected the poet. "Where is the poetry?"

"It seems you never can forget your railroad-poetry," Aromasia remarked smilingly, reading the food buttons.

"Alas! Where is now the poetry of the home!" continued the poet. "In the old days the husband gathered his family around their own table. Now the whole family goes to a restaurant and sits down in a public hall together with total strangers, and eats there. Can this be called family comfort? Do you know what in the old days was meant by domestic bliss?"

"Yes," interjected Aunt Vera, whom Aromasia also had invited to dinner, "with domestic bliss was meant that the housewife should do all the work and perhaps stand by the stove herself, if she wanted to make sure that the food wasn't ruined. She should be the servant of her husband and the whole family. All domestic care, all troubles rested on her. This was the domestic bliss of the old times."

This long extract from the Swedish writer Claes Lundin's delightful Utopian novel *Oxygen och Aromasia* (1879) is very typical of one aspect of the Utopian literature, namely the dream of the country of happiness as the place where all wishes have come true, where everything is orderly and beautifully thought-out, and where one, above all, lives in freedom from want. The beautiful, wonderful Schlaraffenland or Cockaigne or lubberland all rolled into one improbable thing, the country where dissenters are shot at sight and the laws are obeyed immediately or else.

What makes Lundin's novel a strange bird in the peculiar world of the Utopias is its democratic inclination and its humor. Lundin is obviously not taking his Utopia entirely seriously. When the beautiful artist Aromasia plays the scent-organ, the "Odophore," for a group of devoutly groaning members of the local Society, both the scent-organ and the Utopia split wide open with a stench that abruptly terminates the heavenly concert. Lundin's description of the future evening papers *The Rapacious Wolf* and *Next Week's News* are not overly serious either.

Lundin described his Utopia with a pinch of humor, even if it contains all the time-honored ingredients of a true Utopian tale, including space ships (exactly like the *cavorite* sphere later described by H. G. Wells in *First Men on the Moon*), suspended animation, matter-transmitters and (almost) universal peace. Plus an anachronistic dissenter, a rather stupid poet. Weather control and TV telephones also appeared.

It should be noted that this novel was written five years before Hugo Gernsback, the "father of modern science fiction," even was born. Actually, *Oxygen och Aromasia* was at least sixty years before its time, being more modern than any science fiction written in the U.S.A. before 1930, both in imagination and quality of writing. Lundin even considered women as human beings, something that didn't dawn upon most sf writers until the middle of the twentieth century.

Other Utopias are considerably less foreseeing and—of course—not at all interested in the well-being of its poor citizens. As a rule, they show a contempt of men that would give them an honored place in the section for anti-Utopias. The inventors of these narratives from the burning hell have, with few exceptions, regarded themselves as Big Brother himself, who knows best and therefore is best suited to decide what is best for his fellow citizens. Unswerving obedience is the foremost principle of every well-arranged Utopia. I do not know how they have planned to dispose of the citizens that perchance should turn out to have different views on this; probably a firing squad was to be included somewhere.

The real horror in this sub-genre of science fiction is, of course, Plato, the old Nazi, who in his dialogue *The Republic* outlined a Utopia that leaves most others far behind. The first Commandment is naturally obedience before authorities, in this case equivalent to Plato and his friends. Moreover, every citizen's station in the society is fixed since birth, and under no circumstance is someone from the unworthy lower class permitted to ascend to higher positions. Race prejudice is systematized, and put into practical use, following a pattern that later on should be very familiar. After some typical comparisons to the breeding of dogs and the value of "pure" races, Plato turns to Man:

> It follows from our former admissions, that the best men must cohabit with the best women in as many cases as possible and the worst

with the worst in the fewest, and that the offspring of the one must be reared and that of the other not, if the flock is to be as perfect as possible. And the way in which all this is brought to pass must be unknown to any but the rulers, if, again, the herd of guardians is to be as free as possible from dissension. We shall, then, have to ordain certain festivals and sacrifices, in which we shall bring together the brides and the bridegrooms, and our poets must compose hymns suitable to the marriages that then take place. But the number of marriages we will leave to the discretion of the rulers, that they may keep the number of the citizens as nearly as may be the same, taking into account wars and diseases and all such considerations, and that, as far as possible, our city may not grow too great or too small. Certain ingenious lots, then, I suppose, must be devised so that the inferior man at each conjugation may blame chance and not the rulers.

And on the young men, surely, who excel in war and other pursuits we must bestow honors and prizes, and, in particular, the opportunity of more frequent intercourse with the women, which will at the same time be a plausible pretext for having them beget as many of the children as possible. And the children thus born will be taken over by the officials appointed for this . . . The offspring of the good, I suppose, they will take to the pen or crèche, to certain nurses who live apart in a quarter of the city, but the offspring of the inferior, and any of those of the other sort who are born defective, they will properly dispose of in secret, so that no one will know what has become of them. (10)

It is interesting to compare texts and see how near the Nazis came to achieving the ideals of Plato. Jacques Delarue describes in his book *The History of the Gestapo* how the, possibly Plato-inspired, system of the Nazis worked:

. . . The S.S. man did not have the right to marry without the authorization of his superiors. His fiancée had to prove her Aryan descent back to 1800 if she wanted to marry a simple S.S. man or non-commissioned officer, and back to 1750 if she was to marry an officer. Only the *Hauptamt*, the head office, could validate the proofs provided and give the necessary authorization. Furthermore, the girl had to undergo a certain number of medical examinations and physical tests. She must be capable of ensuring issue to the race of Herrenvolk. After the marriage the bride had to attend one of the S.S. special schools, where she was indoctrinated with the political education and "ideology which springs from the idea of racial purity" . . .

Himmler's system achieved its apotheosis with the creation of the Lebensborn—the fountain of life—a sort of human stud farm where young girls selected for their perfect Nordic traits could, free from all

> conjugal bonds, procreate with S.S. men also chosen according to the same criteria. The children born of these unions were fruits of a planned eugenics and belonged to the State, and their education was ensured in special schools. In theory they were destined to form the first generation of pure Nazis, fashioned in the ovum . . . (11)

It should be pointed out that the theory of "racial purity" worked out as badly for the Nazis as it should have for Plato and his philosopher friends. The pure-bred Aryans turned out to have an intellectual standard grossly below the average, and they did show a percentage of mental deficients four or five times higher than the normal. Or perhaps this is the sign of the Nazi/Plato thoroughbred; what do I know?

Other Utopias are somewhat more humanitarian than the Third Reich of Plato. St. Thomas More's *Utopia* (1516) (from the Greek *au topos*, nowhere) is light-years removed from *The Republic*. More has taken over the communistic society from Plato, but actually distributed a little bit of freedom to the people, keeping only ninety percent or so for the king. He is openly anti-militaristic, and even permits diverging religious faiths. The people of Utopia are merry, easy and without fear of the gods, and have a religion which favorably separates from the one of More's own time, foremost in that they maintain that:

> . . . a lesser pleasure might not stand in the way of a greater, and that no pleasure ought to be pursued that should draw a great deal of pain after it; for they think it the maddest thing in the world to pursue virtue, that is a sour and difficult thing; and not only renounce the pleasures of life, but willingly undergo much pain and trouble, if a man has no prospect of a reward? (12)

As for religion, the nice advocate of Free Thought, King Utopus, gave every man of Utopia free liberty to believe in whatever religion suited him:

> . . . only he made a solemn and severe law against such as should so far degenerate from the dignity of human nature as to think that our souls died with our bodies, or that the world was governed by chance, without a wise overruling Providence . . . and they now look on those that think otherwise as scarce fit to be counted men, since they degrade so noble a being as the soul, and reckon it no better than a beast's; thus they are far from looking on such men as fit for human society, or to be citizens of a well-ordered commonwealth. (13)

This, in a nutshell, is the theory of Utopian life and code of conduct, not only for More's novel, but for all Utopian societies: Think what you wish, but think *right*.

More's *Utopia* is divided into two parts. The first is a vigorous attack on social evils of his time—despotism, intrigues, ruinous wars, an almost criminal taxation and a cruel legal system. The second part is the actual Utopian novel—a description of the imaginary communist society on the island of Utopia. The first part of the book is hard and uncompromising; the second is idyllic, and in fact the actual origin of the Utopian never-never land. The complete book is a work of scathing social criticism in which More's England contrasts glaringly to Utopia.

More was later beheaded by his king, Henry VIII, and somewhat later canonized, though not on account of this book.

A century after More, the Italian Dominican friar Tommaso Campanella wrote *The City of the Sun*, which to a great extent is an antithesis to Plato, but with Big Brother still present. Campanella's society is clearly socialistic, based on an authoritarianism that must seem less than desirable for a modern man. Children belong to the State, marriage as an institution is dissolved. All citizens are dressed in identical uniforms. The material prosperity is considerable, but here, as in all other Utopian societies, actual freedom seems to have been caught in a wedge under the writer's enthusiasm. He is obviously incapable of understanding that man might want something more than food, sleep and housing.

Utopian novels have many faults, the most obvious seem to be their single-mindedness and inability to regard man as a thinking, illogical creature with a will of his own. They are sort of sagas, really, or fairy tales, and even though all the classical Utopias—from Plato's dream of the Dorian ideal society over Augustino's Theocracy, Joachim di Fiore's "third society," Thomas More's *Utopia* and on to the ideal creations of Owens, Fouriers, Cabet, Saint-Simon and Huxley—were based on the factual conditions of their times, none has succeeded in making the speculation viable. Except in cases like More's *Utopia*, which clearly is an attack on the appalling social conditions of More's time, all Utopias are little but oversimplified escapist dreams.

In our time, the Utopian novel has found a worthy successor in works like those of Mickey Spillane, with their almost erotic dreams of fulfilled sadism. Not to mention the real Utopian literature of our time, the specialized Utopias of pornography, where everything is possible: the Pornotopia. This is not science fiction, though. What speculation there is, is purely on the monetary side—even though the Pornotopia obviously is fantastic enough.

The big fault with all Utopian literature is that it is illogical and muddily thought-out; it must always be. Chesterton once remarked that:

> The weakness of all Utopias is this, that they take the greatest difficulty of man and assume it to be overcome, and then give an elaborate account of the overcoming of the smaller ones. They first assume that no man will want more than his share, and then are very

> ingenious in explaining whether his share will be delivered by motor car or balloon.

The second objection—and this one might be even more serious—is that Utopias invariably are boring. Again, they must be so; this is in the nature of the Utopia. If everything is tops, what is there to live for? "I don't want comfort," cries Aldous Huxley's John Savage to the World Controller.

> "I want God, I want poetry, I want real danger, I want freedom, I want goodness, I want sin."
>
> "In fact," said Mustapha Mond, "you're claiming the right to be unhappy."

Mr. Savage does, heartily. And through Mr. Savage's reactions toward the apparent Utopia, a Utopia that has all the classical properties including unlimited food, drink and sex, *Brave New World* suddenly comes out as an anti-Utopian novel. The Utopian society described in the Fourth Book of *Gulliver's Travels* is viewed in the same way: The Houyhnhms may have all the reason, but the Yahoos have all the life. Voltaire's Candide voluntarily leaves Eldorado because it is boring. The anachronistic poet in Claes Lundin's *Oxygen och Aromasia* almost becomes mad in the all-too perfect world he is imprisoned in, and dies while trying to escape to the Moon with a newly invented space ship. The perfect Utopia bears in itself the seed of the anti-Utopia. The perfect Utopia is like an army camp: you get fed, clothed and exercised, and nice people do your thinking for you. But who wants to live in an army camp for the rest of his life?

This violently totalitarian attitude is (with few exceptions) characteristic of all Utopias, whether they appear on unknown islands, in the Earth's interior or on the Moon, and could, as far as the implications go, as well be put into the section for horror visions, together with *1984* and *Brave New World*. Plato's *The Republic*, for example, could easily be changed into a true horror novel by making the narrator not one of the ruling elite, but one of those "inferior" citizens whose offspring was to be disposed of. The new Utopian writers are not quite that naïve, and do not persist in constructing their ideal states as concentration camps. In, for example, Ismar Thiusen's *Looking Forward* (1883), it was completely natural that the fair young ladies of the year 3,000 A.D. should be kept locked in, permitted to step outside only in the company of broad-shouldered old hags with daggers in their hands. Nowadays the young women might even go on three-week space tours together with the hero, without any other chaperons than their own accommodating consciences. If the old hag shows up, the hero probably would kick her out. This is, of course, a result of the more liberal outlook on sexuality and personal freedom of our days.

On the whole, the science fiction writers of today entertain a commendably suspicious attitude toward their ideal states, basing their speculations on the sound assumption that man will continue to be what he is, even though his environment will change. He will neither be saint nor slave, and the Utopia must be constructed according to this. In return, Utopia has grown considerably in size, and does hardly circumscribe itself to Earth or an insignificant part thereof. James Hilton's ethereal Shangri-La peacefully dreams away the years in splendid isolation behind impenetrable mountain ranges, but out in the starry void new empires appear—and disappear. The U.S. sf writer Isaac Asimov's well-known trilogy *Foundation* (1942–49) depicts a future that makes all other imagined societies bleak in comparison:

> . . . At the beginning of the thirteenth millennium, this (development) reached its climax. As the center of the Imperial Government for unbroken hundreds of generations and located, as it was, in the central regions of the Galaxy among the most densely populated and industrially advanced worlds of the system, it could scarcely help being the densest and richest clot of humanity the Race had ever seen.
>
> Its urbanization, progressing steadily, had finally reached the ultimate. All the land surface of Trantor, 75,000,000 square miles in extent, was a single city. The population, at its height, was well in excess of forty billions. This enormous population was devoted almost entirely to the administrative necessities of the Empire, and found themselves all too few for the complications of the task. . . . Daily, fleets of ships in the tens of thousands brought the produce of twenty agricultural worlds to the dinner tables of Trantor. . . . (14)

The central theme of all Utopian literature is Power. Power to change the environment, power to maintain the private or human individuality. The novels of Jules Verne belong, with few exceptions, to this branch, as well as most of the science fiction that was written during the time of the late industrialization. It was power to send man to the Moon, power to place man over the natural laws; with the help of human genius, power to create the ideal state on Earth. With a rough generalization, one can say that the Utopian novel dominated science fiction—with shining exceptions like H. G. Wells—until the nineteen thirties, when the Depression quickly put an end to the most naïve hopes for the future. It is interesting, though, to note that H. G. Wells, who started with anti-Utopias like *When the Sleeper Wakes* (1899) and *The Time Machine* (1895), in time became increasingly reactionary, until the scientific progress and evolutionary process whose end results are so gloomily predicted in the early stories, are held forth as the bases for desirable brave new worlds in, for example, *A Modern Utopia* (1905), *Men Like Gods* (1923) and *The Shape of Things to Come* (1933). *A Modern Utopia* describes the modern welfare state, governed by the usual Utopian rational elite, called *Samurai*, and the result is a world ruled by efficiency, proving, as many of Wells's subsequent works did, that he had no fondness for socialism in its classical sense, or even for democracy. This message is also brought forth in the other two mentioned novels, strange as it may seem when one knows that Wells once was an active member of the British Fabian Society, a socialistic movement. In these novels, Wells suddenly returns to the time-honored totalitarian state reminiscent of the government system proposed, among others, by Francis Bacon in *The New Atlantis* and by Plato in *The Republic*; a meritocracy with Science (or Philosophy) as an obedient servant standing behind the Masters. It is Utopia in all respects, chemically free of everything that possibly could make life worth living. The British critic David Lodge has observed regarding *A Modern Utopia* that:

> In a sense it was a generous attempt on Wells's part to imagine a social structure which would make available to everyone the kind of success and happiness he had personally achieved in the teeth of great disadvantages. Or, more cynically, you could call it the paradise of little fat men.

This also goes, in a lesser degree, for Aldous Huxley, creator of one of the most fierce and intelligent anti-Utopian novels, *Brave New World*, who as an old man wrote a straight Utopian novel, *Island* (1961) which is about as stimulating as any of the old stiff-legged and impossible Utopias.

The Utopian novel is escapist, as all dreams of the unattainable must be, and the science fiction writers of today are all too practical to go on escapist Utopian sprees. One of the very few exceptions I know of is the noted sf writer Theodore Sturgeon's novel *Venus Plus X* (1960), which depicts a Utopia in the classic sense, complete with universal brotherhood, understanding, intelligence, love and no dissenters in sight. That the novel still manages to convey a message is entirely due to Sturgeon's obvious skills as a writer, plus the fact that this particular Utopia is built upon sexual and moral standards that in themselves make the novel interesting. Apart from that, this is Schlaraffenland all over again, and no beautiful machinery can make it credible. The societies created by other sf writers are far, far removed from this.

A short story by Robert Sheckley, *Street of Dreams, Feet of Clay* (1969), joyously describes a seemingly perfect Utopia, a sentient city which is programmed to guard its inhabitants from all dangers, and to give them everything they can wish for. It behaves exactly as carpingly patronizing as an anxious mother, and the inhabitants can't wait to get out of it. Another short sf story describes a future where criminals are frozen into suspended animation and left for thawing in some distant Utopian future where people know how to handle them. The protagonist awakes in this future, is taken on a sight-seeing tour of the perfect Utopia, and soon becomes seized by claustrophobia. The continuance of Utopia is guaranteed by a simple surgical incision that is performed while the citizen is still a baby, and secures him a happy and peaceful life, free from unnecessary curiosity and rebelliousness. The protagonist has to choose between going through the operation and becoming a socially well-adjusted individual, or getting thrown out into the wilderness where the scattered remnants of various underdeveloped races live in horrible destitution. He chooses the savages.

In this story the good Utopians enjoyed themselves by spying on the appalling destitution of the savages through hidden TV cameras. In a recent story by Harlan Ellison, *The Prowler in the City at the Edge of the World*, the citizens of a future Utopia fetch Jack the Ripper and force him to prowl the sterile streets, killing and vandalizing, in order to satisfy the Utopians' demands for more and more perverted amusements. The citizens of More's esoteric Utopia were not unacquainted with the idea either. Of course they were strongly opposed to wars and such themselves, and in times of war the foremost task of the priests was to prevent (not preclude: that might put the soldiery out of jobs) unnecessary bloodshed. In the neighboring country Zapolet, however, live heartless, uncivilized brutes who are willing to fight Utopia's wars. The Utopians pay these killers to wage their wars for them, and complacently regard how they butcher each other. For their own part, the Utopians prefer assassinations, and assassins are both honored and well paid.

Imagined societies are still created in science fiction, but they are far from the escapist Utopias of yore. Robert A. Heinlein's and Isaac Asimov's highly complicated future societies are good examples of this. They are, on the whole, better than the societies of today, just as our world on the whole is better than that of a hundred years ago, but they are not perfect. No world will ever be perfect because man isn't, and no *deus ex machina* in the form of a brilliant new religious concept or some wonderful mechanical gadget will ever do the work for him.

When steam power was introduced, it was thought to pave the road to Utopia; well, it didn't, and neither did electricity, even though it certainly made life better. Later, atomic power, worldwide communications and space flight each in its own way contributed to the general welfare, but Utopia is still unattained. It will always be. Utopias make for interesting escapist reading at times, but they certainly have no place in reality.

The English professor John Ronald Reuel Tolkien's epic trilogy *The*

Fellowship of the Ring (1954–55) probably comes as close to a Utopia as anything that has been written during the last fifty years, with its innocent Rousseauian escapism, but even here dangers always lurk in the shadows, threatening to tear the gossamer security into fragments at the first sign of weakness. Also, the story evolves in a mythical ancient past, well before man. When man is mentioned, it is as something threatening, something that will cause the destruction of the fairyland. Utopias, the science fiction writers seem to say, cannot exist. If they, notwithstanding, should exist, they could never work. And if they, against all common sense, should work, they would not be of any use anyway.

QUESTIONS

1. Why is communism or socialism basic to most utopias? Considering that Lundwall sometimes places a "king" at the head of his "communist" society, what might he mean by the terms "communism" and "socialism"?

2. Is it fair to call Plato an "old Nazi"? Why? What elements in Plato's utopia are most objectionable?

3. The Nazi system of sexual pairing was invented in the twentieth century. Is there any place in the world today in which it might be found attractive? If you were an S.S. man, what might be wrong with it?

4. Does the philosophy "Think what you wish, but think *right*" exist anywhere outside of utopian societies? If so, where?

5. Choose one of the following terms as the most appropriate description of the utopian societies discussed by Lundwall: democratic, monarchical, totalitarian, oligarchical, theocratic. Define the term you've chosen and show how it applies to Lundwall's description of utopia.

6. What instances of slanted writing appear in this selection? Is the slanting misleading or informative? Does Lundwall's provocative style add or detract from your enjoyment and learning experience as you read "Utopia"?

7. Is it possible for the human mind to imagine a perfect Utopia? Explain your answer.

The Theory and Practice of Time Travel

Larry Niven

The "time travel" story contains built-in impossibilities, no matter how convincing the author's explanation is made to appear. As such, it illustrates noted SF scholar Sam Moskowitz's observation that "science fiction is a branch of fantasy identifiable by the fact that it eases the 'willing suspension of disbelief' on the part of its readers by utilizing an atmosphere of scientific credibility . . ."

The article that is reprinted below can serve as an example of the kind of speculation that many SF writers engage in as they plan a story or novel. Larry Niven is well suited to be the author of this article, since part of his growing reputation in the SF field rests on his "hard science" and "time travel" stories.

> Speculate: (2) *To ponder a subject in its different aspects and relations: meditate: esp. to theorise from conjectures without sufficient evidence.*
> —*Webster's New Collegiate Dictionary.*

1959

Once upon a time a man was given three wishes. He blew the first two, getting himself in such deep trouble that if he let either wish stand, he would suffer terribly. Now desperate, he cried, "I wish I'd never *had* a fairy godmother!" And the past healed to cancel both wishes.

The first time-travel story was a fairy tale—here drastically condensed.

Its theme is buried deep in the literature. L. Frank Baum used it in *The Wonderful Land of Oz.* Cabell borrowed it for *The Silver Stallion.* Traditionally the protagonist may change the past without actually moving backward in time.

H. G. Wells, one of the fathers of modern science fiction, also fathered the time traveling *vehicle.* This may be the reason Wells' spiritual sons tend to treat time travel as science fiction rather than fantasy. But Wells wrote only of travel into the future. He missed the Grandfather Paradox and all the other derivative paradoxes of travel into the past. His time machine was a mere vehicle, no more remarkable than the gravity-shielding material, Cavorite.

Wells also missed the most important aspect of time travel: wish fulfillment. When a child prays, "Please, God, make it didn't happen," he is inventing time travel in its essence. (He will probably give up the idea when he learns good English. More about that later.) The prime purpose of time travel is to change the past; and the prime danger is that the Traveler might change the past. The man who first thought of travel into the past combined the Wells machine with the fairy tale to produce time travel in its present form.

Time machines come in many forms. Wells' man-carrying vehicle was as open as a bicycle seat, with a magnificent view of time flashing past. Poul Anderson's standard issue time Patrol vehicle could do anything Wells' could, and fly too.

More restricted machines may travel only into the future, or may send only subatomic particles into the past, or may be restricted to things even less substantial: thoughts, dreams, emotional states. Others may move only in quantum jumps of a million or sixty million years. A writer who puts severe limits on his time machine, is generally limiting its ability to change the past in order to make his story less incredible.

The Grandfather Paradox is basic to any discussion of time travel. It runs as follows:

At the age of eighty your grandfather invents a time machine. You hate the old man, so you steal the machine and take it sixty years back into the past and kill him. How can they suspect you?

But you've killed him before he can meet your grandmother. Thus you were never born. He didn't get a chance to build the time machine either.

But then you can't have killed him. Thus he may sire your father, who may sire you. Later there will be a time machine. . . .

You and the machine both do and do not exist. Paradox!

In general we will call any such interference with the past, especially self-cancelling interference, a Grandfather Paradox.

Travel into the past violates certain of what we regard as laws of nature.

(1) A vehicle which travels from the thirtieth century AD to the twentieth, may be regarded as appearing from nowhere. Thus it violates the law of conservation of matter. If the vehicle carries a power source of any kind, it also violates conservation of energy . . . a quibble, as they are both the same law these days.

To say that an equivalent tonnage of matter disappears a thousand years later is no answer. For ten centuries there was an extra time machine around.

But things are even worse if a Grandfather Paradox is involved. One can imagine a centuries-old time machine resting in a museum, inside a glass-and-steel case made from the glass and the steel which would have been used to build the time machine, if anyone had gone ahead and built that time machine, which nobody did, because of interference with the past via that same time machine.

(2) If one cannot send matter through time, perhaps one can send signals—information.

But even this violates conservation of energy. Any signal involves energy in some form.

Furthermore, relativity laws state that information cannot travel faster than *c*, the velocity of light in a vacuum. A signal traveling back through time travels faster than infinity!

(3) Physical time travel clearly violates any law of motion, as motion always relates to time. This affects conservation of momentum, statements about kinetic energy, and even the law of gravity. *Anybody's* law of gravity.

(4) What about drawing information from the future?

If precognition and prophecy are only very accurate guesswork by the subconscious mind, then no laws are violated. But if precognition really has something to do with time—

I cite the Heisenberg Principle. One cannot observe something without affecting it. If one observes the future, there must be an energy exchange of some kind. But that implies that the future one is observing is *the* future; that it already exists; that information is flowing into the past.

I've demonstrated that this violates relativity and conservation of energy. It also involves a Grandfather Paradox, if information drawn from one future is used to create another. And if the information can't be used to change the future, then what good is it?

What was that about the stock market?

(5) Travel into the future is no more difficult than suspended animation and a good, durable time capsule. But you can't go home without traveling into the past.

Does any of this seem like nitpicking? Sure it is. Are we to regard the laws of relativity and conservation as sacred, never to be broken, nor even bent by exceptions? Heaven forbid.

But time travel violates laws more basic than conservation laws.

Our belief in laws of any kind presupposes a belief in cause and effect. Time travel reverses cause and effect. With a Grandfather Paradox operating, the effect, coming before the cause, may cause the cause never to come into effect, with results which are not even self-consistent.

Characters in time-travel stories often complain that English isn't really built to handle time travel. The tenses get all fouled up. We in the trade call this problem Excedrin Headache number $\surd$—3.14159 . . .

To show it in action, I'd like to quote from one of my own stories, "Bird in the Hand." The characters have done catastrophic damage to the past, and are discussing how to repair it.

> "Maybe we can go around you." Svetz hesitated, then plunged in. "Zeera, try this. Send me back to an hour before the earlier Zeera arrives. Ford's automobile won't have disappeared yet. I'll duplicate it, duplicate the duplicate, take the reversed duplicate and the original past you in the big extension cage. That leaves you to destroy the duplicate instead of the original. I reappear after you've gone, leave the original automobile for Ford, and come back here with the reversed duplicate. How's that?"
>
> "It sounded great. Would you mind going through it again?"
>
> "Let's see. I go back to—"

This was less of a digression than it seemed. The English language can't handle time travel. We conclude that the ancestors who made our language didn't have minds equipped to handle time travel. Naturally we don't either; for our thinking is too dependent on our language.

As far as I know, *no* language has tenses equipped to handle time travel. No language on Earth. Yet.

But then, no language was ever equipped to handle lasers, television, or spaceflight until lasers, television, and spaceflight were developed. Then the words followed.

If time travel were thrust upon us, would we develop a language to handle it?

We'd need a basic past tense, an altered past tense, a potential past tense (might have been), an altered future tense, an excised future tense (for a future that can no longer happen), a home base present tense, a present-of-the-moment tense, an enclosed present tense, (for use while the vehicle is moving through time), a future past tense ("I'll meet you at the bombing of Pearl Harbor in half an hour."), a past future tense ("Just a souvenir I picked up ten million years from now"), and many more. We'd need at least two directions of time flow: sequential personal time, and universal time, with a complete set of tenses for each.

We'd need pronouns to distinguish [you of the past] from [you of the future] and [you of the present]. After all, the three of you might all be sitting around the same table someday.

Meanwhile (if, God willing, the word still has meaning), time travel must be considered fantasy. It violates too many of the laws of physics and reason to be thought otherwise.

But it's a form of fantasy superbly suited to games of logic. The temptation to work out a self-consistent set of laws for time travel must be enormous. So many writers have tried it!

Let's look at some of the more popular possibilities:

DEFENSE OF TIME TRAVEL #I: Assume that (1) One can travel *only* into the future. (2) The universe is cyclic in time, repeating itself over and over.

This works! All you've got to do is go into the future past the Big Collapse when the universe falls in on itself, through the Big Bang when it explodes again, and keep going until you reach the area of the past you're looking for. Then you murder Hitler in 1920, or use the H-bomb on the damyankees at Appomatox, or whatever your daydream is. There is no Grandfather Paradox. You merely get a new future.

True, the next version of *you* will not make the trip. You've eliminated his motive. Thus on the *next* cycle the damyankees *will* win the Civil War. Hitler *will* lead Germany into WWII, and so forth. But you've merely introduced a double cycle. There is no paradox.

Further, your time machine need be nothing more than an EXTREMELY durable time capsule.

Objections: Three. First, some people don't believe in cyclic time. (I don't.) Second, locating the proper era is a nontrivial problem when you've got the whole lifetime of the universe to search in. You'd be lucky to find *any* section of human history. Third, removing your time capsule from the reaction of the Big Bang could change the final configuration of matter, giving an entirely different history.

DEFENSE OF TIME TRAVEL #II: Known as the theory of multiple time tracks.

Let there be a myriad of realities, of universes. For every decision made by any form of life, let it be made both ways; or in all possible ways if there are more than two choices. Let universes be created with every choice.

Then conservation of matter and energy holds only for the universe of universes. One can move time machines from one universe to another.

You've got to admit it's flamboyant!

You still can't visit the past. But you can find a universe where things happened more slowly; where Napoleon is *about* to fight Waterloo, or Nero is *about* to ascend the throne. Or, instead of changing the past, you need only seek out the universe where the past you want is the one that happened. The universe you want unquestionably exists. (Though you may search a long, weary time before you find it.)

Ersatz time travel becomes a special case of sidewise-in-time travel, travel between multiple time tracks.

The *what-if* story has fascinated many writers. Even O. Henry wrote at least one. From our viewpoint, sidewise-in-time travel solves conservation laws, Grandfather Paradox, everything.

I *hate* sidewise-in-time travel stories.

Let me show you why.

First, they're too easy to write. You don't need a brain to write alternate-world stories. You need a good history text.

In the second place . . . did you ever sweat over a decision? Think about one that really gave you trouble, because you knew that what you did would affect you for the rest of your life. Now imagine that for every way you could have jumped, one of you in one universe did jump that way.

Now don't you feel silly? Sweating over something so trivial, when you were going to take *all* the choices anyway. And if you think that's silly, consider that one of you still can't decide . . .

In the third place, probability doesn't support the theory of alternate time tracks.

There are six ways a die can fall, right? Which makes thirty-six ways that *two* dice can fall, including six ways to get a seven. Each way the dice can fall determines one universe. Then the chance of your ending in each of the thirty-six universes is one in thirty-six, right?

Then it doesn't matter if the dice are loaded. One chance in thirty-six, exactly, is the odds for each way the dice can fall. One chance in six, exactly, of getting a seven.

Experience, however, shows that it *does* matter if the dice are loaded.

DEFENSE OF TIME TRAVEL #III: The idea of reversing the flow of time isn't nearly as silly as it sounds. I quote from an article in the October 1969 issue of *Scientific American.* "Experiments in Time Reversal," by Oliver E. Overseth.

"All of us vividly recognise the way time flows; we take considerable comfort, for example, in our confidence that the carefully arranged marriage of gin and vermouth is not going to be suddenly annulled in our glass, leaving us with two layers of warm liquid and a lump of ice. It is a curious fact, however, that the laws that provide the basis for our understanding of fundamental physical processes (and presumably biological processes as well) do not favor one direction of time's arrow over another. They would represent the world just as well if time were flowing backward instead of forward and martinis were coming apart rather than being created."

Is the universe really invarient under time reversal? Many physicists think not. Overseth and his partner Roth spent almost two years looking for a case in subatomic physics in which invarience under time reversal is not preserved.

They knew exactly what they were looking for. They were watching (via some very direct instruments) the decay of a lambda particle into a proton plus a pi meson. The anomaly would have been a nonzero value for the beta component of the spin of the proton.

The point is that they failed to find what they were looking for. There have been many such experiments in recent years, and none have been successful. At the subatomic level, one cannot tell whether time is running backward or forward.

Could a determined man reach the past by reversing himself in time and waiting for last year to happen again?

Present theory says that he would reverse both the spin and the charge of every subatomic particle in his body. The charge reversal converts the whole mass to antimatter. BOOM!

Less dramatically, there is conservation of mass/energy. Reverse the direction of travel in time of a human body, and to any physicist it would look like two people have vanished.

Clearly this is illegal. We can't do it that way.

We might more successfully reverse a man's *viewpoint:* send his *mind* backward in time. If there is really no difference between past and future, except in attitude, then it should be possible.

But the traveler risks his memory healing to a *tabula rasa,* a blank slate. When he reaches his target date he might not remember what to do about it.

For there is still entropy: the tendency to disorder in the universe, and the most obvious effect of moving "forward" in time. Entropy is not obvious where few reactions are involved, as in the motion of the planets, or as when a lambda particle breaks down. But the mushroom cloud left by a hydrogen bomb is difficult to return to its metal case. That's entropy.

Any specialist in geriatric medicine knows about entropy.

Let's try something less ambitious.

Suppose we found a clump of particles already moving backward in time. (Exactly what Roth and Overseth and their brethren might find in their experiments, if time-reversal turns out to be valid. Though most expect to find just the opposite.) Now we write messages on that clump. Simple messages. "Blue Ben in the sixth, 4/4/72."

But from our viewpoint, we start by finding a message and end by erasing it! And if it went wrong . . . We find a message: "Blue Ben in the sixth, 4/4/72." We bet on him, and he loses. Now what? Can we unwrite a different message? Or just refuse to erase it at all?

But if it did work, we could make a fortune. And it violates no known physical laws! Practically.

Meanwhile, Roth and Overseth and a number of others are all convinced that there must be exceptions to the symmetry of time. If they find just one, it's all over.

DEFENSE OF TIME TRAVEL #IV: The oldest of all, going back to Greek times. Philosophers call it *fatalism* or *determinism.* A fatalist believes that everything that happens is predetermined to the end of time; that any attempt to change the predetermined future is fated, is a part of the predetermined future itself.

To a fatalist, the future looks exactly like the traditional picture of the past. Both are rigid, inflexible. The introduction of time travel would not alter the picture at all, for any attempt on the part of a time traveler to change the past has already been made, and is a part of the past.

Fatalism has been the basis for many a tale of a frantic time traveler caught in a web of circumstance such that every move he makes acts to bring about just the calamity he is trying to avert. The standard plot sketch is reminiscent of *Oedipus Rex;* when well done it has the same flavor of man heroically battling Fate—and losing.

Notice how fatalism solves the Grandfather Paradox. You can't kill your grandfather, because you *didn't.* You'll kill the wrong man if you try it; or your gun won't fire.

Fatalism ruins the wish-fulfillment aspect of time travel. Anything that averts the Grandfather Paradox will do that. The Grandfather Paradox *is* the wish-fulfillment aspect. *Make it didn't happen.*

The way to get the most fun out of time travel is to accept it for what it is. Give up relativity and the conservation laws. Allow changes in the past and present and future, reversals in the order of cause and effect, effects whose cause never happens . . .

Fatalistic time travel also allows these causative loops, but they are always simple, closed loops with no missing parts. The appearance of a time machine somewhere always implies its disappearance somewhere-and-somewhen else. But with this new, *free will* kind of time travel . . .

We assume that there is only one reality, one past and one future; but that it can be changed at will via the time machine. Cause and effect may loop toward the past; and sometimes a loop is pinched off, to vanish from the time stream. The traveler who kills his six-year-old grandfather eliminates the cause of *himself*, but he and his time machine remain—until someone else changes the past even further back.

Between the deterministic and free will modes of time travel lies a kind of compromise position:

We assume a kind of inertia, or hysteresis effect, or special conservation law for time travel. The past resists change. Breaks in time tend to heal. Kill Charlemagne and someone will take his place, conquer his empire, mate with his wives, breed sons very like his. Changes will be minor and local.

Fritz Leiber used Conservation of Events to good effect in the Change War stories. In "Try and Change the Past," his protagonist went to enormous lengths to prevent a bullet from smashing through a man's head. He was sincere. It was his own head. In the end he succeeded—and watched a bullet-sized meteorite smash into his alter-self's forehead.

Probabilities change to protect history. This is the safest form of time travel in that respect. But one does have to remember that the odds have changed.

Try to save Jesus with a submachine gun, and the gun will *positively* jam.

But if you did succeed in killing your own six-year-old grandfather, you would stand a good chance of taking his place. Conservation of Events requires someone to take his place; and everyone else is busy filling his own role. Except *you*, an extraneous figure from another time. Now Conservation of Events acts to protect you in your new role!

Besides, you're already carrying the old man's genes. . . .

Certain kinds of time travel may be possible; but changing the past is not. I can prove it.

GIVEN: That the universe of discourse permits both time travel and the changing of the past.

THEN: A time machine will not be invented in that universe.

For, if a time machine is invented in that universe, somebody will change the past of that universe. There is just too much future subsequent to the invention of a time machine: too many people with too many good motives for meddling with too many events occurring in too much of the past.

If we assume that there is no historical inertia, no Conservation of Events, then each change makes a whole new universe. Every trip into the past means that all the dice have to be thrown over again. Every least change changes all the history books, until by chance and endless change we reach a universe where there is no time machine invented, ever, by any species.

Then that universe would not change.

Now assume that there *is* an inertia to history; that the past tends to remain unchanged; that probabilities change to protect the fabric of events. What is the simplest change in history that will protect the past from interference?

Right. No time machines!

> Niven's Law: if the universe of discourse permits the possibility of time travel and of changing the past, then no time machine will be invented in that universe.

If time travel is so manifestly impossible, why does every good and bad science fiction writer want to write a new, fresh time travel story?

It's a form of competition. No writer believes that a field is completely mined out. And no field ever is. There is always something new to say, if you can find it.

Time travel can be a vehicle, like a faster-than-light drive. Our best evidence says that nothing can travel faster than light. Yet hard-headed science fiction writers constantly use faster-than-light spacecraft. If a character must reach the Veil Nebula, and if the plot demands that his girl friend be still a girl when he returns, then he must needs travel faster than light. Similarly, it takes time travel to pit a man against a dinosaur, or to match a modern man against King Arthur's knights.

There are things a writer can't say without using time travel.

Then, time travel is so delightfully open to tortuous reasoning. You should be convinced of that by now. The brain gets needed exercise plotting a story in a universe where effects happen before their causes; where the hero and his enemy may be working each to prevent the other's birth; where a brick wall may be no more solid than a dream, if one can eliminate the architect from history.

If one could travel in time, what wish could not be answered? All the treasures of the past would fall to one man with a submachine gun. Cleopatra and Helen of Troy might share his bed, if bribed with a trunkful of modern cosmetics. The dead return to life, or cease to have been at all.

Bothered by smog? Henry Ford could be stopped in time, in time . . .

No. We face insecurity enough. Read your newspaper, and be glad that at least your past is safe.

QUESTIONS

1. If time travel is impossible, how can the notion of traveling through time have any relevance to the "real" world? Need it have any relevance?

2. Which of Niven's four Defenses of Time Travel seems least improbable? Justify your response.

3. The author frequently shifts between the first, second, and third persons in this article. What is the effect of his shifts?

4. Discuss the moral questions involved in time travel.

5. If time travel were possible and if our society decided to change the past, who should decide which changes are to be made? Should it be our politicians, our scientists, our historians, the UN?

6. In what way does James Tiptree avoid the "Grandfather Paradox" in his short story "The Man Who Walked Home"? There is indeed a slight reference to the Grandfather Paradox in the story. What is it and how is it dealt with?

The Obsolescence of Man

Arthur C. Clarke

The title speaks for itself. The following essay is an example of futurist thinking, of an author throwing his ideas forward in time. Arthur C. Clarke presents a case for a pattern of "evolution" that seems, increasingly, to be possible and less depressing for homo sapiens than it might at first appear. The author is widely known for his collaboration with Stanley Kubrick on the movie 2001: A Space Odyssey, *and for his many "classic" SF short stories and novels, including the best-selling* Rendevous with Rama.

About a million years ago, an unprepossessing primate discovered that his forelimbs could be used for other purposes besides locomotion. Objects like sticks and stones could be grasped—and, once grasped, were useful for killing game, digging up roots, defending or attacking, and a hundred other jobs. On the third planet of the Sun, tools had appeared; and the place would never be the same again.

The first users of tools were *not* men—a fact appreciated only in the last year or two—but prehuman anthropoids; and by their discovery they doomed themselves. For even the most primitive of tools, such as a naturally pointed stone that happens to fit the hand, provides a tremendous physical and mental stimulus to the user. He has to walk erect; he no longer needs huge canine teeth—since sharp flints can do a better job—and he must develop manual dexterity of a high order. These are the specifications of Homo sapiens; as soon as they start to be filled, all earlier models are headed for rapid obsolescence. To quote Professor Sherwood Washburn of the University of California's anthropology department: "It was the success of the simplest tools that started the whole trend of human evolution and led to the civilizations of today."

Note that phrase—"the whole trend of human evolution." The old idea that man invented tools is therefore a misleading half-truth; it would be more accurate to say that *tools invented man.* They were very primitive tools, in the hands of creatures who were little more than apes. Yet they led to us—and to the eventual extinction of the ape-men who first wielded them.

Now the cycle is about to begin again; but neither history nor prehistory ever exactly repeats itself, and this time there will be a fascinating twist in the plot. The tools the ape-men invented caused them to evolve into their successor, Homo sapiens. The tool we have invented *is* our successor. Biological evolution has given way to a far more rapid process—technological evolution. To put it bluntly and brutally, the machine is going to take over.

This, of course, is hardly an original idea. That the creations of man's brain might one day threaten and perhaps destroy him is such a tired old *cliché* that no self-respecting science-fiction writer would dare to use it. It goes back, through Capek's *R.U.R*, Samuel Butler's *Erewhon*, Mary Shelley's *Frankenstein* and the Faust legend to the mysterious but perhaps not wholly mythical figure of Daedalus, King Minos' one-man office of scientific research. For at least three thousand years, therefore, a vocal minority of mankind has had grave doubts about the ultimate outcome of technology. From the self-centered, human point of view, these doubts are justified. But that, I submit, will not be the only—or even the most important—point of view for much longer.

When the first large-scale electronic computers appeared some fifteen years ago, they were promptly nicknamed "Giant Brains"—and the scientific community, as a whole, took a poor view of the designation. But the scientists objected to the wrong word. The electronic computers were not *giant* brains; they were dwarf brains, and they still are, though they have grown a hundredfold within less than one generation of mankind. Yet even in their present flint-ax stage of evolution, they have done things which not long ago almost everyone would have claimed to be impossible—such as translating from one language to another, composing music, and playing a fair game of chess. And much more important than any of these infant *jeux d'esprit* is the fact that they have breached the barrier between brain and machine.

This is one of the greatest—and perhaps one of the last—break-throughs in the history of human thought, like the discovery that the Earth moves round the Sun, or that man is part of the animal kingdom, or that $E = mc^2$. All these ideas took time to sink in, and were frantically denied when first put forward. In the same way it will take a little while for men to realize that machines can not only think, but may one day think them off the face of the Earth.

At this point you may reasonably ask: "Yes—but what do you mean by *think?*" I propose to sidestep that question, using a neat device for which I am indebted to the English mathematician A. M. Turing. Turing imagined a game played by two teleprinter operators in separate rooms—this impersonal link being used to remove all clues given by voice, appearance, and so forth. Suppose one operator was able to ask the other any questions he wished, and the other had to make suitable replies. If, after some hours or days of this conversation, the questioner could not decide whether his telegraphic acquaintance was human or purely mechanical, then he could hardly deny that he/it was capable of thought. An electronic brain that passed this test would, surely, have to be regarded as an intelligent entity. Anyone who argued otherwise would merely prove that he was less intelligent than the machine; he would be a splitter of nonexistent hairs, like the scholar who proved that the *Odyssey* was not written by Homer, but by another man of the same name.

We are still decades—but not centuries—from building such a machine, yet already we are sure that it could be done. If Turing's experiment is never carried out, it will merely be because the intelligent machines of the future will have better things to do with their time than conduct extended conversations with men. I often talk with my dog, but I don't keep it up for long.

The fact that the great computers of today are still high-speed morons, capable of doing nothing beyond the scope of the instructions carefully programmed into them, has given many people a spurious sense of security. No machine, they argue, can possibly be more intelligent than its makers—the men who designed it, and planned its functions. It may be a million times faster in operation, but that is quite irrelevant. Anything and everything that an electronic brain can do must also be within the scope of a human brain, if it had sufficient time and patience. Above all, it is maintained, no machine can show originality or creative power or the other attributes which are fondly labeled "human."

The argument is wholly fallacious; those who still bring it forth are like the buggy-whip makers who used to poke fun at stranded Model T's. Even if it were true, it could give no comfort, as a careful reading of these remarks by Dr. Norbert Wiener will show:

> This attitude (the assumption that machines cannot possess any degree of originality) in my opinion should be rejected entirely. . . . It is my thesis that machines can and do transcend some of the limitations of their designers. . . . It may well be that in principle we cannot make any machine, the elements of whose behaviour we cannot comprehend sooner or later. This does not mean in any way that we shall be able to comprehend them in substantially less time than the operation of the machine, nor even within any given number of years or generations. . . . This means that though they are theoretically subject to human criticism, such criticism may be ineffective until a long time after it is relevant.

In other words, even machines *less* intelligent than men might escape from our control by sheer speed of operation. And in fact, there is every reason to suppose that machines will become much more intelligent than their builders, as well as incomparably faster.

There are still a few authorities who refuse to grant any degree of intelligence to machines, now or in the future. This attitude shows a striking parallel to that adopted by the chemists of the early nineteenth century. It was known then that all living organisms are formed from a few common elements—mostly carbon, hydrogen, oxygen, and nitrogen —but it was firmly believed that the materials of life could not be made from "mere" chemicals alone. There must be some other ingredient—some essence or vital principle, forever unknowable to man. No chemist could ever take carbon, hydrogen, and so forth and combine them to form any of the substances upon which life was based. There was an impassable barrier between the worlds of "inorganic" and "organic" chemistry.

This *mystique* was destroyed in 1828, when Wöhler synthesized urea, and showed that there was no difference at all between the chemical reactions taking place in the body, and those taking place inside a retort. It was a terrible shock to those pious souls who believed that the mechanics of life must always be beyond human understanding or imitation. Many people are equally shocked today by the suggestion that machines can think, but their dislike of the situation will not alter it in the least.

Since this is not a treatise on computer design, you will not expect me to explain how to build a thinking machine. In fact, it is doubtful if any human being will ever be able to do this in detail, but one can indicate the sequence of events that will lead from H. sapiens to M. sapiens. The first two or three steps on the road have already been taken; machines now exist that can learn by experience, profiting from their mistakes and—unlike human beings—never repeating them. Machines have been built which do not sit passively waiting for instructions, but which explore the world around them in a manner which can only be called inquisitive. Others look for proofs of theorems in mathematics or logic, and sometimes come up with surprising solutions that had never occurred to their makers.

These faint glimmerings of original intelligence are confined at the moment to a few laboratory models; they are wholly lacking in the giant computers that can now be bought by anyone who happens to have a few hundred thousand dollars to spare. But machine intelligence will grow, and it will start to range beyond the bounds of human thought as soon as the second generation of computers appears—the generation that has been designed, not by men, but by other, "almost intelligent" computers. And not only designed, but also built—for they will have far too many components for manual assembly.

It is even possible that the first genuine thinking machines may be *grown* rather than constructed; already some crude but very stimulating experiments have been carried out along these lines. Several artificial organisms have been built which are capable of rewiring themselves to adapt to changing circumstances. Beyond this there is the possibility of computers which will start from relatively simple beginnings, be programmed to aim at specific goals, and search for them by constructing their own circuits, perhaps by growing networks of threads in a conducting medium. Such a growth may be no more than a mechanical analogy of what happens to every one of us in the first nine months of our existence.

All speculations about intelligent machines are inevitably conditioned —indeed, inspired—by our knowledge of the human brain, the only thinking device currently on the market. No one, of course, pretends to understand the full workings of the brain, or expects that such knowledge will be available in any foreseeable future. (It is a nice philosophical point as to whether the brain can ever, even in principle, understand itself.) But we do know enough about its physical structure to draw many conclusions about the limitations of "brains"—whether organic or inorganic.

There are approximately ten billion separate switches—or neurons—inside your skull, "wired" together in circuits of unimaginable complexity. Ten billion is such a large number that, until recently, it could be used as an argument against the achievement of mechanical intelligence. About ten years ago a famous neurophysiologist made a statement (still produced like some protective incantation by the advocates of cerebral supremacy) to the effect that an electronic model of the human brain would have to be as large as the Empire State Building, and would need Niagara Falls to keep it cool when it was running.

This must now be classed with such interesting pronouncements as, "No heavier than air machine will ever be able to fly." For the calculation was made in the days of the vacuum tube (remember it?), and the transistor has now completely altered the picture. Indeed—such is the rate of technological progress today—the transistor itself is being replaced by still smaller and faster devices, based upon abstruse principles of quantum physics. If the problem was merely one of space, today's electronic techniques would allow us to pack a computer as complex as the human brain on to a single floor of the Empire State Building.

Interlude for agonizing reappraisal. It's a tough job keeping up with science, and since I wrote that last paragraph the Marquardt Corporation's Astro Division has announced a new memory device which could store inside a six-foot cube *all information recorded during the last 10,000 years.* This means, of course, not only every book ever printed, but *everything* ever written in *any* language on paper, papyrus, parchment, or stone. It represents a capacity untold millions of times greater than that of a single human memory, and though there is a mighty gulf between merely storing information and thinking creatively—the Library of Congress has never written a book—it does indicate that mechanical brains of enormous power could be quite small in physical size.

This should not surprise anyone who remembers how radios have shrunk from the bulky cabinet models of the thirties to the vest-pocket (yet much more sophisticated) transistor sets of today. And the shrinkage is just gaining momentum, if I may employ such a mind-boggling phrase. Radio receivers the size of lumps of sugar have now been built; before long, they will be the size not of lumps but of grains, for the slogan of the micro-miniaturization experts is "If you can see it, it's too big."

Just to prove that I am not exaggerating, here are some statistics you can use on the next hi-fi fanatic who takes you on a tour of his wall-to-wall installation. During the 1950's, the electronic engineers learned to pack up to a hundred thousand components into one cubic foot. (To give a basis of comparison, a good hi-fi set may contain two or three hundred components, a domestic radio about a hundred.) . . . At the beginning of the sixties, the attainable figure [was] around a million components per cubic foot; [in the] 1970['s], when today's experimental techniques of microscopic engineering have begun to pay off, it may reach a hundred million.

Fantastic though this last figure is, the human brain surpasses it by a thousandfold, packing its ten billion neurons into a *tenth* of a cubic foot. And although smallness is not necessarily a virtue, even this may be nowhere near the limit of possible compactness.

For the cells composing our brains are slow-acting, bulky, and wasteful of energy—compared with the scarcely more than atom-sized computer elements that are theoretically possible. The mathematician John von Neumann once calculated that electronic cells could be ten billion times more efficient than protoplasmic ones; already they are a million times swifter in operation, and speed can often be traded for size. If we take these ideas to their ultimate conclusion, it appears that a computer equivalent in power to one human brain need be no bigger than a matchbox.

This slightly shattering thought becomes more reasonable when we take a critical look at flesh and blood and bone as engineering materials. All living creatures are marvelous, but let us keep our sense of proportion. Perhaps the most wonderful thing about Life is that it works at all, when it has to employ such extraordinary materials, and has to tackle its problems in such roundabout ways.

As a perfect example of this, consider the eye. Suppose *you* were given the problem of designing a camera—for that, of course, is what the eye is—which *has to be constructed entirely of water and jelly,* without using a scrap of glass, metal, or plastic. Obviously, it can't be done.

You're quite right; the feat is impossible. The eye is an evolutionary miracle, but it's a lousy camera. You can prove this while you're reading the next sentence.

Here's a medium-length word:—photography. Close one eye and keep the other fixed—repeat, *fixed*—on that center "g." You may be surprised to discover that—unless you cheat by altering the direction of your gaze—you cannot see the whole word clearly. It fades out three or four letters to the right and left.

No camera ever built—even the cheapest—has as poor an optical performance as this. For color vision also, the human eye is nothing to boast about; it can operate only over a small band of the spectrum. To the worlds of the infrared and ultraviolet, visible to bees and other insects, it is completely blind.

We are not conscious of these limitations because we have grown up with them, and indeed if they were corrected the brain would be quite unable to handle the vastly increased flood of information. But let us not make a virtue of a necessity; if our eyes had the optical performance of even the cheapest miniature camera, we would live in an unimaginably richer and more colorful world.

These defects are due to the fact that precision scientific instruments simply cannot be manufactured from living materials. With the eye, the ear, the nose—indeed, all the sense organs—evolution has performed a truly incredible job against fantastic odds. But it will not be good enough for the future; indeed, it is not good enough for the present.

There are some senses that do not exist, that can probably never be provided by living structures, and that we need in a hurry. On this planet, to the best of our knowledge, no creature has ever developed organs that can detect radio waves or radioactivity. Though I would hate to lay down the law and claim that nowhere in the universe can there be organic Geiger counters or living TV sets, I think it highly improbable. There are some jobs that can be done only by vacuum tubes or magnetic fields or electron beams, and are therefore beyond the capability of purely organic structures.

There is another fundamental reason living machines such as you and I cannot hope to compete with nonliving ones. Quite apart from our poor materials, we are handicapped by one of the toughest engineering specifications ever issued. What sort of performance would you expect from a machine which has to grow several billionfold during the course of manufacture—and which has to be completely and continuously rebuilt, molecule by molecule, every few weeks? This is what happens to all of us, all the time; you are not the man you were last year, in the most literal sense of the expression.

Most of the energy and effort required to run the body goes into its perpetual tearing down and rebuilding—a cycle completed every few weeks. New York City, which is a very much simpler structure than a man, takes hundreds of times longer to remake itself. When one tries to picture the body's myriads of building contractors and utility companies all furiously at work, tearing up arteries and nerves and even bones, it is astonishing that there is any energy left over for the business of thinking.

Now I am perfectly well aware that many of the "limitations" and "defects" just mentioned are nothing of the sort, looked at from another point of view. Living creatures, because of their very nature, can evolve from simple to complex organisms. They may well be the only path by which intelligence can be attained, for it is a little difficult to see how a lifeless planet can progress directly from metal ores and mineral deposits to electronic computers by its own unaided efforts.

Though intelligence can arise only from life, it may then discard it. Perhaps at a later stage, as the mystics have suggested, it may also discard matter; but this leads us in realms of speculations which an unimaginative person like myself would prefer to avoid.

One often-stressed advantage of living creatures is that they are self-repairing and reproduce themselves with ease—indeed, with enthusiasm. This superiority over machines will be short-lived; the general principles underlying the construction of self-repairing and self-reproducing machines have already been worked out. There is, incidentally, something ironically appropriate in the fact that A. M. Turing, the brilliant mathematician who pioneered in this field and first indicated how thinking machines might be built, shot himself a few years after publishing his results. It is very hard not to draw a moral from this.

The greatest single stimulus to the evolution of mechanical—as opposed to organic—intelligence is the challenge of space. Only a vanishingly small fraction of the universe is directly accessible to mankind, in the sense that we can live there without elaborate protection or mechanical aids. If we generously assume that humanity's potential *Lebensraum* extends from sea level to a height of three miles, over the whole Earth, that gives us a total of some half billion cubic miles. At first sight this is an impressive figure, especially when you remember that the entire human race could be packaged into a one-mile cube. But it is absolutely nothing, when set against Space with a capital "S." Our present telescopes, which are certainly not the last word on the subject, sweep a volume at least a million million million million million million million million million million times greater.

Though such a number is, of course, utterly beyond conception, it can be given a vivid meaning. If we reduced the known universe to the size of the Earth, then the portion in which *we* can live without space suits and pressure cabins is about the size of a single atom.

It is true that, one day, we are going to explore and colonize many other atoms in this Earth-sized volume, but it will be at the cost of tremendous technical efforts, for most of our energies will be devoted to protecting our frail and sensitive bodies against the extremes of temperature, pressure, or gravity found in space and on other worlds. Within very wide limits, machines are indifferent to these extremes. Even more important, they can wait patiently through the years and the centuries that will be needed for travel to the far reaches of the universe.

Creatures of flesh and blood such as ourselves can explore space and win control over infinitesimal fractions of it. But only creatures of metal and plastic can ever really conquer it, as indeed they have already started to do. . . .

It may well be that only in space, confronted with environments fiercer and more complex than any to be found upon this planet, will intelligence be able to reach its fullest stature. Like other qualities, intelligence is developed by struggle and conflict; in the ages to come, the dullards may remain on placid Earth, and real genius will flourish only in space—the realm of the machine, not of flesh and blood.

A striking parallel to this situation can already be found on our planet. Some millions of years ago, the most intelligent of the mammals withdrew from the battle of the dry land and returned to their ancestral home, the sea. They are still there, with brains larger and potentially more powerful than ours. But (as far as we know) they do not use them; the static environment of the sea makes little call upon intelligence. The porpoises and whales, which might have been our equals and perhaps our superiors had they remained on land, now race in simpleminded and innocent ecstasy beside the new sea monsters carrying sixteen megatons of death. Perhaps they, not we, made the right choice; but it is too late to join them now.

If you have followed me so far, the protoplasmic computer inside your skull should now be programmed to accept the idea—at least for the sake of argument—that machines can be both more intelligent and more versatile than men, and may well be so in the very near future. So it is time to face the question: Where does that leave man?

I suspect that this is not a question of very great importance—except, of course, to man. Perhaps the Neanderthalers made similar plaintive noises, around 100,000 B.C., when H. sapiens appeared on the scene, with his ugly vertical forehead and ridiculous protruding chin. Any Paleolithic philosopher who gave his colleagues the right answer would probably have ended up in the cooking pot; I am prepared to take that risk.

The short-term answer may indeed be cheerful rather than depressing. There may be a brief golden age when men will glory in the power and range of their new partners. Barring war, this age lies directly ahead of us. As Dr. Simon Remo put it recently: "The extension of the human intellect by electronics will become our greatest occupation within a decade." That is undoubtedly true, if we bear in mind that at a somewhat later date the word "extension" may be replaced by "extinction."

One of the ways in which thinking machines will be able to help us is by taking over the humbler tasks of life, leaving the human brain free to concentrate on higher things. (Not, of course, that this is any guarantee that it will do so.) For a few generations, perhaps, every man will go through life with an electronic companion, which may be no bigger than today's transistor radios. It will "grow up" with him from infancy, learning his habits, his business affairs, taking over all the minor chores like routine correspondence and income-tax returns and engagements. On occasion it could even take its master's place, keeping appointments he preferred to miss, and then reporting back in as much detail as he desired. It could substitute for him over the telephone so completely that no one would be able to tell whether man or machine was speaking; a century from now, Turing's "game" may be an integral part of our social lives, with complications and possibilities which I leave to the imagination.

You may remember that delightful robot, Robbie, from the movie *Forbidden Planet.* (One of the three or four movies so far made that anyone interested in science fiction can point to without blushing; the fact that the plot was Shakespeare's doubtless helped.) I submit, in all seriousness, that most of Robbie's abilities—together with those of a better known character, Jeeves—will one day be incorporated in a kind of electronic companion-secretary-valet. It will be much smaller and neater than the walking jukeboxes or mechanized suits of armor which Hollywood presents, with typical lack of imagination, when it wants to portray a robot. And it will be extremely talented, with quick-release connectors allowing it to be coupled to an unlimited variety of sense organs and limbs. It would, in fact, be a kind of general purpose, disembodied intelligence that could attach itself to whatever tools were needed for any particular occasion. One day it might be using microphones or electric typewriters or TV cameras; on another, automobiles or airplanes—or the bodies of men and animals.

And this is, perhaps, the moment to deal with a conception which many people find even more horrifying than the idea that machines will replace or supersede us. It is the idea, already mentioned in the last chapter, that they may combine with us.

I do not know who first thought of this; probably the physicist J. D. Bernal, who in 1929 published an extraordinary book of scientific predictions called *The World, the Flesh and the Devil.* In this slim and long out-of-print volume (I sometimes wonder what the sixty-year-old Fellow of the Royal Society now thinks of his youthful indiscretion, if he ever remembers it) Bernal decided that the numerous limitations of the human body could be overcome only by the use of mechanical attachments or substitutes—until, eventually, all that might be left of man's original organic body would be the brain.

This idea is already far more plausible than when Bernal advanced it, for in the last few decades we have seen the development of mechanical hearts, kidneys, lungs, and other organs, and the wiring of electronic devices directly into the human nervous system.

Olaf Stapledon developed this theme in his wonderful history of the future, *Last and First Men,* imagining an age of immortal "giant brains," many yards across, living in beehive-shaped cells, sustained by pumps and chemical plants. Though completely immobile, their sense organs could be wherever they wished, so their center of awareness—or consciousness, if you like—could be anywhere on Earth or in the space above it. This is an important point which we—who carry our brains around in the same fragile structure as our eyes, ears, and other sense organs, often with disastrous results—may easily fail to appreciate. Given perfected telecommunications, a fixed brain is no handicap, but rather the reverse. Your present brain, totally imprisoned behind its walls of bone, communicates with the outer world and receives its impressions of it over the telephone wires of the central nervous system—wires varying in length from a fraction of an inch to several feet. *You would never know the difference if those "wires" were actually hundreds or thousands of miles long, or included mobile radio links, and your brain never moved at all.*

In a crude way—yet one that may accurately foreshadow the future—we have already extended our visual and tactile senses away from our bodies. The men who now work with radioisotopes, handling them with remotely controlled mechanical fingers and observing them by television, have achieved a partial separation between brain and sense organs. They are in one place; their minds effectively in another.

Recently the word "Cyborg" (cybernetic organism) has been coined to describe the machine-animal of the type we have been discussing. Doctors Manfred Clynes and Nathan Kline of Rockland State Hospital, Orangeburg, New York, who invented the name, define a Cyborg in these stirring words: "an exogenously extended organizational complex functioning as a homeostatic system." To translate, this means a body which has machines hitched to it, or built into it, to take over or modify some of its functions.

I suppose one could call a man in an iron lung a Cyborg, but the concept has far wider implications than this. One day we may be able to enter into temporary unions with any sufficiently sophisticated machines, thus being able not merely to control but to *become* a spaceship or a submarine or a TV network. This would give far more than purely intellectual satisfaction; the thrill that can be obtained from driving a racing car or flying an airplane may be only a pale ghost of the excitement our great-grandchildren may know, when the individual human consciousness is free to roam at will from machine to machine, through all the reaches of sea and sky and space.

But how long will this partnership last? Can the synthesis of man and machine ever be stable, or will the purely organic component become such a hindrance that it has to be discarded? If this eventually happens—and I have given good reasons for thinking that it must—we have nothing to regret, and certainly nothing to fear.

The popular idea, fostered by comic strips and the cheaper forms of science fiction, that intelligent machines must be malevolent entities hostile to man, is so absurd that it is hardly worth wasting energy to refute it. I am almost tempted to argue that only *un*intelligent machines can be malevolent; anyone who has tried to start a balky outboard will probably agree. Those who picture machines as active enemies are merely projecting their own aggressive instincts, inherited from the jungle, into a world where such things do not exist. The higher the intelligence, the greater the degree of cooperativeness. If there is ever a war between men and machines, it is easy to guess who will start it.

Yet however friendly and helpful the machines of the future may be, most people will feel that it is a rather bleak prospect for humanity if it ends up as a pampered specimen in some biological museum—even if that museum is the whole planet Earth. This, however, is an attitude I find impossible to share.

No individual exists forever; why should we expect our species to be immortal? Man, said Nietzsche, is a rope stretched between the animal and the superhuman—a rope across the abyss. That will be a noble purpose to have served.

QUESTIONS

1. How does Clarke's use of anthropological and cybernetic concepts affect the tone of the essay? How does it affect its scientific credibility?
2. Is the title slightly ironic?
3. Do you think that Clarke's description of the "electronic companion" is the least believable part of his essay? Why or why not?
4. In what ways can a cyborg be frightening? Is Anne McCaffrey's "The Ship Who Sang" a frightening story?
5. Is the essay, despite the final paragraphs, depressing? Give reasons for your answer.
6. How does Clarke echo the essay's main themes in his movie *2001*?
7. Discuss "The Last True God" in light of this essay's ideas.

The Outer Limits of Space

Edward Edelson

The facts of science may often dwarf the imaginings of fiction. Just as it appears incredible that we have invented atomic warfare and have walked on the moon, so is it incredible that we may have also seen, through our telescopes, the boundaries of the universe. It is science, not science fiction, that brought us white holes and black holes, quasars, tachyons, theories and probable facts for creation and destruction as overwhelming as any born from the imagination. Edward Edelson, science editor of The New York Daily News, *here outlines part of the knowledge that has already altered our perspectives on life and the universe.*

Science, in its brash, spirited explorations of the far reaches of the cosmos, has suddenly, to its own amazement, arrived at what may be the ultimate boundary—the very edge of the universe.

Astronomers at the California Institute of Technology, employing telescopes that measure and analyze the optical waves and radio waves emanating from various heavenly bodies, believe they have reached their limit. As far as they can tell, the signals they are studying come from the outermost rim of the universe—a point in space-time that, by the esoteric rules of modern cosmology, is close to the origin of the universe.

Even if no other notable event had occurred, this discovery alone would make our decade memorable in the long history of mankind's struggle to understand the universe. But this is no isolated breakthrough in knowledge. It is only a small part of an incredibly productive epoch in astronomy, a few decades packed with events that have shown scientists a universe filled with objects that stretch our former understanding of the world's physical laws.

There are, for instance, quasars—distant and massive bodies whose ability to produce *more energy than a billion suns* is still not understood.

There are pulsars, burnt-out remnants of stars, so dense that *a cubic inch weighs a billion tons* yet whirling on their axes faster than a top.

There are so-called black holes, even denser remains of stars, whose gravitational pull is strong enough to make them literally invisible because not even light waves can escape.

And there are the other remarkable inhabitants of the universe: clouds of gas and dust where stars are being born; galaxies, containing billions of stars, which appear to be torn apart by violent upheavals; paired stars that orbit each other in intricate loops—all set against the background of a quiet flow of radiation left over from the origin of the universe.

Put it all together—something that theorists have been busy doing for more than a decade—and you have the first reasonably comprehensive picture of the universe, from its beginning some 12 or 13 billion years ago, through the long evolutionary process that gives us what we see today, and on into the future.

Most of this new understanding comes from data gathered by new instruments that have enormously expanded scientists' reach into the universe. Three decades ago an astronomer did essentially what Galileo did in the seventeenth century: He studied the light from stars and galaxies. Today the astronomer uses huge dishes and arrays of antennae that gather in radio waves from the cosmos, and he sends into orbit instruments that detect ultraviolet rays, X rays, gamma rays, and other radiation blocked by the earth's atmosphere.

A lot remains to be learned, of course. Astronomers would like to be able to predict the ultimate fate of the universe: perhaps infinite expansion, perhaps contraction and collapse. They still need a better understanding of how quasars obtain their immense supply of energy and where quasars fit into the scheme of the universe. And there are puzzling anomalies here and there, phenomena that a handful of revisionist astronomers say might eventually call for a new set of physical laws.

Much excitement centers on quasars, which have managed to remain unexplainable and controversial for many years. Astrophysicists have been trying to fit quasars into the accepted picture of a universe that is expanding, like a balloon being blown up. According to this model, an observer standing on the surface of the balloon would see all other observers moving away from him, the velocity of their flight increasing with their distance from him. That situation—in three dimensions—describes our universe, with one notable addition: Most of the objects in the universe emit light, which allows their velocity relative to the earth to be measured.

Measurement is simple: The faster the flight, the more light is stretched out toward the red, or longer, end of the spectrum. By the rules of expansion of the universe, the bigger this "red shift," the farther away the object. Over many decades astronomers have measured a cosmic body's red shift to determine its distance from the earth.

In 1962 Cal Tech astronomers Allan Sandage and Thomas Matthews identified an innocuous-looking minor star as the source of powerful radio waves. But when they tried to measure the radio source's distance by its red shift, they got nowhere, for an odd reason: The light waves emitted by the star did not fit any known pattern. It took a few years for two other Cal Tech scientists, Maarten Schmidt and Jesse L. Greenstein, to solve the puzzle. They found that the star's red shift was much greater than any previously known, which meant that the star was much farther away than any other.

It was a solution that caused more problems: If the star was that distant, it would have to be putting out incredible amounts of light to be visible—as much energy as 10 trillion suns. That discovery lifted this innocuous-looking star into a class of its own. It was dubbed a "quasi-stellar radio source," which was soon abbreviated to quasar.

Some 200 quasars have now been discovered, and a simple interpretation of their red shift indicates that almost all of them are farther away than any other class of objects. A typical galaxy not too far from earth (by astronomical standards) will have its visible light shifted by perhaps 20 percent; to put it another way, the red shift is 0.20. Some extremely distant galaxies have red shifts of perhaps 0.40. But the closest known quasar has a red shift of 1.50, and most of them have red shifts of about 2.0—or a red shift of 200 percent!

Only during the past few months have astronomers reported the discovery of several quasars whose red shifts are in the neighborhood of 3.5, far greater than that of any others known so far. These quasars are moving away from the earth at an appreciable fraction of the speed of light. They are almost unquestionably the most distant objects known. Their distance from us is perhaps 12 billion light-years.

And beyond those quasars is—nothing.

At least this is the interpretation of Sandage and other Cal Tech scientists. They believe that the light emitted by these quasars started out not long after the birth of the universe and that the most distant quasars are also the oldest observable objects, bodies that were among the first to be formed out of the chaos that was the birth of the universe.

"Does the absence of larger red shifts mean that the time horizon has been breached and that we look back further than the time of first-galaxy formation?" Sandage asks. "If so, we are now observing not only a matter horizon in space but the edge of the universe of galaxies in time as well. That we can, in principle, see the edge of the world is amazing. That we may have already done so may be unique."

An alternate explanation already exists, one that is even more revolutionary than the discovery of the edge of the universe. Some astronomers believe that the red shifts of quasars are not what they seem to be. These astronomers—and they are decidedly in the minority—think that something other than distance and velocity produces the enormous red shifts of some quasars. What could that something be? Perhaps a physical phenomenon of unknown nature, one that would require an explanation beyond the accepted rules of physics.

One astronomer, Halton Arp of Cal Tech, has carefully collected perhaps a dozen cases in which the standard rule—red shift equals distance—appears to be violated. Arp has celestial photographs showing apparent connections between quasars, galaxies, and other bodies that have completely different red shifts. According to Arp's interpretation, these objects are indeed side by side; yet their red shifts are far apart, which means that something incomprehensible to physicists is affecting the red shift. And if two objects at the same cosmic distance can have varying red shifts, Arp says, "some of our fundamental assumptions are wrong."

Most astronomers think it is Arp's fundamental assumption that is wrong. The consensus is that his collection of curious objects consists mostly of coincidences—bodies that appear to be side by side in the two-dimensional view offered by photographic plates but that are actually many light-years apart in the third dimension, distance from earth. Arp is doggedly trying to mass enough instances of discrepant red shifts to disprove that view, but the conventional wisdom is against him.

At the moment most astronomers believe that the red shift is just what it appears to be, a belief that allows them to talk in definite terms about the age of the universe. This means they have resolved one of the most enduring debates in astronomy, the cosmological argument over the origin and fate of the universe.

The cosmological question got its start in 1927, when a Belgian mathematician, Abbé Georges Lemaître, proposed that all the mass in the universe had once been packed into a single point—a superatom, so to speak—which had then exploded, sending matter streaming out in all directions. Lemaître's proposal gained new vigor when an American astronomer, Edwin P. Hubble, discovered in 1929 that the universe was, indeed, expanding. But in 1948 two British scientists, Hermann Bondi and Thomas Gold, proposed an alternative explanation.

They said the expansion of the universe came from an entirely different cause: the continuous creation of matter. Rather than assuming a universe whose very existence hinges on a singular event, Bondi and Gold proposed a universe that has always been as it is today, with new matter popping into existence to replace the galaxies that go rushing off into infinity. The resolution of the debate between Lemaître's "big bang" cosmology and the "steady state" universe proposed by Gold and Bondi (and expanded by Fred Hoyle) had to wait for the arrival of radio astronomy.

In 1931 a Bell Laboratories engineer named Carl G. Jansky, studying the propagation of radio waves through the atmosphere, found that after every known terrestrial source of static was accounted for, some background noise still could not be eliminated. Tracking the background radio waves, Jansky found that they came from beyond the earth—apparently from the center of the galaxy.

It was not until after World War II that astronomers began building radio telescopes to make a systematic study of radio waves from the cosmos. That opened a new window on the universe and sent revolutionary winds blowing through the astronomical community.

The beginning of the end of the cosmological debate came in 1965, when Princeton astronomers Robert H. Dicke and P. J. Peebles said that if the big bang had really occurred, there should be some leftover radiation surging through the universe. Immediately radio astronomers at Bell Laboratories said "Eureka!" for the Peebles-Dicke theory explained the strange background radiation they were picking up on their radio telescope.

Today almost all astronomers believe that this background radiation is the final dying glow of the big bang.

Now the debate is over a different question: the ultimate fate of the universe. There are those who believe that the universe will go on expanding forever, until its components slip away into infinity. And there are those who believe that the expansion will first slow down, then stop, then turn into a contraction that will end literally in a universal collapse.

It all depends on the mass of the universe; there is a critical mass at which the gravitational pull will keep the galaxies from moving beyond a certain limit. Once that limit is reached, the contraction begins. And so the fate of the universe depends, in non-scientific terms, on its weight.

How do you weigh a universe? Sandage's group has been trying to measure the rate at which distant galaxies are separating, thus determining the mass of those galaxies and hence of the universe. So far the available information indicates that the universe has only one-thirtieth of the mass needed to prevent infinite expansion, but the measurements are so tentative that no one takes them as anywhere near final. Perhaps in twenty years the universe will be weighed to everyone's satisfaction. Meanwhile, astronomers can speculate.

Some astrophysicists, among them John Wheeler of Princeton University, stand by the latter theory—that the universe will eventually slow its expansion, begin to contract, and ultimately collapse into a superdense object whose existence was first postulated by Einstein. Einstein's theory of relativity dealt on a grand scale with velocities and masses far beyond anything encountered on earth. Under such conditions, the theory said, strange things happen.

For example, according to the theory, a body could be so immense that it would collapse under its own weight and would keep on collapsing forever. Its gravitational field would become so strong because of the concentration of matter that light waves could not escape. At the same time this object would be the source of an immense energy output, because it would pull nearby objects into itself, ripping them apart violently and turning 40 percent of their mass into energy.

That aspect of Einstein's theory received new attention in 1970, when Wheeler and a collaborator, Remo Ruffini, wrote a scientific paper on these so-called black holes, describing their strange features and pointing out that the natural life cycle of many stars may end in the creation of black holes.

What finally happens to a star, astrophysicists know, is a function of that star's mass, which in turn governs the amount of energy it produces. For most of a star's life, the inward pull of the star's mass is balanced by the outward push of the energy produced by nuclear fusion. As energy output declines, that balance is upset and the star contracts.

A star the size of the earth (which is average by stellar standards) comes to a relatively dull end. It burns up the hydrogen it uses as fuel,* expands briefly, then contracts to a cold, dense "white dwarf."

Stars with masses 40 percent greater than the sun's have a much more interesting end—one that provides one of the most fascinating phenomena in space. These stars stage a more spectacular explosion, the kind that creates a brilliant outflaring called a supernova. Then they condense to supermassive bodies called neutron stars; a cubic inch of a neutron star can weigh a billion tons.

Until 1968 neutron stars existed only in theory. But in that year British astronomers detected surprisingly regular bursts of intense radio waves from space—waves so regular that it was thought at first that they might come from another civilization. The truth was different but almost as fascinating.

It developed that these so-called pulsars that gave off these radio waves are neutron stars. And they are *spinning* neutron stars, which whirl beams of radio waves into the universe as they rotate at rates of perhaps 100 times a minute.

Weird as the pulsars are, the black holes are more so. At least a pulsar stops collapsing at some point, as its energy output reaches a new balance with its gravitational pull. But for stars whose mass is three or four times greater than the sun's, nothing can counterbalance the pull of gravity. The collapse goes on forever, and a black hole is the result.

Even though a black hole by definition is invisible, astronomers believe they have found several. An astronomer finds an invisible object by looking at two star systems, searching for a pair of which one star cannot be seen but is obviously influencing the other star's orbit. At the same time, he looks for the high-energy output expected from a black hole. The first star to be more or less firmly identified as a black hole is Cygnus X-1, a member of a two-star system in the constellation Cygnus, the Swan.

---

* Squeezing hydrogen atoms to form helium, and thus releasing energy, is the basic mechanism that lights up the stars.

Wheeler believes that the universe, in billions of years, will become one massive black hole, in a collapse in which the known laws of the universe will be "not broken but transcended." To this, astrophysicist Robert M. Hjellming adds a fillip: He proposes that black holes in our universe are "white holes" in a neighboring universe and that matter which vanishes from a black hole here reappears in a white hole there. This could mean that the ultimate collapse envisioned by Wheeler would end with the universe almost literally turning itself inside out, starting the cycle of expansion and contraction all over again.

All this may sound incredible, but is it much more incredible than pulsars, quasars, and black holes? Some of the strangest speculations of astronomers have become established dogma in the past few decades.

While they spare time for such speculation, astronomers also are trying to tidy up the details of the universe. Perhaps the greatest unknown is the nature of quasars—the source of the immense amounts of energy they emit. The current belief is that quasars are the nuclei of young galaxies, sowing their energetic wild oats before settling down to the sober business of galactic evolution. If this is so, a study of quasars can tell scientists much about the origin of galaxies and the universe because, as Sandage points out, "With quasars we see the conditions in the cosmos as they were close to creation." It is one of the fascinations of modern astronomy that it lets its practitioners look ahead to the end of the universe and back to its birth in one all-inclusive sweep of theory and imagination.

QUESTIONS

1. If the universe has an end, is the concept of infinity negated? What effect might a finite universe have on perceptions of reality? on the concept of God?

2. Is a finite universe more logically consistent with the "big bang" or with the "steady state" theory? Explain your answer.

3. Explain the concept of black holes and neutron stars. Do you find these phenomena "interesting," "weird," or "frightening"? What is the concept behind Robert Hjellming's notion of "white holes" in a "neighboring universe"? What is the concept of a "mirror universe"? Do these bits of scientific speculation give you a sense of unreality?

4. Edward Edelson writes as a science editor of a major newspaper. Does this make his essay more convincing than if written by an SF writer? Which presents a more disturbing "end-of-the-world" image, Edelson's essay or Heinlein's short story?

Topics for Shorter and Longer Papers

1. Is nature a malevolent or benevolent force in science fiction? Is science fiction in favor of adapting to or "conquering" nature? Are nature and science seen as "enemies" in this genre? Write a paper discussing the attitudes toward nature reflected in science fiction.

2. What are the chances for the world's survival if the ecological balances in nature are upset? Research books and articles on ecology, population, depletion of natural resources, and the problems of economic growth; write a paper discussing the possibilities for human survival on the planet. How does science fiction deal with this topic?

3. In the near future it may be possible to take a single cell and from it grow a complete organ or even a complete human being. This scientific capability is new and troubling. Research the processes involved in cloning and consider some of the problems it may pose. Write a paper discussing the social, religious, psychological, and political questions raised by cloning. Consider the ways in which science fiction might deal with the possibility of a laboratory produced human.

4. It is already possible to control human behavior by neurosurgery and psychological conditioning. Write a paper discussing the way this possibility has been treated in science fiction, from Aldous Huxley's *Brave New World* to the "The Ship Who Sang."

5. What is the difference between fantasy and science fiction? Which is closer to mainstream literature? Compare these different literary types.

6. Reread Leslie Fiedler's "Cross the Border, Close the Gap." Keeping Fiedler's comments in mind, make a comparative study of "pop" and "serious" literature. Focus on their differences and similarities, for there are many, and describe the different kinds of satisfaction each provides. Do not concern yourselves with such problems as trying to determine which is the superior form of literature. Also, do not confine yourselves to the literature of this book or, for that matter, to science fiction. However, do consider Fiedler's assertion that "the new novel must be antiart as well as antiserious." Try also to determine if pop literature satisfies Fiedler's demand any better than serious, "modernist" literature by authors such as James Joyce or Henry Miller.

7. The origins of SF are in the early nineteenth century's Gothic tales, a subgenre of Romantic fiction. SF has changed considerably since Mary Wollstonecraft Shelley wrote her tale of terror. And this change has given rise to the question of whether the genre is a species of Romanticism or Realism. Explore the meanings of these two terms and discuss which one would best suit science fiction.

8. Make a survey of mad scientists in science fiction. Determine if they are heroes or villains, if they are responsible for their actions, and if outside forces pushed their experiments out of control or if the dire results were inherent in the experiments from the beginning. Does science fiction present every scientist as at least a little mad? Is science fiction hostile to science? What position does SF take toward the idea that knowledge is good for its own sake? You might begin by reading Mary Shelley's *Frankenstein.*

9. Make a survey of Christ figures in science fiction. Note any deviations from the legend. How effective are these stories? Is a Judeo-Christian background necessary for their comprehension? Do they suggest a religious orientation on the part of their writers? Read *Stranger in a Strange Land* by Robert Heinlein and *The Idiot* by Fyodor Dostoevsky. Compare Michael Valentine Smith to Prince Myshkin.

10. What is the attitude of science fiction toward innocence? Why are children so often given unusual powers of telepathy, prevision, telekinesis, or other kinds of extrasensory force? How is the "adult" world seen in relation to these children? Are they more often the hope or the doom of this world?

11. From the time of the ancient Greeks, with their Argonauts, to our own day, with our astronauts, people have tended to convert their histories into myths. One of the favorite motifs of all mythologies is the journey. Make a study of this motif in classical myth, the Arthurian legends, our own Wild West stories, and science fiction. Try to draw as many parallels between the different treatments of the motif as you can. Try also to relate the mythic elements to whatever historical information is available. Read the critical writings that discuss the journey or Quest motif (most of which will deal with elite literature) and apply the insights you gain from this reading to all four treatments of the motif. Throughout your study keep notes and then write a paper on the journey in myth and history.

12. What is the nature of love between man and woman in pre-1969 science fiction? Has the inclusion of sex since then changed the basic relationship? What attitude does science fiction take toward the family? Toward parent-child relationships? Discuss courtship, marriage, and the family in science fiction. Contrast the way these subjects are treated in contemporary mainstream literature.

13. Trace attitudes toward the media in science fiction. In stories of regressive civilizations, the printing press is almost always reinvented. In stories of the future, is the printed word always obsolete? How typical is the attitude of Ray Bradbury in *Fahrenheit 451*? In what varied ways is television used in science fiction? What new media does science fiction propose for the future? What is the function of the mass media in science fiction?

14. If we divide science fiction into space fiction and Earth fiction,

which is more relevant to our everyday lives? Which comes closer to pure entertainment? Which do you think would be more acceptable to the literary establishment?

15. In a paper, trace the portrayal of robots from Karl Capek's *R.U.R.* to Isaac Asimov's *I, Robot* and beyond. The robot can be either hero or villain, benefactor or enemy. What qualities determine its role? Do most authors come to any conclusions about the inherent goodness or badness of robots?

16. What godlike attributes are inherent in the popular conception of robots? Could the god in "A Vision of Judgment" be a robot? What is the difference between a robot and a machine? Between a robot and a human? If people believed their god to be a robot and still worshipped it, what would this say about humanity?

17. How do Clarke's theories in "The Obsolescence of Man" apply to Helva in "The Ship Who Sang"? To the robot in "The Last True God"?

18. "The Artist of the Beautiful" deals both directly and by implication with the concept of beauty. What is the place of beauty in science fiction?

19. Do a paper on "alternate world" science fiction, of the type presented in R. A. Lafferty's "Interurban Queen." What other ways might we have taken? How realistic is it to expect the future to resist change?

20. In "The Marriage of Heaven and Hell" William Blake, the English poet, wrote:

> Without Contraries is no progression. Attraction and Repulsion, Reason and Energy, Love and Hate, are necessary to Human existence.
>
> From these contraries spring what the religious call Good & Evil. Good is the passive that obeys Reason. Evil is the active springing from Energy.
>
> Energy is Eternal Delight.

At a later point in the same work Blake wrote:

> Drive your cart and your plow over the bones of the dead.
> The road of excess leads to the palace of wisdom.
> Prudence is a rich, ugly old maid courted by Incapacity.
> He who desires but acts not, breeds pestilence.

Write a paper discussing the content of Lafferty's "Interurban Queen" in terms related to Blake's prose poem.

21. Comic books such as *Forever People* qualify as pop literature. Reread the selection and state the story line in one or two sentences. Do the same with one of the SF stories in the book. Are there similarities in simplicity or complexity of plot, characterization, theme? Do you have

any difficulty in telling which are the "good guys" and which are the "bad guys?" What about plot development? Do you feel any uncertainty about where the story is "going"? Is the point of the story unclear at any time? Compare the SF story and the comic to Hawthorne's "The Artist of the Beautiful" in terms of plot, characterization, and theme. Is the structure of Hawthorne's tale similar to or different from the other two works? In your paper take the Hawthorne story as an example of elite literature and the comic book as its polar opposite and discuss the validity of this distinction in relation to science fiction.

22. What are the differences and similarities between the people of Kornbluth's and Vonnegut's futures? Do both authors have the same purposes in treating the future with a touch of humor? Is either future likely to happen?

23. What inventions are predicted directly or by implication in this book? What do the writers feel should be eradicated or controlled? How can we avoid the future dangers projected by science fiction? What are some dangers that have not been covered in this volume? Write a paper discussing whether anything can be done to prevent the end of the world so often predicted in science fiction.

24. Do you agree that the events and problems related in the *About Now* section of this book are the major ones affecting contemporary times? Write a short paper describing what you would add or subtract.

Further Topics

Below is a list of possible subjects for extended discussions and for papers based on material both in this book and in other areas of science fiction and future studies. Many of the suggested topics can be utilized with only *Looking Ahead* for reference. Others will require further reference and reading. Students should be sure to check with their instructor for topic approval, advice on the paper's type (essay, critical study, research paper, and so on.) Ask, too, advice on manuscript form, length, focus, and style.

1. There's No Such Thing as Science Fiction.
2. The Use of Poetic Devices in Science Fiction
3. Science Fiction: The Black Sheep of Literature
4. The Politics of Science Fiction
5. The Treatment of Ethnic Minorities in Contemporary Science Fiction
6. A Science Fiction Bestiary
7. Science Fiction in Films and Television
8. Science Fiction and Modern Technology: Luddites of the Twentieth Century
9. The Utopian Vision in Science Fiction
10. Point of View in Science Fiction: The Teller of the Tale

11. Walt Disney as a Creature of Science Fiction
12. The Creature from the Lagoon: Otherworldly Beings in Science Fiction
13. Science Fiction in Advertising
14. Propaganda in Science Fiction
15. The Role of Women in Science Fiction
16. Astronauts: Real and Imagined
17. The Maternal Computer: A Study of Helva of "The Ship Who Sang" and Aunt Jane of "Stranger Station"
18. The Fanzine Phenomenon
19. The Hugo and Nebula Awards: A Study in Critical Evaluations of SF
20. Hard-Core SF, How It Differs from Other Kinds of Science Fiction
21. Time Travel: The Remaking of History Past, Present, and Future
22. Fact Stranger Than Fiction: A Response to Edward Edelson's "The Outer Limits of Space"
23. Science Fiction Poetry: From Homer's Cyclops to Dick Allen's *Anon*
24. Etiquette and Fashion: A Study of Decorum in Science Fiction
25. Predictions of Things to Come: Modern Day Inventions Foreseen by Science Fiction
26. The World's End: The Apocalyptic Vision of Science Fiction

A Chronology of Science Fiction

The chronology has two functions. First, it indicates the antecedents and history of SF as it develops, "comes of age," and begins joining mainstream literature. Second, the chronology provides a brief and graphic reminder of how recent most of the inventions and events are that have shaped contemporary lives.

Eighth century B.C. Homer. *Odyssey.*
Fourth century B.C. Plato. *Timaeus, Critias.*
Second century A.D. Lucian of Samosta. *Icaromenippus, True History.*

c. 1456	GUTENBERG PRINTS THE MAZARIN BIBLE FROM MOVABLE TYPE.
1492	COLUMBUS REDISCOVERS AMERICA.
1515–16	Thomas More. *Utopia.*
1532	Ariosto. *Orlando Furioso.*
1610	Galileo. *Sidereus Nuncius.*
1627	Francis Bacon. *The New Atlantis.*
1634	Johann Kepler. *Somnium.*
1638	Bishop Francis Godwin. *The Man in the Moone.*
1650	Cyrano de Bergerac. *Voyage to the Moon.*
1726	Jonathan Swift. *Gulliver's Travels.*
1818	Mary Wollstonecraft Shelley. *Frankenstein.*
1822	FIRST PHOTOGRAPH.
1833	Edgar Allan Poe. "Ms. Found in a Bottle."
1847	THOMAS EDISON BORN.
1864	Jules Verne. *Journey to the Center of the Earth.*
1876	TELEPHONE INVENTED.
1877	PHONOGRAPH INVENTED.
1879	FIRST PRACTICAL ELECTRIC LIGHT.
1887	H. Rider Haggard. *She.*
1888	Robert Louis Stevenson. *The Strange Case of Dr. Jekyll and Mr. Hyde.*
1895	H. G. Wells. *The Time Machine.*
1898	H. G. Wells. *War of the Worlds.*
1903	WRIGHT BROTHERS MAKE KITTY HAWK FLIGHT.
1905	Albert Einstein. "Special Theory of Relativity."
1906	RADIO MADE PRACTICAL.
1911	Hugo Gernsback. *Ralph 124C41+.*
1912	Edgar Rice Burroughs. *Under the Moons of Mars.* Arthur Conan Doyle. *The Lost World.*

1913	Edgar Rice Burroughs. *Tarzan of the Apes.*
1914–18	FIRST WORLD WAR.
1916	Albert Einstein. "General Theory of Relativity."
1920	H. P. Lovecraft. *From Beyond.*
1921	Karel Capek. *R.U.R.*
1926	Hugo Gernsback founds *Amazing Stories.*
	ROBERT GODDARD FLIES FIRST ROCKET.
1928	Philip Francis Nowlan. *Armageddon 2419* A.D. (Buck Rogers).
1929	HUGO GERNSBACK COINS "SCIENCE FICTION."
1930	Olaf Stapledon. *Last and First Men.*
	Philip Wylie. *Gladiator.*
1932	Aldous Huxley. *Brave New World.*
1934	Stanley G. Weinbaum. *A Martian Odyssey.*
1936	Karel Capek. *War With the Newts.*
1937	John Campbell becomes editor of *Astounding Stories.*
	J. R. R. Tolkien. *The Hobbit.*
1938	C. S. Lewis. *Out of the Silent Planet.*
1939–45	SECOND WORLD WAR.
1939	Orson Welles's broadcast of *The War of the Worlds.*
1941	PENICILLIN'S ANTIBIOTIC POWERS PUT TO USE.
1945	ATOMIC BOMB.
1946	MASS CONSUMER TELEVISION BECOMES PRACTICAL.
1949	George Orwell. *1984.*
	The Magazine of Fantasy and Science Fiction.
1950	*Galaxy.*
1951	Marshall McLuhan. *The Mechanical Bride.*
	HUGE TELEVISION INFLUENCE INCREASINGLY FELT.
1952	Kurt Vonnegut, Jr. *Player Piano.*
1953	Albert Einstein. "United Field Theory."
1955	Judith Merril, ed. *1st Annual, The Best of SF.*
1957	SPUTNIK.
1960	GROWTH OF CIVIL RIGHTS MOVEMENT.
1961	Rachel Carson. *The Silent Spring.*
	Robert Heinlein. *Stranger in a Strange Land.*
1963	PRESIDENT JOHN F. KENNEDY ASSASSINATED.
1965	NORTHEAST POWER BLACKOUT.
	Frank Herbert. *Dune.*
1966–69	MAJOR INFLUENCE OF FOLK ROCK.
	ANTI-VIETNAM WAR PROTESTS.
1967	Harlan Ellison, ed. *Dangerous Visions.*
1968	Arthur C. Clarke and Stanley Kubrick. *2001: A Space Odyssey.*
	MARTIN LUTHER KING ASSASSINATED.
	ROBERT KENNEDY ASSASSINATED.

1968	INTENSIFICATION OF "DRUG CULTURE."
	Paul Erlich. *The Population Bomb.*
	APPARENT HIGH POINT OF AMERICAN MATERIALISTIC WEALTH.
1969	NEIL ARMSTRONG WALKS ON THE MOON.
1970	Alvin Toffler. *Future Shock.*
	STUDENTS KILLED AT KENT STATE.
	"JESUS FREAKS."
	COMMUNES.
1971	WINDING DOWN OF VIETNAM WAR.
	WOMEN'S LIBERATION.
	SMILE BUTTONS!
1972	SF "Academic Revolution."
	Club of Rome. *The Limits to Growth.*
	HOLIOGRAPH.
	CLOSE-UP PICTURES FROM MARS.
	TACHYON THEORIES POPULARIZED.
	WHITE HOLE AND BLACK HOLE THEORIES.
	AIRPLANE HIJACKS.
	BIOFEEDBACK.
1973	WATERGATE SCANDAL INTENSIFIES.
	THE ENERGY CRISIS.
	SKYLAB.
	ZERO POPULATION GROWTH APPEARS REACHED IN AMERICA.
	EDGE OF SPACE AND TIME SEEMINGLY DISCOVERED.
	END OF DRAFT IN U.S.A.
	STOCK MARKET BEGINS ITS PLUNGE.
	VICE PRESIDENT SPIRO AGNEW RESIGNS.
1974	WORLDWIDE FOOD SHORTAGES.
	THE NEW MORALITY APPEARS TO ALMOST BECOME THE NORMAL MORALITY.
	PROLIFERATION OF DOOMSDAY AND GODS FROM SPACE BOOKS.
	TRUCK DRIVER STRIKES PARALYZE MANY AMERICAN SUPER-HIGHWAYS.
	THE YEAR OF THE KIDNAP.
	THE NEW ALCOHOLISM.
	WORLDWIDE INFLATION.
	PRESIDENT NIXON RESIGNS PRESIDENCY OF U.S.A.
	NUMEROUS MONASTERIES FOUNDED.

Suggestions for Further Reading and Viewing

Below is a four-part bibliography, designed for readers who are creating a small basic library of SF, futurism, and related works. More extensive bibliographies are found in many of the works cited below.

Useful works of SF criticism are included, as well as the major works that can lead to an understanding of present and future planetary concerns.

The listing of short-story anthologies is brief, since the outstanding anthologies produced by the Science Fiction Writers of America have considerably reduced the number of collections readers must buy in order to be familiar with the "classic" shorter works of SF.

The list of novels is as nearly complete as we could make it—after much consultation and checking of similar lists.

Finally, we have included a list of popular and significant SF movies. Most of the worst SF films have been eliminated from this list, although some have been retained. These low quality films seem to us significant indicators of popular consciousness.

There will, of course, be arguments with this "basic" bibliography. The reading-viewing list inevitably reflects the subjective tastes of the editors, as well as gaps in our readership and viewing. We do not doubt that many excellent works have been left out due to oversight. But we hope that the readers of this book will subtract and add according to their own standards of criticism. They should certainly feel free to revise, substitute, and expand their collections beyond what we have provided here.

The Future

Anderson, David D., ed. *Sunshine and Smoke: American Writers and the American Environment*. Lippincott, 1971.

Bateson, Gregory. *Steps to an Ecology of Mind*. Ballantine, 1972.

Bateson, M. C. *Our Own Metaphor*. Alfred A. Knopf, 1972.

Bell, Daniel. *The Coming of the Post-Industrial Society*. Basic Books, 1973.

Bell, David, ed. *Toward the Year 2000*. Beacon, 1968.

Blau, Sheridan D., and Rodenbeck, John von B., eds. *The House We Live In: An Environment Reader*. Macmillan, 1971.

Clarke, Arthur C., *Profiles of the Future*. Bantam, 1964.

———. *Report from Planet Three*. Harper & Row, 1972.

Collins, Michael. *Carrying the Fire*. Farrar, Straus & Giroux, 1974.
Commoner, Barry. *The Closing Circle*. Bantam, 1972.
Cox, Harvey. *The Secular City*. Collier-Macmillan, 1965.
Erlich, Paul R. *How to Be a Survivor*. Ballantine, 1971.
———. *The Population Bomb*. Ballantine, 1968.
Freud, Sigmund. *Civilization and Its Discontents*. Doubleday, 1930.
Fromm, Erich. *The Anatomy of Human Destructiveness*. Holt, Rinehart and Winston, 1973.
Fuller, R. Buckminster. *Operating Manual for Spaceship Earth*. Southern Illinois University Press, 1969.
———. *Utopia or Oblivion: The Prospects for Humanity*. Bantam, 1969.
Gorney, Roderic. *The Human Agenda*. Bantam, 1973.
Hever, Kenneth. *How the Earth Will Come to an End*. Collier, 1963.
Kahn, Herbert. *Thinking About the Unthinkable*. Avon, 1969.
Kahn, Herbert, and Weiner, Anthony. *The Year 2000: A Framework for Speculation on the Next 33 Years*. Macmillan, 1967.
Kostelanetz, Richard, ed. *Social Speculations: Visions for Our Time*. William Morrow, 1971.
Leeming, David Adams. *Flights: Readings in Magic, Mysticism, Fantasy, and Myth*. Harcourt Brace Jovanovich, 1974.
Lorenz, Konrad. *Civilized Man's Eight Deadly Sins*. Harcourt Brace Jovanovich, 1974.
McHale, John. *The Ecological Crisis*. Braziller, 1970.
———. *The Future of the Future*. Braziller, 1969.
McLuhan, Marshall. *Understanding Media*. McGraw-Hill, 1965.
Mailer, Norman. *Of a Fire on the Moon*. Signet, 1971.
Meadows, Donella H.; Meadows, Dennis L.; Randers, Jørgen; and Behrens, William, III. *The Limits to Growth*. Universe Books, 1972.
Oltmans, William L., ed. *On Growth: The Crisis of Exploding Population and Resource Depletion*. G. P. Putnam's Sons, 1974.
Ostrawder, Sheila, and Schroeder, Lynn. *Psychic Discoveries Behind the Iron Curtain*. Bantam, 1971.
Teilhard de Chardin, Pierre. *The Future of Man*. Harper (Torchbooks), 1969.
Thompson, William Irwin. *Passages About Earth*. Harper & Row, 1974.
Toffler, Alvin. *Future Shock*. Bantam, 1970.
———, ed. *The Futurists*. Random House, 1972.
Toynbee, Arnold. *A Study of History* (Abridged Edition). Oxford, 1946.
Yeats, William Butler. *A Vision*. Collier, 1966.

Criticism and Anthologies

Aldiss, Brian. *Billion Year Spree: The True History of Science Fiction*. Doubleday, 1973.

Allen, Dick, ed. *Science Fiction: The Future.* Harcourt Brace Jovanovich, 1971.
Amis, Kingsley. *New Maps of Hell.* Harcourt Brace Jovanovich, 1960.
Bailey, J. O. *Pilgrims Through Space and Time.* Greenwood Press, 1972.
Baxter, John. *Science Fiction in the Cinema.* Paperback, 1970.
Clareson, Thomas. *Science Fiction: The Other Side of Realism.* Bowling Green, 1971.
Franklin, Bruce, ed. *Future Perfect: American Science Fiction of the Nineteenth Century.* Oxford, 1966.
Gifford, Dennis. *Science Fiction Film.* Studio Vista/Dutton Paperback, 1971.
Johnson, J. W., ed. *Utopian Literature: A Selection.* Modern Library, 1968.
Lundwall, Sam. *Science Fiction: What It's All About.* Ace Books, 1971.
Mackenzie, Norman, and Mackenzie, Jeanne. *H. G. Wells: A Biography.* Simon & Schuster, 1974.
Moskowitz, Sam. *Explorers of the Infinite.* World, 1963.
———. *Seekers of Tomorrow.* Ballantine, 1967.
Philmus, Robert. *Into the Unknown.* University of California Press, 1970.
Wilson, Robin Scott, ed. *Those Who Can: A Science Fiction Reader.* Mentor, 1973.
Wolf, Jack C., and Fitzgerald, Gregory, eds., *Past, Present and Future Perfect.* Fawcett, 1973.
Wollheim, Donald. *The Universe Makers.* Harper & Row, 1971.

Short Story Collections

Asimov, Isaac, ed. *The Hugo Winners.* Doubleday, 1962, 1971.
Ballard, J. G. *Chronopolis: The Science Fiction of J. G. Ballard.* Berkeley, 1971.
Bova, Ben, ed. *The Science Fiction Hall of Fame.* Vol. II, A., B. Avon, 1973.
Ellison, Harlan. *Dangerous Visions.* Berkeley, 1967.
———, ed. *Again, Dangerous Visions.* Signet, 1973.
McCaffrey, Anne. *The Ship Who Sang.* Mercury, 1961.
The Nebula Awards Series. Harper & Row. Various years.
Silverberg, Robert, ed. *The Science Fiction Hall of Fame.* Vol. I. Avon, 1970.
Wells, H. G. *Twenty-Eight Science Fiction Stories.* Dover, 1934.

A Basic SF Novel Collection

Aldiss, Brian. *The Long Afternoon of Earth.*
Anderson, Pohl. *Brain Wave.*

———. *Tau Zero.*
———. *Vault of the Ages.*
Anthony, Piers. *Macroscope.*
Asimov, Isaac. *The Caves of Steel.*
———. The Foundation Trilogy.
———. *I, Robot.*
Bacon, Sir Francis. *New Atlantis.*
Barth, John. *Giles Goat-Boy.*
Beagle, Peter S. *The Last Unicorn.*
Bellamy, Edward. *Looking Backward.*
Bester, Alfred. *The Demolished Man.*
———. *The Stars My Destination.*
Blish, James. *A Case of Conscience.*
———. *Cities in Flight.*
Boulle, Pierre. *Planet of the Apes.*
Bradbury, Ray. *Fahrenheit 451.*
———. *The Martian Chronicles.*
Brown, Frederic. *What Mad Universe.*
Brunner, John. *Stand on Zanzibar.*
Budrys, Algis. *Rogue Moon.*
Burgess, Anthony. *A Clockwork Orange.*
Butler, Samuel. *Erewhon.*
Capek, Karel. *R.U.R.* (play)
Clarke, Arthur C. *Against the Fall of Night.*
———. *Childhood's End.*
———. *The City and the Stars.*
———. *2001: A Space Odyssey.*
Clement, Hall. *Mission of Gravity.*
DeCamp, L. Sprague. *Lest Darkness Fall.*
Delany, Samuel R. *The Einstein Intersection.*
Dick, Philip K. *The Man in the High Castle.*
Dickson, Gordon R. *Soldier, Ask Not.*
Disch, Thomas. *Camp Concentration.*
Doyle, Arthur Conan. *The Lost World.*
Farmer, Philip José. The Riverworld Series.
Finney, Charles G. *The Circus of Dr. Lao.*
Finney, Jack. *Time and Again.*
Gernsback, Hugo. *Ralph* 124C41+
Golding, William. *The Inheritors.*
———. *The Lord of the Flies.*
Goulart, Ron. *After Things Fell Apart.*
Harrington, Alan. *The Revelations of Dr. Modesto.*
Harrison, Harry. *Make Room, Make Room.*
Heinlein, Robert. *Beyond This Horizon.*
———. *Stranger in a Strange Land.*

Henderson, Zelda. The People Series.
Herbert Frank. *Dune.*
Huxley, Aldous. *Brave New World.*
Keyes, Daniel. *Flowers for Algernon.*
LeGuinn, Ursula. *The Left Hand of Darkness.*
Leiber, Fritz. *The Wanderer.*
Lewis, C. S. Out of the Silent Planet Trilogy.
Lovecraft, H. P. *The Colour Out of Space.*
Matheson, Richard. *I Am Legend.*
Merle, Robert. *The Day of the Dolphin.*
Merritt, A. *The Moon Pool.*
Miller, Walter M. *A Canticle for Leibowitz.*
Moorcock, Michael. *Behold the Man.*
Moore, Ward. *Bring the Jubilee.*
More, Thomas. *Utopia.*
Niven, Larry. *Ringworld.*
Nowlan, Philip Francis. *Armageddon 2419 A.D.*
Orwell, George. 1984.
Panshin, Alexei. *Rite of Passage.*
Percy, Walker. *Love Among the Ruins.*
Pohl, Frederik (with Cyril M. Kornbluth). *Gladiator-at-Law.*
———. *The Space Merchants.*
Pyncheon, Thomas. *The Crying of Lot 49.*
———. *Gravity's Rainbow.*
Rand, Ayn. *Atlas Shrugged.*
Russ, Joanne. *And Chaos Died.*
Shelley, Mary Wollstonecraft. *Frankenstein.*
Shute, Nevil. *On the Beach.*
Silverberg, Robert. *The World Inside.*
Simak, Clifford. *City.*
———. *Cosmic Engineers.*
Skinner, B. F. *Walden II.*
Smith, E. E. (Doc). The Lensman Series.
———. The Skylark Series.
Stapledon, Olaf. *Last and First Men.*
———. *Odd John.*
Sturgeon, Theodore. *More Than Human.*
Swift, Jonathan. *Gulliver's Travels.*
Tolkien, J. R. R. The Lord of the Rings Trilogy.
Twain, Mark. *A Connecticut Yankee in King Arthur's Court.*
Vance, Jack. *The Dragon Masters.*
Van Vogt, A. E. *Slan.*
———. *The Weapon Shops of Isher.*
———. *The World of Null-A.*
Verne, Jules. *From the Earth to the Moon.*

———. *Twenty Thousand Leagues Under the Sea.*
Vonnegut, Kurt, Jr. *Cat's Cradle.*
———. *Player Piano.*
———. *The Sirens of Titan.*
Wells, H. G. *In the Days of the Comet.*
———. *The First Men in the Moon.*
———. *The Food of the Gods.*
———. *The Invisible Man.*
———. *The Island of Dr. Moreau.*
———. *The Time Machine.*
———. *The War of the Worlds.*
Wilson, Colin. *The Philosopher's Stone.*
Wylie, Philip. *Gladiator.*
———. *After Worlds Collide.*
——— (with Edwin Balmer). *When Worlds Collide.*
Wyndhem, John. *The Day of the Triffids.*
Zamyatin, Eugene. *We.*
Zelazny, Roger. *Lord of Light.*

Science Fiction Movies

Aelita (1924)
Alphaville (1965)
The Andromeda Strain (1970)
The Angry Red Planet (1960)
Barbarella (1967)
The Beast from 20,000 Fathoms (1953)
Beneath the Planet of the Apes (1970)
The Birds (1963)
The Blob (1958)
The Bride of Frankenstein (1935)
Buck Rogers (1939)
The Cabinet of Dr. Caligari (1919)
Captain Nemo and the Underwater City (1969)
The Colossus of New York (1958)
The Conquest of Space (1955)
The Creature from the Black Lagoon (1954)
Cyborg 2087 (1966)
The Damned (1961)
Day of the Dolphin (1973)
The Day of the Triffids (1963)
The Day the Earth Stood Still (1951)
Destination Moon (1950)
Dr. Jekyll and Mr. Hyde (1941)
Doctor No (1972)

Doctor Strangelove, or How I Learned to Stop Worrying and Love the Bomb (1964)
Doctor Who and the Daleks (1965)
Donovan's Brain (1953)
Dracula (1931)
Earth II (1971)
Earth Versus the Flying Saucers (1956)
Fahrenheit 451 (1966)
Fail Safe (1964)
Fantasia (1939)
Fantastic Voyage (1966)
The First Men in the Moon (1964)
Five Million Miles to Earth (1968)
Flash Gordon (1936)
The Fly (1958)
The Forbidden Planet (1956)
The Forbin Project (1970)
Frankenstein (1931)
Frankenstein in 3D (1974)
From the Earth to the Moon (1964)
Godzilla (1955)
The Golden Voyage of Sinbad (1974)
Gorgo (1960)
The Hellstrom Chronicle (1971)
The Incredible Shrinking Man (1957)
Invasion of the Body Snatchers (1956)
The Invisible Man (1933)
It Came from Outer Space (1953)
Journey to the Center of the Earth (1959)
Killdozer (1974)
King Kong (1933)
The Last Man on Earth (1964)
Lost Horizon (1937)
The Lost World (1925)
The Manchurian Candidate (1962)
Marooned (1970)
Metropolis (1926)
Mothra (1962)
The Mummy (1932)
Mutiny in Outer Space (1965)
The Mysterians (1958)
Mysterious Island (1961)
The Next Voice You Hear (1950)
The Omega Man (1971)
On the Beach (1959)

Panic in the Year Zero (1962)
The Planet of the Apes (1968)
The Purple Monster Strikes (1945)
Red Planet Mars (1952)
Riders to the Stars (1954)
Robinson Crusoe on Mars (1964)
Rocketship XM (1950)
Rodan (1956)
Seven Days in May (1964)
The Shape of Things to Come (1936)
Silent Running (1972)
Soylent Green (1973)
Superman (1948)
Them (1954)
The Thing (1951)
This Island Earth (1955)
The Time Machine (1950)
Tobor the Great (1954)
Turn of the Screw (1961)
Twenty Million Miles to Earth (1957)
The Twenty-Seventh Day (1957)
Twenty Thousand Leagues Under the Sea (1955)
2001: *A Space Odyssey* (1968)
War of the Worlds (1953)
Westworld (1973)
When Worlds Collide (1951)
Wild in the Streets (1968)
The Wolfman (1941)
The World, The Flesh, and the Devil (1959)
Zardoz (1974)

A B 5 C 6 D 7 E 8 F 9 G 0 H 1 I 2 J 3